CliffsNotes

AP®

World History

CRAM PLAN™

CliffsNotes®

AP® World History

CRAM PLAN™

James Zucker, M.A.

Contributor: *Joy Mondragon-Gilmore, Ph.D.*

Houghton Mifflin Harcourt
Boston • New York

About the Author

James Zucker is a highly regarded history teacher who currently teaches at Loyola High School and UCLA Extension in Los Angeles, California. He has taught AP World History for ten years and is a consultant for the College Board helping to train teachers in the Advanced Placement World History framework, history disciplinary practices and thinking skills, and key concepts. Mr. Zucker received his B.A. in History and Political Science and his M.A. in Social Studies from Loyola Marymount University.

Acknowledgments

I would like to thank the many great teachers and mentors who have helped me in my personal and educational development. Thank you to Thomas Goepel, Philip Klinkner, Joseph Tiedemann, and Tassie Hadlock for your encouragement and opening my eyes to the world of imagination and critical thinking.

Dedication

This book is dedicated to Tammy Michelle Zucker, my best friend and inspiration, who continues to believe in me as a teacher and father to our two amazing daughters, Brianna and Katelyn.

Editorial

Executive Editor: Greg Tubach
Senior Editor: Christina Stambaugh
Production Editor: Jenny Freilach
Copy Editor: Lynn Northrup
Technical Editor: Dominique Craft
Proofreader: Susan Moritz

CliffsNotes® AP® World History Cram Plan™

Copyright © 2018 by Houghton Mifflin Harcourt Publishing Company
All rights reserved.

Library of Congress Control Number: 2017949050

ISBN: 978-0-544-92611-0 (pbk)

Printed in the United States of America
DOC 10 9 8 7 6 5 4 3 2 1

For information about permission to reproduce selections from this book, write to trade.permissions@hmhco.com or to Permissions, Houghton Mifflin Harcourt Publishing Company, 3 Park Avenue, 19th Floor, New York, New York 10016.

www.hmhco.com

Table of Contents

Preface

Congratulations! You've made the decision to take charge of the AP World History course. Very few people your age make the choice to take on such a demanding class and national test. You have decided to challenge yourself. There are a lot of rewards that will come out of this choice. You are not only learning time management, but you are also learning the critical thinking skills needed for college success, as well as some important historical content that will make you much more informed about other fields of academic study. Most importantly, you are developing a strong sense of self-confidence that is well deserved because of your perseverance.

Whether you are looking for a quick reference guide, an in-depth reference, or an occasional refresher of one or more topics of world history, it is contained in this book. This guide is a supplement to your textbook and your teacher's lectures. Too often, students find themselves lost in the massive accumulation of historical facts and wish they had a copy of the teacher's lecture notes. The review chapters are very much like lecture notes. Each chapter contains the essential information necessary for understanding AP World History, or WHAP.

CliffsNotes AP World History Cram Plan is an easy-to-follow cram plan study guide that provides the maximum benefit in a reasonable amount of time. Although this study guide is not meant to substitute for a formal high school AP history class, it provides you with important learning tools to refresh your understanding of the general and specific topics outlined in the AP course curriculum framework and key concepts. The skills and concepts defined in this study guide will not only help you pass the WHAP exam, but will also provide you with exam-oriented approaches and practice material to help you evaluate your strengths and areas of improvement. If you follow the lessons and strategies in this book and study regularly, you will deepen your understanding of world history, which will strengthen your performance on the exam.

Navigating This Book

CliffsNotes AP World History Cram Plan is organized as follows:

- **Introduction to the AP World History Exam** — A general description of the WHAP exam, exam format, scoring, question types, chronological periods, reasoning skills, themes, and frequently asked questions.
- **Chapter 1: Two-Month Cram Plan** — A study calendar that provides a detailed suggested plan of action for preparing for the WHAP exam 2 months before your exam.
- **Chapter 2: One-Month Cram Plan** — A study calendar that provides a detailed suggested plan of action for preparing for the WHAP exam 1 month before your exam.
- **Chapter 3: Test-Taking Strategies** — Invaluable test-taking strategies to help prepare you for the WHAP multiple-choice and free-response question types, along with information about working with documents.
- **Chapter 4: Diagnostic Test** — A shortened version of the WHAP practice exam in Chapter 11, the Diagnostic Test introduces you to the WHAP question types, evaluates your areas of strength and weakness to help you focus your study, and provides you with a baseline starting point.

- **Chapter 5: Period One: Technological and Environmental Transformations (to c. 600 B.C.E.)**
- **Chapter 6: Period Two: Organization and Reorganization of Human Societies (c. 600 B.C.E. to c. 600 C.E.)**
- **Chapter 7: Period Three: Regional and Interregional Interactions (c. 600 C.E. to c. 1450)**
- **Chapter 8: Period Four: Global Interactions (c. 1450 to c. 1750)**
- **Chapter 9: Period Five: Industrialization and Global Integration (c. 1750 to c. 1900)**
- **Chapter 10: Period Six: Accelerating Global Change and Realignments (c. 1900 to the Present)**
- **Chapter 11: Full-Length Practice Exam:** Includes answers and in-depth explanations for multiple-choice questions and sample responses and scoring guidelines for the short-answer, long-essay, and document-based questions.

How to Use This Book

You're in charge here. You get to decide how to use this book. You can read it cover to cover, or just look for the information that you want and then put the book back on the shelf for later use. Most people find it useful to start by learning *general* reasoning skills, themes, and historical periods to develop a broad understanding of world history before memorizing *specific* facts, concepts, and evidence.

Here are some of the recommended ways to use this book.

- Create a customized study "action plan." Be time-wise, because your study plan depends on the total amount of time until the exam date. Preview the cram plan calendars in chapters 1 and 2 to organize your study time.
- Don't take shortcuts. It is always good to know what you are up against, but be careful with this information. Being informed about the scoring and format can help with strategic studying, but it can also lead to a game-playing mindset. Don't try to outmaneuver the test and take shortcuts to eliminate studying certain sections. Rather, use the information presented in this study guide to supplement the in-depth knowledge that is gained by studying for the entire exam.
- Read (and then reread) the Introduction to become familiar with the exam format, time periods, reasoning skills, themes, and question types.
- Review the test-taking strategies and working with documents information in Chapter 3.
- Take the Diagnostic Test (Chapter 4) to assess your strengths and weaknesses.
- Get a glimpse of what you'll gain from a chapter by reading through the headings referenced at the beginning of each chapter.
- Follow the recommended sequence of time periods (chapters 5–10). Within each chapter, take detailed notes on the pages of this book to highlight important facts and topics related to the WHAP key concepts.
- Pay attention to the intermingled callout features in chapters 5–10 that focus on what you need to study to pass the WHAP exam.
  - **Key Facts** — Lists the significant facts of a topic for a quick study reference.
  - **Did you know?** — Covers interesting information about people, places, and events to aid in your overall understanding of a point in history.

- **Heads Up: What You Need to Know** — Summarizes details about specific content that may be on the actual WHAP exam.
- **Test Tip** — Offers quick strategies and tips for approaching exam questions.
- **Historiography** — Offers different scholarly viewpoints so that you can "think like a historian" to reconstruct, debate, or critically think about topics that shape our history over time. For example, the causes and consequences, comparisons and contrasts, and similarities and differences of historical events.

- Use the "Chapter Review Practice Questions" to gauge your grasp of questions on the WHAP exam and strengthen your critical thinking skills. Although it is tempting to look ahead at the answer explanations, try to simulate testing conditions by answering the questions and writing your DBQ responses before reviewing the explanations. Initially, it may be difficult, but this strategy will reinforce your learning, particularly for writing DBQ responses.
- Test your knowledge more completely by taking the Full-Length Practice Exam in Chapter 11.

If you have moments of self-doubt, keep reminding yourself that even though the material is challenging, it is manageable. Take a deep breath, and know that you can do this by using the content, tips, and practice questions offered in this study guide.

Finally, the lessons and strategies you are learning in this book will help you throughout your high school and college learning experiences. If you make the commitment to follow the lessons and practice regularly, you will not only statistically increase your odds for passing the WHAP exam, but you will also learn skills that will help you manage future college coursework!

Introduction to the AP World History Exam

Teachers and students alike will find *CliffsNotes AP World History Cram Plan* to be a valuable course supplement. This compact book is packed with information about what to expect on the exam, how to approach the questions, how to plan your study time, and how to study the six major time periods. To enhance your learning, a diagnostic test and a full-length practice exam provide practice questions with complete answer explanations.

As you begin your preparation, know that while the AP World History (WHAP) exam is challenging, it is manageable. Students may feel overwhelmed by the class because the world history curriculum covers . . . well, everything in history. It encompasses over 10,000 years of human history and examines the history of every significant region, empire, and human civilization.

The WHAP exam will ask students to understand the big ideas, themes, and significant events within each time period. You do not need to memorize specific dates, battles, and events. Rather, you will be asked to analyze the important changes, continuities, comparisons, and contrasts within and between significant groups and regions. This "big picture" approach makes the exam both manageable and thought-provoking. *CliffsNotes AP World History Cram Plan* takes the guesswork out of how to approach questions. So take a deep breath, and know that you can do this.

You should familiarize yourself with the structure of the exam before exploring the content of the exam. The following sections cover the exam format, scoring, question types, historical periods, history disciplinary practices and reasoning skills, and themes.

Exam Format

There are a total of 55 multiple-choice questions on the WHAP exam, and you must respond to three short-answer questions, one document-based essay question, and one long-essay question. The entire exam is 3 hours and 15 minutes. The chart below summarizes the format of the exam. Multiple-choice questions are combined with free-response questions for a combined scaled score of 1–5.

Note: Format and scoring are subject to change. Visit the College Board website for updates: http://apcentral.collegeboard.com.

Section	Question Type	Time	Number of Questions	Percent of Total Grade
Section I: Part A	Multiple-Choice Questions	55 minutes	55 questions	40% (Note: Multiple-choice questions are graded on a curve.)

Continued

Section	Question Type	Time	Number of Questions	Percent of Total Grade
Section I: Part B	Short-Answer Questions	40 minutes	3 questions (Note: Answer the first two questions and then choose 1 question from 2 choices.)	20%
Section II: Part A	Document-Based Question	60 minutes (includes a 15-minute reading period)	1 question	25%
Section II: Part B	Long-Essay Question	40 minutes (Note: DBQ and LEQ questions appear in the same section. Use the 15-minute mandatory reading period to read and plan BOTH essays.)	1 question (Note: Choose 1 question from 3 choices.)	15%
TOTALS:		3 hours, 15 minutes	55 multiple choice 5 essays	100%

Scoring

Scores on your WHAP exam will be based on the number of questions you answer correctly for two separate sections.

Section I: Multiple-choice and short-answer questions are 60% of your overall score.

Section II: Document-based and long-essay questions are 40% of your overall score.

Based on the combination of the two sections, the scores are converted into a grading scale of 1 to 5. A score of 5 is the best possible score. Most colleges consider a score of 3 or better a passing score. If you receive a passing score, the WHAP exam can be applied as a college course equivalent—two-semester units will apply toward your college bachelor's degree as a world history course.

As a reference, in 2017, more than 50% of students who took the WHAP exam scored a 3 or higher.

AP Score	Score Translation
5	Extremely well qualified
4	Well qualified
3	Qualified
2	Possibly qualified
1	No recommendation

The WHAP exam is graded on a curve, particularly the multiple-choice questions. Oftentimes, students panic when they get back their first practice exam. "A 65% on the multiple choice? I'm failing!" In reality, a 65% on the multiple-choice questions can be good enough for a 4 or even a 5 on the entire exam, depending on your score on the other sections. Note: For multiple-choice questions, no points are deducted for incorrect answers. If you don't know the answer, take an educated guess because there is no penalty for guessing.

Question Types

The WHAP question types are multiple-choice, short-answer, document-based, and long-essay. Questions measure your knowledge of the main concepts within the content of the six chronological periods, your ability to analyze primary and secondary documents, your ability to relate the broader historical context, and your ability to apply reasoning skills. As you approach each of the four question types, consider the following points to receive your best possible score.

- What are the main points within the context of a particular historical period?
- What is the broader historical context (what happened before, during, and after)?
- What are the relevant significant themes?
- What supporting evidence will strengthen your analysis?
- What are the reasoning skills?

Section I of the WHAP exam includes both multiple-choice and short-answer questions.

> TEST TIP: Chapter 3 details test-taking strategies for multiple-choice questions and free-response questions. Take your time to study Chapter 3 closely.

Multiple-Choice Questions

Multiple-choice questions require that you read and analyze a passage or graphic image and draw reasonable conclusions based on your knowledge of world history and your interpretation of the document. Documents are primary or secondary sources (text or graphic image) that college history students might use in their research. Each question draws from the WHAP key concept outlines and your knowledge of world history.

Key points about multiple-choice questions:

- Multiple-choice questions comprise 40% of your overall score.
- The exam contains 55 multiple-choice questions.
- The questions are grouped into sets. Each set contains one sourced-based prompt (text or graphic image) and two to five questions.
- Questions ask you to analyze, interpret, or find evidence from a primary or secondary source (historical text, quotation, graph, chart, map, political cartoon, art, or image).
- Select one answer from among four choices in each question.
- No points are deducted for incorrect answers; therefore, there is no penalty for guessing.

Short-Answer Questions (SAQs)

The SAQs are similar to multiple-choice questions, but consist of short written responses. Short-answer questions give students an opportunity to demonstrate what they know by describing examples of historical evidence in a concise response that answers the question. If you answer all parts of the question and apply reasoning skills, the SAQs are a great section to increase your score.

One question is taken from a primary source, one question is taken from a secondary source (text or graphic image), and one question has no source.

Question	Type of Source	Task	Historical Period
SAQ 1	Secondary source	Analyze a historian's argument.	Periods 3–6
SAQ 2	Primary source	Analyze the original source and respond by using the reasoning skills of comparison or continuity and change over time.	Periods 3–6
Choose only ONE of the following (not both):			
SAQ 3	No source	Respond to the question by using the reasoning skills of comparison or continuity and change over time.	Periods 1–3
SAQ 4			Periods 4–6

Key points about short-answer questions:

- Short-answer questions comprise 20% of your overall score.
- The exam contains four short-answer questions, but you are only required to answer three short-answer questions. You must answer the first two short-answer questions, and then choose one from the last two questions. Select the period you know more about. It's your choice!
- No thesis statement is required in your written response.
- Write a short analysis that responds to a question with a secondary source, a primary source, or no source. If the question contains a primary or secondary source, you must identify, describe, explain, or provide evidence from the document found in a graph, text, map, or image source.
- Use at least one reasoning skill in your written response (comparison or continuity and change over time).
- Each short-answer question contains *three* tasks. You must respond to all three tasks to receive full credit.

Scoring Rubric for the Short-Answer Questions	
SAQ Score (per question)	**Scoring Criteria**
3 points	The written response accomplishes all **three** tasks in the question.
2 points	The written response accomplishes **two** tasks in the question.
1 point	The written response accomplishes **one** task in the question.
No points	The written response accomplishes **none** of the tasks in the question, or is completely blank.

Document-Based Question (DBQ)

DBQs require that you write an essay with *specific* historical evidence in support of your argument. You will need to analyze (not summarize) the documents, explain the broader historical context, follow a line of reasoning, and provide historical examples to construct your response.

Key points about the document-based question:

- The document-based question comprises 25% of your overall score.
- The exam contains one document-based question.

- The document-based question contains six or seven documents of historical sources in text (speeches, reports, laws, declarations), graphs, charts, maps, artifacts, political cartoons, art, or images.
- Write an essay response to identify, describe, explain, or provide evidence from three to six documents.
- Each point is earned independently. For example, you can earn a point for a historically defensible thesis, but fail to earn a point for not providing an example beyond the documents.
- Write a response that considers the relationship among the topic question, your thesis argument, and the documents.
- Write a response that addresses all points in the scoring criteria as described by the College Board (see the chart below).

Scoring Rubric for the Document-Based Question		
Task	**Scoring Criteria**	**Possible Points**
Thesis and Claim	Presents a historically defensible thesis that establishes a line of reasoning **(1 point)**. (Note: The thesis must make a claim that responds to *all* parts of the question and must *not* just restate the question. The thesis must consist of at least one sentence, either in the introduction or the conclusion.)	1 point
Contextualization	Explains the broader historical context of events, developments, or processes that occurred before, during, or after the time frame of the question **(1 point)**. (Note: Must be more than a phrase or reference.)	1 point
Evidence	**Evidence from the Documents:** Uses at least *six* documents to support the argument in response to the prompt **(2 points)**. OR Uses the content of at least *three* documents to address the topic prompt **(1 point)**. (Note: Examples must describe, rather than simply quote, the content of the documents.)	3 points
	Evidence Beyond the Documents Uses at least one additional piece of specific historical evidence beyond those found in the documents that is relevant to the argument **(1 point)**. (Note: Evidence must be different from the evidence used in contextualization.)	
Analysis and Reasoning	Uses at least *three* documents to explain how each document's point of view, purpose, historical situation, and/or audience is relevant to the argument **(1 point)**. (Note: References must ex.plain how or why, rather than simply identifying.)	2 points
	Uses historical reasoning and development that focuses on the question while using evidence to corroborate, qualify, or modify the argument **(1 point)**. (Examples: Explain the nuances of an issue by analyzing multiple variables; explain what is similar and different; explain the cause and effect; explain multiple causes; explain both continuity and change; explain connections across periods of time; corroborate multiple perspectives across themes; qualify or modify the argument by considering alternative views or evidence.)	
Total Possible Points		**7 points**
Note: Each point is earned independently by task. You must respond to **all** tasks to receive full credit.		

Long-Essay Question (LEQ)

The final part of the exam is one long-essay question. Just like the DBQ, the long-essay question requires that you write an essay with *specific* historical evidence in support of your argument. LEQs focus on reasoning skills and often require a great deal of contextualization about broad trends in history—the big picture. You need to consider not only overall trends, but also historiographical arguments, long-term developments, and overall characterizations.

Key points about the long-essay question:

- The long-essay question comprises 15% of your overall score.
- Long-essay questions are drawn from broad topics on the key concept outlines.
- The exam contains three long-essay questions from different time periods, but you will choose only one question to write your essay response (periods 1–2, periods 3–4, or periods 5–6). Focus on the time period that is most familiar.
- Each point is earned independently. For example, you can earn a point for a strong thesis, but fail to earn a point for not applying historical reasoning to explain specific evidence.
- Write a response that addresses all points in the scoring criteria as described by the College Board (see the chart below).

Scoring Rubric for the Long-Essay Question		
Task	**Scoring Criteria**	**Possible Points**
Thesis and Claim	Presents a historically defensible thesis that establishes a line of reasoning **(1 point)**. (Note: The thesis must make a claim that responds to *all* parts of the question and must *not* just restate the question. The thesis must consist of *at least* one sentence, either in the introduction or the conclusion.)	1 point
Contextualization	Describes the broader historical context of events, developments, or processes that occurred before, during, or after the time frame of the question **(1 point)**. (Note: Must be more than a phrase or reference.)	1 point
Evidence	Supports the argument in response to the prompt using specific and relevant examples of evidence **(2 points)**. OR Provides specific examples of evidence relevant to the topic of the question **(1 point)**. (Note: To earn 2 points, the evidence must *support* your argument.)	2 points
Analysis and Reasoning	Demonstrates a complex understanding of the historical development that addresses the question and uses evidence to corroborate, qualify, or modify the argument **(2 points)**. (Examples: Explain the nuances of an issue by analyzing multiple variables; explain what is similar and different; explain the cause and effect; explain multiple causes; explain both continuity and change; explain connections across periods of time; corroborate multiple perspectives across themes; qualify or modify the argument by considering alternative views or evidence.) OR Uses historical reasoning (comparison, causation, or continuity and change over time) to frame and develop the argument while focusing on the question **(1 point)**. (Note: Must be more than a phrase or reference.)	2 points
Total Possible Points Note: Each point is earned independently by task. You must respond to **all** tasks to receive full credit		6 points

Historical Periods

The content of the exam is connected to the six major time periods. These time periods are very manageable once you understand the big picture overview. Students who are successful on the exam can easily connect themes and topics within the chronological context of the period, era, or century.

As you review the time periods in the table below, keep in mind that certain time periods receive more emphasis than others. Your review and study for the exam should reflect those percentages. Note: The two short-answer questions and the document-based question (DBQ) focus on periods 3–6.

Overview of Historical Periods				
Era	Period	Percent of Exam	Century	Description
Prehistory	Period 1: to c. 600 B.C.E.	5%	Human beginnings to the 6th century B.C.E. (Before the Common Era)	**Technological and environmental transformations.** This time period was when humans changed from tribal to sedentary societies.
Classical to the Early Middle Ages	Period 2: c. 600 B.C.E. to c. 600 C.E.	15%	6th century B.C.E. to 6th century C.E. (of the Common Era)	**Organization and reorganization of human societies.** This time period is noted for humans settling into large and consolidated empires.
Post-Classical to the Middle Ages	Period 3: c. 600 C.E. to c. 1450	20%	6th century to the mid-15th century	**Regional and transregional interactions.** The Post-Classical Era saw empires expand into land-based empires that conquered tributary states.
Early Modern World	Period 4: c. 1450 to c. 1750	20%	mid-15th century to the mid-18th century	**Global interactions.** The Early Modern Era saw the European Black Death, religious warfare, the rise of new monarchies, and the rise of exploration and global trade.
Modern World	Period 5: c. 1750 to c. 1900	20%	mid-18th century to 20th century	**Industrialization and global integration.** The Modern Era ushered in a series of events connected to the Industrial Revolution, including the Scientific Revolution, Enlightenment, imperialism, and nationalist movements.
Modern World to Post-Modern World	Period 6: c. 1900 to the present	20%	20th century to the present	**Accelerating global change and realignment.** The 20th century has seen the development of independence movements, global free trade and the transition from two World Wars, a great depression, and a Cold War to the 21st-century problem of terrorism.

AP History Disciplinary Practices and Reasoning Skills

To be successful on the exam, you must make sure that you are clear on AP disciplinary practices and reasoning skills identified by the College Board. These skills are the heart of every question. If you become familiar with these skills, you can focus, predict, and respond to all of the questions on the WHAP.

Disciplinary Practice 1: Analyzing historical evidence. Analyze and explain the significance of historical evidence from primary sources and secondary sources. Ask yourself, "What is the point of view, historical situation, and/or audience of the source?" and "Is the source credible, or does it have limitations?" (See p. 30 for a description of primary and secondary sources.)

Disciplinary Practice 2: Argument development. To develop your free-response argument, you should: (a) defend your thesis/claim based on historical facts, (b) support your thesis using specific (and relevant) evidence, (c) use one of the reasoning skills listed below make a connection to the evidence, and (d) consider alternative evidence to qualify or modify your argument.

AP History Reasoning Skills		
Skill	Description	Critical Thinking Questions
Contextualization	Historical context is the key to the WHAP exam. If you understand this skill, you will be far ahead of other students. Context not only refers to a document source, but more importantly to the <u>time period surrounding or inspiring the creation of the document</u> (author, purpose, point of view, situation, and audience). People who study history have often argued that humans study history to make sure we don't make the same mistakes that were made in the past. That's a pretty good reason, but there is a problem with this theory. It assumes that the people who live today think just like the people of the past. Some people believe that if humans study long enough, they will solve problems from today based on solutions from past history. However, the people of the past were not the same as the people of today. In fact, most people who lived long ago were almost like a foreign culture. People who lived long ago had different ideas and values, lived in a different *context,* and saw the world in a very different way from the world today. In order to understand history, we must think about the context in which people lived. For WHAP documents, it's all about understanding *historical context* and the author's intended purpose for writing the document in the time frame that it was written.	❑ Can I describe what was happening in the world when a particular event occurred? ❑ Can I connect a particular historical event to broader trends and developments (social, religious, political, economic)? ❑ How did the interactions among different people, time periods, and regions shape how the author of a document was influenced?
Comparison	Comparison involves <u>comparing and contrasting</u> historical perspectives about an event so that you can draw conclusions about your findings. This skill is probably the core of everything in world history. It's the glue that holds the reasoning skills together. To compare and contrast: (1) list similarities and differences of an issue, (2) group the similarities and differences around a core issue, (3) look at the "core" compare/contrast issues, and (4) give *reasons* for the compare/contrast issues.	❑ What are the similarities and differences of core issues (events or developments) between periods, regions, or empires? (Can these be grouped by themes?) ❑ Can I reasonably explain why one nation was affected by an issue differently than another nation?

Skill	Description	Critical Thinking Questions
Causation	Causation uses the skill of cause and effect. It involves providing *reasons* for the causes of complex issues that resulted in unexpected developments (called turning points in history). A good way to simplify this skill is to think about the logical sequence: (a) what happened *before* the event, (b) what happened *during* the event, and (c) what happened *after* the event—or cause, event, effect.	❑ Can I identify several reasons that prompted an event or development? (And the short-term and long-term consequences?) ❑ Can I prioritize the causes and consequences? ❑ Can I build an argument by providing a clear and specific chain of events leading up to the event?
Continuity and Change	Think of continuity and change over time as another level of causation. Continuity and change over time involves recognizing "patterns" in a society that tend to stay the same over time or change over time. These patterns are consistent across the larger big picture of history. You are expected to recognize and evaluate established patterns, and changes in patterns, of historical developments.	❑ Can I identify what is the same and what is different in a society or time period? ❑ Can I identify similar patterns or differences in other societies? ❑ Can I identify the main reasons (causes) that led to decision-making changes in these societies?

Examples of Reasoning Skills

Contextualization

It's important to understand the context of a document to be able to make an interpretation. In the following example, the context of a single sentence can change the author's intended meaning.

In 1900, Japanese industrialization leader Tsurumi Shunsuke wrote, "The person who takes employment in the factory is an unattached component of the family." If this quote is taken out of context from Shunsuke's entire document, you might think that in 1900, people in Japanese factories were self-centered individuals who did not care about their families. However, if we put this quote into the broader context of the first part of the document, you may find a different interpretation of Shunsuke's writings:

> They all come from farming communities. People from families that are working their own land, or are engaged in tenant farming but have surplus workers, come to the cities and industrial centers to become factory workers. Income from the farms provides for the family needs and subsistence of the parents and siblings. The person who takes employment in the factory is an unattached component of the family.

Notice how the context of the document changes the meaning or, at the very least, gives us a better sense of what the author intended. Now the sentence appears to mean that families had individuals who would leave to work in the factories to supplement the income of the farming family. This means that the individual being described is not selfish, but is actually trying to support the family by gaining more income.

Now, let's put this document in historical context. Historical context means that we need to look at what was happening in Japan in the 1900s and how this affected the author's intended meaning. During the early 1900s, the Japanese leadership had changed to the Meiji Restoration. The Meiji Restoration tried to industrialize Japan in order to compete with Western nations' trade. The Meiji Restoration also created an empire in Southeast Asia to compete with the American and British empires. Since the document is written in 1900, you can probably guess that the intended audience included workers, women's groups, ethnic groups, parliaments, movements, etc.

Does this historical information change the document's meaning? Traditional Japanese farmers believed in the importance of family obligations. They also believed in important social roles for boys and girls. Boys typically were seen as the honorary individuals who would enter the sphere of public work and leadership. Girls were supposed to grow up to be mothers and raise children. However, industrialization caused changes among these traditional roles. Peasant girls were leaving the home to go work in the cities, and this disrupted the traditional Japanese identity and social roles.

Therefore, since this document was written by a Japanese authority who gave support to industrialization, you might guess that his purpose was to justify industrialization while also arguing that this change is still upholding the traditional Japanese family values. Thus, the document's purpose is really about creating a modern nation-state in Japan. Notice how the analysis of a single sentence has changed by using multiple levels of context.

The takeaway from this example is this: On the WHAP exam, always remember to analyze what the document is doing in its *historical context* (author, purpose, point of view, and audience). Don't just restate, paraphrase, or summarize a document. Otherwise, you may miss the whole point of the document.

Comparison

Comparing and contrasting is at the core of what we do in history. For example, compare and contrast what comes before and after a point in history, compare and contrast how documents are influenced by a historical period, and compare and contrast one period to another period in history. This skill overlaps with most of the major reasoning skills, as you will see in the following example.

Example free-response question:

> **Question:** Compare and contrast the political systems in Latin America and the Middle East during the 19th century.

Compare: During the 19th century, both Latin America and the Middle East (1) inspired nationalism, (2) sought independence from the West, (3) were ruled by strong authority figures, and (4) tried to modernize their economies.

Contrast: During the 19th century, (1) Latin American governments tried to unite people with national identities, and Middle Eastern governments dealt with the break-away nationalist groups. (2) Latin American governments were centralized, and Middle Eastern governments tried to decentralize. (3) Latin American governments were ruled by military leaders, and Middle Eastern governments were ruled by religious leaders. (4) Latin American governments dealt with land inequalities, and Middle Eastern governments tried to unite religious sects.

Overall Comparison: Both Latin American and Middle Eastern governments used nationalism to unite their people against Western imperialism.

Overall Contrast: While Latin American governments tried to solve inequalities through centralized rulers, Middle Eastern governments used religion to unify their people.

In this example, we have created a list of the core comparisons and contrasts, grouped this list by theme, and provided an overall comparison and contrast. With this information, you can create core issues with supporting examples to include in your response.

Causation

In free-response questions, it is sometimes helpful to distinguish between *correlations* (is associated with by relationship) and *causations* (prompts an effect). A correlation does not necessarily cause something to result. For example, before World War I, Germany had a correlation to a powerful military. Germany's military was ready for war, but the military did not cause the war.

When you discuss the cause-and-effect sequence on the WHAP exam, be sure to keep in mind the short-term and long-term causes, and remember that most events have multiple causes and multiple consequences. The following steps will help you with causation questions.

1. Identify not one, but several, causes and effects for any historical question.
2. Prioritize the significant causes and effects by period or turning point to help to build the rest of your argument.
3. Provide a clear and coherent reason for your prioritization of the causes and effects.

Continuity and Change

As you study world history, you will learn that almost every society has "social tensions" between continuity of traditional conventions and change of new developments. For example, China has been a dynamic and powerful society throughout world history. However, China has an internal *tension* of continuity and change.

Continuity: On one hand, throughout time, China retained a constant reverence for ancestors and a respect for social stability taught in traditional Confucian family relationships.

Change: Yet, China was constantly changing due to its trade interactions over the Silk Roads. This changed the Chinese economy, but new ethnic groups also brought the influences of Buddhism, the steppe people, and other social and political changes.

How is it possible that a society can have both tremendous changes and a constant desire for social stability at the same time? Well, this is the point of the continuity and change reasoning skill.

Themes

History is not just about memorizing facts and dates; it's also about understanding the themes that people had in common from different time periods. All of the topics covered on the WHAP exam refer to conceptual themes. Most colleges and universities expect students to master these themes and to understand *why* particular developments occurred in the context of a larger historical big picture. These themes will guide your studying and help you group documents for your DBQ essay response.

The good news is that the College Board has identified five themes that give us the framework for understanding the big picture and why certain social, political, economic, and cultural developments transpired, or why they were repeated in history. You can use these to both guide your studying and predict what will be asked on the exam. Success on the WHAP exam will depend on the connections you make between the content and the deeper understandings of thematic developments relevant to the history of the world.

TEST TIP: To help you stay focused on the big picture and connections across periods and regions, use the acronym SPRITE to remember the subject matter of the historical themes—social, political, religious, ideological, technological, and economic.

Theme	Subject Matter	Description	Example
Interaction Between Humans and the Environment	Environment and Technology	The environment influenced early societies, but societies also had a great impact on the environment, particularly as a result of migration, industrialization, and disease. The human impact on the environment increased as humans explored the world and established trade routes. This drove the global economy and introduced new cultures, beliefs, and technologies. However, exploration also introduced new diseases that annihilated some regions.	What were the environmental advantages or disadvantages of industrialization over time?
Development and Interaction of Cultures	Culture and Religion	The development and spread of new beliefs, ideas, science, art, technology, and knowledge among regions was integral to the exchange of world religions, cultures, philosophies, and political ideologies.	How did religion change or influence the political, social, and economic systems of a society?
State Building, Expansion, and Conflict	Politics and Government	The formation and organization of governments is at the foundation for stability (or instability) within regions, empires, and nations. Based on political hierarchical systems of government, alliances, conflicts, and revolutions were impacted across regions and the world. This influenced nationalism, expansion, relationships, and dissolutions of nations, empires, and kingdoms.	How have state governments influenced conflicts and alliances?
Creation, Expansion, and Interaction of Economic Systems	Economics	The approaches to agricultural production, trade, labor systems, commerce, industrialization, and economics brought advantages and disadvantages for regions. Humans were motivated by production and trade because there were economic benefits, but prosperity also caused conflicts across regions and introduced capitalist and socialist systems. It also brought coerced labor systems and economic poverty.	How has trade and commerce changed over time?

Theme	Subject Matter	Description	Example
Development and Transformation of Social Structures	Social	Societies formed with social roles, norms, and structures over time. Hierarchies were formed based on social and economic classes, racial and ethnic norms, gender roles, and family kinship. These norms influenced political, economic, and cultural values of societies.	How have social roles for women changed over time?

Frequently Asked Questions about the WHAP Exam

Q: Who administers the AP World History exam?

A: The College Board prepares and scores the WHAP exam. For further information regarding exam administration, contact *Advanced Placement Program (AP)*, P.O. Box 6671, Princeton, NJ 08541-6671, (888) 225-5427 or (212) 632-1780, e-mail: apstudents@info.collegeboard.org, http://apcentral. collegeboard.com.

Q: Are there prerequisites to taking the WHAP exam?

A: No. However, you should be able to read college-level textbooks and write grammatically correct and complete sentences.

Q: How do I register for the WHAP exam?

A: If your school offers the WHAP course, contact your AP teacher or coordinator to register. If your school does not offer the WHAP course, visit http://apcentral.collegeboard.com for more information.

Q: Can I take the WHAP exam more than once?

A: Yes, but you may not retake the exam within the same year. If you take the exam a second time, both scores will be reported unless you cancel one score.

Q: What do I bring to the exam?

A: Bring several no. 2 pencils with erasers for the multiple-choice questions, and bring several pens with black or dark-blue ink for the free-response questions. Bring your 6-digit school code. Bring a watch that does not have Internet access, does not beep, and does not have an alarm. If you do not attend the school where you are taking the exam, bring identification (school-issued photo ID or government-issued ID).

Q: What items am I not allowed to bring to the exam?

A: You cannot bring electronic equipment (cell phone, smartphone, listening devices, cameras, or any other electronic devices). You cannot bring books, highlighters, notes, food, or drinks.

Q: Can I bring scratch paper?

A: No; however, the exam booklets will not be graded, so you can take notes, organize your essay, and write down key words in the margins of your exam booklet.

Q: When is the WHAP exam?

A: The WHAP exam is given in May.

Q: Can I cancel, withhold, or change my report recipient score?

A: Yes, you can request to cancel your scores at any time before the deadline. Contact AP Services for deadlines and policies.

Q: How long does it take to receive my score?

A: Once you sign up for a College Board account at www.collegeboard.org/register, you can receive your scores online sometime in July. You will receive an e-mail reminding you how to access your scores. You will be asked to enter your AP number (the 8-digit number on the labels inside your AP Student Pack), or your student identifier to access your scores.

Q: Should I guess on the WHAP exam?

A: Yes. There is no penalty for wrong answers. Your score is based on the number of questions you answer correctly. If possible, use the elimination strategy (see p. 24) for multiple-choice questions to increase your chances of guessing the correct answer. Don't leave any questions unanswered.

Chapter 1

Two-Month Cram Plan

The calendar below details a two-month action plan for the WHAP exam. The first step is to determine how much time you have to prepare and then pick the plan that fits your schedule: two-month plan or one-month plan (see pp. 19–20 for a one-month plan). Ask yourself, "How many hours a week can I realistically devote to preparing for the exam?" Be specific. For example, you may be able to study on Tuesdays, Thursdays, and Fridays from 4:00 to 6:00 p.m.; or you may only have time on Saturdays and Sundays from 8:00 to 11:00 a.m. It doesn't matter what plan you pick; what matters is that you stick to the schedule to get your best possible results.

Two-Month Cram Plan	
8 weeks before the exam	**Study Time:** 3 hours ❑ Chapter 4: Take the Diagnostic Test and review the multiple-choice answer explanations. ❑ Compare your essay responses to the free-response essay scoring guidelines rubrics. ❑ Browse the WHAP official website: https://apstudent.collegeboard.org/apcourse/ap-world-history. ❑ Read the Introduction. ❑ Study the WHAP exam format (pp. 1–2).
7 weeks before the exam	**Study Time:** 2–3 hours ❑ Take notes as you study and memorize the WHAP history disciplinary practices and reasoning skills (pp. 8–11). ❑ Take notes as you study and memorize the WHAP historical periods (p. 7). ❑ Take notes as you study and memorize the WHAP themes (pp. 11–13). ❑ Chapter 3: Read and study the test-taking strategies. **Study Time:** 3 hours at least two times a week (or as often as your schedule permits) ❑ Chapter 5: Read and take notes on Period One, "Technological and Environmental Transformations (to c. 600 B.C.E.)." ❑ Use additional resources to read more about general and specific topics discussed in Chapter 5. ❑ Reread the "AP World History Key Concepts" for Period One on pp. 69–70. ❑ Answer the chapter review multiple-choice practice questions after you have read the entire chapter.
6 weeks before the exam	**Study Time:** 3 hours at least two times a week (or as often as your schedule permits) ❑ Chapter 6: Read and take notes on Period Two, "Organization and Reorganization of Human Societies (c. 600 B.C.E. to c. 600 C.E.)." ❑ Use additional resources to read more about general and specific topics discussed in Chapter 6. ❑ Reread the "AP World History Key Concepts" for Period Two on p. 86. ❑ Answer the chapter review multiple-choice practice questions after you have read the entire chapter.
5 weeks before the exam	**Study Time:** 3 hours at least two times a week (or as often as your schedule permits) ❑ Chapter 7: Read chapter and take notes on Period Three, "Regional and Interregional Interactions (c. 600 C.E. to c. 1450)." ❑ Use additional resources to read more about general and specific topics discussed in Chapter 7. ❑ Reread the "AP World History Key Concepts" for Period Three on p. 108. ❑ Answer the chapter review multiple-choice practice questions after you have read the entire chapter. ❑ Answer the chapter review DBQ question after you have read the entire chapter. Compare your response to the scoring guidelines and sample response.

Continued

4 weeks before the exam	**Study Time:** 3 hours at least two times a week (or as often as your schedule permits) ❑ Chapter 8: Read chapter and take notes on Period Four, "Global Interactions (c. 1450 to c. 1750)." ❑ Use additional resources to read more about general and specific topics discussed in Chapter 8. ❑ Reread the "AP World History Key Concepts" for Period Four on pp. 136–137. ❑ Answer the chapter review multiple-choice practice questions after you have read the entire chapter. ❑ Answer the chapter review DBQ question after you have read the entire chapter. Compare your response to the scoring guidelines and sample response.
3 weeks before the exam	**Study Time:** 3 hours at least two times a week (or as often as your schedule permits) ❑ Chapter 9: Read chapter and take notes on Period Five, "Industrialization and Global Integration (c. 1750 to c. 1900)." ❑ Use additional resources to read more about general and specific topics discussed in Chapter 9. ❑ Reread the "AP World History Key Concepts" for Period Five on pp. 168–169. ❑ Answer the chapter review multiple-choice practice questions after you have read the entire chapter. ❑ Answer the chapter review DBQ question after you have read the entire chapter. Compare your response to the scoring guidelines and sample response.
2 weeks before the exam	**Study Time:** 3 hours at least two times a week (or as often as your schedule permits) ❑ Chapter 10: Read chapter and take notes on Period Six, "Accelerating Global Change and Realignments (c. 1900 to the Present)." ❑ Use additional resources to read more about general and specific topics discussed in Chapter 10. ❑ Reread the "AP World History Key Concepts" for Period Six on p. 200. ❑ Answer the chapter review multiple-choice practice questions after you have read the entire chapter. ❑ Answer the chapter review DBQ question after you have read the entire chapter. Compare your response to the scoring guidelines and sample response.
7 days before the exam	**Study Time:** 5 hours ❑ Chapter 11: Take the full-length practice exam and review your answers and the explanations and sample responses. ❑ Based on your performance, identify topics and their corresponding chapters that require further review. ❑ Use additional resources to read more about general and specific topics discussed in the practice exam.
6 days before the exam	**Study Time:** 3 hours ❑ Based on your review, target general and specific topics. ❑ Review Chapter 3 again, "Test-Taking Strategies." ❑ Practice writing responses to two short-answer questions and one document-based question (or one long-essay question) using the scoring guidelines on pp. 4–6 to score your essay. Note: Previous free-response question topics can be found online at https://apstudent.collegeboard.org/apcourse/ap-world-history/exam-practice.
5 days before the exam	**Study Time:** 2 hours ❑ Review WHAP Key Concepts for Period One (pp. 69–70) and Period Two (p. 86). ❑ Study and target specific topics as needed.
4 days before the exam	**Study Time:** 2 hours ❑ Review WHAP Key Concepts for Period Three (p. 108) and Period Four (pp. 136–137). ❑ Study and target specific topics as needed.
3 days before the exam	**Study Time:** 1–2 hours ❑ Review WHAP Key Concepts for Period Five (pp. 168–169). ❑ Study and target specific topics as needed.

2 days before the exam	**Study Time:** 1–2 hours ❑ Review WHAP Key Concepts for Period Six (p. 200). ❑ Study and target specific topics as needed. ❑ Reread any material you feel is necessary.
1 day before the exam	❑ Relax. You are well-prepared to score well on the exam. ❑ Get plenty of sleep the night before the exam.
Morning of the exam	❑ Eat a balanced, nutritious breakfast with protein. ❑ Keep your usual habits. Don't try something new today. ❑ Bring your photo ID, ticket for admission (if received), watch (that does not have Internet and does not beep), your 6-digit school code, several sharpened no. 2 pencils with erasers, and a few pens with black or dark-blue ink. Note: Cell phones, scratch paper, books, smartwatches, and food/drinks are not allowed at the testing center.

Chapter 2

One-Month Cram Plan

The calendar below details a one-month action plan for the WHAP exam. The first step is to determine how much time you have to prepare and then pick the plan that fits your schedule: two-month plan or one-month plan (see pp. 15–17 for a two-month plan). Ask yourself, "How many hours a week can I realistically devote to preparing for the exam?" Be specific. For example, you may be able to study on Tuesdays, Thursdays, and Fridays from 4:00 to 6:00 p.m.; or you may only have time on Saturdays and Sundays from 8:00 to 11:00 a.m. It doesn't matter what plan you pick; what matters is that you stick to the schedule to get your best possible results.

One-Month Cram Plan	
4 weeks before the exam	**Study Time:** 3–4 hours ❑ Chapter 4: Take the Diagnostic Test and review the multiple-choice answer explanations. ❑ Compare your essay responses to the free-response essay scoring guidelines rubrics. ❑ Browse the WHAP official website: https://apstudent.collegeboard.org/apcourse/ap-world-history. ❑ Read the Introduction. ❑ Study the WHAP exam format (pp. 1–2). ❑ Take notes as you study the WHAP history disciplinary practices and reasoning skills (pp. 8–11). ❑ Take notes as you study the WHAP historical time periods (p. 7). ❑ Take notes as you study the WHAP themes (pp. 11–13). ❑ Chapter 3: Read this chapter on test-taking strategies. **Study Time:** 3 hours at least two times a week (or as often as your schedule permits) ❑ Chapter 5: Read chapter and take notes on Period One, "Technological and Environmental Transformations (to c. 600 B.C.E.)." ❑ Answer the chapter review multiple-choice practice questions after you have read the entire chapter. ❑ Chapter 6: Read chapter and take notes on Period Two, "Organization and Reorganization of Human Societies (c. 600 B.C.E. to c. 600 C.E.)." ❑ Answer the chapter review multiple-choice practice questions after you have read the entire chapter.
3 weeks before the exam	**Study Time:** 3 hours at least two times a week (or as often as your schedule permits) ❑ Chapter 7: Read chapter and take notes on Period Three, "Regional and Interregional Interactions (c. 600 C.E. to c. 1450)." ❑ Answer the chapter review multiple-choice practice questions after you have read the entire chapter. ❑ Answer the chapter review DBQ question after you have read the entire chapter. Compare your response to the scoring guidelines and sample response. ❑ Chapter 8: Read chapter and take notes on Period Four, "Global Interactions (c. 1450 to c. 1750)." ❑ Answer the chapter review multiple-choice practice questions after you have read the entire chapter. ❑ Answer the chapter review DBQ question after you have read the entire chapter. Compare your response to the scoring guidelines and sample response.

Continued

	Study Time: 3 hours at least two times a week (or as often as your schedule permits) ❏ Chapter 9: Read chapter and take notes on Period Five, "Industrialization and Global Integration (c. 1750 to c. 1900)." ❏ Answer the chapter review multiple-choice practice questions after you have read the entire chapter. ❏ Answer the chapter review DBQ question after you have read the entire chapter. Compare your response to the scoring guidelines and sample response. ❏ Chapter 10: Read chapter and take notes on Period Six, "Accelerating Global Change and Realignments (c. 1900 to the Present)." ❏ Answer the chapter review multiple-choice practice questions after you have read the entire chapter. ❏ Answer the chapter review DBQ question after you have read the entire chapter. Compare your response to the scoring guidelines and sample response.
7 days before the exam	**Study Time:** 5 hours ❏ Chapter 11: Take the full-length practice exam and review your answers and the explanations and sample responses. ❏ Based on your performance, identify topics and their corresponding chapters that require further review. ❏ Use additional resources to read about general and specific topics discussed in the practice exam.
6 days before the exam	**Study Time:** 2 hours ❏ Based on your review, target general and specific topics. ❏ Review Chapter 3 again, "Test-Taking Strategies." ❏ Practice writing a response to one document-based question or one long-essay question using the scoring guidelines on pp. 4–6 to score your essay. Note: Previous free-response question topics can be found online at https://apstudent.collegeboard.org/apcourse/ap-european-history/exam-practice.
5 days before the exam	**Study Time:** 2 hours ❏ Review WHAP Key Concepts for Period One (pp. 69–70) and Period Two (p. 86). ❏ Study and target specific topics as needed.
4 days before the exam	**Study Time:** 2 hours ❏ Review the WHAP Key Concepts for Period Three (p. 108) and Period Four (pp. 136–137). ❏ Study and target specific topics as needed.
3 days before the exam	**Study Time:** 1–2 hours ❏ Review the WHAP Key Concepts for Period Five (pp. 168–169). ❏ Study and target specific topics as needed.
2 days before the exam	**Study Time:** 1–2 hours ❏ Review the WHAP Key Concepts for Period Six (p. 200). ❏ Study and target specific topics as needed. ❏ Reread any material you feel is necessary.
1 day before the exam	❏ Relax. You have covered all of the material necessary to score well on the exam. ❏ Get plenty of sleep the night before the exam.
Morning of the exam	❏ Eat a balanced, nutritious breakfast with protein. ❏ Keep your usual habits. Don't try something new today. ❏ Bring your photo ID, ticket for admission (if received), watch (that does not have Internet and does not beep), your 6-digit school code, several sharpened no. 2 pencils with erasers, and a few pens with black or dark-blue ink. Note: Cell phones, scratch paper, books, smartwatches, and food/drinks are not allowed at the testing center.

Chapter 3

Test-Taking Strategies

This chapter was developed as a guide to introduce *general* and *specific* test-taking guidelines, approaches, and strategies that will be useful on the WHAP exam.

General Test-Taking Strategies

To be successful on the WHAP exam, you must spend time learning about the exam and how best to approach it, study to increase your knowledge, and practice answering simulated questions.

Consider the following general strategies:

- Stick to the College Board key concepts.
- Think and reason historically.
- Know the historical periods.
- Know the important historical turning points.
- Know the significant themes.

Stick to the College Board Key Concepts

Take the guesswork out of what to expect on the exam and follow the guidelines for the College Board key concepts. The key concepts are the well from which *all* questions are drawn. The WHAP course content can seem overwhelming at first, with so many dates, events, people, movements, clashes, and alliances, along with a variety of geographic changes to follow. Take a deep breath and understand that the College Board has provided key concepts in the *AP World History Course and Exam Description* that can help you focus on what is testable. It is true that you must acquire knowledge of significant historical events, people, and trends, but as you prepare to take the WHAP exam, the key to your success begins with understanding the College Board guidelines and key concepts.

Think and Reason Historically

Historians study evidence from historical texts in order to interpret and draw conclusions about history. Students who are successful on the WHAP exam use some of the same skills that historians use. These skills are called *higher-order thinking skills*. Higher-order thinking skills challenge you to think about and draw conclusions as you approach each question. Refer to pp. 8–11 for comprehensive descriptions and examples of AP history reasoning skills.

You can make these reasoning skills more manageable by organizing them into four important overarching categories that historians use:

1. Historians look to see how the context of a particular time period uniquely impacted the ideas, actions, and social positions in a society (*contextualization*).
2. Historians look for common similarities and differences from other time periods (*comparison*).

3. Historians look for the causes and effects by asking *why* things happened when they did (*causation*).
4. Historians look for common themes (patterns) that link historical events and changes across different periods of world history (*continuity and change over time*).

Know the Historical Periods

Students who are successful on the exam can identify what preceded and what followed particular events. Use the College Board time frames as bookends. Refer to the "Overview of Historical Periods" table on p. 7 to make sure you recognize periods, eras, centuries, and their topics. To help you focus on topics within historical periods, pay attention to the "Key Facts" headings in chapters 5–10. Focus on the rulers (dynasties) for each time period, political ideologies, and conflicts. Knowing the rulers or dynasties will give you clues for drawing meaningful comparisons between each time period.

Know the Important Historical Turning Points

While history occurs on a continuum of cause and effect, it can be viewed in smaller chunks, with each period of time set apart from others by *turning points* (events that clearly distinguish the beginning and end of each historical period). An overview of the College Board historical periods and themes tells you that although wars are certainly part of the world story, the emphasis on the WHAP exam is on causes, outcomes, and consequences, NOT on strategies or tactics of particular battles. In other words, time spent memorizing all of the details may be time and effort wasted. To be successful on the exam, it is important to pay careful attention to the road map that the College Board has provided and familiarize yourself with the major turning points in history.

Know the Significant Themes

Students must have a general understanding of how to link historical developments to principal themes, patterns, and broad trends in world history. This is often challenging for students. If you can remember that the WHAP exam is about seeing the big picture, and not about specific details, you should be able to identify the most important themes across different time periods and regions. You will also be able to use the themes to decode questions and eliminate answer choices. As a reminder, the five significant themes are interaction between humans and the environment; the development and interaction of cultures; state building, expansion, and conflict; creation, expansion, and interaction of economic systems; and the development and transformation of social structures (see pp. 11–13).

> **TEST TIP:** The following memory aid will help you stay focused on the big picture. Use the acronym SPRITE to remember the historical themes—social, political, religious, ideological, technological, and economic.

Why is knowing the themes important? Because these themes help you to analyze questions. As a teacher, I have found that most AP students have excellent memorization abilities. However, you may have noticed this last year that taking notes and memorizing them did not work when studying for Advanced Placement exams. There is an easy explanation for this. Most classes in early education are based on memorization and comprehension skills. This is really important because you need those skills to retain information in both your short- and long-term memories. However, in Advanced Placement classes, you are asked to do something different—you must be able to *analyze*. But before you can analyze a question, you must have basic knowledge about the historical themes.

If you keep your eye on the thematic big picture, you will be able to predict future developments connected to the same theme. For example, the theme of *interaction between humans and the environment* in early civilizations gives you a clue that you should discuss the relationship of human beings to their geographic natural surroundings. This theme is especially important to help you connect ideas related to humans forming early societies when hunter-gatherers migrated to find food and shelter.

Specific Test-Taking Strategies

When attacking the questions on the WHAP exam, it's important to consider the types of questions you are being asked and the best strategies to tackle these questions. This section discusses specific test-taking strategies for multiple-choice questions and free-response questions.

Once you are familiar with the structure of the exam, the reasoning skills, and the themes, you can start to study. The studying you are going to do will be more strategic and based on critical reasoning. This type of studying will help you predict what types of questions you will face—which will be a huge benefit in your success on the exam. Memorization is good for solidifying key terms, issues, ideas, and events in your long-term memory, but the test will ask you to analyze questions based on critical reasoning skills. Therefore, if you start to use these skills before you even take the exam, you are way ahead of the curve. Now let's talk about specific test-taking strategies for the WHAP exam.

Strategies for Multiple-Choice Questions

Instructions for multiple-choice questions will appear in your exam booklet, but here are specific strategies to help you work through the multiple-choice questions quickly, accurately, and efficiently.

- Budget your time wisely.
- Use the elimination strategy.
- Mark the answer sheet correctly.
- Read each question and document carefully.
- Watch for "attractive distractors."
- Be on alert for EXCEPT and NOT questions.
- Make an educated guess if necessary.
- Practice, practice, practice.

Budget Your Time Wisely

You have 55 minutes to answer 55 multiple-choice questions. You might calculate that you have about 1 minute per question, but this does not include the time it takes to read a passage or analyze an image. Some questions may take more time, while others may take less time. Students who spend too much time dwelling on a single question don't get the score they deserve because they leave insufficient time to answer other questions they could get right. With sufficient practice, you will almost automatically know when a question is taking too much time and when to take an educated guess and move on to the next question. There is no penalty for guessing, so make sure you answer every question.

Use the Elimination Strategy

Take advantage of being allowed to mark in your exam booklet. Eliminate one or more answer choices to narrow down your choices. Remember that, statistically, your chances improve if you can eliminate at least one answer choice. For example, if you can eliminate one answer choice, you have a 25% greater chance of answering the problem correctly. If you can eliminate two answer choices, you will have a 50% chance of answering correctly.

Keep this marking system very simple and mark the answers in your exam booklet (no need to erase the markings because you are allowed to write in your exam booklet). Practice this strategy as you take practice exams in this study guide.

Use a question mark (?) to signify that a choice is a possible answer, use a diagonal line (/) to cross out an answer choice that is incorrect, and leave the choice blank if you are uncertain. This strategy will help you avoid reconsidering those choices you've already eliminated. Notice that in the example below, you've just narrowed your chances of answering correctly to 50%.

? A.

B.

C.

D.

Mark the Answer Sheet Correctly

Make sure that your marked responses on the bubble answer sheet match your intended response. When answering questions quickly, it is common to select the wrong answer choice by mistake. Students who skip questions might make the mistake of continuing to mark their answers in sequence and forget to leave a blank space for the unanswered questions. To avoid this mistake, mark your answers (and any other notes) in the exam booklet before you fill in the answer sheet. If necessary, you will be able to double-check your answers.

Read Each Question and Document Carefully

Don't work so quickly that you make careless errors. Read actively and take notes as you read each document and multiple-choice question (see pp. 30–32 for more information about analyzing a document). Do not make a hasty assumption that you know the correct answer without reading the whole question, the document, and all the answer choices. The hurried test-taker commonly selects an incorrect answer when jumping to a conclusion after reading only one or two of the answer choices in the easy questions. Don't let the easy questions mislead you. You must look at all of the answer choices in order to select the *best* answer.

Watch for "Attractive Distractors"

Watch out for answer choices that look good but are not the *best* answer choice, called *attractive distractors*. Attractive distractors are usually the most common wrong answers. Just because an answer choice is a true statement does not mean that it is the best choice. Let me explain what I mean. National standardized tests have moved away from memorization, comprehension, and even some problem-solving skills. Students are now tested on *content knowledge* and *critical reasoning* rather than memorization skills. You will not be tested on discrete facts like specific dates, author names, events, or even battles. The downside is that you are going to have make *interpretations* for everything in the multiple-choice section.

This means that you may not find one true answer that distinguishes itself in contrast to the other answer choices. Rather, you may have three answer choices that "distract" you from the correct answer because they may appear like the correct choice, but these distractors are not good enough to be the best answer. The facts and concepts presented on the exam are often in subtle variations of the selected answer choices, making it difficult for test-takers to narrow down the correct answer.

Here are some examples of attractive distractor answer choices that should be eliminated:

- Answer choices that only answer *part* of the question and do not directly answer the entire question.
- Answer choices that are not related to the correct time period.
- Answer choices that are not using the correct AP history reasoning skill.
- Answer choices that are not related to both the document and question.

Be on Alert for EXCEPT and NOT Questions

Another common mistake is misreading a question that includes the words *except* or *not*. A negative question reverses the meaning of the question and asks for the opposite to be true in order to select the correct answer. Negative questions can initially be confusing and challenge your thinking. It is helpful to write down brief notes to avoid misreading a question (and therefore answering it incorrectly). Simply write down what you must answer in the question. To help answer a negative question, treat the answer choices as true or false statements, searching for the answer choice that is false.

Make an Educated Guess If Necessary

Remember, there is no penalty for guessing. If you don't know the answer to a multiple-choice question, make an educated guess to get a general range for your answer. If possible, try to eliminate some of the answer choices to increase your chances of choosing the right answer. You have nothing to lose and, quite possibly, something to gain.

Many students believe that if they just follow the right formula, they will be able to select a "good" answer. Please do not fall into the "formula" mindset because this is not a math class; it is a history class. Math is based on analytical skills, and history is based on interpretive skills. When using math analytical skills, you follow a formula to break down the elements needed to determine the "right" answer. When using history interpretive skills, you have to (a) look at all the elements—your knowledge of world history, the document, question, and answer choices and (b) and tie those elements together to determine the best possible relationship.

Interpretive skills always involve a level of *opinion* and *subjectivity*—known as an educated guess. If you get stuck on a question, you may want to reread the question if time permits. The answer may become apparent when you take a second look. If not, make an educated guess by eliminating one or more of the choices that you believe are incorrect and proceed to the next question. If you have time, you can always go back to rethink the marked questions and change the answers.

Example

1. From the founding of each religion, Christians and Muslims shared a belief in:

    A. Principle of separation of church and state
    B. The legal equality of women and men
    C. Equality of opportunity
    D. Belief in an omnipotent God

Let's use four steps to make an educated guess to lead us to the correct answer choice: underline, predict, eliminate, and guess.

Step 1: Underline (or circle) key words in the question—usually AP history reasoning skills and issues. Based on this information, you probably determined that you are looking for a *comparison skill* and the issue of *Christianity and Muslim beliefs*. Here is what you may have underlined.

From the <u>founding</u> of each <u>religion</u>, <u>Christians and Muslims</u> shared a <u>belief</u> in:

Step 2: Predict. What are the beliefs of Christians and Muslims?

> Muslims = one God, holy book, justice
>
> Christianity = one God, holy book, salvation

Step 3: Eliminate incorrect answer choices based on your findings.

Choices A and B can be immediately eliminated. Choice A, *principle of separation of church and state*, can be eliminated because you know that Islam is a political and religious belief system. Even if Christianity was not, this would still mean that Christianity and Islam don't share this belief. Choice B, *the legal equality of women and men,* can be eliminated because both religions were formed during a patriarchal period that was in favor of male leaders.

Step 4: Make a reasonable educated guess.

You have narrowed your chances of selecting the correct answer to 50%, choice C or choice D. Choice C, *equality of opportunity,* and choice D, *belief in an omnipotent God,* require an educated guess based on historical reasoning. Reasonably, choice C is about another time period, probably modern. Therefore, choice D makes the most sense since both religions are about monotheism and the power of one God. The correct answer is choice D.

Practice, Practice, Practice

The College Board recommends consistent practice to attain a higher score. This is why we have included practice questions throughout this study guide: Chapter 4 (diagnostic test), chapters 5–10 (review chapters), and Chapter 11 (full-length practice exam). These practice questions include answers and thorough explanations. Be sure to practice in the exam format as often as possible. To benefit from further practice, you can purchase previously administered AP World History exams at https://store. collegeboard. org. Just keep in mind that some of these exams may not reflect the most recent format of AP World History.

Strategies for Free-Response Questions

Unlike old-school history that is just about memorizing facts, dates, and names, for free-response questions students must do what historians do—interpret historical evidence while reasoning historically. When given historical documents, data, or images, you must be able to provide evidence while constructing a clear argument to support your claims. You must also be able to bring together historical knowledge in the form of an essay, with strong writing conventions on display.

This section gives you strategies for the three types of free-response questions:

- Short-Answer Questions (3 questions, 9 points, 20% of your score)
- Document-Based Question (1 question, 7 points, 25% of your score)
- Long-Essay Question (1 question, 6 points, 15% of your score)

Essay Writing

To write effective free-response essays, stay focused on the AP essay scoring rubrics, follow the essay-writing strategies in the table below, and practice writing essays.

NOTE: Sample essays are available at the end of review chapters 7–10 and on the College Board website found on the AP World History Course Homepage: http://apcentral.collegeboard.com/apc/members/exam/exam_information/232215.html.

Checklist for Answering Free-Response Questions			
Strategy	Short-Answer Questions (SAQs)	Document-Based Question (DBQ)	Long-Essay Question (LEQ)
1. Stay focused on the question.	✓	✓	✓
2. Prewrite to organize your essay.	✓	✓	✓
3. Link AP history reasoning skills.	✓	✓	✓
4. Link the broader historical context (key time periods and principal themes).	✓	✓	✓
5. Link documents to your essay to (a) cite evidence/examples, (b) provide the document's point of view, and (c) corroborate, qualify, or modify your argument.	✓	✓	
6. Write a strong thesis statement that relates to the question.		✓	✓
7. Write an essay with a clear line of reasoning using the standard essay writing format: introduction, body, and conclusion.		✓	✓

The example below applies the specific strategies listed above to organize your essay responses. The following question will help you understand what the AP Readers ARE NOT expecting, and what the AP Readers ARE expecting for you to succeed.

Example:
Directions: Analyze the question below and use some of the steps in the table above to organize your response.

Analyze the changes and continuities of legal systems in affecting social relationships in empires during 600 B.C.E. to 600 C.E.

When you read this question, you may recognize that you need to discuss the relationship between legal codes and empires, but you are probably also thinking that the WHAP exam is extremely challenging. It looks like you are expected to talk about all of the empires in a thousand-year period! However, you are not expected to discuss every empire for over 1,200 years, and you are not expected to list every detail and event that occurred during that period of time. The WHAP exam is not about obscure facts. Instead, you are expected to discuss the relationship between legal codes and empires, and you are expected to develop a broad picture of the changes that occurred during this time period.

Using the strategies, your prewriting notes might include some of the following.

- Identify the *targeted reasoning skill* that is being asked for in the question. In this case, you will need to address patterns of change and patterns of continuity over time.
- Identify the broad, big picture *contextual themes* of this time period related to the question. This question is about the broader themes of politics and the relationship with social hierarchies.
- Discuss *specific examples* from this time period to support your argument (remember, at least one example must be beyond what was found in the documents). You should be able to identify major topics like Hammurabi's Law Code, Roman law, Mosaic Law, and the Qin Empire's use of law for Chinese Legalism.
- Write a clear *interpretation* or *analysis* in the body of your essay. This should include the law and social hierarchies.

Now, with the information above, you should be able to write an effective essay. Remember, the WHAP exam is NOT impossible. The key to being prepared is to follow these steps and think about the big picture, not the unnecessary details and isolated facts.

Now, let's discuss each of the free-response strategies in more detail.

Stay Focused on the Question

One of the most important strategies is that your essay must stay focused on the question and address *all parts* of the question prompt. To help you stay focused, underline or circle key words in the question prompt before you start writing. For example, if the question reads, "Explain the political and social consequences of 20th-century capitalism," you must respond to *both* parts of the question—political and social consequences. Too often students lose points because they don't respond to all parts of the question.

Note: The WHAP exam asks you to choose between two or three questions in the long-essay and short-answer sections. This is an opportunity for you to focus on a time period that is most familiar. For the LEQ, choose one of the three long-essay questions from different time periods (periods 1–2, periods 3–4, or periods 5–6). For the SAQ, you are expected to answer the first two questions from periods 3–6, and then choose to answer either question 3 or question 4 which address two different time periods (periods 1–3 or periods 4–6).

Prewrite to Organize Your Essay

Think before you write by brainstorming, planning, and prewriting to organize your thoughts. The technique of brainstorming means that you should write down all ideas and examples that come to your mind. After you brainstorm, organize those ideas in a logical sequence of events. These ideas should emphasize important points, offer historical evidence, and provide the historical context related to the question prompt. (Note: For the DBQ and LEQ, the exam allows 15 minutes to read documents, take notes, and plan both essays.)

To help you organize your ideas, consider some of the broad themes represented in the acronym SPRITE (social, political, religious, ideological, technological, and economic). SPRITE issues are common themes that have emerged in almost every nation and time period in world history.

If you're stuck and can't think of ideas, read the question a few times and think about one of the AP history reasoning skills. For example, consider the causes and consequences of the historical turning points, or the common similarities and differences in themes during the time period and another time period. Remember that free-response questions are generally designed so that you can receive at least partial credit if you have some knowledge of the subject. Partial responses will get partial credit. Even a response that receives 1 point will be added to your total points. One point may not seem like much now, but earning 1 point is better than zero.

Link AP History Reasoning Skills

AP history reasoning skills are at the heart of all WHAP questions. Every essay must include at least one of the four targeted AP history reasoning skills described on pp. 8–11.

- *Causation* (What was the cause/effect of an event?)
- Long-term patterns of *continuity and change over time* (What was the big picture? What changed or stayed the same?)
- *Comparison* (What were the similarities and differences of an event?)
- *Contextualization* (What was the broader historical significance of the event?)

Refer to the chart below for each free-response question.

Free-Response Question Type	Commonly Assessed Reasoning Skill(s)
Short-Answer Questions (SAQs)	SAQ questions commonly assess the AP history reasoning skills of *comparison* or *continuity and change over time*.
Document-Based Question (DBQ)	The DBQ question can assess any of the AP history reasoning skills: *causation*, *continuity and change over time*, or *comparison*.
Long-Essay Question (LEQ)	The LEQ question commonly assesses the AP history reasoning skills of *causation*, *comparison*, or *continuity and change over time*.

Link the Broader Historical Context (Time Periods and Principal Themes)

Remember to keep your eye on the big picture. Identify and connect the question topic to the broader historical context of different time periods and principal themes. What preceded and what followed the events and developments? Study the historical time periods on p. 7 to help you focus on the big picture of chronological events.

Link Documents to Your Essay

One of the main objectives of the WHAP exam is testing your ability to work with documents in multiple-choice questions, short-answer questions, and document-based questions. This means that you will have to quickly read over a document source or graphic image, and then organize your answer based on some pretty in-depth critical reasoning.

On free-response document-based questions, you will be required to read short passages, interpret images, or make sense of a graph, chart, table, or map to link documents to your essay so that you can attain your highest possible score by (a) creating groups of common themes in your essay, (b) relating the documents to a historical period, (c) citing evidence that matches the context of the documents to your essay topic,

(d) referencing the document's point of view or purpose in your essay, (e) citing at least one additional piece of outside historical evidence, and (f) drawing conclusions about the meaning of the documents to support the argument.

This may seem like a pretty difficult task because these types of questions may challenge your thinking processes. However, these questions may also provide you with an opportunity to excel on the WHAP exam because all of the documents are related to the question prompt. According to the College Board, "there are no irrelevant or deliberately misleading documents." The real issue is how to decode all of the documents so that you can connect them to the questions. The good news is that the documents are giving you the information that you need to answer the questions.

How do you accomplish this? What I strongly suggest is that you stop looking at the exam as a test, and start looking at the exam as a puzzle. Your job is to decode the puzzle. The test-makers have given you most of the pieces of the puzzle, and it is your job to figure out how to complete the puzzle by filling in the missing pieces.

Primary and Secondary Sources

Before you can figure out the puzzle and decode a document, it's important to be familiar with the differences between primary and secondary document sources. A *primary source* is an original passage, speech, or image that was composed, spoken, or illustrated during a specific time period. Primary sources give you an "inside view" of the particular event by someone who directly witnessed or experienced the historical event. For example, primary sources include artifacts, letters, diaries, correspondence, books, speeches, and art. A *secondary source* is a "secondhand" account told by a third party who interpreted or wrote about the primary source. For example, secondary sources are often published by historians in historiographies.

Analyzing Documents: A Five-Step Process

Analyzing documents requires that you evaluate a variety of primary and secondary sources and then draw conclusions about the meaning or relevance of the documents. As you analyze the documents, ask yourself, "Can I show how these documents are related to my thesis, and can I provide reasons, examples, and proof from the specific facts in these documents?"

The following five-step process will help you analyze the documents: Decode the documents; read the documents; group the documents into thematic categories; cite evidence from at least three to six of the documents and at least one outside piece of evidence not found in the documents to corroborate, qualify, or modify the argument; and cite the document's point of view or purpose from three of the documents.

1. **Decode the documents.** First, you must decode the documents by previewing the documents and circling or underlining key points. This will help you match information from the documents to your essay question. As you look through the documents, think about how each document might fit with your tentative thesis. Write notes from the documents in the margins of your test booklet, but remember that you don't have a lot of time to take comprehensive notes. Try to keep notes to one or two words and abbreviate when possible. Don't worry about neatness because you will not be graded on your notes. Just get a general sense of each document so that you can refer to your notes.

   Think like a historian when you decode the documents. Use the acronym CAFE to help you remember how to approach documents by looking for **c**ontext, **a**udience, and important information in the **f**irst sentence and the **e**nding sentence.

C	Context	Historians don't look at what a document says when first looking at a document. Rather, they look at the overall historical *context* to interpret the document. What is context? Context is the author's intended purpose for creating the document. Find the context by asking some of the following questions (remember to take notes as you answer these questions): ■ Are there headings showing the title, author, and date of the document? ■ Who is the author of the document (male/female, nationality, title, social status)? ■ What is the document's main purpose or the author's point of view? ■ Can I paraphrase the author's main ideas in my own words? ■ Can I determine one piece of evidence from the document that supports (corroborates or qualifies) my argument or one that weakens (modifies) my argument? If you know the world history time periods, you should have a general sense of events that took place when the document was written, and you should be able to make an educated guess of the major events, ideas, themes, and issues that surrounded the document when it was written. This information also helps you to understand the author's point of view and to determine what came before and what came after this period (*continuity and change over time*).
A	Audience	Use the information from the context to try to determine the audience that the author is addressing. Ask yourself, in the context of the passage, *who* is the author addressing, *why* is the author addressing this particular audience during this particular time period, and *how* the audience might have influenced the author's work. Keep in mind that until modern history, most people could not read or write. This information narrows the document's intended audience to literate and educated people. This means that before modern history, documents were typically written for nobles, aristocrats, government leaders, rulers, court officers, or business leaders.
F	First Sentence	Once you establish the context and the audience, you can begin briefly reading the source. Read the first sentence and continue to take notes.
E	Ending Sentence	Now read the last sentence of the passage. Many authors insert main ideas in the first and last sentences of their writing because it is the thesis of the argument and the conclusion of the argument.

After you have completed the CAFE process to interpret each document, quickly scan the rest of the document to see if you missed anything, but remember you are just trying to get an overall idea or gist of the document. Reading, scanning, and taking abbreviated notes should take you less than a minute per document. This step is critical to help you set up your essay response.

2. **Read the documents.** Use speed reading, an important tool when test taking. In order to avoid reading every word, you must have the mindset that you will not need to know every detail, statistic, date, or emperor in the document. Rather, look for the overall gist of the document so that you can draw general conclusions. This is an important strategy because you are only being tested on what the questions are asking about in the document. In some cases, the implications of the document may be more important than the actual details in the document.

3. **Group the documents into thematic categories.** It is likely that you will not be familiar with the author or his work, but after decoding the context, this information should help you make an educated guess to determine a relationship between the document and the categorical theme(s) related to your thesis statement. As you analyze each document and take notes, ask yourself two questions: "What is the main point of the document?" and "How does the document relate to the question prompt?" This information will help you group the documents into general or specific thematic groups.

Readers want to see that your essay has specific groupings that logically support your thesis. For example, a generalized grouping might be, "The social roles during the 18th century." A specific grouping on this topic might be, "Documents 1, 3, and 5 characterize women's roles during 18th-century industrialization and the impact on the labor industry."

Note: If you don't have time to read through the entire document, remember that many authors insert main ideas in the first and last sentences of their writing because it is the thesis and the conclusion of the passage. Start with the first and last sentences to get a gist of what the author is trying to convey.

4. **Cite evidence from at least three to six of the documents (and at least one piece of evidence not found in the documents).** To receive the highest score possible, you need to be able to explain the fundamental issues related to the question with supporting evidence from at least three to six documents to support your main thesis and at least one additional piece of historical evidence beyond those found in the documents. When given historical documents, data, or images, you must be able to provide evidence and historical knowledge while constructing a clear argument to support your claims. (Note: Make sure that you use quotation marks around direct quotes when citing information from the documents.)

Don't worry about second-guessing the AP Readers regarding what evidence they expect to be included in your written response. AP Readers take into account that AP teachers use a variety of approaches to select and prioritize evidence that they present to students in class. The only expectation from the Readers is that the evidence is *valid* and *relevant* to the question prompt, identifies specific points that you are trying to defend or refute, and references the correct number of documents in the scoring criteria.

Note: Remember to add the document number when referencing evidence in your essay. For example, "Document 3 vividly describes the brutal methods that were used by the Spanish in their conquest and rule of the Caribbean islands."

5. **Cite the document's point of view or purpose from three of the documents.** After you've scanned the documents using CAFE, it's time to read the documents to gather more information and discuss the point of view from at least three DBQ documents. A surprising number of students neglect this step and lose points on their DBQ essays because they do not successfully address the point of view from three documents. It is not enough to cite the title of a document; you must explain the author's perspective (what influenced or inspired the author to create the document). As you read and take notes in the margins of the document, think about why the author produced the document during the specific period of time. What is the meaning of the document from the author's perspective? For example, "Document 5 demonstrates the author's point of view in the political cartoon, 'Big Brother is Watching You.' The context of this unifying theory of totalitarian governance was characterized by Joseph Stalin's reign in the 20th century."

Write a Strong Thesis Statement

The introduction of your response should include a convincing thesis statement that tells the AP Reader the main points of your argument within a historical context of world history, the question prompt, and the documents. The thesis statement must be historically defensible. A strong opening paragraph tells the Reader what to expect in the body of your essay and lets the Reader know that you are (1) addressing the central issues of the question prompt, (2) addressing all parts of the question, (3) using multiple pieces of historical evidence or examples, (4) following a line of logical reasoning, and (5) including pertinent themes, periods, and AP history reasoning skill(s) such as context, comparison of similarities and differences, causes and effects, or the changes (or no changes) over time periods.

To earn your best possible score, carefully read the question prompt and use key points from the question prompt in your thesis statement. Do not just restate the question in the thesis statement. AP Readers are looking for your own original thinking. After you read the question prompt, what thoughts jump out at you? Can you provide concrete facts to support your ideas? Write down these ideas as you brainstorm to prewrite a tentative thesis. Underline or circle what you will need to locate in the document(s) and use this information to formulate your thesis statement.

Remember, the brainstorming stage is tentative; you can always adjust the thesis statement once you have gathered all of the information from the documents. Try to avoid a long introduction and aim to keep it about the same length as your conclusion.

Use the Standard Essay Writing Format

Write a clear and legible essay using a general essay writing format:

- Introduction with a strong thesis statement that focuses on the question prompt
- Body with examples and evidence that are historically defensible
- Conclusion

Paragraph one: The introduction of your essay should focus on a line of reasoning, and (a) present a strong main thesis within a historical context, (b) list supporting point #1, (c) list supporting point #2, (d) list supporting point #3, etc.

Paragraphs two, three, and four: Divide the body of your essay into separate supporting points. The body must develop historical evidence by showing *proof, examples, evidence, analysis,* or *interpretations* of the points in your introduction. This includes evidence that corroborates, qualifies, or modifies your thesis. Think about the thematic big picture of major developments and events to support your argument, and think about the key turning points that caused shifts in developments. Remember that a strong argument not only provides supporting evidence, but also addresses alternative explanations. It is sometimes helpful to use "who, what, where, why, and when" to support your points. And remember to show a connection between each paragraph and your thesis statement.

> Paragraph Two – Develop point #1
>
> Paragraph Three – Develop point #2
>
> Paragraph Four – Develop point #3

Note: Continue this process if you have more than three supporting points.

Paragraph Five: Finish with your conclusion. A lengthy conclusion is not necessary, but your conclusion should expand on important points from your thesis. The Reader will look to the introduction and the conclusion. Therefore, if you make a mistake at the beginning of the essay, you have a second chance to provide substance from your thesis at the end.

Let's take an example and show how the document analysis process works. This following passage can appear as a multiple-choice, short-answer, or document-based question.

Example

Source: Han Feizi, Chinese Legalist Scholar, 3 B.C.E.

The sage in governing the people considers the springs of their action, never tolerates their wicked desires, but seeks only for the people's benefit. Therefore, the penalty he inflicts is not due to any hatred for the people but to his motive of loving the people. If penalty triumphs, the people are quiet; if reward overflows, culprits appear. Therefore the triumph of penalty is the beginning of order; the overflow of reward, the origin of chaos.

Fill in the chart below based on your findings.

C (Context)	**Look at the *author and date* of the document and then determine the context of the document.** The author is Han Feizi, a Chinese Legalist Scholar, and the passage was written in 3 B.C.E. What do you know about the author? My guess is not that much. It would be difficult to remember every individual in world history. However, you can make some inferences based on the other information. For example, you can see that he is a scholar from the Chinese Legalism tradition. Remember, Chinese Legalism was a philosophy that was popular after the period of the Era of Warring States. Chinese Legalism was in conflict with the other Chinese philosophy, Confucianism. Just based on the author and date, you may be able to make inferences. You can guess that this is a pro-Legalist text. You can guess that it is going to be about the key issue of Legalism: social stability. And, it is probably going to praise a strong leader.
A (Audience)	**Try to determine the audience of the document.** This next step is tougher. You are not really given any information about the audience, but you can make an educated guess. You know that the audience cannot be the general public of China since most people at that time were farmers and uneducated. This population would not be able to read a philosophical treatise. Since you know that this document was written after the Era of Warring States, you can guess that the passage must be directed to the people in China who would be most affected by that conflict—nobles and the emperor. From this information, you may guess that the audience for this document is the educated elite who are seeking answers to the general conflict in China.
F (First Sentence)	**Skim the first sentence.** *The sage in governing the people considers the springs of their action, never tolerates their wicked desires, but seeks only for the people's benefit.* You can probably see that the first sentence is about the need to create social order.
E (Ending Sentence)	**Now skim the ending sentence.** *Therefore the triumph of penalty is the beginning of order; the overflow of reward, the origin of chaos.* The ending sentence seems to put an emphasis on providing strong punishments to those who create instability.

Now, let's interpret the information to draw some conclusions about this document.

- The document is about the need for a strong leader.
- The document calls for rewards and punishments for social order.
- The document follows the Era of Warring States.

Now we can answer the question(s) knowing that this document is about an attempt to create loyalty amongst the nobles to a centralized emperor for social order.

The following strategic plan of attack summarizes the strategies for all three free-response question types:

A Strategic Plan of Attack

Read the question TWICE and note the directions, prompts, and document sources.

↓

PREWRITE. Gather information from the question, sources, or documents by marking and taking notes about key points. Organize your ideas by prewriting an outline (or list) to prioritize important points and evidence from sources and documents.

↓

WRITING SHORT-ANSWER RESPONSES

No thesis statement.

Answer all three points in each question to receive full credit.

Answer three questions—the first two questions and then choose ONE of the last two questions (the period you know more about).

Keep your answers brief and address historical evidence from the primary or secondary sources (if included).

Use interpretation to historically explain the *content knowledge* related to the question.

Use reasoning skills to address similarities and differences, causes and effects, or changes and continuities over time.

WRITING A DOCUMENT-BASED RESPONSE

Develop a thesis statement that is a historically defensible claim, establishes a line of reasoning, and responds to *all* parts of the question.

Support your argument by showing relationships among the question, thesis, and evidence.

Describe the broader historical context of events, developments, and processes. (What happened before, during, or after that time frame?)

Group the documents and make connections among the documents to corroborate, qualify, or modify the argument.

For the highest possible score, identify, interpret, and cite specific examples from six documents to support your argument.

Provide examples of the author's point of view, historical situation, purpose, or audience from at least three documents.

Use targeted reasoning skills (comparison, causation, or continuity and change over time).

Support your argument using at least one piece of outside historical evidence not mentioned in the documents.

WRITING A LONG-ESSAY RESPONSE

Choose ONE of the three question options (the period you know more about).

Develop a thesis argument that is a historically defensible claim and establishes a line of reasoning.

Explain how the historical context influenced the topic.

For the highest possible score, support your argument with specific facts and examples that corroborate, qualify, or modify your argument.

Relate the topic to broader historical events, developments, or processes (before, during, or after the time frame of the question).

Incorporate a targeted reasoning skill (comparison, causation, or continuity/change).

↓

PROOFREAD AND EDIT. Leave yourself a few minutes to correct errors and make minor revisions.

Working with Graphic Images

Graphic images are commonly used on the WHAP exam for multiple-choice questions, short-answer questions, and document-based questions. Some students become concerned about working with images because they believe they cannot interpret artifacts, art, pictures, political cartoons, maps, graphs, charts, and tables.

The overall strategy in working with images is to take your time as you interpret the image and follow the steps below. The steps may seem time-consuming, but trust the process. When you first start to work with images, it will require more time. As you practice the process, you will internalize the steps and interpretation will move much quicker. Just remember to always look for the reasoning skills and the historical issues.

1. Scan the question(s) and underline key words to see what types of reasoning skills and issues you are being asked to interpret. By scanning the questions first, you can filter out insignificant elements of the image.

2. Look for clues in the graphic image by quickly brainstorming all ideas that come to mind about what you see. When interpreting graphs, charts, and tables, always read the title, labels, and values (if available). This information can provide you with important information about the answer. For example, graphs showing you historical trends, increases, decreases, averages, and frequencies can help you make predictions about the answer.

3. Compare the question(s) to the image to see how these details relate to one another.

4. Use the elimination strategy (see p. 24) to narrow your choices.

Example 1: Multiple-Choice Question
Use the graph below to answer the question that follows.

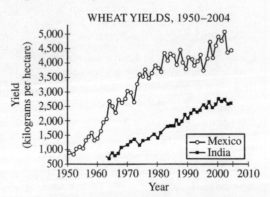

Source: Food and Agriculture Organization of the United Nations (FAO), 2005.

1. Which of the following best explains the different rates of food production in developing countries?

   A. Mexico was fully industrialized, while India remained an agricultural economy into the 1970s.

   B. Mexico was open to international trade, while India closed itself off from the globalized market.

   C. Mexico used the methods and technologies from the Green Revolution before they were implemented in India.

   D. The Mexican political system was more stable than India's system due to India's participation in the Soviet Union's communist alliance.

Now, let's use four steps to lead us to the correct answer choice.

Step 1: Scan the question and underline key words.

For example:

> Which of the following best explains the <u>different rates</u> of <u>food production</u> in <u>developing countries</u>?

By scanning the question you probably determined that the AP history reasoning skills are *comparison* and *causation.* These skills show you that you are comparing and contrasting, and you are looking for the *cause* of the different rates. The primary issue is food production in the developing world.

Step 2: Look for clues in the graph. Remember: For graphs, you will be looking for increases, decreases, or trends.

> **Title and headings:** Wheat yields in Mexico and India
>
> *x*-axis: Years in increments of ten years, 1950–2010
>
> *y*-axis: Wheat yields in kilograms

Step 3: Compare the relationship to make an interpretation. Take your time to examine the details. The details of the graph show you that both Mexico and India saw an increase in wheat production since the mid-20th century. However, Mexico increased its rate of wheat production faster than India.

Step 4: Use the elimination strategy. We know that the two countries are in the developing world. We know that the graph is about wheat production. We can see that both countries had an increase in wheat production. And, we can see the difference in the rate of production. However, we don't really have an answer to the question. The question asked to explain the reason for the difference. Here is where the elimination strategy helps. Remember a key principle of test taking: You are not looking for the right answer; you are looking for the *best possible answer.*

Choices A and B can be eliminated. Choice A can be eliminated very quickly based on our knowledge that most developing countries remained primarily agricultural throughout the 20th century and struggled to industrialize. Choice B can be eliminated since we know that countries tended to be open to trade following World War II due to the incentives of the International Monetary Fund and World Bank. This narrows your choices to C or D. Choice D can be eliminated since India was a part of the non-aligned movement and never joined directly with the Soviet Union. In addition, an alliance with the Soviet Union does not explain why India's wheat production increased. Choice C is the only possible choice since the Green Revolution occurred during this time period. It explains the development of wheat production since it started first in Mexico. Choice C also provides the best possible answer to the question of causation for explaining the differences in wheat production.

Example 2: Short-Answer Question

Use the image below to answer the question that follows.

Source: *Emperor Meiji* (1880) by
Takahashi Yuichi, Imperial
Collection.

2. **(a)** Identify and explain one significant <u>change</u> in Japanese culture after 1853 C.E. as depicted in
the picture.

   (b) Identify and explain one additional <u>change</u> in Japanese culture after 1853 C.E. as depicted in
the picture.

   (c) Identify and explain one <u>continuity</u> in Japanese political practices after 1853 C.E.

Short-answer graphic questions assess your ability to show historical content knowledge of the graphic
image while following explicit directions of the task.

Skills for a good short-answer response include: (1) carefully read the directions and answer all parts of the
question or you may only receive partial credit, (2) brainstorm to form an interpretation about the basic
details of the image, (3) determine the historical context of the image—what is the significance of the image,
and (4) address the reasoning skill—comparison or continuity and change over time.

Use the chart below to answer short-answer questions with images.

Skill	Part (a)	Part (b)	Part (c)
Directions Always follow the specific directions.	Identify what changed in Japanese culture after 1853.	Identify one additional change in Japanese culture after 1853.	Identify what stayed the same in Japanese political practices after 1853.
Details of image Ask yourself, "Who is Emperor Meiji and what does his clothing tell me?"	Emperor Meiji's clothing reflects Western European cultural and military ideas.		
Historical context Ask yourself, "What do I know in the historical context of 19th-century Japanese culture and politics?"	Meiji adopted Western European style of clothing that was a significant shift from previous empires to a modernized Western culture. Historically, Meiji transformed Japanese culture from a Tokugawa shogun (military government) to Western European culture (advanced technologies and military), helping Japan move toward new innovations in the 20th century.		
Reasoning skill Ask yourself, "What is the historical reasoning skill?"	Change over time	Change over time	Continuity over time

After formulating some ideas, provide a short-answer response that describes or references the image in your response and provides a historical interpretation of the image related to the question.

Sample Response

(a) The picture of the Meiji Emperor demonstrates a change in clothing exemplified by the more Western style of leadership and military uniforms. This was due to the Western and Japanese exchange of cultural values.

(b) The picture of the Meiji Emperor also demonstrates how the emperor adopted Western values of professional military and the political system of organization. This can be seen in the standard use of cultural symbols for hierarchy and authority.

(c) While Emperor Meiji adopted Western attitudes to build up Japan's military and industry, Japanese authorities continued to stress social hierarchy and the importance of respecting the leader of the country as a symbol of national unity for all of the different classes. This meant that the local governors, samurai, and peasants continued to see the emperor as the representative of the entire island of Japan.

Chapter 4

Diagnostic Test

This chapter contains a diagnostic test that will give you valuable insight into the types of questions that may appear on the WHAP exam. It is for assessment purposes only and is NOT a full-length practice exam. Additional practice questions are included at the end of each period review chapter (chapters 5–10) and a full-length practice exam is included in Chapter 11.

As you take this diagnostic test, try to simulate testing conditions and time limits for each of the following sections:

Section	Diagnostic Test	Actual Exam
Section I: Part A—Multiple-Choice Questions	25 questions, 25 minutes	55 questions, 55 minutes
Section I: Part B—Short-Answer Questions	2 questions, 25 minutes	3 questions, 40 minutes
Section II: Part A—Document-Based Question	1 question, 60 minutes	1 question, 60 minutes
Section II: Part B—Long-Essay Question	1 question, 40 minutes	1 question, 40 minutes

Answer Sheet for Multiple-Choice Questions

1 Ⓐ Ⓑ Ⓒ Ⓓ
2 Ⓐ Ⓑ Ⓒ Ⓓ
3 Ⓐ Ⓑ Ⓒ Ⓓ
4 Ⓐ Ⓑ Ⓒ Ⓓ
5 Ⓐ Ⓑ Ⓒ Ⓓ

6 Ⓐ Ⓑ Ⓒ Ⓓ
7 Ⓐ Ⓑ Ⓒ Ⓓ
8 Ⓐ Ⓑ Ⓒ Ⓓ
9 Ⓐ Ⓑ Ⓒ Ⓓ
10 Ⓐ Ⓑ Ⓒ Ⓓ

11 Ⓐ Ⓑ Ⓒ Ⓓ
12 Ⓐ Ⓑ Ⓒ Ⓓ
13 Ⓐ Ⓑ Ⓒ Ⓓ
14 Ⓐ Ⓑ Ⓒ Ⓓ
15 Ⓐ Ⓑ Ⓒ Ⓓ

16 Ⓐ Ⓑ Ⓒ Ⓓ
17 Ⓐ Ⓑ Ⓒ Ⓓ
18 Ⓐ Ⓑ Ⓒ Ⓓ
19 Ⓐ Ⓑ Ⓒ Ⓓ
20 Ⓐ Ⓑ Ⓒ Ⓓ

21 Ⓐ Ⓑ Ⓒ Ⓓ
22 Ⓐ Ⓑ Ⓒ Ⓓ
23 Ⓐ Ⓑ Ⓒ Ⓓ
24 Ⓐ Ⓑ Ⓒ Ⓓ
25 Ⓐ Ⓑ Ⓒ Ⓓ

Section I

Part A—Multiple-Choice Questions

Multiple-choice questions are grouped into sets. Each set contains one source-based prompt (document or image) and two to five questions.

25 questions

25 minutes

Questions 1–3 refer to the following passage.

> "The Tathagata," the Buddha continued, "does not seek salvation in austerities, but neither does he for that reason indulge in worldly pleasures, nor live in abundance.
>
> The Tathagata has found the middle path. There are two extremes, O Bhikkhus, which the man who has given up the world ought not to follow the habitual practice.
>
> On the one hand, of self-indulgence which is unworthy, vain and fit only for the worldly-minded and the habitual practice. On the other hand, of self-mortification, which is painful, useless and unprofitable."
>
> —Source: Buddha, 6th century B.C.E.

1. Based on your knowledge of world history, which of the following best explains the context for why Buddha offered this insight?

   A. Buddha was attempting to criticize the infiltration of foreign beliefs that resulted from contacts of interregional trade.

   B. Buddha was attempting to reform the Hindu religion by offering a new egalitarian spiritual path for all believers.

   C. Buddha was attempting to criticize the existence of a priestly class.

   D. Buddha was calling for a return to the original spiritual sources of the faith.

2. In the centuries following Buddha's death, which of the following best illustrates how Buddhist beliefs spread out and became accepted?

   A. Buddhism remained isolated to India because of the multiple competitive belief systems in the region.

   B. Buddhism spread out to the known world through sea trade.

   C. Buddhism was diffused by Ashoka through the Silk Roads.

   D. Buddhism became the state religion of the Chinese dynasties.

3. Based on your knowledge of world history and the <u>third paragraph</u>, which of the following best explains why Buddhism struggled in China?

   A. Buddhism's belief in nirvana came into conflict with China's emphasis on real-world social obligations.

   B. Buddhism's doctrines favoring the caste system conflicted with Chinese egalitarian beliefs.

   C. Buddhist beliefs did not allow for any trade of material goods.

   D. Buddhist monks stressed that followers had to leave their families for the monastic life.

Questions 4–6 refer to the following passage.

One day, Wang Tsun resigned from his post and set out for the capital to take the imperial examination. As he was approaching the capital, he met Hsu T'ang, who was seeing some friends off at the outskirts of the city.

"Eh," Hsu T'ang asked him, "what are you doing here in the capital?"

"I have come to take the imperial examination," answered the former functionary.

Upon hearing this, Hsu T'ang angrily declared, "How insolent you are, you lowly clerk!" Although they were now fellow candidates for the imperial examination, Hsu T'ang treated him with contempt. But in the end, Wang Tsun passed the examination and became very famous. Hsu T'ang did not pass until five years later.

—Source: The Examination System during the T'ang Dynasty, 8th century B.C.E.

4. Which of the following best describes the Chinese practice referenced in the passage?

    A. The story is about the significance of filial duties and obligations.

    B. The characters emphasize the need for hierarchy and social order.

    C. The emperor is praised for having complete authority to maintain stability.

    D. The civil service test is promoted as a way to find the individual with the best merit.

5. Based on your knowledge of world history, which of the following Chinese philosophies might oppose the ideas expressed in the passage?

    A. Daoism, because it taught that natural harmony was necessary for spiritual fulfillment

    B. Confucianism, because it stressed the importance of filial obligations to establish practical relationships

    C. Chinese Legalism, because it argued that the emperor needed absolute power to keep selfish people under social order

    D. Buddhism, because it overlapped with Chinese beliefs providing a spiritual afterlife in nirvana

6. Which of the following conclusions can be drawn about the consequence of the practice described in the passage?

    A. Chinese peasants were able to compete and move up the social ladder.

    B. The Chinese emperor was able to consolidate power and stop nobles from competing for power over the land.

    C. The Chinese were able to stop the Northern steppe invaders from entering China.

    D. The Chinese nobility trained and educated their sons to retain positions of power for family honor.

Questions 7–9 refer to the following two sources.

Source 1

It has been heard repeatedly that you have subjected the upright community of Muhammad to your devious will, that you have undermined the firm foundation of the Faith, that you have unfurled the banner of oppression in the cause of aggression, that you no longer uphold the commandments and prohibitions of the Divine Law, that you have incited your abominable Shi'a faction to unsanctified sexual union and to the shedding of innocent blood, that like they "Who listen to falsehood and consume the unlawful" (Quran V:42) you have given ear to idle deceitful words and have eaten that which is forbidden . . .

—Source: "The Letters of Sultan Selim I and Safavid Shah Isma'il I," 1514 C.E.
Sultan Selim of the Ottoman Empire to Shah Isma'il of the Safavid Empire.

Source 2

Now to being: Your honored letters have arrived one after another, for "No sooner has a thing doubled than it has tripled." Their contents, although indicative of hostility, are stated with boldness and vigor. The latter gives us much enjoyment and pleasure, but we are ignorant of the reason for the former. In the time of your late blessed father when our royal troops passed through the lands of Rum to chastise the impudence of Ala' al-Dawla Dhul Qadr, complete concord and friendship was shown on both sides. Moreover, when your majesty was governor at Trebizone there existed perfect mutual understanding. Thus now, the cause of your resentment and displeasure yet remains unknown. If political necessity has compelled you on this course, then may your problems soon be solved.

—Source: "The Letters of Sultan Selim I and Safavid Shah Isma'il I," 1514 C.E. Shah Isma'il of the Safavid Empire response to Sultan Selim of the Ottoman Empire.

7. Taken together, which of the following best expresses the context of a historical conflict between the leaders of the Ottoman Empire and the Safavid Empire in 1514?

   A. Both leaders fought over access to sea-based trade routes.
   B. Both leaders expressed a desire to stop minority groups from breaking away for their own nationalist identification.
   C. Both leaders were attempting to reform the dominant religious sect of their empires.
   D. Both leaders identified with different religious sects in the religion of Islam.

8. Which of the following best identifies the historical advantage of the author of the passage in Source 1?

   A. The Ottoman Empire was equipped with a navy fleet, while the Safavid Empire was landlocked.
   B. The Ottomans lacked a policy for integrating minority groups into their empire.
   C. The Safavids did not have a strong and coherent national identity.
   D. The Ottomans lacked a national army, while the Safavids had a professional military.

9. Which of the following contradicts the notion that both empires were in a constant state of tension?

   A. The Ottomans were constantly attempting to expand their eastern boundaries.
   B. The Safavids invited foreign advisers to help with checking and balancing the nobles.
   C. The Ottomans and Safavids were connected through trade along the Silk Roads.
   D. The Ottomans and Safavids were a part of two distinct Islamic sects, the Sunni and Shiite.

Questions 10–12 refer to the following image.

Source: Cuneiform Clay Tablet. Mesopotamia,
Iraq, c. 3000 B.C.E.

10. Which of the following best supports the purpose of the cuneiform tablet in sedentary societies?

    A. It demonstrates the outgrowth of artists who were patronized by higher classes.
    B. It was an example of recordings used for both historical and practical purposes.
    C. It was a part of walled defenses against invaders and flooding.
    D. The cuneiform's graphics validate the lack of written languages in early societies.

11. During the period of sedentary societies, which of the following social groups were associated with the images depicted on the cuneiform tablet above?

    A. Local farmers to differentiate themselves from centralized control
    B. Hunters and gatherers to record images of their migration with animals
    C. Bureaucrats who were in a position to record the production of food surpluses
    D. Explorers who recorded expeditions in different regions

12. Which of the following was an alternative form of record-keeping used by other societies during the same time period?

    A. Holy books used by priests and scholars to express their religious beliefs
    B. Legal codes recorded by emperors to create social order in their hierarchies
    C. Oral stories told by storytellers and hunter and gatherer groups to teach about genealogies and cultural values
    D. Stone tablets used by Ashoka on trade routes to inform people about his religious and cultural norms

Questions 13–15 refer to the following passage.

Many eyes, I am afraid, are irretrievably lost, and several poor wretches must remain forever totally blind. Dysentery too, that fellest of all diseases in the Negro race, is at work amongst them, and will undoubtedly commit fearful ravages.

Five hundred and seventy-two Africans were found on board. What the number was at starting there is no means of ascertaining. One of the crew, a slave, who acted on board in the capacity of a cook, and who preferred being captured by Englishmen to escaping with his master, told me that many had died and were thrown overboard during the passage.

The exact number taken on board, however, he could not tell. In all probability, it was not under seven hundred; but of course this is only mere conjecture.

—Source: Thomas Nelson, "Remarks on the Slavery and the Slave Trade of Brazil," 1846.

13. Nelson's reaction in the <u>first paragraph</u>, ". . . will undoubtedly commit fearful ravages," is best understood in the historical context of which of the following?

   A. The headright system that had colonists in the Americas pay for indentured servant labor
   B. The trade of African slave labor from Western Africa to the Islamic Middle East through the Trans-Saharan trade route
   C. The migration of Asian labor into India and South Africa during the Industrial Revolution
   D. The Triangle Trade of African labor to the West Indies for sugar production

14. Which of the following offers the best interpretation about what made the slave system unique in contrast to other forms of coerced labor?

   A. The individuals were forced into labor and then received their freedom after 7 years of labor.
   B. The slaves were defined as property in order to extract natural resources for mercantile trade.
   C. The individuals were used to send tribute back to the capital of the empire.
   D. The Africans were placed in segregated hometowns and then provided labor in the South African townships.

15. Based on your knowledge of world history and the passage, which of the following most accurately identifies the reason for the introduction of slavery?

   A. European nations competed with each other in the mercantile global market for the extraction of natural resources.
   B. European nations needed explorers who would be willing to seek out alternative trade routes to China.
   C. European nations needed cheap labor for factory production in the Industrial Era.
   D. European nations used cheap native labor in Mexico to extract silver for the global market.

Questions 16–18 refer to the following passage.

In England, exclusive of Wales, it is only in some of the colliery districts of Yorkshire and Lancashire that female Children of tender age and young and adult women are allowed to descend into the coal mines and regularly to perform the same kinds of underground work, and to work for the same number of hours, as boys and men; but in the East of Scotland their employment in the pits is general; and in South Wales it is not uncommon.

—Source: "Women Miners in the English Coal Pits. Great Britain, Parliamentary Papers, Vol. XVI, 1842.

16. Based in a historical context, which of the following changes prompted the British Parliament to write the document above?

   A. The feudal land lords used a three-field system to produce a surplus of food.
   B. The cottage system allowed for individuals to make products based on the investments of local traders.
   C. The Black Death led to more people moving into urban centers.
   D. The Industrial Revolution led to urbanization and more mass manufacturing.

17. Based on your knowledge of world history, which of the following best describes how the majority of English reformers tried to resolve the problems identified in the British Parliamentary Papers?

    A. They led revolutionary movements based on Marxism and anarchism.
    B. They used labor unions and political legislation to reform wages and working conditions.
    C. They fought for a laissez-faire approach to capitalist markets.
    D. They argued for destruction of new technology and a return to agricultural organization.

18. Which of the following accurately represents the impact of social reactions to the problems described in the British Parliamentary Papers?

    A. England changed back to an agricultural society.
    B. The English industrial system developed only two social classes, owners and impoverished workers.
    C. English workers argued for industrial social leaders to have more freedom for investment and economic production and expansion.
    D. Women led social movements and then began to argue for expanded suffrage.

Questions 19–21 refer to the following image.

Source: "McDonald's in the Middle East."

19. Based on your knowledge of world history, which of the following best describes the main point of the image above?

    A. McDonald's and other transnational companies are seeking out cheap labor in the developing world.
    B. Technology has now replaced many of the manufacturing and menial jobs done by human labor in the past.
    C. Western culture is converging with other societies through globalization.
    D. Global cultures are mostly distinct and divergent from one another.

20. Which of the following provides the best explanation as to why this image can be captured in the 21st century?

    A. The lowering of tariffs under the GATT and the WTO has led to more globalized trade.
    B. Arab nationalist movements have tried to unite the Middle East around a common pan-Arab movement.
    C. Previously colonized countries in the developing world have demanded their self-determination.
    D. Religious traditionalist and fundamentalist beliefs have become more prominent around the globe after the Cold War.

21. Based on your knowledge of world history, which of the following historical events is most similar to the image above?

    A. The Ming Dynasty's decision to tell Zheng He not to explore areas outside of China
    B. The Ottomans' search for spiritual purity following their loss at the naval Battle of Lepanto
    C. The Mongols' reopening and protection of the Silk Roads that connected various cultures ranging from China to Eastern Europe
    D. Aurangzeb's closing down of Hindu temples in Northern India during the Mughal Empire to pursue purity in Islam

Questions 22 and 23 refer to the following passage.

The violence which has ruled over the ordering of the colonial world, which has ceaselessly drummed the rhythm for the destruction of native colonial forms and broken up without reserve the systems of reference of the economy, and the customs of dress and external life, that same violence will be claimed and taken over by the native at the moment when, deciding to embody history in his own person, he surges into the forbidden quarters. To wreck the colonial world is henceforward a mental picture of action which is very clear, very easy to understand and which may be assumed by each one of the individuals which constitute the colonized people. To break up the colonial world does not mean that after the frontiers have been abolished, lines of communication will be set up between the two zones. The destruction of the colonial world is no more and no less than the abolition of one zone, its burial in the depths of the earth or its expulsion from the country.

—Source: Frantz Fanon, "The Wretched of the Earth," 1963.

22. According to the passage above, Fanon was responding to the historical context of which of the following?

    A. The Spanish and Portuguese initiation of a triangle trade in slavery between Europe, Africa, and the Americas
    B. The exploration of the Americas by Europeans in search of an alternative trade route to China
    C. The European use of the developing world for the extraction of raw resources
    D. The lowering of tariffs after the GATT to increase globalized trade

23. Which of the following best explains one way that colonizers justified the global imperialism described in Fanon's passage?

    A. The post-WWII belief about increasing global trade for the purpose of isolating communism
    B. The European use of science, called social Darwinism, to justify supposed racial hierarchies
    C. Nationalist ideologies in the developing world that promoted self-determination
    D. Cultures diffused and spread to a variety of regions over the Silk Roads and Indian Ocean trade routes.

Questions 24 and 25 refer to the following passage.

Moreover, purely consensual trade with less densely populated parts of the Old World—a strategy being pursued by all the core areas of Eurasia, often on a far larger scale than pre-1800 western Europe could manage—had limited potential for relieving these resources bottlenecks. But the New World had greater possibilities, in large part due to the effects of global conjunctures. First, epidemics seriously weakened resistance to European appropriation of these lands. Second, the transatlantic relationship that followed conquest and depopulation—mercantilism and especially the African slave trade—made the flow of needed resources to Europe self-catalyzing in ways that consensual trade between Old World regions was not; it anticipated, even before industrialization, the self-perpetuating division of labor between primary products exporters and manufacturing regions in the modern world. Thus the world's first "modern" core and its first "modern" periphery were created in tandem . . .

—Source: Kenneth Pomeranz, "The Great Divergence: China, Europe, and the Making of the Modern World Economy," 2000.

24. Which of the following best summarizes why Pomeranz believes that Europe was able to subdue the Western Hemisphere?

   A. He argues that the main reason was the appeal of European beliefs in nationalism and local rule.
   B. He argues that European professional militaries overwhelmed the native populations.
   C. He maintains that Europe's scientific discoveries allowed it to use new technologies to explore.
   D. He argues that epidemics made European settlement and trade expansion more accessible.

25. Which of the following best supports Pomeranz's argument?

   A. Europeans used new medicines and steam technology to subdue colonies.
   B. African slave labor was used in the West Indies for the production of sugarcane to supply the mercantile trade.
   C. Europeans used new scientific discoveries from China for navigation.
   D. The Black Death led to peasant labor going into urban centers for work.

IF YOU FINISH BEFORE TIME IS CALLED, CHECK YOUR WORK ON THIS SECTION ONLY. DO NOT WORK ON ANY OTHER SECTION IN THE TEST.

Part B—Short-Answer Questions

2 questions

25 minutes

Reading Time: 5 minutes (brainstorm your thoughts and organize your responses)

Writing Time: 20 minutes

Directions: The short-answer questions will not require that you develop and support a thesis statement. Use complete sentences—bullet points or an outline are unacceptable. Answer **all** parts of the question to receive full credit.

> NOTE: The following short-answer questions are for instructional purposes only and may not reflect the format of the actual exam. On the actual exam, there are four short-answer questions, but you are only required to answer three questions. Answer the first two questions, and choose to answer either the third or fourth question. Questions 1 and 2 are based on sources with texts, images, graphs, or maps from periods 3–6. Question 3 (periods 1–3) and Question 4 (periods 4–6) have no sources.

Question 1. Use the two passages below and your knowledge of world history to answer all parts of the question that follows.

Source 1

As the ancient Annals explained, the boundary between insiders and outsiders can be mutually penetrable in different times and under different circumstances. Understanding this aspect of Chinese culture can be especially valuable in making sense of China's internal and international policies; the relationship between the Chinese Communist and Nationalist parties provides a modern example. After their initial period of cooperation ended in 1927, the two became enemies and were entangled in a bloody civil war until the Japanese launched its overall invasion of China a decade later. Threatened by a common outsider, the parties launched a second united front. But when the Japanese were out of the picture at the end of World War II, the Communists and Nationalists reverted to their adversarial positions and, with the establishment of the People's Republic of China in 1949, the Nationalists fled to Taiwan.

—Source: Haiwang Yuan, "This is China: The First 5,000 Years," 2010.

Source 2

As we will see, China's withdrawal of the most powerful navy on earth from periodic patrols on and around the Indian Ocean turned out to be of immense importance for the course of world history. For now, though, we have to ask why the Chinese court abandoned the Indian Ocean. The short answer is that political struggles within China, struggles that had been going on for some time at the imperial court between those who wanted the voyages to continue and those who wanted China to apply its resources to the greater threat of the Mongols to the north, finally resolved themselves in favor of the latter when the emperor died in 1435. From that point forward, the Chinese state abandoned the seas, paid attention to how an agrarian economy could feed a growing population, and saw their main enemy as being the nomads roaming the steppe to the north. Rebuilding and lengthening the Great Wall became of greater importance to China's rulers than continuing the expensive voyages of the Treasure Ships.

—Source: Anonymous

1. **(a)** Compare the two interpretations and briefly explain the primary reason for China's social tension that has developed since the Modern Age.
   (b) Explain ONE difference between the two passages regarding China's foreign relationships.
   (c) Provide ONE piece of historical evidence that would support Yuan's interpretation of internal Chinese tensions.

Question 2. Use the graph below and your knowledge of world history to answer all parts of the question that follows.

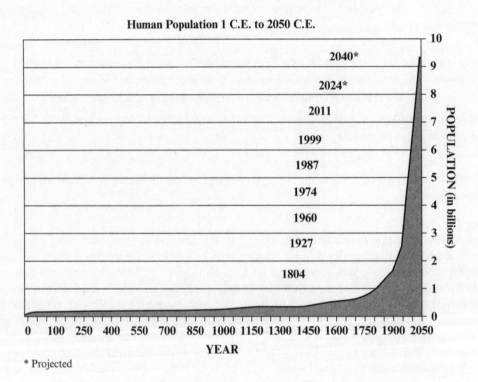

Human Population 1 C.E. to 2050 C.E.

* Projected

—Source: https://populationeducation.org/content/population-information

2. **(a)** Identify and explain ONE historical <u>change</u> in food production that influenced human population growth after 1750, as shown on the graph.
   (b) Identify and explain ONE piece of historical evidence that reflects a <u>continuity</u> in the projections in the graph about global population growth.
   (c) Identify and explain ONE piece of historical evidence that might <u>change</u> the results of the projections in the graph about global population growth.

IF YOU FINISH BEFORE TIME IS CALLED, CHECK YOUR WORK ON THIS
SECTION ONLY. DO NOT WORK ON ANY OTHER SECTION IN THE TEST.

Section II

Part A—Document-Based Question

1 question
60 minutes

Reading Time: 15 minutes (brainstorm your thoughts and organize your response)
Writing Time: 45 minutes

Directions: The document-based question is based on the seven accompanying documents. The documents are for instructional purposes only. Some of the documents have been edited for the purpose of this practice exercise. Write your response on lined paper and include the following:

- **Thesis.** Present a thesis that supports a historically defensible claim, establishes a line of reasoning, and responds to all parts of the question. The thesis must consist of one or more sentences located in one place—either the introduction or the conclusion.
- **Contextualization.** Situate the argument by explaining the broader historical events, developments, or processes that occurred before, during, or after the time frame of the question.
- **Evidence beyond the documents.** Support or qualify your argument by explaining at least one additional piece of specific historical evidence not found in the documents. (Note: The example must be different from the evidence used to earn the point for contextualization.)
- **Analysis.** Use at least three documents that are relevant to the question to explain the documents' point of view, purpose, historical situation, and/or audience.
- **Historical reasoning.** Use historical reasoning to show relationships among the documents, the topic question, and the thesis argument. Use evidence to corroborate, qualify, or modify the argument.

Based on the documents that follow, answer the question below.

Question 1: Analyze how Islam spread and managed multiple religious, political, and social groups from 1300 to 1700 C.E.

Document 1

> **Source: Map of Ottoman Empire in 1680 C.E.**
>
>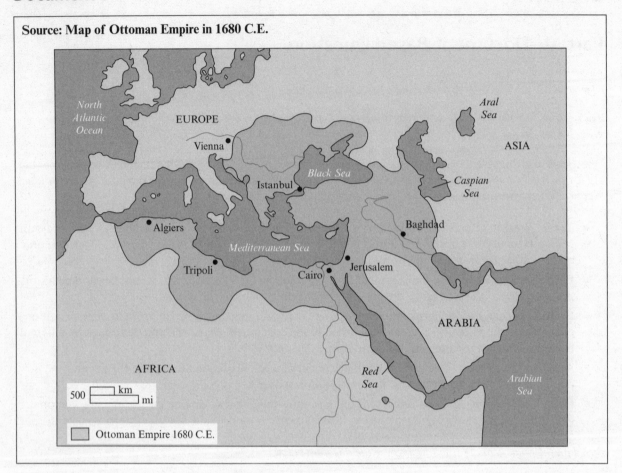

Document 2

> **Source: Ogier Ghiselin de Busbecq, Hapsburg Ambassador to Suleiman the Magnificent, Constantinople, from letters sent to the Austrian Emperor, 1554 to 1562 C.E.**
>
> The sultan's hall was crowded with people, . . . but there was not a single man in that Great Assembly who owed his position to anything but merit. No distinction is attached to birth among the Turks. . . . In making his appointments, the Sultan pays no regard to wealth or rank, nor does he take into consideration recommendations or popularity. He considers each case on its own merits, and examines carefully into the character, ability, and disposition of the man whose promotion is in question. . . . Those who receive the highest offices from the Sultan . . . do not believe that high qualities are either natural or hereditary, nor do they think that they can be handed down from father to son, but that they are partly the gift of God, and partly the result of good training [in state schools], great industry, and unwearied zeal. . . . Among the Turks, therefore, honors, high posts, and judgeships are the rewards of great ability and good service. If a man be dishonest, or lazy, or careless, he remains at the bottom of the ladder. This is the reason that they are successful in their undertakings . . . and are daily extending the bounds of their empire.

Document 3

Source: Ibn Battuta describes the Muslim African kingdom of Mali, 1352 C.E. Battuta was a Muslim scholar who documented his journeys in the Islamic world. Here he shows his high regard for the Islamic sultan.

The Negroes possess some admirable qualities. They are seldom unjust, and have a greater abhorrence of injustice than any other people. Their sultan shows no mercy to anyone who is guilty of the least act of injustice. There is complete security in their country. Neither traveler nor inhabitant need worry about robbers or men of violence. They do not confiscate the property of any white man who dies in their country, even if it be uncounted wealth. On the contrary, they give the money to some trustworthy white person in the community until the rightful heir takes possession of it.

Document 4

Source: Ibn Khaldun, "The Muqaddimah," circa 1350 C.E. Arab historian who wrote about the political and social issues of civilizations.

When one considers what God meant the Caliphate to be, nothing more needs to be said about it. God made the Caliph his substitute to handle the affairs of his servants. He is to make them do the things that are good for them and forbid them to do those that are harmful. He has been directly told so. A person who lacks the power to do a thing is never told to do it.

Document 5

Source: Eskandar Beg Monshi, "History of Shah Abbas the Great," the chief secretary and advisor to Abbas I, shah of Safavid Empire (Persia), 1587–1629 C.E. The shah was considered the strongest ruler of the empire.

His history had official approval and was based on his own observations and interviews with officials, soldiers, merchants, and travelers for the work. The welfare of his people was always a prime concern of the Shah, and he was at pains to see that the people enjoyed peace and security, and that oppression by officialdom, the major cause of anxiety on the part of the common man, was totally stamped out in his kingdom. Substantial reductions were made in the taxes due . . . first, the tax on flocks in Iraq, amounting to nearly fifteen thousand Iraqi toman, was remitted to the people of that province, and the population of Iraq, which is the flourishing heart of Iran and the seat of government, by this gift was preferred above the other provinces. Second, all divan levies were waived for all Shiites throughout the empire during the month of Ramadan. The total revenues for one month, which according to the computation of the divan officials amounted to some twenty thousand toman, were given to the people as alms. The object was that they should be free from demands for taxes during this blessed month, which is a time to be devoted to the service and worship of God.

Document 6

Source: François Bernier: An Account of India and the Great Moghul, 1655 C.E. Bernier, a French traveler and representative of King Louis XIV for the French East India company, wrote a book about his travels for 12 years in the Mughal Empire during the time of Emperor Aurangzeb.

The persons thus put in possession of the land, whether as timariots, governors, or contractors, have an authority almost absolute over the peasantry, and nearly as much over the artisans and merchants of the towns and villages within their district; and nothing can be imagined more cruel and oppressive than the manner in which it is exercised. There is no one before whom the injured peasant, artisan, or tradesman can pour out his just complaints; no great lords, parliaments, or judges of local courts, exist, as in France, to restrain the wickedness of those merciless oppressors, and the Kadis, or judges, are not invested with sufficient power to redress the wrongs of these unhappy people. This sad abuse of the royal authority may not be felt in the same degree near capital cities such as Dehly and Agra, or in the vicinity of large towns and seaports, because in those places acts of gross injustice cannot easily be concealed from the court.

Document 7

Source: Guru Nanak, founder of the Sikh religion, circa 1450 C.E. "We are all one, created by One Creator of all creation."

IF YOU FINISH BEFORE TIME IS CALLED, CHECK YOUR WORK ON THIS SECTION ONLY. DO NOT WORK ON ANY OTHER SECTION IN THE TEST.

Part B—Long-Essay Question

1 question

40 minutes

Directions: Write your response on lined paper. You must demonstrate your ability to use specific, historical evidence and write an effective essay to support your argument. Your essay is considered a first draft and may contain some grammatical errors that will not be counted against you. However, to receive full credit, your essay must demonstrate historically defensible content knowledge and the following:

- **Thesis.** Provides a thesis that is a historically defensible claim, establishes a line of reasoning, and responds to all parts of the question—rather than merely restating or rephrasing the question. The thesis must consist of one or more sentences and must be located in one place—in the introduction or the conclusion.

- **Contextualization.** Describes how the historical context is relevant to the question. Relates the topic to broader historical events, developments, or processes that occurred before, during, or after the time frame. (Note: Must include more than a phrase or reference.)

- **Evidence.** Supports and develops the argument by identifying specific and relevant historical examples of evidence related to the topic of the question.

- **Historical reasoning.** Uses historical reasoning (comparison, causation, or continuity/change over time) to structure the argument that addresses the question.

- **Analysis.** Demonstrates a complex understanding of the historical development that focuses on the question to corroborate, qualify, or modify the argument. (For example, analyze multiple variables, explain similarities/differences, explain cause/effect, explain multiple causes, explain both continuity and change, explain connections across periods of time, corroborate multiple perspectives across themes, or consider alternative views.)

Write ONE essay on the topic that follows.

> **NOTE: On the actual exam, you will choose ONE essay from three different time periods.**

Question 2: Compare the ways in which state political systems governed their territories between the Post-Classical Era (c. 600–c. 1450) and the Early Modern Era (c. 1500–c. 1750). (*AP History Reasoning skill: Comparison*).

IF YOU FINISH BEFORE TIME IS CALLED, CHECK YOUR WORK ON THIS SECTION ONLY. DO NOT WORK ON ANY OTHER SECTION IN THE TEST.

Answer Key for Multiple-Choice Questions

1. B	6. D	11. C	16. D	21. C
2. C	7. D	12. C	17. B	22. C
3. A	8. A	13. D	18. D	23. B
4. D	9. C	14. B	19. C	24. D
5. B	10. B	15. A	20. A	25. B

Answer Explanations

Section I

Part A—Multiple-Choice Questions

1. **B.** Remember that Siddhartha Gautama's name was changed to "Buddha" when he became the original "enlightened one." The Buddhist movement was a reform movement of Hinduism that used many of the Hindu beliefs, but criticized the inequality of the caste system, as indicated in choice B. The traditions of Buddhism did not stress a cultural purity for China, and therefore did not criticize other beliefs (choice A); criticisms of other beliefs arose from Neo-Confucian leaders during the Ming Dynasty. Buddhists did not criticize the priestly class and often called for a monastic life (choice C). Buddhism was not based on the holy books or written sources of Hinduism (choice D).

2. **C.** The Mauryan Empire under Ashoka sent out Buddhist monks along the Silk Roads, choice C. Buddhism was not isolated (choice A); it was mixed with Chinese beliefs like Confucianism. Buddhism spread primarily over land, not sea routes (choice B). Buddhism never became a state faith (choice D); it was eventually mixed with Confucianism to form Neo-Confucianism.

3. **A.** Buddhism's belief in escaping this world for nirvana came into conflict with the Confucian emphasis of practical filial pieties and obligations mentioned in the third paragraph, "unworthy . . . fit only for the worldly-minded and habitual practice," choice A. Buddhism criticized the inequality of the caste system (choice B). Buddhism criticized the obsession with material goods but was not against all trade (choice C). Buddhism did call for a monastic life but was tolerant of family life as well (choice D).

4. **D.** The passage is about families competing to do well on the civil service exam to show merit, choice D. While one of the themes of Confucianism is filial or family obligations, it is not a theme of the passage (choice A). Confucianism also stresses the importance of social order, but this passage is not about social hierarchy (choice B). There is no reference in the passage to Chinese Legalism's emphasis on the emperor's power (choice C).

5. **B.** This passage is similar to Confucianism's stress on the individual upholding his family's honor through competition on the civil service exam, choice B. The passage is about merit and competition, and Daoism stresses individual harmony based on the natural order (choice A). This passage does not express the absolute authority of the emperor (choice C). Choice D is incorrect because it is about Neo-Confucianism, which mixed the practicality with the rewards of the afterlife in nirvana.

6. **D.** Chinese families saw the civil service exam as a way to prove their honor. The nobility would hire teachers to train their sons for the exam, choice D. In theory, the civil service exam was open to all people, but peasants could not afford the training for the exam (choice A). Nobles used the exam to advance up the social ladder (choice B). The civil service exam was not relevant to the problem of the steppe invaders (choice C); the Northern wall system was used to slow down the steppe peoples.

7. **D.** The Ottomans identified with the Sunni sects and the Safavids identified with the Shiite sects, thus creating conflict between the empires, choice D. Only one leader did not have access to the sea (choice A); the Ottomans had access to the Mediterranean Sea, but the Safavids were landlocked. Greeks, Bosnians, and Egyptians did break away from the Ottoman Empire, but it was in the late 1800s, not the 1500s (choice B). There were no reform movements within either empire at this time (choice C).

8. **A.** The Ottomans had a strong navy due to their location in Northern Africa by the Mediterranean, but the Safavids were landlocked in the Persian area, choice A. The Ottomans used a variety of methods of cooptation and integration for their Christian and Jewish minorities (choice B), including the Janissary, Devshirme, and Millet systems. Shah Abbas created a unified Safavid Empire under the Shiite faith system (choice C). The Ottomans had a strong professional army and navy (choice D).

9. **C.** The Ottomans and Safavids did peaceably trade over the Silk Roads. This would be an avenue of peace between the two societies, and contradicts the notion that they were constantly in a state of tension, choice C. Indeed, the Ottomans were constantly fighting the Safavids with the hope of expanding into the Central Asian areas (choice A). The Safavids did invite foreign advisers to create internal checks and balances with the nobles (choice B), but this had nothing to do with the Ottomans. The Ottomans and Safavids were a part of two sects of Islam, and this created tension between the two empires (choice D).

10. **B.** Cuneiform was used for recording of irrigation and surpluses of food, choice B. Patronizing of artists occurred during the Renaissance (choice A). This tablet was used for recording, not for the construction of walls (choice C). The tablet shows that pictures and languages were used for written records (choice D).

11. **C.** Bureaucrats who managed irrigation and food surpluses were the ones who learned the different recording practices, choice C. Farmers were not literate during this period (choice A). Hunters and gatherers did record their migrations, but this was done on cave walls, not on stone tablets (choice B). Exploration and recording happened much later in world history (choice D).

12. **C.** Storytelling was a sacred practice taught in hunter and gatherer groups who did not use written languages, choice C. Holy books required literate priestly classes who learned the language of the empire (choice A). Legal codes were written in order to solidify the leader's power (choice B). Ashoka spread his rule through written legal codes on tablets placed throughout Northern India and on the Silk Roads (choice D).

13. **D.** The first paragraph is describing the devastating effects of the Trans-Atlantic slave trade that took Africans to the West Indies, Brazil, and North America for the production of sugarcane for mercantile markets, choice D. The headright system (choice A) was not a coercive form of labor; it provided passage for English poor to the American colonies. They worked for the investor families and then gained freedom after 7 years of indentured servitude. The passage is about African slavery; it is not about the Trans-Saharan slave trade between Africa and the Middle East (choice B). Asian and Indian laborers traveled around the world during the Industrial Revolution to find agricultural jobs; this was not coercive labor (choice C).

14. **B.** The unique aspect of the Trans-Atlantic slave trade was taking human beings and defining them as property, choice B. This was done to ensure relatively free labor for nation-states looking to extract resources for manufacturing. The description in choice A is for indentured servitude for English citizens. Tribute (choice C) was primarily done by land-based empires like the Aztec and Chinese dynasties; this allowed local areas to retain some sovereignty but admit allegiance to a central empire. Africans were segregated in the 20th century into South African townships (choice D); however, this is not what the passage was describing nor is it the right time period.

15. **A.** Slavery was a product of the competing nation-states looking to extract raw resources like sugar for mass production. The profits were then used to invest in their militaries and expand into colonial areas for more resources, choice A. European exploration (choice B) came before the Trans-Atlantic slave trade. Slave trade developed when Europeans needed a cheap labor source for harvesting crops, after the Industrial Era (choice C). Choice D describes the encomienda system, but the passage is describing a sea-based trade of humans for slavery.

16. **D.** The Industrial Revolution was spurred on by the discovery and use of coal. This led to mining for children and women working in the mines as mentioned in the passage, choice D. The change in farming that allowed for a rotation of crops happened during the 1500s, long before women and children entered into mining (choice A). The cottage system (choice B) was a way of investing and making single-item products during the 1500s. The Black Death (choice C) did cause a decline in labor and a rise in prices for labor and urbanization, but all of this happened before the outgrowth of mining.

17. **B.** British workers used collective bargaining and passed laws ensuring labor protections, choice B. There were radical movements like Marxism and anarchism (choice A), but they did not gain enough popularity among the British public. British workers did not accept a complete hands-off approach to government regulation (choice C). Choice D is describing the Luddites, a small and radical group of reformers who wanted to destroy technology and return to farming.

18. **D.** Women who entered the workforce joined unions, and middle-class women argued for women's higher education and the right to vote, choice D. England never went back to a primarily agricultural state (choice A); it became the leader of the Industrial Revolution. The English system developed a prosperous and large middle class (choice B). English workers did want a system with competition and new innovations (choice C), but they also believed in government regulations and collective bargaining by workers.

19. **C.** The image depicts a transnational company, McDonald's, fitting into the culture and language of the Middle East; this is an example of cultural convergence, choice C. It is true that transnational companies are seeking out cheaper labor in the developing world, but the image does not portray labor, (choice A). Technology has replaced many menial jobs, moving many developed nations into service-based economies, but the image does not represent that (choice B). The image represents how globalization is causing a mixture of cultures; cultural divergence (choice D) is just the opposite.

20. **A.** The 1947 meeting that established the General Agreement on Tariffs and Trade (GATT), and the 1995 World Trade Organization (WTO) lowered tariffs and allowed for greater movement of transnational companies, choice A. Arab nationalist movements (choice B) were strong during the 1950s to the 1970s and operated at the political and military levels, not the international consumer level. After WWI, developing countries demanded independence and self-determination, but the image is about the globalization of trade (choice C). Religious traditionalists have become more prominent around the world. While religious individuals are shown in the image, this does not explain the influence of McDonald's and transnational corporations (choice D).

21. **C.** The Mongols' reopening of the Silk Roads was done through conquering, but it led to the diffusion of culture and technology, choice C. The Ming decision to stop the sharing of culture and trade is just the opposite of what's depicted in the image (choice A). The Ottomans' choice to stop the import of Western technology for Islamic purity is the opposite of what's depicted in the image (choice B). Aurangzeb's actions in Mughal India are the opposite of the diffusion demonstrated in the image (choice D).

22. **C.** Fanon was writing about the effects of European imperialism, including the use of the developing world's resources in an unequal manner, choice C. Fanon was responding to the effects of imperialism, not the Trans-Atlantic slave trade (choice A). The exploration of the Americas was a part of the 1600s, not the 20th century when Fanon was writing his critique (choice B). Fanon was talking about European imperialism, not globalization (choice D).

23. **B.** Europeans had used a scientific definition of race to justify their "civilizing" of the developing world, choice B. The freeing of the developing world was seen as necessary to defeat communism (choice A), but this question is asking about global imperialism. Nationalist ideologies were used to fight against, not justify, European imperialism (choice C). Cultural diffusion (choice D) would be the opposite of the justification for subduing cultures and societies in the developing world.

24. **D.** Pomeranz argues that disease opened up frontiers and made it easier for European populations to move into these freed-up zones, choice D. Pomeranz was arguing that disease, demographic movements, and luck were the reasons for European success, not ideas (choice A). Pomeranz does not argue that military superiority was the reason for European successes during exploration (choice B). Pomeranz is arguing *against* the idea that unique European scientific discoveries led to successful colonization (choice C).

25. **B.** The European movement of African labor and the use of the labor to extract resources fits into Pomeranz's argument about demographics and labor, choice B. Choice A is about the successes of European imperialism in the 1800s. Pomeranz did not argue about the diffusion of new technologies from Asia (choice C), although this is historically accurate. Peasant labor did go into cities after the Black Death (choice D), but this was a century before colonization and exploration.

Part B—Short-Answer Questions

Question 1

Reasoning skill: *comparison (and contrast)*.

The first part of this analysis is to understand the arguments of the two historians about Chinese development. Yuan and the other author are both arguing about internal tensions in Chinese society. Yuan argues that China has developed a fear of outsiders due to the problems of foreign invaders from the Northern steppe region. The other historian argues that the Chinese Confucian elders decided to stop exploration to retain cultural purity and stop the invasions from the Mongols. These two passages provide a number of comparisons and contrasts that will help to answer the prompts.

The second part is to understand what you are being asked to do. Part (a) asks you to compare the two historians' interpretations on internal social issues in China. Part (b) asks you to explain one brief contrast (difference) in the historical interpretations about foreign relations, and Part (c) asks you to fulfill the task by supporting the historian Yuan with historical context.

To receive full credit, you must address all three parts. The sample responses for parts (a), (b), and (c) in the table below are for instructional purposes only. On the actual exam, you must write ONE complete short-answer essay.

Part	Task	Explanation	Sample Response
(a)	Compare the two passages and explain the primary reason for China's social tension since the Modern Age.	Part (a) can be answered by comparing the two authors' views regarding China's fear of outsiders. Both passages express social tension, but Yuan's argument refers to China's ongoing internal tension over fears of foreign influence. Your response should demonstrate this idea by referring to the fear of Mongol invasions.	Both sources demonstrate that an internal tension in China was the fear of outside influence due to invasions from the steppe region such as by the Mongols or from foreign invaders like Japan during WWII.
(b)	Identify ONE difference between the two passages related to China's foreign relationships.	Part (b) can be answered by focusing on the different groups within China's society. Yuan argues that the internal social tension in China between political parties was developed through foreign invasions. However, the second passage argues that China's foreign relations were influenced through long-term trade relationships.	Yuan argues that the Chinese fear of outsiders was due to foreign invasions, and the second passage argues that Chinese Confucian elders feared a loss of cultural purity due to global trade and exploration.
(c)	Identify ONE example that supports Yuan's interpretation of internal Chinese tensions.	Part (c) can be answered by relating a specific example from the broader historical context of Chinese world history. Yuan argues that foreign invasions created a fear of outsiders. Therefore, your answer might include the steppe invaders.	The steppe invaders coming into China had an influence on internal tensions very early, as seen by the invasions in the Qin Dynasty that led to the development of the Great Wall system early in Chinese classical history.

Question 2

Reasoning skill: *continuity and change over time*.

This graph may challenge your ability to analyze and interpret data about changes in the human population over time. The tasks are asking you to explain why the changes in population growth occurred. Remember, the question is asking you to support your interpretation within a reasonable historical context.

To receive full credit, you must address all three parts.

Part	Task	Explanation	Sample Response
(a)	Identify what caused the change in food production that influenced human population growth after 1750.	Part (a) is asking you to explain the main change in why human population growth takes off after the mid-1700s. You will need to provide a clear but concise cause-and-effect relationship about specific changes that occurred over time.	Population growth expanded at such a fast rate after the mid-1700s due to the Industrial Revolution since new technology helped to produce greater food surpluses.
(b)	Identify ONE piece of historical evidence that supports the continuity of projections in the graph about population growth.	Part (b) is asking you to support your argument in Part (a) by providing a specific piece of evidence from the historical context. You can provide many examples of new types of innovation in technology and food production.	The creation of the diesel engine, the discovery of fossil fuels, and the use of new fertilizers all allowed for the mass production of food for growing populations living in urban areas.
(c)	Identify ONE piece of evidence that might change the results of the projections in the graph about population growth.	Part (c) is asking you to show that you can see multiple historical interpretations, and that you can weigh or compare different viewpoints that might change the results of the projections. You will need to provide an alternative piece of evidence that challenges your argument.	The projections in the graph assume that other variables will remain the same. A catastrophic event, such as a global war or pandemic, could dramatically slow population growth.

Section II

Part A—Document-Based Question

DBQ Scoring Guide

To achieve the maximum score of 7, your response must address the scoring criteria components in the table below.

Scoring Criteria for a Good Essay	
Question 1: Analyze how Islam spread and managed multiple religious, political, and social groups from 1300 to 1700 C.E.	
Scoring Criteria	**Examples**
A. THESIS/CLAIM	
(1 point) Presents a historically defensible thesis that establishes a line of reasoning. (Note: The thesis must make a claim that responds to *all* parts of the question and must *not* just restate the question. The thesis must consist of *at least* one sentence, either in the introduction or the conclusion.)	The introduction and thesis of your essay should (a) analyze the causes for the spread of Islam and (b) briefly list the three categories: the first supporting point (religion), the second supporting point (politics), and the third supporting point (social relationships). Note: Do not just restate the question in the thesis statement, and remember to stay on topic. The thesis provides a specific argument about how Islamic leaders used forms of merit and tolerance to form a unified community. Notice that the sample response has a clear and specific thesis that addresses all parts of the prompt and follows a line of reasoning (religion, politics, and social groups).

Continued

B. CONTEXTUALIZATION	
(1 point) Explains the broader historical context of events, developments, or processes that occurred before, during, or after the time frame of the question. (Note: Must be more than a phrase or reference.)	To construct your argument, recall any information from the broader historical context that you can remember about how Islamic empires began, spread, and then had diverse populations. What happened before, during, and after Islam spread? This essay provides specific context about the faith and religion of Islam. The student provides background for the context, origins, and spread of Islam. In addition, the basic background for the argument's claims about Islam's management of multiple groups and religions is provided.
C. EVIDENCE	
Evidence from the Documents **(2 points)** Uses at least *six* documents to support the argument in response to the prompt. OR **(1 point)** Uses the content of at least *three* documents to address the topic prompt. (Note: Examples must describe, rather than simply quote, the content of the documents.)	To receive the highest points for this category, you must include at least six documents related to the question. As depicted in Document 1, the map of the Ottoman Empire and Document 2, letters from the Ambassador to Suleiman, the essay discusses how different Islamic leaders incorporated minority groups and different ethnic and religious people in their government. The argument discusses how they both included techniques of tolerance and religious purity. The writer provides specific examples in each paragraph to describe the historical context. The writer refers to the merit system in the Ottoman Empire (Documents 1 and 2) for the Janissary Corps. The writer also provides context for India as a location that struggled with combining the different Hindu and Muslim populations. The essay then discusses the context of the Safavids and Mughals (Documents 4, 5, and 6) who sought a more pure definition of Islam.
Evidence Beyond the Documents **(1 point)** Uses at least one additional piece of specific historical evidence beyond those found in the documents relevant to the argument. (Note: Evidence must be different from the evidence used in contextualization.)	Document 7 depicts the nonviolent and serene qualities of Guru Nanak, the founder of Sikhism. To provide evidence beyond the documents, you might want to provide specific historical evidence about the founder of the Sikh religion. Nanak grew up in a Hindu family surrounded by Islamic neighbors. He spoke out for equality of humanity and peace within the region. Nanak exemplifies the unification of religious, political, and social worlds during the 15th century. Note: Even if you weren't familiar with Guru Nanak's biography, notice that the illustration depicts a holy or divine person who appears to be fostering peace.
D. ANALYSIS AND REASONING	
(1 point) Uses at least *three* documents to explain how each document's point of view, purpose, historical situation, and/or audience is relevant to the argument. (Note: References must explain how or why, rather than simply identifying.)	The documents are mostly analyzed for their purpose. However, some of the documents provide the author's point of view. For example, the analysis of Document 3 shows the point of view of the Islamic explorer Ibn Battuta who wants to justify the spread of Islam in Africa. In Document 4, the analysis is that of an Islamic scholar who wants to justify Islamic authority as based on religion and justice. Document 6 was written by a European emissary who criticized the Mughal empire for his home audience as a place of intolerance.

D. ANALYSIS AND REASONING	
(1 point) Uses historical reasoning and development that focuses on the question while using evidence to corroborate, qualify, or modify the argument. (Examples: Explain what is similar and different; explain the cause and effect; explain multiple causes; explain connections within and across periods of time; corroborate multiple perspectives across themes; or consider alternative views.)	This particular prompt is asking about how societies were able to create religious, political, and social order by including different groups of people. This is a cause and effect question so you will want to see how the documents address that relationship and then corroborate, qualify, or modify your argument (see Documents 1, 2, 3, 4, and 5).

Sample Response

In 600 C.E., the prophet Muhammad preached a "new" message of the religious principles of Islam when he wrote the holy book, the Quran. Muhammad claimed to have received a revelation from Allah, or God, that was meant to unite the various tribes in the Saudi Arabian desert. Muhammad attracted thousands of followers to a message that promised spiritual equality to all people. After his death, the religion of Islam spread to Northern Africa and throughout the Middle East. Islam was split between two sects, Sunni and Shiite. Future Islamic ki]ngdoms, or Caliphates, faced the problems of managing both this internal split and the multiple different ethnic, religious, political, social, and cultural groups in the region. Successful Islamic empires in the region maintained their religious identity while forming relationships with individuals of other groups through merit and tolerance.

Some historians would argue that in the context of history, the Islamic Caliphates were able to create order through the political authority of the sultan (Documents 2, 3, and 4). In Document 4, Ibn Khaldun seems to express this point of view when he argues that the political authority is a product of Islam's religious teachings. However, this argument does not explain how Islamic leaders were able to accommodate many different groups into the political management of the empires.

Islam was able to spread over a wide geographic region while being comprised of numerous different ethnic groups. By 1300 C.E., Islamic empires included regions in India, the Middle East, Northern African, and Western Africa. The spread of Islam posed a problem for Islamic empires since most people in these regions were not Muslim. Document 1 corroborates this by showing how the largest Islamic empire, the Ottomans, included Christian, Jewish, and other non-monotheistic regions. In Document 2, Busbecq explained to the audience of the European Hapsburg Empire that the Ottoman Sultan made appointments through good training and a merit based system, and not through wealth, rank, or hereditary. His description showed that the Ottoman Turks were able to bring together different people into their government by valuing "great ability and good service" for civil service positions. This was most likely a reference to the Ottoman Janissary Corps that used individuals from various faiths to advise the Sultan.

Islam was most successful when its leaders found a way to incorporate the beliefs and traditions of all the people into overseeing and participating in the empire (Documents 2, 4, 5, and 6). Document 3 was written by Ibn Battuta, who expressed a point of view of admiration for the incorporation of West Africans into the Islamic faith. Battuta wrote to fellow Muslims in the Middle East about the positive contribution of West African Muslims in the kingdom of Mali. Mali had been consolidated under the rule of Mansa Musa, who connected Islam in Western Africa to the trade networks of the Trans-Saharan and the Silk Roads. Similarly, in Northern India, the faiths of Hinduism and Islam often melted together to create a stronger unity. Document 7 depicts the new leadership of Guru Nanak, who created the Sikh religion in Northern India to unite the Muslims and Hindus in one faith. This was similar to the attempt by Akbar the Great to create the Divine Faith in the hope of uniting all people of different faiths in India to unite the country.

However, an alternative view is that some Islamic leaders attempted to rule their empires through religious purity and nationalism. The Safavids built their empire around the favoring of the Shiite sect of Islam. Shah Abbas did this in order to unite his small kingdom against his neighboring rival, the Ottomans. In Document 5, Beg Monshi justifies the rule of Shah Abbas by pointing out how the central leader treated the Shia population with fairness in the area of taxation. This represents how Shah Abbas used the Shiite identity to centralize the empire and unify it under one common Islamic identity. Document 6 was written by a European representative who was criticizing the Mughal Empire for its lack of checks on the Muslim authorities. This was the time of Aurangzeb, the grandson of Akbar the Great. Aurangzeb tried to also create a unified and pure Islamic India. He did this by ending any tolerance to Hindus, stopping interfaith marriages, and closing Hindu temples. In both of these cases, Islamic leaders used a more monolithic and pure definition of Islam to unify the empire and maintain control.

Islamic empires had a complex history. Some attempted to use a more narrow form of Islam to create unity based on an exclusive definition of the faith. However, during the 14th to the 18th centuries, many other empires attempted to create unity by allowing for tolerance and inclusion of other faiths in the political structures.

Part B—Long-Essay Question

Long-Essay Scoring Guide

Each point is earned independently. (For example, you can earn a point for developing your argument and earn a point for providing evidence.) To achieve the maximum score of 6, your response to ONE topic should use the scoring criteria that follow as a checklist to make sure you have included all of these elements in your essay.

Scoring Criteria for a Good Essay	
Question 1: Compare the ways in which state political systems governed their territories between the Post-Classical Era (c. 600–c. 1450) and the Early Modern Era (c. 1500–c. 1750).	
Scoring Criteria	**Examples**
A. THESIS/CLAIM	
(1 point) Presents a historically defensible thesis that establishes a line of reasoning. (Note: The thesis must make a claim that responds to *all* parts of the question and must *not* just restate the question. The thesis must consist of *at least* one sentence, either in the introduction or the conclusion.)	The introduction of your essay should present a strong main thesis by briefly introducing the content of the historical reasoning skill of both comparison and contrast of "governance" related to the Post-Classical Era and the Early Modern Era. Make sure your thesis follows a clear line of reasoning to show differences (or similarities) in the way governments ruled their empires or nation-states.

B. CONTEXTUALIZATION

(1 point) Describes the broader historical context of events, developments, or processes that occurred before, during, or after the time frame of the question. (Note: Must be more than a phrase or reference.)	It is important to cite and discuss specific examples related to the broader historical context. This is particularly important in this question because you are comparing two different time periods and two different ways in which governments ruled its regions. For example, you must compare the Post-Classical Era to the Early Modern Era. Brainstorming ideas will help you accumulate examples to address in your response. List the context of events and developments of state governance that occurred before, during, or after those two time periods and cite specific examples.

C. EVIDENCE

Evidence from the Documents **(2 points)** Supports the argument in response to the prompt using specific and relevant examples of evidence. OR **(1 point)** Provides specific examples of evidence relevant to the topic of the question. (Note: To earn 2 points, the evidence must *support* your argument.)	Provide evidence for your comparisons of the two periods. For example, Post-Classical period themes for governance: land-based empires, tributary systems, migration of people from the steppe region, spread of religions and use of religions for governance, law codes, trade routes (Silk Roads, Indian Ocean, Trans-Saharan, and Mediterranean), and diffusion of culture. Early Modern Era themes for governance: nation-states and nationalism, explorers, colonization, trade routes, mercantile trade, or enlightened monarchies. Now, you can start to think of multiple ways to develop your response with examples from a variety of different empires and kingdoms.

C. ANALYSIS AND REASONING

(2 points) Demonstrates a complex understanding of historical development that addresses the question and uses evidence to corroborate, qualify, or modify the argument. (Examples: Explain what is similar and different; explain the cause and effect; explain multiple causes; explain connections within and across periods of time; corroborate multiple perspectives across themes; and consider alternative views.) OR **(1 point)** Uses historical reasoning (comparison, causation, or continuity/change over time) to frame and develop the argument while focusing on the question. (Note: Must be more than a phrase or reference.)	Always remember to incorporate the reasoning skill. In this case, it's comparison and contrast. Examples: (1) One possible response would be to compare the methods of governance and then think of how the two periods were different from each other. (2) One of the greatest turning points is the development of nation-states in the Early Modern Era as a new form of governance and investment. (3) You might point out how the fragmentation of Europe led to kingdoms (nation-states) with centralized power that created investment possibilities for explorers to seek out alternative trade routes to the Silk Roads and the Indian Ocean. (4) Contrast these Early Modern Era nation-states to land-based empires of the Post-Classical Era that created large empires based upon tributary trade and exchange.

Sample Response

From 1500 to 1750, the large land-based empires of the Post-Classical Era were replaced by nation-states of the early Modern Era with different forms of governance based on investment and exploration. China expanded its empire from c. 600 to c. 1450 in the early empires of the Sui, T'ang, and Song Dynasties where its leaders conquered areas like Vietnam and Korea, placing them in a tributary relationship. In comparison, during the 1700s, the European nation-states used exploration and colonies to establish regions for resource extraction. These resources were used to expand European investment for future colonies. One of the similarities of governance in both periods was that both land-based empires and nation-states sought out territories for raw resources. While Post-Classical empires managed their regions through expansion and the creation of tributary states with local conquered tribes, Early Modern nation-states invested in sea-based exploration in order to create colonies for resource extraction.

Both land-based empires and nation-states expanded out into new regions in order to accumulate natural and other resources that they did not possess. For example, China's powerful and prosperous Qing Dynasty expanded west into Mongolia, Korea, Vietnam, and Tibet. China had the dominant military and was able to conquer these regions. The Chinese Empire created trade networks that connected the northern expanses of China to the south. As early as c. 618, China created the Grand Canal to serve as a more efficient transportation route for trade in the empire, and the Canal was widely used by merchant ships and explorers. The conquered regions paid tribute back to China in order to acknowledge China's ultimate control in the region. Similarly, in the Early Modern Era, European nations used trade networks and military power to gain resources that they did not have. Spain and Portugal's explorations discovered the Mesoamerican region in the 1500s and set up local extensions of their nation-states. They used the investment power of the Spanish and Portuguese nation-states to set up colonies for the extraction of resources like silver, sugar, and tobacco. Next, France and England established their colonial possessions in North America. The French and English colonists traded with local native populations for resources including fur, timber, and materials for textiles. In all of these examples, the land-based empires and nation-states shared a common need for basic resources.

However, the reasons for acquiring these resources differed between land-based empires and nation-states. Land-based empires used tributes to demonstrate political authority, while nation-states used tributes for manufacturing raw resources and economic gain. For example, in the Post-Classical Era, gunpowder empires in the Middle East conquered local regions for trade. But the main purpose was to show the dominance of the centralized authority. The Ottoman Empire used its navy and gunpowder to stretch from Northern Africa to Iran. The empire encompassed hundreds of local ethnic and religious groups. The millets, or local communities, were allowed to run their own societies. But the millets had to pay a tribute back to the sultan to recognize his ultimate authority. On the other hand, in the Early Modern Era, the Spanish, Portuguese, English, and French settled colonies in the American region in order to attain raw resources for the purpose of economic gain by manufacturing and trading these resources back in Europe. Spain tried to do this by creating New Spain, a group of military and religious outposts in the Americas. Spain used encomiendas to extract gold and silver to be used as currency for international markets. France established New France, a group of trading outposts along the Mississippi River. Later, France used the fur trade for the market of hats and clothes in Europe. England set up New England, a group of family settlements in the Americas. England used timber to produce ships for mercantile trade. England also used cotton production for the manufacturing of textiles. The purpose for all of the nation-states was to acquire natural raw resources to ship back to Europe for mass manufacturing of materials and goods. So, the change in the 1600s was from political legitimacy to economic manufacturing.

While Post-Classical empires used tributary taxes to establish their authority over conquered territories, the Early Modern Era nation-states utilized mercantile and sea-based trade with colonies to expand their influence and advance economically.

Chapter 5

Period One: Technological and Environmental Transformations (to c. 600 B.C.E.)

Period One explores the beginning of life on earth.

- Big History: The Big Bang and Human Life
- Sedentary Societies
- Early Civilizations and Empires

Overview of AP World History Period One

You may be asking yourself, "What is the point of studying this period in history? What could the people of really . . . really . . . really . . . old stuff have to say to us today?" In reality, the collection of past events, even from thousands of years ago, helped to shape important social, religious, and political structures in our world today. The origins of human history are actually very intriguing. There are some very important themes and issues from this time period that you should consider.

But first, let's take a look at the AP World History curriculum framework and key concepts to give you a checklist of the topics that reference the WHAP exam. Use this chart as a guide to make mental connections between the key concepts and the topics covered in this chapter.

The information contained in this chart is an abridged version of the concept outline with topic examples. Visit https://apstudent.collegeboard.org/apcourse/ap-world-history/ for the complete WHAP course curriculum descriptions and key concepts.

AP World History Key Concepts (to c. 600 B. C. E.)	
KEY CONCEPT 1.1: BIG GEOGRAPHY AND THE PEOPLE OF EARTH **The term Big Geography draws attention to the global nature of world history. Throughout the Paleolithic period, humans migrated from Africa to Eurasia, Australia, and the Americas. Early humans were mobile and creative in adapting to different geographical settings from savanna to desert to tundra. Humans also developed varied and sophisticated technologies.**	Archeological evidence indicates that during the Paleolithic era, hunting-foraging bands of humans gradually migrated from their origin in East Africa to Eurasia, Australia, and the Americas, adapting their technology and cultures to new climate regions. Humans developed increasingly diverse tools—including fire. People lived in small groups that structured social, economic, and political systems.

Continued

KEY CONCEPT 1.2: THE NEOLITHIC REVOLUTION AND EARLY AGRICULTURAL SOCIETIES **Beginning about 10,000 years ago, some human communities adopted sedentary and agriculture lifestyles, while others pursued hunter-forager or pastoralist lifestyles in several different parts of the world. The switch to agriculture created a more reliable food supply. As populations increased, patriarchy and forced labor systems developed, giving elite men concentrated power.**	The Neolithic Revolution led to the development of more complex economic and social systems. Possibly as a response to climatic change, permanent agricultural villages first emerged in the eastern Mediterranean. People in each region domesticated locally available plants and animals. Agricultural communities had to work cooperatively to clear land and create water systems. Pastoralism and agriculture drastically affected the environment. Agriculture and pastoralism began to transform human societies. Pastoralism and agriculture led to more reliable and abundant food supplies and led to specialization of labor, including new classes of artisans and warriors (and the development of elites). Technology led to improvements in agricultural production, trade, and transportation.
KEY CONCEPT 1.3: THE DEVELOPMENT AND INTERACTIONS OF EARLY AGRICULTURAL, PASTORAL, AND URBAN SOCIETIES **The appearance of the first urban societies 5,000 years ago laid the foundations for the development of complex civilizations; these civilizations shared several significant social, political, and economic characteristics.**	Core and foundational civilizations developed in a variety of geographical and environmental settings, where agriculture flourished: **Mesopotamia** in the Tigris and Euphrates River Valleys; **Egypt** in the Nile River Valley; **Mohenjo-daro** and **Harappa** in the Indus River Valley; **Shang** in the Yellow River Valley; **Olmec** in Mesoamerica; and **Chavin** in Andean South America. The first states emerged within core civilizations in Mesopotamia and the Nile River Valley. States were powerful new systems of rule that mobilized surplus labor and resources over large areas. Rulers of early states often claimed divine connections to power. Rulers also relied on the support of military, religious, or aristocratic elites. As states grew and competed for land and resources, the more favorably situated had greater access to resources, produced more surplus food, and experienced growing populations, enabling them to undertake territorial expansion and conquer surrounding states. Culture played a significant role in unifying states through laws, language, literature, religion, myths, and monumental art. Systems of record keeping arose independently; states developed legal codes that reflected hierarchies; new religious beliefs developed; interregional exchanges of culture and technology grew.

Important Themes, Terms, and Concepts

The list below shows important themes, terms, and concepts that you should be familiar with on the WHAP exam. Please don't memorize each concept now. Place a check mark next to each topic as it is studied and refer to this list as often as necessary. After you finish the review section, reinforce what you have learned by working the practice questions at the end of this chapter. The answers and explanations provide further clarification into the perspectives of the beginning of humankind.

Themes, Terms, and Concepts You Should Know	
SOCIAL	
Term/Concept	**Brief Description**
Patriarchy	A social system ruled by men. In sedentary societies, men held the power in every way, excluding women.
Matriarchy	A social system ruled by women.
Tribe	A group of people who were united by a common culture with social, religious, economic, or family ties.
Clan	A group of people who were united by a kinship with a common ancestor. Sedentary societies were often organized around family clans.
Caste system	A religious hierarchy found only in India. It was started by the Aryan invaders into India (see "Hinduism" in Chapter 6).
POLITICAL	
Term/Concept	**Brief Description**
Theocracy	"Theo" means God, and "cracy" means government. Theocracy is a government that operates by religious authority in the name of God (divine rule).
Monarchy	A political system of government whereby the head of government is a single person such as a king or queen. Governmental power is passed on by heredity from generation to generation.
Big Man	A Big Man was the influential leader of a group of followers. He had the highest status within the group (tribe, village, or city-state).
City-state	A sovereign city (and its surrounding territory) with its own government.
Village	A small settlement group of residents smaller than a town.
Hierarchy	A system of social order. It is a vertical system defining inequalities. It is based on class, gender, race, and religious beliefs.
Priestly class	A ruling or powerful class of leaders. They gain their power through religious status.
RELIGIOUS	
Term/Concept	**Brief Description**
Polytheism	A religious system that favors the belief in multiple gods. Usually it refers to the gods being represented through nature.
Naturalism	A religious system that believes in multiple gods. The gods are represented through animals, nature, and totems.

Continued

Animism	A religious system that believes in multiple gods. The gods are revealed through animal groups.
Monotheism	A religious system that believes that there is one god. Typically that god is outside of the universe hat created it. For example, Judaism, Christianity, and Islam.

IDEOLOGICAL

Term/Concept	Brief Description
Ancestor worship	This practice began during the Shang Dynasty. It emphasized the importance of reverence for ancestors. Ancestor worship was significant for the foundations of filial piety or family obligations in Chinese dynasties.
Mandate of Heaven	The Zhou Dynasty in China started this belief to justify its rebellion against the Shang. The belief stated that the emperor held on to power if he was judged to be righteous by the gods in the afterlife.
Epic of Gilgamesh	An epic poem about the Mesopotamian kingdoms. It is believed to be the earliest surviving literary work and addresses the finality of life. It explains the power and chaos of the gods in Mesopotamia.

TECHNOLOGY

Term/Concept	Brief Description
Cuneiform	One of the first systems of writing found in the classical world from the Sumerian kingdom in Mesopotamia.
Hieroglyphics	One of the earliest forms of writing. It was largely made up of pictographs and found in the Egyptian society.
Pictographs	A form of writing based on pictures. It was found on cave walls used by hunter-gatherers. It was also found in Egyptian hieroglyphic writings.
Papyrus	A form of paper that was used for writing in ancient Mediterranean societies.
Paleolithic Age	The "Old Stone Age" of society. About 200,000 years ago, humans hunted and gathered in small family groups.
Neolithic Age	The "New Stone Age" of society. Humans used metallurgy to develop iron and bronze tools. This allowed humans to settle into sedentary societies next to a river system.
Metallurgy	The process of mixing minerals together to create a new, stronger form of metal that was used for farming and warfare.
Iron and bronze	The products of metallurgy used these metals for farming and warfare.

ECONOMICS

Term/Concept	Brief Description
Surpluses of food	The products of sedentary societies. They were able to produce more food than the number of people. This allowed for the growth of populations.
Trade routes: Mediterranean, steppe region	The early trade routes in the Classical Era included the land-based Silk Roads and the sea-based Indian Ocean.
Cereal grains	Include wheat, barley, sorghum, rye, and millet. These nutritious grains allowed for the growth of populations in Africa and the Middle East.
Division of labor	Societies created specialized tasks that led to different jobs for people in society. This created class systems.

Chapter Review

WHAP Period One covers three main eras from c. 8000 B.C.E. to c. 600 B.C.E.: the beginning of humans in the Paleolithic period (Stone Age), human migration and the development of early agriculture in the Neolithic period, and prehistoric agricultural and pastoral human societies.

The WHAP is divided into six time periods. The list below should help you visually and conceptually identify what preceded and what followed particular developments.

WHAP Time Period	Era	Time Period
Period One	Prehistory	to c. 600 B.C.E.
Period Two	Classical Antiquity to the Early Middle Ages	c. 600 B.C.E. to 600 C.E.
Period Three	Middle Ages	c. 600 C.E. to c. 1450
Period Four	Early Modern History	c. 1450 to c. 1750
Period Five	Modern History	c. 1750 to c. 1900
Period Six	Modern History to Post-Modern History	c. 1900 to the present
Note: B.C.E. = Before Common Era; C.E. = Common Era		

Big History: The Big Bang and Human Life

About 13.7 billion years ago, something really interesting happened. All of the material of the universe came together and exploded in a really Big Bang. When the material came together, it was literally the size of a dot in a room. Now, just consider that for a moment. The entire universe fit into the size of a dot on your finger. In the span of a few fractions of a second, our universe doubled in size hundreds of times and at a speed faster than the speed of light. The explosion then moved the material out at incredible speeds and it took another 500,000 years for the universe to slow down and start to form stars, planets, and the conditions that would make it possible to support life.

Did you know? Do you know how scientists determined the age of Earth and the age of human life? Scientists study and measure the amount of *radiocarbon* (radioactive element) in Earth's oldest rocks, plants, animals, and human remains. The measurement of carbon atoms in living organisms is called *radiocarbon dating*. The oldest rock (zircon) was found in Australia and the oldest fossil of human remains was found in Africa.

The Beginning of Earth

Planet Earth was formed 4.6 billion years ago, but scientists have determined that human life only started about 200,000 years ago. The oldest form of human life, *Homo sapiens* (wise man in Latin), appears to have started in Central Africa during the *Paleolithic period* (called the Old Stone Age).

Early Humans

Early humans from this period tended to live together in tribes of 20 to 30 people. As humans advanced to the *Neolithic period* (called the New Stone Age) about 9000 to 3500 B.C.E., they migrated and were continually on the move in search of food. Based on the images discovered on cave walls, we know that these early humans hunted wild animals, fished, and gathered roots, seeds, and berries to survive.

Source: Cave Painting of Tassili n'Ajjer, 15,000–10,000 B.C.E.

The common stereotype of these early humans was that they barely survived. Humans were so primitive and so lacking in basic technology that they barely could find enough food. But this assumption has been challenged by scientist Jared Diamond and his work about human history.

HISTORIOGRAPHY. *Many historians and scholars study a particular topic such as a country, person, or event to understand the "history of history." Historiography makes it possible to reconstruct, debate, and critically think about topics that shape our history over time. After studying early human survival, Jared Diamond, a UCLA professor, argued that the evidence from skeletons of early humans and their current descendants suggested that tribes and nomads did much better than scientists originally hypothesized. According to Diamond, evidence shows that early humans survived because of their geographic environments: good climate, rich soil, water systems, and plenty of animals for hunting.*

Key Facts about Early Humans

Early humans were egalitarian. The skeletons of hunter-gatherer tribes show that these early humans consumed a variety of food sources. And, current-day tribal examples show that people in the tribes tended to live in a very **egalitarian** (equal) manner. Even though there were roles for men and women, women tended to have a stronger position in these tribes. The responsibilities of the tribe were shared among all members.

Early humans developed technology. Humans developed new forms of technology in the Neolithic Age. The most important was the process of **metallurgy,** which allowed humans to mix minerals and create metals like **iron and bronze.** These metals could be used for farming, building, and creating weaponry.

Early humans practiced agriculture. Technology allowed humans to migrate, settle down in villages, domesticate animals, and, most importantly, farm a surplus of food. Early forms of farming were important to human survival. Planting agricultural crops was a much more efficient way to produce food, rather than performing the time-consuming process of gathering berries, roots, and nuts.

Early humans formed clans. Human societies became organized around tribes or **clans** or family obligations. While it is true that the clan members treated other clan members well, they were inclined to see people outside of the clan as the enemies. In addition, scientific findings suggested that the humans who lived in these early clans were not quite as healthy as their nomadic counterparts. When scientists studied skeletons from this time period, it appeared that most people who lived in these villages or *sedentary societies* (groups of people who settle down to live in one spot) tended to be small, fragile, and unhealthy.

Early humans organized social hierarchies. Most hunter-gatherer groups were **matrilineal.** This meant that descendants were defined as coming from the mother's side of the family. This did not mean that women led the tribes (**matriarchy**), it meant that women were given a special place of advising and power in the tribes. The sedentary societies, however, established certain types of social hierarchies. Men became the leaders in every way, including symbolically. This type of **patriarchy** defined all power in society as centered on fathers and other male figures. Women became relegated to a second-class status defined through child bearing and rearing in the household.

Early humans practiced naturalism. Humans commonly based religious beliefs on multiple gods who were revealed through the animal world.

Critical Thinking Question: Did the agricultural revolution help or harm humans?

The advent of early agriculture during the Neolithic period should have been a human advancement toward a better life, right? Well, Diamond argues that it depends on who you were in early civilizations. He claims that the agricultural revolution may be the worst "catastrophe from which we have never recovered," and was the start of disease, social class inequality, and sometimes starvation.

Throughout history, if you were part of the rich, land-owning, or governing classes, then the agricultural revolution was awesome because crops yielded far more food and profits for the landowners. But if you were the poor slaves or laborers who worked the farmland, then you tended to get the least variety of nutritious foods in your diet. This led to disease and poor health.

Let's compare and contrast the two arguments below.

Agricultural Revolution Helped Humans	Agricultural Revolution Harmed Humans
On one hand, the agricultural revolution allowed the lives of early humans to improve because hunter-gatherers no longer spent laborious hours each day gathering small amounts of food. Once humans developed technology, which has evolved over time, it allowed many more people to become independent from nature because farmers were able to produce, store, and manufacture larger quantities of food. Because of the agricultural revolution, today's humans can now eat abundant and varied foods.	On the other hand, you could argue that over time the agricultural revolution: (1) Led to poor health because farmers primarily planted starchy foods (wheat, rice, and corn). It also spread diseases and parasites from the agriculture (plants and animals). (2) Created inequalities in class. It forced women into a more subservient position in the patriarchal (male-dominated) societies. It also created incentives for landowners to treat slaves and the landless in a negative way. (3) Led to starvation if crops failed.

So, what is the answer? Did the initial agricultural revolution help or harm most humans? Well, it is not clear. It depends on what you value. If you value equality and community, you might say that Professor Diamond is correct: It helped the rich, land-owning, or governing classes, but not the poor and the slaves who worked the land. But if you value progress, technological innovation, and long-term development, you might disagree with Professor Diamond.

Either way, the beginnings of human history appear much more complex and controversial than you might have first imagined. And, it is easy to see how we are still struggling with some of these same issues today. We live in a developed country with advances in technology, surpluses of food, complex uses of energy, and vast opportunities. But what about the developing world south of our hemisphere? Are they receiving these benefits as well? Or are they like the poor and the landless of the sedentary societies, hoping to receive some of the advantages of the developed countries? There is no clear answer, but it shows how world history can inspire debates about technology, energy, economic growth, and social classes even today.

TEST TIP: In the above discussion about Professor Diamond's theories, we used the reasoning skill of continuity and change over time. We made a connection between the hunter-gatherer and sedentary societies of the past and the continuity of the current global inequalities between the developed and developing world. This is an example of what you can do in making connections across time periods and locations on the WHAP exam.

Sedentary Societies

Biological Old Regime (BOR)

At the beginning of human history, we tended to live in what world history researchers call the **Biological Old Regime (BOR).** The BOR was a period when humans were very much controlled by the natural processes of nature and the environment. This comes before the big Industrial Revolution of the 1700s and 1800s, when we discovered different forms of energy, especially **fossil fuels.** The BOR was likely to be dominated by humans' use of energy from wind, water, and fire. All three of these resources had incredible potential for human development, but they were also limited by location, intensity, and regularity.

Environment

While discussing the environment may not seem relevant to the prehistory time period when societies were just beginning to organize, it's important to remember that the decisions of early humans have impacted our modern-day global environment. Think about WHAP exam questions that connect the reasoning skill of "continuity and change over time" of the past to the global environment of today. The migrations of early humans were influenced by the environment, and many modern-world human innovations were inspired by the environmental influences.

This discussion leads us to an important critical thinking question.

Critical Thinking Question: Are humans controlled by nature or is nature controlled by humans?

To answer this question, think about the current climate change debate. On one side of the argument, consider if the daily lives of humans are influenced by nature. On the other side, consider if humans have influenced nature, for better or worse.

Compare and contrast the two arguments below.

Nature Controls Humans	Humans Control Nature
Analysis of early human beginnings seems to give a very strong argument for nature's control over human life. Early humans' first survival needs, along with food and water, was to seek shelter from the effects of nature: heat, snow, wind, rain, lightning, earthquakes, and uncontrolled fires. Note that the need for food and water, the need to seek shelter from harsh climate, and the topography of land continue to affect most human decisions, everything from governmental management to religious/cultural beliefs. Nature has even dictated what climate people prefer to live in. This side of the argument shows that nature controls human beings.	Analysis of this side of the argument shows that humans adapted to their environments to survive from nature. Humans planted, plowed, and irrigated land for agriculture. And to survive and flourish, humans created new technologies using water, wind, fire, and natural resources (built homes, dams, air conditioners, heaters, and modes of transportation). However, this has led to unintended consequences for nature. Humans have polluted the earth, air, and water with waste and chemicals. For example, greenhouse gas emissions, such as CO_2, are trapping heat in Earth's atmosphere, causing Earth's average temperature to increase. To counter some of man's negative effects on nature, new technologies are now constantly being invented and improved. So, maybe one conclusion of this side of the argument is that humans influence nature through innovation because of their necessity to adapt to nature.

Migration

As humans moved out of Africa into Eurasia, they were affected by the changes in the climate as the earth heated and cooled. One of the biggest changes was the cycling of cooling and heating of the earth. The earth often tilted toward or away from the sun during a period of 40,000 years, causing either greater warming or more cooling. As the earth tilted closer to the sun during orbit, the ice receded. These changes led to massive migrations of people to warmer climates, especially in Mesopotamia.

> **TEST TIP:** The geography of ancient civilizations can sometimes be confusing because the names of some continents and countries have changed over time. For example, in ancient history, Eurasia was geographically located in Mesopotamia (the modern-day Middle East: Iraq and parts of Iran, Syria, and Turkey), Egypt, India, and China.

Migrations of people led to two major changes: search for water sources and social and political order.

Search for water sources. The first major change was the need to find water sources. The world's earliest civilizations settled down into **villages** and **city-states** along river systems such as the **Fertile Crescent.** The Fertile Crescent stretched from the Mediterranean Sea to the Persian Gulf. It got its name because the soil was rich, and the land was shaped like a half-moon. The big river systems in Mesopotamia (means land between rivers) were the **Tigris/Euphrates** Rivers, and in Egypt it was the **Nile River.**

Social and political order. Settlements along the river banks led to social and political organization. These were small political and social organizations run by a strong male leader. The leader was typically called a **Big Man** because he was able to rise to power and maintain power based on his charisma and personality. To meet the need for water and other resources, humans developed governments that would manage the resources for their populations and resolve conflicts with neighboring populations. This created governmental bureaucracies. These bureaucracies needed security so they established police or military forces for protection and order.

Theocracy

Every human society has had some form of religion. Early humans felt the need to make sense of the world that surrounded them so they formed a system of government based on their religious beliefs in gods. The system of a government under a god's divine rule was called a **theocracy** (in Greek "Theo" means God, and "cracy" means government). Mesopotamian and Egyptian literature offers evidence that myths and legends describing the nature and power of gods played an important part in early human civilizations. For example, the Tigris and Euphrates rivers tended to flood sporadically and without warning. Humans who lived in these areas created myths about gods that were like fickle humans who wanted power. In Egypt, the Nile River was constant and predictable; these gods were portrayed as just and balanced in their control over people.

Humans formed a variety of spiritualties in early civilizations. Most came to believe in **pantheism,** the belief that God exists in everything on the earth. This was complemented by **polytheism,** the belief in multiple gods. Typically, these gods were manifested through **naturalism** (the belief that the spiritual world and gods were found in nature). These beliefs would eventually differ with the development of **monotheism,** the belief in one god. Most societies developed a **priestly class,** a group of leaders who justified their authority based on being messengers of the spirits.

Early Civilizations and Empires

Humans moved to find areas that were better suited for larger populations. Humans began trading systems in the Middle East and along the Eastern African coastline. For example, the Bantu nomadic tribes moved from Western Africa and set up port cities that would eventually link up with civilizations from Eastern Africa, the Middle East, and India. This led to a diffusion of cultures, mixtures of populations, and sharing of goods and services over one of the largest trade zones in human history. In social living groups, humans began class systems that ranked the hierarchical status of a group of people when compared to other groups of people.

The major areas for civilizations and development included Europe, Africa, India, the Middle East, and Southeast Asia. Examples include the Mohenjo-Daro, Indus River Valley, Tigris/Euphrates, and the Yalu River civilizations.

> **TEST TIP: An important reasoning skill on the WHAP exam is the comparison and contrast between the major civilizations that were formed in the early human civilizations. When reading world history material, you should be constantly asking yourself about similarities and differences. And equally important, you should be considering "why" those civilizations were similar or different.**

Similarities among Early Civilizations

As you can see, these civilizations formed over a vast group of regions. However, there were several similarities among them.

Similarities among Early Civilizations	
Irrigation Systems	All of these civilizations developed irrigation systems.
Written Record Systems	Most of the early civilizations developed written record systems. Some examples include **hieroglyphics, cuneiform, pictographs,** and character-based languages. Recording systems were used to record food storage, governmental records, and histories.
Metallurgy	All of the early civilizations practiced **metallurgy,** the melting together of different metals to form iron and bronze.
Trade	All of the early civilizations interacted with each other in trade.

But what were the differences?

Differences among Early Civilizations

We know that different areas developed different belief systems and social organization. Let's look at some key facts.

Key Facts about Early Belief Systems and Social Organization

- India developed a complex belief system called Hinduism that included a variety of social **castes** or levels of a hierarchy. These early dynasties included the Mohenjo-Daro, the Mauryan, and the Gupta.
- Chinese dynasties developed a respect for ancestors that included a devotion or **ancestor worship** of ancient family members. Their dynasties included the Xia.
- China's Zhou Dynasty also developed the **Mandate of Heaven** or justification of leadership based on an emperor's righteous behavior.
- Africa developed three major empires, including Nubia, Kush, and Axum. These kingdoms traded with one another, causing a flow of goods and a diffusion of ideas. This led to both new centralized kingdoms and small port cities with competitive merchants.
- The Sumerian society (first major Mesopotamian civilization) developed a centralized kingdom with classes that allowed for the development of a surplus of food.
- The Babylonians (Mesopotamian civilization) added on to this system a codified system of laws under King Hammurabi that allowed for a legal justification of class- and gender-based hierarchies.
- The Middle East developed a series of religious beliefs in strong father-figure gods, which eventually led to a belief in monotheistic religions, including Judaism, Christianity, and Islam.

So, why are there differences in these beliefs and social organizations? There really is no one answer. All of these societies were at the center of developing trade routes like the Mediterranean and the routes in Central Asia. Societies traded their **food surpluses** across these routes.

Let's consider the context. India was at the center of major crossroads for trade and invasions, so a belief system that allowed for both social organization and diversity of populations became necessary. China developed quickly into a vast and diverse set of dynasties that needed social order and defense from Northern invaders. Respect for the elders provided for social order and relationships. The Middle East was dominated by tribal groups that traded with one another but were in conflict over scarce resources and water. So a father-figure god and charismatic Big Man leader, both in the divine and in politics, provided for a social order and hierarchy. Note that the differences could have been highly influenced by context, geography, resources, and diversity of population.

Critical Thinking Question: Why would such diverse human populations develop civilizations with such similar characteristics over such a large and diverse geography?

There are a few possibilities. All human populations were affected by climatic changes that forced movement or migration. These human populations needed to find good water sources. Once they did, they needed to establish water management systems to irrigate large areas of land, both for themselves and for conflicts with other groups. Establishing a water management system required a system of government with bureaucracies. These bureaucracies needed to keep records. Thus, writing was born.

As humans settled down into civilizations with water, they needed to have a way to produce food. They used the water for increased agricultural production, which in turn required the creation of new tools. Therefore, experimentation with irrigation systems control, agricultural production, and social organization led to experimentation with technology. As food surpluses were developed, there was an incentive for trade with other populations.

So, how do we sum all of this up? Here is one possible thesis using the reasoning skill of causation: *Human migration and desire for resources created the need for innovation in both technology and social organization.*

Heads Up: What You Need to Know

We have already covered a lot of territory, and this is just Period One. Here's a summary of the common themes and issues for Period One.

1. Human migration was caused by climatic changes, and this led to sedentary societies along river systems.

2. Humans developed new forms of metals like bronze and iron to create tools for farming and weapons for military protection.

3. Humans created water management systems and developed irrigation systems.

4. Humans developed labor systems to create surpluses of food for growing populations.

5. Sedentary societies created government bureaucracies, writing systems, monuments to authorities, and religious justifications for their civilizations.

6. Humans created trading systems that included land routes and sea routes in the Middle East.

Chapter Review Practice Questions

The practice questions show the types of questions that may appear on the exam. On the actual exam, the questions are grouped into sets. Each set contains one sourced-based prompt and two to five questions.

Questions 1–3 refer to the following image.

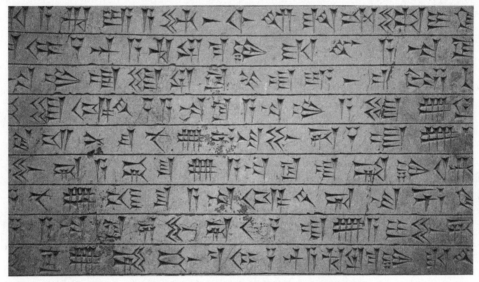

Source: Cuneiform from Sumeria in the Ancient Middle East, 3200 B.C.E.

1. Which statement below best explains the purpose of the drawings recorded in the image above?

   A. The image above would have come from a hunter-gatherer society, trying to explain animal migrations.

   B. The symbols in the image above would have developed from a loosely organized tribal society.

   C. The symbols in the image above would have been used for recording purposes for surpluses of food.

   D. The symbols in the image above were randomly created and show a lack of social organization.

2. Which of the following is an accurate depiction of how a historian would use the image above to make interpretations about societies?

   A. A historian would be unable to make any accurate interpretations since the recordings are not clear.

   B. A historian could use these recordings to understand the social class, order, and occupations of those people who made the symbols.

   C. A historian would attempt to impose our current understanding of religion and politics on the recordings of the past.

   D. The recordings would demonstrate that the society lacked a clear language due to the use of symbols.

3. Which of the following best explains how the image above demonstrates a turning point in the development of human societies?

    A. The recordings show that humans had developed bureaucracies with educated elites who could record changes in productivity.

    B. The image demonstrates that humans had migrated as hunter-gatherers to catch their hunted prey.

    C. The recordings demonstrate that human societies had accepted a new monotheistic spirituality to explain their surroundings.

    D. The symbols in the recording clearly demonstrate a fear of the gods and nature due to flooding in the surrounding area.

Questions 4–6 refer to the following passage.

An eye for an eye, a tooth for a tooth. If a man puts out the eye of another man, put his own eye out. If he knocks out another man's tooth, knock out his own tooth. If he breaks another man's bone, break his own bone.

If he puts out the eye of any man's slave, he shall pay one half of its value.

If a man marry a woman, and she bear sons to him; if then this woman die, then shall her father have no claim on the dowry, this belongs to her sons.

If anyone fails to meet a claim for debt, and sell himself, his wife, his son and daughter for money or gives them away to forced labor; they shall work for three years in the house of the man who bought them, or the proprietor, and in the fourth year they shall be set free.

—Source: Adapted from the *Code of Hammurabi,* 1754 B.C.E.

4. Which of the following best describes the major impact of the Babylonian law codes?

    A. The codes helped to create standards for trade between empires.

    B. The laws were used to unify the empire around a single religious belief system.

    C. The law codes provided justification for the class and gender relationships between the people.

    D. The codes were used for fair land distribution between the peasants.

5. How would a historian use the following law code to determine gender relationships in Babylonia?

If a man marry a woman, and she bear sons to him; if then this woman die, then shall her father have no claim on the dowry, this belongs to her sons.

    A. Historians could interpret the use of the dowry and its distribution to determine the way that the society would define a woman's social worth.

    B. Historians could argue that women held a high position due to the significance of nature gods.

    C. A historian could interpret the role of women through the law's justification of female jobs in the public sector.

    D. Historians could argue that women held high positions as advisers to the monarch of the empire.

6. Which of the following examples is most similar to the *Code of Hammurabi*?

   A. The Roman Triumvirate took power away from the Senate in order to develop military control over the empire.

   B. Byzantine Emperor Justinian established a set of standards to unite the fortress of the kingdom of Byzantine under his leadership.

   C. The Han Dynasty ruled by reinforcing strong family relationships.

   D. The Muslim Caliphates managed minorities by labeling them as *dhimmis* (protected people) through a military replacement tax.

Answers and Explanations

1. **C.** The use of written recordings during the beginnings of societies was a way to keep a record of food surpluses. People settled next to river systems. This allowed for irrigation, which led to the creation of food surpluses, larger populations, and class systems. Such societies required management of people and food distributions. Societies created writing or pictographs like cuneiform in order to record and account for the creation of food, trade, and exchange of produce.

2. **B.** Historians use writings and recording systems to decipher class systems. A recording system during this time period required literacy. This would mean the creation of specialized labor and training for these positions. So, historians would begin asking who would have the leisure time, class status, and training to achieve these higher positions. This path of questioning leads to conclusions about class structure organized around landownership.

3. **A.** Leaders who could learn to read and write would need time for training in this activity. This would not be possible or necessary in a hunter-gather society that tended to move with the migration of animals. But this also leads to a question of who would be trained in these activities. It would be leaders who could manage food production. This leads to the creation of government bureaucracies and offices to manage societies.

4. **C.** The Code of Hammurabi had many purposes. However, the content of this particular passage relates to both class and gender relationships. The codes helped to set up legal standards for the behavior of the different classes. Typically, the poorer classes and women found that they were put under more severe and strict rules and that their actions had more punitive consequences.

5. **A.** The law code in question is about the dowry. Dowries were given at this time in order to pay for giving a daughter to another family. The perspective at the time was that most societies imposed limitations on women. Women were not allowed to own property and women were not allowed to work in the public sector. (Note: There were exceptions like in Babylon where women had considerable rights compared to other societies. Babylonian women could own businesses and engage in trade.) So, the daughter's family was paying the husband's family to take her on. This represents how sedentary societies defined a woman's role primarily in the private household. And, this shows how women were limited to reproductive responsibilities in society.

6. **B.** The Justinian Code established in Byzantine was most similar to the Code of Hammurabi. Emperor Justinian established the law code to create a clear hierarchy. He especially needed this in order to create a strong social order. Justinian feared that Byzantine was vulnerable in its position on the Dardanelles Strait since it was surrounded by water on one side and attacks from people from the steppe region on the other side. The code allowed for a strict adherence to the emperor's power.

Chapter 6
Period Two: Organization and Reorganization of Human Societies (c. 600 B.C.E. to c. 600 C.E.)

Period Two explores how humans established and organized sedentary societies through mutually shared ideas, beliefs, and trades.

- Worldview
- Axial Beliefs: Hinduism, Buddhism, Confucianism, Chinese Legalism, and Daoism
- Mediterranean Beliefs: Judaism, Christianity, and Islam.
- Empires and Governance: China, India, Greek City-States, and Rome
- Trade

Overview of AP World History Period Two

Period Two is one of my favorite periods in world history. In this time period, the civilizations were not technologically sophisticated, but these early sedentary societies emerged into powerful states and empires.

Centuries ago, sedentary people were asking some fundamental questions about life and *why* people do the things they do. They developed shared beliefs based on the answers to these questions, and these beliefs offered a community bond that supported social and political decisions. Asking questions continues to be important in our understanding of the world in which we live. Questions help to establish a point of view about who we are, what we value, and what our relationship is to others in a community—these philosophical questions refer to our historical *worldview,* the historical point of view of people from around the world.

Before we expand our discussion of worldview, let's review the WHAP curriculum framework key concepts for Period Two. Use the chart that follows as a guide to help you make mental connections between the key concepts and the topics covered in this chapter.

The information contained in this chart is an abridged version of the AP World History concept outline with topic examples. Visit https://apstudent.collegeboard.org/apcourse/ap-world-history/ for the complete WHAP course curriculum descriptions and key concepts.

AP World History Key Concepts (c. 600 B.C.E. to c. 600 C.E.)	
KEY CONCEPT 2.1: THE DEVELOPMENT AND CODIFICATION OF RELIGIOUS AND CULTURAL TRADITIONS **As states and empires increased in size, contacts between regions multiplied and human communities transformed their religious and ideological beliefs and practices.**	Religions and belief systems provided a social bond and an ethical code to live by. New belief systems and cultural traditions emerged and spread, often asserting universal truths. Belief systems influenced and reinforced political, economic, and occupational stratification, offering new roles and status to some men and women. For example, Confucianism emphasized filial piety, and some Buddhists and Christians practiced a monastic life. Religious and political authorities often merged as rulers (some of whom were considered divine). Rulers used religion, along with military and legal structures, to justify their rule and ensure its continuation. Religion and belief systems also generated conflict. Other religious and cultural traditions continued and in some places were incorporated into major religious traditions.
KEY CONCEPT 2.2: THE DEVELOPMENT OF STATES AND EMPIRES **As the early states and empires grew in number, size, and population, they frequently competed for resources and came into conflict with one another.**	The number and size of key states and empires grew dramatically as rulers imposed political unity on areas where previously there had been competing states. Key states and empires that grew included **Southwest Asia:** Persian empires; **East Asia:** Qin and Han empires; **South Asia:** Mauryan and Gupta empires; **Mediterranean region:** Phoenicia, Greek city-states, and Hellenistic and Roman empires; **Mesoamerica:** Teotihuacan and Mayan city-states; **Andean South America:** Moche; and **North America:** from Chaco to Cahokia. (Note: Students should know the location and names of the key empires and states.) Empires and states developed new techniques of imperial administration based, in part, on the success of earlier political forms. Imperial governments centralized legal systems, promoted trade, and projected military power over larger areas. Unique social and economic dimensions developed in imperial societies in Afro-Eurasia and the Americas. Imperial cities served as centers of trade, public performance of religious rituals, and political administration for states and empires. The social structures of empires displayed hierarchies: cultivators, laborers, slaves, artisans, merchants, elites, or caste groups. The Roman, Han, Persian, Mauryan, and Gupta empires encountered political, cultural, and administrative difficulties that they could not manage, which eventually led to their decline, collapse, and transformation into successor empires or states.
KEY CONCEPT 2.3: EMERGENCE OF INTERREGIONAL NETWORKS OF COMMUNICATION AND EXCHANGE **With the organization of large-scale empires, transregional trade intensified, leading to the creation of extensive networks of commercial and cultural exchange.**	Land and water routes became the basis for interregional trade, communication, and exchange networks in the Eastern Hemisphere including Eurasian Silk Roads, Trans-Saharan caravan routes, Indian Ocean sea lanes, and Mediterranean sea lanes. New technologies facilitated long-distance communication and exchange. Alongside the trade in goods, the exchange of people, technology, religious and cultural beliefs, food crops, domesticated animals, and disease pathogens developed across extensive networks of communication and exchange.

Important Themes, Terms, and Concepts

The list below shows important themes, terms, and concepts that you should be familiar with on the WHAP exam. Please don't memorize each concept now. Place a check mark next to each topic as it is studied and refer to this list as often as necessary. After you finish the review section, reinforce what you have learned by working the practice questions at the end of this chapter. The answers and explanations provide further clarification into the perspectives of the societies and empires during the Classical Period.

Themes, Terms, and Concepts You Should Know	
SOCIAL	
Term/Concept	**Brief Description**
Hierarchy	A social organization of society that defines certain people as either in a superior or inferior position.
Classes and land ownership	A group classification of people organized around an economic categorization based on the acquisition of property.
Plebeians versus patricians	The Roman social designation of either workers on the land (plebeians) or owners of the land (patricians).
POLITICAL	
Term/Concept	**Brief Description**
Polis	The political organization of people in city-states, usually used in reference to ancient Greece.
Republic	A political organization based on people choosing representatives.
Empire	A political organization based on a central authority that acquires surrounding civilizations for resources.
Mauryan Empire (c. 322 to 185 B.C.E.)	The first Indian empire to centralize authority in Northern India.
Ashoka (ruled 268 to 232 B.C.E.)	The Mauryan emperor who centralized Northern India through violence and then used the religion of Buddhism to establish cultural unity.
Gupta Empire (c. 320 to 550 C.E.)	The second Indian empire to centralize power in Northern India. The Gupta balanced centralized power with local governors.
Era of Warring States (475 to 221 B.C.E.)	The period in China characterized by decentralized power and a conflict between local governors.
Qin Dynasty (221 to 206 B.C.E.) Han Dynasty (206 B.C.E. to 220 C.E.)	The Qin Empire ruled China with strong authority under Chinese Legalism. The Han used Confucianism and filial obligations to rule China.

Continued

POLITICAL	
Term/Concept	**Brief Description**
Olmec Empire (1500 to 400 B.C.E.) **Toltec Empire** (500 to 1200 C.E.)	These were the first two empires in the Mesoamerican region that established strong centralized authorities and trade markets.
Mayan Empire (c. 2000 B.C.E. to c. 900 C.E.)	A confederation of kingdoms that traded with one another in Central America.
Moche	A religious movement in Peru that eventually led to the formation of the Incan Empire.
Teotihuacan	The central city or capital of the Aztec Empire.
RELIGIOUS	
Term/Concept	**Brief Description**
Judaism	A monotheistic faith established in the Middle East. Jewish faith teaches the belief in one God who created a covenant or agreement with the Hebrew people. This led to a series of laws and scriptural writings stored in the Jewish scriptures, or Pentateuch.
Christianity	A reform movement of Judaism established by the central figure, Jesus. Christians professed a belief in Jesus being the Messiah or savior. His teachings led to the establishment of the Catholic and Protestant churches.
Mahayana	A reform movement of Buddhism that emphasizes helping others through the Bodhisattva path and delaying nirvana. Gained popularity in Tibet and China.
Theravada	A reform movement of Buddhism that allows for the use of meditation and rituals to reach nirvana; associated with Southeast Asia.
IDEOLOGICAL	
Term/Concept	**Brief Description**
Athenian philosophy	A group of philosophers who taught that the world could be understood through rational investigation, discussion, inquiry, and argumentation.
Socrates (470 to 399 B.C.E.)	The Greek philosopher who established the use of discussion or Socratic dialogue as a way to question and discover reality.
Plato (428 to 347 B.C.E.)	The Greek philosopher and student of Socrates who argued that there was an external and absolute world of forms or ideals that we could be inspired by.
Aristotle (384 to 322 B.C.E.)	The Greek philosopher and student of Plato who argued that we discover truth by examining the real world.
Confucianism	The Chinese philosophy of Confucius found in the Analects that argues for a practical social order based on filial obligations.

ECONOMICS	
Term/Concept	Brief Description
Silk Roads	A group of land-based trade routes that connected China to Eastern Europe and Northern Africa.
Indian Ocean trade route	A sea route of trade that connected India, China, the Middle East, and Eastern Africa.
Andean Mountains trade route	A trade route found along the Andean Mountains in Peru that connected kingdoms and civilizations within South America.
Trans-Saharan trade route	A trade route that connected North Africa to the Middle East.

Chapter Review

WHAP Period Two covers human civilizations of the Classical Antiquity Period through the Early Middle Ages (c. 600 B.C.E. to 600 C.E.). Broad areas of discussion include the civilizations' (1) axial beliefs, (2) empires and governance, and (3) trade systems.

As the world population steadily grew, networks, migrations, and exchanges interfaced across regions. Humans began forming beliefs, attitudes, and values about the world including social, economic, religious, and political systems. As you read through material about the organization of civilizations, stay focused on the big picture and how these early systems laid the foundation for the world we know today.

> TEST TIP: To help you stay focused on the big picture and connections across periods and regions, use the acronym SPRITE to remember the subject matter of the historical themes—social, political, religious, ideological, technological, and economic.

Worldview

The concept of worldview is important to both philosophy and history. The term *worldview* was coined by philosopher Immanuel Kant when he talked about the "power of the perception" of the human mind. The definition of worldview is a lot like it sounds. It is a set of beliefs about central issues in life. These beliefs form a way of looking at the world so that we can judge reality. Our perceptions of reality influence ideas, attitudes, and interactions of individuals and societies within each uniquely different time period.

HISTORIOGRAPHY. *In the context of history, think about how worldview has led to many conflicts, revolutions, and wars. Historically, leaders had certain worldviews, and these beliefs impacted how they responded to or instigated conflicts. Many historians and philosophers continue to study how people think and understand worldview over time based on the context of the time period in which people lived. After all, each civilization is a reflection of people's shared understandings of the world. To help historians study worldview, they ask questions related to ontological, epistemological, and moral systems of the world.*

Key Facts about Understanding Worldview

Ontology. Ontological questions ask, "What is the nature of being, or existence?" These types of questions usually ask about the similarities or differences in the nature of being human. For example, are humans essentially good or bad, or are humans purely material or spiritual beings?

Epistemology. Epistemological questions ask, "What are the methods for attaining knowledge or information?" For example, is human knowledge gained through religious, scientific, or rationalistic methods? For some people, religious texts are the foundation for inspiring virtuous knowledge. For others, science and research are the basis for factual, evidence-based knowledge. Still, for others, rational thought of mind is the basis for using logic and reason to answer questions.

Moral and ethical systems. Ontological and epistemological questions are the foundation for moral and ethical systems. In moral systems, people develop mental rules about what they ought to do. For some people, moral systems are absolute and provide right and wrong evaluations of their actions. For others, moral systems are about the natural consequences of good or bad behavior. Still, for many others, morality exists as social codes, or *normative codes,* created by societies.

The beliefs, or worldviews, that we are talking about are linked to a philosophical concept called *axial beliefs,* which are discussed in the next section.

Axial Beliefs

The term **axial beliefs** was suggested by German philosopher Karl Jaspers when he referred to the Axial Age (or Pivotal Age) from 800 to 200 B.C.E. The Axial Age was a turning point in history when humans reflected upon their beliefs, views, and thoughts about what we now know as religion, spirituality, and philosophy. In early civilizations, these beliefs independently and simultaneously arose in different parts of the world.

To understand the term *axial,* think about the axle on a car—the axle is the center for rotating the wheels on a car. Axial beliefs were at the center of how societies were formed and how they operated. These beliefs arose as people settled down into sedentary societies, which was no coincidence.

Establishing axial beliefs formed a major shift in human thinking. Individuals began to ask major questions about human nature, individual responsibilities, and collective responsibilities just as societies were developing major states and empires. Why? People needed to form an understanding and a justification for the shared context that they inhabited, and rulers began to merge their political authority with these beliefs to justify their laws (see "Theocracy" in Chapter 5, p. 78). At times, these beliefs justified the social roles and reinforced political and economic positions that were held in society. At other times, these beliefs challenged social roles, causing conflicts and struggles among societies.

Heads Up: What You Need to Know

The Axial Age was critical to the moral, spiritual, social, and political development of societies. On the WHAP exam, be sure that you can identify the Eastern beliefs of Hinduism, Buddhism, Confucianism, Chinese Legalism, and Daoism (pp. 91–94). You should also be familiar with the Abrahamic monotheistic beliefs of Judaism and Christianity (p. 94) and Islam (pp. 116–118). The three main similarities in Eastern beliefs that helped to form values in early civilizations are:

- **Change is fundamental to humankind.** The historical reason for this might be because people in India and China were at the center of trade routes where major transformations took place.
- **Letting go and acceptance.** The historical reason for this might be because India and China were at the center of diverse interactions with many different ethnic groups.
- **Achieving balance and harmony.** The historical reason for this might be because there was a need for social order among large dynasties and kingdoms.

Hinduism

Hinduism is the oldest of the axial beliefs. It started in Indià about 2500–1500 B.C.E. (the Hindu Vedism Period). Hinduism is a somewhat complex belief system that practices meditation and studies ancient texts, essays, and poems (called the *Upanishads*). The five elements (strands) that help to shape Hindu traditions are doctrine, practice, society, story, and devotion.

Key Facts about Hinduism

Hindu scripture. What makes Hinduism difficult to understand is that it is not contained in holy texts like the ones that most of us in the West are familiar with. Rather, Hinduism is explained through a series of Sanskrit philosophical and religious teachings written in the Upanishads as stories, poems, and hymns that are recognized as *Vedas* (divine knowledge). This doctrine is now found in an extract of the Upanishads called the *Bhagavad-Gita,* or *Gita* (Hindu religious scriptures), which are not connected in a linear fashion. Rather, they are a series of moral stories by unknown authors about the gods and truths of nature and the universe.

Hindu gods. How many gods are there? You are probably thinking thousands. Actually, for the truly enlightened according to Hinduism, there are zero gods. How is that possible?

Hindu brahma. According to Hinduism, there is an impersonal energy that created all things and connects all things. This is known as *brahma* (creator of god). Brahma manifested all life and matter. When this happened, time and space exploded into cycles. These cycles eventually manifested in the diversity of life that we see and are a part of in the world and the universe.

Hindu karma. The purpose of life in Hinduism is to get back to the harmony and connectedness of brahma, and this is achieved by following our *karma* (the law of cause and effect). For example, if we do what is good, we achieve an escape from the wheel of life. If we do what is bad, we remain connected to the wheel and its suffering. Since all of reality is about cause and effect, there must be an effect caused by our actions. According to Hinduism, if we cannot escape the wheel of life, we need to return to it in order to learn and eventually escape. How do we learn?

Hindu caste system. According to Hinduism, we learn by entering a *caste* (hierarchy) system of life that helps us to be purified of our bad karma. This is the caste system that includes the *Brahmas* (priests), *Kshatriyas* (warriors), *Vaisyas* (skilled merchants), *Sudras* (farmers), and *Untouchables* (outcasts). As we learn, we are reincarnated into a new life to learn again. Since all energy and matter come from the *dharma* (the right way of living), it cannot be wasted or lost until it returns to its origin in the complete connection of all beings.

Buddhism

Buddhism was a reform movement of Hinduism that grew out of a philosophy in present-day Nepal (India) in 500 B.C.E. Buddhism is not a religion, but a philosophical tradition that focuses on spiritual insight into the true nature of life.

Key Facts about Buddhism

Buddhism was founded by Siddhartha. According to tradition, Buddhism was based on the teachings of a prince of India named **Siddhartha Gautama.** Siddhartha was the original enlightened one, or **Buddha.** He grew up in complete luxury, and his father wanted to protect him from all suffering. Then one day Siddhartha traveled out past his palace walls and found people suffering from poverty, disease, and death. Siddhartha left the worldly comforts in the castle to find *enlightenment* (an awakening of wisdom and truth). He became an *ascetic*—one who sacrificed all earthly desires—but found this to be too extreme. When he came to this dead end, he changed his path to search for truth. He went to the desert and meditated under the Bodhi Tree to seek the true nature of things. It is there that he found enlightenment. He spent the next 45 years teaching *dharma* (the right way of living to be free of suffering). Siddhartha also established *sangha* (a community of monks).

Buddhism and suffering. Siddhartha, or the first Buddha, taught enlightenment through the **Four Noble Truths.** (1) Life's primary problem is suffering. (2) Suffering is caused by desire and attachment. (3) Suffering is defined as holding on to or attaching to life when it is constantly changing. This attachment is not understood by most people. Therefore, the main obstacle for people is ignorance, but enlightenment will help those who are hindered by obstacles. (4) Buddha's solution was to follow the right thinking and right action that would lead to a detachment and the freedom of letting go of the changes in the world. Eventually, this detachment would lead to a detachment from life itself and a return to the ultimate source of peace and harmony—*nirvana* (the highest state of enlightenment).

Buddhism and compassion. To achieve enlightenment, people must develop an overall attitude and action of compassion. Why compassion? Compassion is the ability to understand the needs of others. This means the letting go of the self. In fact, the ultimate action by a truly enlightened Buddha is to achieve nirvana (the end of all suffering), then to let go of nirvana and come back to the material reality in order to help others let go.

Confucianism

Confucianism is a political and social philosophy based on the teachings of Master Kung, or **Confucius.** It is often characterized as a "way of life" rather than a religion. The teachings of Confucius are known as the *Analects of Confucius* (a collection of short philosophical writings). Confucianism was started around 550–479 B.C.E. in China during a time of great political upheaval and social instability. Confucianism was formed at a time of the decline of the Chinese feudal system.

TEST TIP: On the WHAP exam, you may be asked to compare and contrast the ancient Chinese feudal hierarchy system with the European feudal system in the Early Middle Ages. Feudalism was a political, social, and economic system of landownership.

Chinese feudalism evolved between 1122 B.C.E. and 256 B.C.E. It was a landownership system, whereby the emperor of China had all of the power. Although the emperor owned all of the land, he granted parcels to lords and nobles in return for allegiance. However, the lords and nobles were unable to work their lands (farms) and protect their lands from outside invasions. The lords and nobles recruited peasants and commoners to work on their lands.

Key Facts about Confucianism

Confucianism was based on social harmony. In China, Confucius wrote the *Analects* in order to solve the problem of social disorder and corruption. Confucius lived at a time when China had experienced centuries of civil wars. He saw corrupt leaders manipulating the people and using their power for selfish ends. Confucius claimed that humans were basically good, but they needed a way to be protected from the selfish actions of leaders who misused their powers.

Confucianism was based on filial piety. Confucius called for a society that was based on family or *filial piety* hierarchical relationships (respect for one's father, elders, and ancestors). He believed that if people were related to one another like parents and siblings, they could develop obligations and duties to one another that would ensure both social stability and fair treatment. A Confucian society is like a family, with the emperor as the father figure. The family is a microcosm example of an empire at the local level. Each person is obligated to one another.

Confucianism was not a religion. Confucius once said that he did not know if there was a god or gods, but he needed to form a practical system of governance that worked for everyone. For Confucius, private religious beliefs were acceptable, but public beliefs and actions should be based on what works to yield social order, or *practical thinking*. Practical thinking was defined as a social order that treats all people fairly with mutual respect, appreciation, and kindness.

Chinese Legalism

Chinese Legalism was a social-political system that was popular during the Qin Dynasty (221–207 B.C.E.) under Qin Shi Huang. Although Chinese Legalism declined after this period, the ideas of Chinese legalist thinkers have remained an important part of China's history.

Key Facts about Chinese Legalism

Chinese Legalism philosophy. In contrast to Confucianism, the scholars of Chinese Legalism believed that humans were all basically corrupt and selfish. These philosophers wrote that the only way to control humans was through a strong, absolute leadership of the emperor. Chinese legalists sought to achieve "a rich state and powerful army" to create a stable society. You might ask, "Can't the emperor also be corrupt?" Yes, so the emperor was surrounded by wise advisers who kept the emperor in check. If the emperor was not wise and did not show virtuous leadership, he was overthrown.

Chinese Legalism under the Qin Dynasty. Under Qin Shi Huang, military power was used to unify the Warring States period. He created a unified measurement system for trade and a universal taxation system. Huang's authoritarian rule created anger and resentment from the nobles. After his death, they rebelled and created a new political system based upon the Confucian philosophy.

Daoism

Daoism (also known as *Taoism*) is a religious and philosophical system in China that started during the 4th century. It emphasized a positive attitude of living in balance (harmony) with the *dao* (the way or the path)—a balance between humans and nature. The philosophy of Daoism continues to be practiced in China's culture and traditions today and has influenced Chinese poetry, architecture, and medical practices.

Key Facts about Daoism

Daoism text is based on opposites. Lao-Tzi wrote the *Tao Te Ching* (Chinese philosophical and religious text of Daoism) in circa 600 B.C.E. He argued that all of life is based on opposites. These opposites include life and death, violence and peace, male and female, and the yin and the yang. According to the *Tao Te Ching,* all of these opposites are in a fine balance of life.

Daoism and the Third Way. According to Daoism, the individual must find this balance in the humility of life to experience the peace and harmony of the balance. Lao-Tzi called this the *Third Way* (or the way of nature). When we think of nature, we might think of it as the biological nature around us. Actually, he meant that there is a spiritual reality that we can find when we are in harmony, and we experience this harmony by letting go of our desire to control reality.

Mediterranean Beliefs

In the Mediterranean region (the Middle East), a new type of fundamental belief system arose called **monotheism** (the belief in one God who created the universe). Monotheistic religions (sometimes called "Abrahamic" or "Semitic" religions) include Judaism, Christianity, and Islam.

Judaism. Judaism originated in c. 1500 B.C.E. in the land of Canaan. Jewish people believed that their ancient ancestors came into contact with God, Yahweh (Hebrew for God), through the patriarchs of Abraham. Yahweh then gave the Jewish people a set of codified laws, the Ten Commandments, which provided an agreement between them and God.

Christianity. Christianity originated in Palestine (1st century C.E.) as a reform movement to Judaism. It has three major branches: Roman Catholic, Eastern Orthodox, and Protestant. Christianity is based on the life and teachings of Jesus, a Jewish man who claimed to be the son of God. It spread throughout the Roman world and Greek culture from the doctrines of Jesus' twelve apostles, like the Apostle Paul. Christianity is now the largest religion in the world.

Islam. Islam was a movement that claimed to be the final revelation of monotheism (see Chapter 7, pp. 116–118 for an in-depth description of Islam).

Empires and Governance

Students frequently complain that Period Two has so many names, dates, and empires to remember, and it tends to get really boring. To help you get through this section, let's look at the bigger themes and think about a story that most everyone is familiar with—*Star Wars*. If you watch the movies, you know what happened. In *Star Wars,* a group of planets makes an alliance with a grand group of planets. This alliance forms a senate to make decisions together, but the alliance gets so large that it can be manipulated by corrupt leaders. Eventually the senate falls due to the manipulation of some bad guys who use the dark side of the force. Okay, the last part about the force cannot really be applied to world history, but the first part does apply to the WHAP exam.

Did you know? The *Star Wars* model can be applied to the real-world organization of empire governments. In almost all cases of empires, the model of *Star Wars* works really well. Follow this line of reasoning:

1. A group of people form a small community based on farming and trade.
2. For defensive purposes and wealth accumulation, the farming communities join together and are ruled by some charismatic leader(s).
3. Charismatic leaders form a centralized kingdom or land-based empire.
4. Leaders often become corrupt and power-driven, causing a rebellion, or they lack defense against foreign intruders.

Let's see how this model plays out below in the real world.

TEST TIP: As humans became organized, early empires expanded dramatically in number and size. On the WHAP exam, it is important to be familiar with the names and geographic locations of early key empires and states: China, India, Greek city-states, and Rome.

China (Qin and Han Empires in East Asia)

China's ancient civilizations began as groups of farming communities, which expanded in time throughout East Asia. The ruling house, or dynasty, changed over time, often when the existing dynasty was overthrown.

TEST TIP: China's dynasties are listed in the table that follows, but the two most important dynasties to remember for the WHAP exam are the Qin Dynasty and the Han Dynasty in East Asia.

Ruling House	Description
Xia Dynasty (2100 to 1600 B.C.E.)	The Xia Dynasty is the first dynasty in China that started as a farming community. Some historians consider the Xia Dynasty to be a mythical legend because it is difficult to link history to the Xia.
Shang Dynasty (1600 to 1046 B.C.E.)	The Shang Dynasty is the earliest dynasty confirmed by archaeological evidence. Eventually, the farming communities formed under the Shang Dynasty, which consolidated power and justified their power through *ancestor worship* (the Chinese custom of worshiping dead ancestors whose spirits were believed to have the power to influence the fate of the living world). Silk weaving was invented and Chinese writing was developed. The Shang power caused resentment among the landed nobles, and the imperial power of the Zhou farther up the Yellow River rebelled against the Shang rule.
Zhou Dynasty (1046 to 256 B.C.E.)	The Zhou Dynasty justified its rebellion against the Shang as the *Mandate of Heaven* (heaven grants the emperor the right to rule). Under this belief, an emperor was allowed to rule if he was just and fair. If not, the gods would cause him to fall. The Zhou did fall into disarray for thousands of years during the Era of Warring States. During the Zhou rule, irrigation was introduced and iron casting was invented. Confucius began his philosophical and social teachings.

Continued

Ruling House	Description
Qin Dynasty (221 to 206 B.C.E.)	Known for ending feudal decentralization of the Warring States period. Eventually the Qin Dynasty centralized all political power in the emperor under the philosophy of **Chinese Legalism,** but this led to resentment from the nobles, who rebelled. During this dynasty, a new tax system and laws were designated to free slaves (serfdom) so that slaves would pay taxes. Construction of the **Great Wall of China** began during the Qin Dynasty.
Han Dynasty (206 B.C.E. to 220 C.E.)	The Han Dynasty rebelled against the Qin rule and continued a centralized empire. Known for establishing trade routes and a **tributary system** (demanding payments from neighboring regions) along the Eurasian Silk Roads to the Mediterranean from India and Persia to China. These trade routes passed along culture and established Buddhism in China. The Han Dynasty used Confucianism to create a balance between the emperor and nobles based on filial piety, obligations, and traditions. The Han Dynasty started the **civil service examination** to ensure strong government candidates.

India (Mauryan and Gupta Empires in South Asia)

India is such a large region that we classify it as its own subcontinent. The two important empires to remember for the WHAP exam are the Mauryan and Gupta empires in South Asia.

Empire	Description
Harappa and Mohenjo-Daro	Originally, India had a group of farming communities called Harappa and Mohenjo-Daro. It's not known for certain what happened to these communities. Most likely they collapsed due to changes in the environment. However, it is known that their descendants were assimilated into waves of migrants from the Eastern European and *steppe regions*. (Note: Steppe is a vast grassland that has enough rain for grass, but not enough for trees to grow.) At this time, migrants or Aryans (Indo-Europeans) came down into the northern areas of India and created a caste system that justified their labor specialization and social hierarchy. The Aryan culture spread throughout India.
Mauryan Empire (c. 322 to 185 B.C.E.)	The Mauryan Empire emerged when Chandragupta Maurya united Aryan kingdoms into one civilization, but it was one of the charismatic leaders, **Ashoka,** who built the empire into a powerful dynasty. He used military force to unite the different peoples of Northern India. When he saw the effects of his military brutality, Ashoka turned to a new religious movement, Buddhism, as a way to peaceably unite the people under a common identity. Ashoka was known for his Buddhist stone carvings on **Rock and Pillar Edicts** that instructed Mauryans to live lives of righteousness and charity. Ashoka sent out Buddhist missionaries along the Silk Roads trade route to create a peaceful connection with China. Mauryans traded silk, cotton, and elephants along the trade route.
Gupta Empire (320 to 550 C.E.)	When Ashoka's Mauryan Empire began to collapse, a new Gupta Empire arose. While not entirely successful, the Gupta were able to provide some centralization of the empire under a new government. They did this through a common language, common national identity, and standardization of trade. Hinduism was the dominant belief system, and the caste system was strictly enforced. During the Gupta Empire, many mathematical scholars emerged with important advancements (i.e., decimal system, pi, and zero).

Greece and Rome (Mediterranean Region)

In the Mediterranean during the Classical period, two civilizations ruled the region, Greece and Rome.

Greek City-States (Athens and Sparta)

The Mycenaeans (c. 1600–1000 B.C.E.) migrated into the Greek peninsula. They formed a series of city-states in an isolated, rocky, and poor land in Greece. Eventually two city-states (called *polis,* which means "city" in Greek) rose to prominence: the **Athenians** and the **Spartans.** The ancient Greek city-states of Athens and Sparta had significant political, cultural, and economic differences.

Key Facts about the Greek City-States

Athenians. The Athenians formed a democratic government by 450 B.C.E., in which the wealthy nobles and aristocrats held control of the land and government. The only people allowed to vote or publicly debate were citizens born in Athens. Athenian political developments have influenced modern-day Western European and the United States' democracy; historians call this period the **Hellenic Period.**

Spartans. The Spartans were known as a warrior society. They created a military dictatorship that was ruled by just a few landowners and nobles. Most Spartans could not hold a government position, especially the labor class of slaves (called *helots*), but people had a duty to the state. Loyalty to the state came before anything else. Young boys entered military training and a state-sponsored education program by age 7.

Delian and Peloponnesian leagues. The Greek city-states were dragged into a fight between the Persian Empire and the Ionians. The Greek city-states had to fight the Persians in two separate wars until they were able to retain their independence, but this led to a power struggle within the city-states. The Athenians led a new confederation called the **Delian League** (468 B.C.E.) to fight the Persian Empire. The Spartans created their own competitive group called the **Peloponnesian League.**

The Peloponnesian War. The conflict between the two leagues eventually led to the Peloponnesian War (441–404 B.C.E.), weakening Athens and reshaping the ancient Greek world. Sparta became the leading power of Greece, but the economic cost of war severely destabilized both city-states. Sparta was unable to unite all of the Greek city-states, and this left the Greek peninsula open to outside invaders.

Alexander the Great. Most of the Greek city-states eventually united under King Philip of Macedon in 338 B.C.E. When King Philip died, his son Alexander became a powerful ruler of Macedonia. Alexander was a good example of a charismatic leader of the period and was a brilliant military leader who continued to unite the Greek city-states. He became the king of Persia (Iran today), Babylon (Iraq today), and Asia. Alexander was tutored by Aristotle, who taught him philosophy, poetry, science, and politics. Historians say he was successful due to his intelligence and charisma. His empires conquered territories reaching as far east as India and as far south as Egypt.

Alexander's legacy was that he helped to spread Greek culture, language, and religion throughout the Middle East. During Alexander's expeditions and invasions, he spread Greek culture throughout Central Asia, causing Hellenism or a *syncretism* of Greek beliefs and arts (syncretism is the mixing of different beliefs that have been diffused from a variety of civilizations). However, because Alexander never established a new leader in the event of his death, his empires collapsed after he died. Alexander ruled over the Greek city-states from 336–323 B.C.E. and died at the young age of 32 from malaria. When he died, his empire collapsed into multiple regions including the Seleucids and Ptolemaic empires under the Roman Empire. This division eventually led to the weakening of Alexander's Macedonian empires.

Heads Up: What You Need to Know

On the WHAP exam, it's important to know about ancient Greek contributions and achievements.

- **Philosophy:** Ancient Greek philosophers Socrates, Plato, and Aristotle contributed to philosophical thoughts of logic, science, ethics, and politics. Plato's ideas about the Republic helped kings form ideal governments.

- **Mathematics and science:** Greek contributions include medicine (Hippocrates), science of atoms (Democritus), geometry (Pythagoras and Euclid), astronomy (Aristarchus), and geographic maps (Eratosthenes).

- **Literature:** Ancient Greeks are famous for inventing and performing plays of tragedy and comedy. For example, Homer (*The Iliad* and *The Odyssey*) and Sophocles (*Oedipus Rex*).

- **Architecture:** The Greeks built the *Parthenon,* a temple on a hill called the *Acropolis*. They also introduced the first lighthouse to safely guide ships to port and water-driven wheels called watermills.

- **Olympic Games:** The Greeks started the modern-day Olympics for athletes around the world at a festival at Olympia to honor the god Zeus.

The Roman Empire

The Roman Empire was one of the greatest civilizations in world history. This geographic area was centered in the city of Rome in 500 B.C.E., but is now known as the Western European region.

Key Facts about the Roman Empire

The Roman Republic. After the Roman aristocracy overthrew the Etruscans (509 B.C.E.), the citizens of Rome created the Roman Republic. The definition of a Roman citizen evolved over the time period of the Roman Republic, and then the Roman Empire. Roman society was split into two groups, patricians and plebeians.

Patricians and plebeians. At first, Roman citizenship was only granted to aristocrats and nobles, called patricians. **Patricians** were descendants from the original tribes of Rome and were landowners with large estates. The citizens selected two consuls to rule over them, and only men could vote. A second class of citizens was called **plebeians** (farmers who did not own as much land and craftsmen). They were free (not slaves) and were the average working citizens of Rome. Although they worked hard and paid their taxes, plebeians could not vote. Over time, some plebeians were included into the Senate. However, the eventual problem was having enough land to support the larger population. This led to geographic expansion, more power for the military, and the creation of an empire with a strict class system. This period of civil unrest was the beginning of the transition from the Roman Republic to the Roman Empire.

Tribunes given senate power. During this period, the plebeians made political gains and won the right to become members of government and write *codifications* (laws) into the **Twelve Tables** (legislative Roman laws that protected human rights and property). As Romans acquired land, they handed more and more senate power to their *tribunus* (*tribune* in English), who were the Roman elected officials comprised of plebeians and the military generals.

TEST TIP: On the WHAP exam, it is important to be familiar with the Roman Twelve Tables because these legislative laws have influenced legal systems throughout the Western world. You will not need to know the specific laws, but you should know that the Romans used the Twelve Tables to codify legal norms and class responsibilities.

The rise of the Roman Empire. The Roman Republic tried to resolve its internal land inequalities through expansion. Roman generals amassed soldiers by promising rewards of land from those areas that were conquered. The First *Triumvirate* (military-political alliance of three men) included Pompey, Caesar, and Crassus. After a series of successive wars, Rome surrendered its power from the Republic's Senate to Julius Caesar, as dictator of the Republic. After Caesar's assassination, his adopted heir, Octavian (later known as Caesar Augustus), rose to power. Rome became an empire under its first Roman emperor, Caesar Augustus, who ruled from 27 B.C.E. to 14 C.E.

Did you know? The Hellenistic culture of the Greeks (cosmopolitan culture of the Hellenistic Period) was popular among the Romans. Historians say that even though the Romans conquered the Greeks, it is the Greek "culture" that conquered Rome.

Rome's accomplishments. Under Julius Caesar's dictatorship (49 B.C.E. to 44 B.C.E.), the Roman Republic was known for its expansion over three continents and for its control over Western Europe and Northern Africa. It was the largest empire in the world, creating an internal infrastructure of roads, highways, and aqueducts. In fact, the Roman Colosseum still stands today. The Roman Empire changed from a civilian force to an unmatched military army with select generals. The Roman Empire took the *Twelve Tables,* a codification of universal laws under the Republic, and applied them in a much more complex way to the conquered territories. The Romans spread their language. Latin became the basis for the Romance languages of Spanish, French, and Italian.

Did you know? Christianity started in the Roman Empire after the birth of Jesus in the 1st century. It began as a reform movement of Judaism. However, until the reign of Constantine (312–337 C.E.), Christians were condemned and killed. The Emperor Constantine issued the **Edict of Milan** (religious tolerance) so that Christians could practice Christianity throughout Western (Rome) and Eastern (Byzantium) Europe. Christianity spread throughout the region and the Roman Catholic Church (Christian) dominated Europe's politics, morals, philosophy, science, and education from 590 to 1515 C.E.

Rome's road to peace. Rome had several civil wars during its years as a Republic. As generals gained more military and political power, the soldiers became loyal to their commanders instead of to the Roman Senate. This created civil wars. The Senate decided to appoint General Julius Caesar as dictator in 46 B.C.E., but then tried to get him to step down. Caesar was murdered on March 15, 44 B.C.E. (foretold by a psychic, "the Ides of March"). Caesar Augustus (Octavian) became the Emperor of the Roman Empire and a period of peace and stability called the **Pax Romana** (27 B.C.E. to 180 C.E.) followed.

The decline of the powerful Roman Empire (180–476 C.E.) is an important topic in world history. You should be familiar with the reasons that the empire collapsed.

- **Invasions.** The rapid growth of the Roman Empire made it necessary for the Roman army to protect its borders from invaders. Unfortunately, the empire was so large that it was difficult to protect from invaders (barbarians and German tribes).

- **Economic decline.** The Roman Empire experienced a breakdown in the labor force. Rome became dependent on foreign trade to feed its population, and its infrastructure began to decline. In addition, territorial expansions required that the government impose more and more taxes on the people to maintain its army. This created economic warfare between the rich and the poor.

- **Political weakness.** The leadership was comprised of aristocrats and the military. The military became corrupt and disloyal to the government. Eventually, rulers were unable to manage this large geographic area without the help of loyal military leaders.

- **Division.** The emperor **Diocletian** tried to solve the problem of Rome's decline by splitting Rome into Western Rome and Eastern **Byzantium**. This laid the foundation for the **Byzantine Empire,** but that was only a temporary solution to the problem of Rome's decline.

- **Class system.** There was a decline of citizenry and a growing gap between the rich and the poor. The civic morale declined because there was a strict class system. Citizens felt discouraged and their feelings of patriotism declined.

- **Christianity.** Christianity's values conflicted with the empire's authoritarian values. This later changed when Constantine tried to unite Rome by adopting Christianity as the empire's main religious identity.

Trade

Now, let's focus on the common practice that humans have been doing since pretty much the beginning of time—trade. Consider a world without trade. In a world without trade, we would be stuck with only what we have in our local area. We would not get to try things that are new and exotic. Our learning would be limited to what we are most familiar with in our local area, and we may be wary of trying new, unfamiliar things. That means that we would not be able to create as many technological innovations, and jobs would be limited, which in turn means a lot less economic growth. In other words, we would either stagnate or impede our own development.

Benefits of trade:

- New exotic, luxury, and varied types of goods and services from other cultures
- New developments in science and health (spices were not only used for food, but for medicine)
- The transfer of distinctive customs, culture, language, and religious ideas from foreign traders
- New competition with other regions leading to economic gains

- New ideas that helped people to think "outside the box" to create new technologies and innovations
- New forms of communication and transportation that led to a faster dissemination of ideas

Let's go over some of the early forms of trade that developed between human communities.

Early Trade Route Networks		
Trade Route	**Description**	**Exchanges**
Mediterranean Sea Network (600 B.C.E. to 600 C.E.)	The first trade started along the Mediterranean Sea and Persian Gulf followed transregional routes through Mesopotamia and Egypt (Middle East). People moved through the Middle East and formed small villages and sedentary societies along river systems.	Agriculture, animals (camels and donkeys), frankincense, myrrh, papyrus, wool, and copper.
Eurasian Silk Roads Network (100 B.C.E. to 1500 C.E.)	The Eurasian Silk Roads were the first networks to join the East and West worlds. The Han Dynasty expanded trade when it started to create land-based trade routes that became the Silk Roads. The Silk Roads were among the most famous trade routes because these multiple roads crisscrossed from Western China into India, across the Middle East, and into the Mediterranean to create a major network for trading goods and services.	The early Eurasian Silk Roads focused on luxury items. Silk textiles, metals (bronze), woolen goods, carpets, tapestries, precious stones (jade), medicine, spices, teas, sugar, furs, animals (horses), porcelain, perfumes, and agriculture (pomegranates, figs, onions, string beans, and carrots). In addition to carrying goods, the Silk Roads became notable for transferring ideas, religions, customs, and new forms of technology.
Trans-Saharan Desert Network (300 C.E. to 1450 C.E.)	West African kingdoms controlled important caravan trade routes that connected West Africa and North Africa across the Sahara Desert. The Trans-Saharan trade routes were formed along the geographic centers of the desert's oases. The camels made large caravans possible because they could store water for 2–3 days in their humps.	Salt, gold, animals (sheep, goats, cattle, camels), pottery, wool, precious stones (obsidian), and exchanges of culture and customs.
Indian Ocean Network (500 B.C.E. to 1500 C.E.)	The Indian Ocean was the first ocean to be crossed for trade. It was the largest East-West trade route, which went from Eastern Africa to Western India and the Southern Middle East. The trade route was used by the Mauryan Empire in India, the Han Empire in China, and the Roman Empire in the Mediterranean.	Gold, ivory, iron, silk, porcelain, paper, food, migrations, and religious ideas: Buddhism and Hinduism.

The Silk Roads

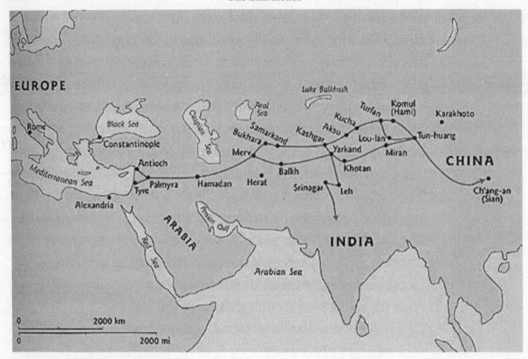

Source: The Silk Roads Trade Map

Trade routes carried everything from agricultural goods to religious ideas. The trade routes created the incentives to develop new forms of transportation and communication. Boats were built to carry large loads of goods across the ocean. The Indian Ocean trade route had the advantage of carrying large bulk goods on boats like lumber. The Silk Roads had the advantage of connecting empires by land, and the Trans-Saharan route used domesticated camels to carry large loads across Northern Africa due to their ability to store water. Amazingly, throughout this time period, trade routes remained peaceful.

TEST TIP: A good understanding of trade can help you on the WHAP exam. There is a strong likelihood that there will be a question that deals with trade either directly or indirectly. This study guide covers trade for each period in chapters 6 to 10.

Here are a few ideas to keep in mind if you encounter an AP history reasoning skill question about trade.

- Trade is a "continuity" throughout world history due to the diffusion of ideas and innovations.
- Trade is a "cause-and-effect" relationship since it has an impact on almost all parts of human life.
- Trade has "caused" governments to manage and regulate trade to connect political-state development to the exchange.
- The "context" of the ideas of trade has been diffused to almost all religious, political, cultural, philosophical, technological, and economic systems of the world.
- The "comparison" of the periods and regions of trade is important to understanding the rise and decline of civilizations and empires.

Heads Up: What You Need to Know

To summarize Period Two, look through the following major themes, commonalities, and turning points that are important to remember for the WHAP exam.

- The social relationships of sedentary and large empires were hierarchical. This hierarchy tended to include an emperor, priestly class, merchants, artisans, landowners, and peasants.

- The political development was centralized through the power of the emperor. Emperors justified their rule through legal codes and religious belief systems.

- The societies developed new belief systems called the axial beliefs. These religious worldviews aimed to answer questions about the meaning of life, the purpose of the individual, and the role of the community. Axial beliefs included Hinduism, Buddhism, Confucianism, Daoism, Judaism, Christianity, and Islam.

- The development of new forms of technology included metals, military weapons, and maritime transportation that promoted exchanges along new trade routes.

- The economies of societies continued to develop trade along routes including the Eurasian Silk Roads, Indian Ocean, Mediterranean Sea, Trans-Saharan Desert, and Andean Mountain ranges. These trade routes connected sedentary societies, spread cultural traditions, and centralized empires.

Chapter Review Practice Questions

The practice questions show the types of questions that may appear on the exam. On the actual exam, the questions are grouped into sets. Each set contains one source-based prompt and two to five questions.

Questions 1–3 refer to the following passage.

Question: If Buddhism is the greatest and most venerable of ways, why did the great sages of the past and Confucius not practice it? In the Confucian Classics one mentions it. Why then, do you love the Way of the Buddha and rejoice in outlandish arts? Can the writings of the Buddha exceed the Classics and commentaries and beautify the accomplishments of the sages?
Answer: All written works need not necessarily be the words of Confucius. To compare the sages to the Buddha would be like comparing a white deer to a unicorn, or a swallow to a phoenix. The records and teachings of the Confucian Classics do not contain everything. Even if the Buddha is not mentioned in them, what occasion is there for suspicion?

—Source: Anonymous Chinese scholar, "The Disposition of Error," China, 500 C.E.

1. The passage above represents what primary conflict in China during the Classical Age?

    A. The fight between the nobles and emperor over control of the land
    B. The rise of new bureaucrats into positions through the use of the civil service exam
    C. The conflict between Confucianists and Buddhists over focusing on practical governance versus detaching from material reality
    D. The Confucian leaders' acceptance of outside cultural influences made possible through trade

2. Which statement best reflects why this conflict was occurring in China during the Classical Age?

    A. Northern steppe invaders were coming into China and conquering the Northern territories.

    B. Buddhist missionaries were traveling the Silk Roads into China spreading the new faith.

    C. Zheng He had brought back new ideas and products from his voyages to India and Eastern Africa.

    D. China's expansion into Vietnam and Korea had led to local peasant rebellions.

3. Which of the following best explains how Confucian leaders responded to the problem that was discussed in the passage above?

    A. The Confucian leaders accepted the new ideas as part of the Chinese traditions.

    B. Buddhism was able to dominate due to its acceptance by the emperor.

    C. Buddhists were accepted, but they were given a special tax that was meant as a disincentive to people converting to the new faith.

    D. The Confucian leaders mixed the notion of merit with a reward of eternal life, which came to be known as Neo-Confucianism.

Questions 4–6 refer to the following image.

Source: Temple of Borobudur, c. 8th–9th centuries C.E.

4. Which of the following represents the consequence of trade in Southeast Asia based on the image above?

    A. The isolation of kingdoms in the fear of losing cultural purity

    B. The dominance of one Confucian belief system

    C. Syncretism of a variety of faiths and cultures that were diffused through global trade

    D. The creation of military fortresses to defend trade routes against competing kingdoms

5. Which of the following best describes how the differing ideas that led to this monument have spread into Southeast Asia?

   A. Monks brought these ideas over the Silk Roads.
   B. The Indian Ocean trade route transported goods and ideas into this region.
   C. Asian governments invested in merchant and military fleets to dominate these regions.
   D. Kingdoms in Southeast Asia cut off trade and developed cultural purity from within their boundaries.

6. Which statement below is similar to the monument shown in the image above?

   A. The Portuguese introduced cannons along the Indian Ocean trade route during the 1600s C.E. in order to create economic dominance.
   B. New global trade due to lowered tariffs in the 21st century has led to a convergence of cultures.
   C. The expansion of the Mongols led to the protection of the Silk Roads and transfer of goods and services over land.
   D. The Confucian leaders stopped Zheng He's expeditions for fear of outside cultural influences.

Answers and Explanations

1. **C.** Confucianists were suspicious of Buddhists because Confucianism stressed practical issues over spiritual ones. Confucian leaders feared that Buddhist spirituality would lead to a lack of pragmatic grounded work and solutions from peasants.

2. **B.** Buddhists came to China over the Silk Roads. They came due to Ashoka and the Indian dynasties sending these missionaries both to the East and West to spread these religious ideals. This led to cultural diffusion of Indian beliefs to Southeast Asia.

3. **D.** Confucians initially responded by exiling Buddhists and imprisoning followers of Buddhism. Eventually they mixed the two beliefs through Neo-Confucianism. The idea was that proper Confucian behavior would be rewarded with achieving eternal life.

4. **C.** The temple of Borobudur is found in Indonesia. It is an excellent example of the diffusion of Buddhism to other countries.

5. **B.** The Indian Ocean was the main route of cultural diffusion because it connected India to Africa, the Middle East, and Southeast Asia.

6. **B.** This question is an example of causation. Therefore, the answer we are looking for is about cultural diffusion due to increased trade. Globalization is the closest example of the answers since it is a relatively free trade without barriers to trade goods or ideas.

Chapter 7

Period Three: Regional and Interregional Interactions (c. 600 C.E. to c. 1450)

With improved transportation, civilizations of the Post-Classical Period migrated, traded, and networked throughout the world.

- East and Southeast Asian Civilizations
- Central Asia and the Middle East
- Africa
- Europe
- The Crusades
- Gunpowder Empires
  - Ottoman Empire (1301–1922)
  - Safavid Empire (1501–1722)
  - Mughal Empire (1526–1748)
- Mesoamerica

Overview of AP World History Period Three

Period Three is called the Post-Classical Era that most people know as the Middle Ages or the Dark Ages. Sounds like a pretty bad period of time, but actually the events that transpired set the stage for much of what we know today as modern history. Many of the classical civilizations collapsed or declined by this time, but they left behind important traditions and systems of organization.

While some people might think of this period as a time of stagnation, this was a time when innovations in trade, technology, and culture expanded and advanced. These innovations were largely due to the networks of trade and interaction among civilizations.

As you read through this chapter, focus on relations among world civilizations and pay attention to the key leaders and how their political, social, or religious ideologies may have impacted trade and relations with other civilizations.

The WHAP curriculum framework and key concepts for Period Three explain important developments that emerged during this time period. Use the chart that follows as a guide to help you make mental connections between the key concepts and the topics covered in this chapter.

The information contained in this chart is an abridged version of the concept outline with topic examples. Visit https://apstudent.collegeboard.org/apcourse/ap-world-history/ for the complete WHAP course curriculum descriptions and key concepts.

AP World History Key Concepts (c. 600 C.E. to c. 1450)	
KEY CONCEPT 3.1: EXPANSION AND INTENSIFICATION OF COMMUNICATION AND EXCHANGE NETWORKS **A deepening and widening of networks of human interaction within and across regions contributed to the cultural, technological, and biological diffusion within and between various societies.**	Improved transportation technologies and commercial practices led to an increased volume of trade and expanded the geographical range of existing and newly active trade networks. The movement of peoples caused environmental and linguistic effects. Cross-cultural exchanges were fostered by the intensification of existing networks of trade and communication, or the creation of new ones. For example, Christianity in Europe, Neo-Confucianism and Buddhism in East Asia, Hinduism and Buddhism in Southeast Asia, Islam in Sub-Saharan Africa and Asia, and Toltec/Mexico or Inca traditions in Mesoamerica and Andean America. There was continued diffusion of crops and pathogens, including epidemic diseases like the bubonic plague along the trade routes.
KEY CONCEPT 3.2: CONTINUITY AND INNOVATION OF STATE FORMS AND THEIR INTERACTIONS **State formation and development demonstrated continuity, innovation, and diversity in various regions.**	Empires collapsed in different regions of the world, and in some areas were replaced by new imperial states or political systems. Interregional contacts and conflicts between states and empires encouraged significant technological and cultural transfers, including transfers between T'ang China and the Abbasids, transfers across the Mongol Empire, transfers during the Crusades between the Muslims and Christians, and transfers during Chinese maritime activity led by Ming Admiral Zheng He.
KEY CONCEPT 3.3: INCREASED ECONOMIC PRODUCTIVE CAPACITY AND ITS CONSEQUENCES **Changes in trade networks resulted from and stimulated increasing productive capacity, with important implications for social and gender structures and environmental processes.**	Innovations stimulated agricultural and industrial production in many regions. For example, the *chinampa* field systems, the *waru waru* agricultural techniques in the Andean areas, the horse collar, three-field rotation, improved terracing, and swamp draining. The fate of cities varied greatly, with periods of significant decline and periods of increased urbanization buoyed by rising productivity and expanding trade networks. Despite significant continuities in social structures and in methods of production, there were also some important changes in labor management and in the effect of religious conversion on gender relations and family life.

Important Themes, Terms, and Concepts

The list that follows shows important themes, terms, and concepts that you should be familiar with on the WHAP exam. Please don't memorize each concept now. Place a check mark next to each topic as it is studied and refer to this list as often as necessary. After you finish the review section, reinforce what you have learned by working the practice questions at the end of this chapter. The answers and explanations provide further clarification into the interrelationships among early civilizations.

Themes, Terms, and Concepts You Should Know

SOCIAL

Term/Concept	Brief Description
Dhimmis	Jewish and Christian communities in the Islamic caliphates. They were given some protections, but they were expected to pay a jizyah or military replacement tax to the sultan.
Polygyny	The practice of marrying several wives for the purpose of reproduction.
Feudalism	The social system in the Post-Classical world of landowners renting land to peasant workers.
Vassals and serfs	The two classes of the Post-Classical world. The vassals owned the land, and the serfs sold their labor through rent to the vassals.
Patriarchy	A cultural and social system in which power is defined through fathers and "masculine" values.
Kowtow	The Chinese practice of bowing to the emperor as one approached him in order to show subordination to his power.
Foot binding	The practice of upper-class women having their feet broken and bound. This started in the T'ang Dynasty in China. It created a class divide between upper-class women and middle-class merchant women.

POLITICAL

Term/Concept	Brief Description
Caeseropapism	The practice of the emperor choosing the bishops. This was only practiced in Byzantium, where the emperor gave a blessing to the bishops chosen by the patriarch, the leader of the Eastern Orthodox church. It led to a centralization of power for the emperor..
Caliphates	Islamic kingdoms and empires after the death of the Prophet Muhammad.
Abbasids	The second Islamic caliphate. It was a Shiite caliphate. Its capital was in Baghdad.
Umayyads	The first Islamic caliphate. It was a Sunni kingdom. Its capital was in Damascus.
Sultan	The leader of the Ottoman Empire. He was considered to be the messenger of Allah and the Prophet Muhammad.
Baghdad	The capital of the Shiite caliphate, the Abbasids.
Damascus	The capital of the Sunni caliphate, the Umayyads.
Ghana	Post-Classical African empire involved in gold mining and trade on the Western coast.
Mali	Western African kingdom that would centralize the tribes. It became the Western end to the Trans-Saharan trade route.
Mansa Musa	The king who united Mali on the Western coast of Africa with the Middle East. He established a trade route between these two regions that expanded the gold trade. And, he brought Islam to Western Africa.
Sundiata	He centralized the tribes into the kingdom of Mali and created the conditions for Mansa Musa to create the Trans-Saharan trade route.
Sui, T'ang, and Song dynasties	The Post-Classical dynasties for China. They similarly looked to expand outward into areas like Vietnam, Korea, Tibet, and Manchuria.
Yuan Dynasty	The dynasty in China created by the Mongol invasion. It would be led by Genghis Khan's grandson, Kublai Khan.
Daimyo	Local governors in Japan. They would rule over a small province. They fought with the emperor for local control. For most of Japan's history, they held most of the power.

Continued

POLITICAL	
Term/Concept	**Brief Description**
Taika reforms	The Japanese emperor tried to centralize Japan by initiating the Taika reforms. These were a series of laws that created a merit-based system similar to the Confucian system in China.
Fujiwara	One of the Japanese clans that attempted to unite the Japanese island.
Bushido code	A political/cultural system of nationalism in Japan that tried to unite the local clans into one Japanese identity.
Charles Martel (686 to 741)	The French king who stopped the Islamic invasion from Spain into France at the Battle of Tours.
Charlemagne (742 to 814)	The French emperor who united much of Europe during the early 9th century. He created the Treaty of Verdun, but it was signed after his death by his son. Charlemagne's vision was to resurrect the Roman Empire, but his son later divided the empire to create the basis of the modern boundaries of European nation-states.
Holy Roman Empire	Charlemagne had hoped to resurrect the Roman Empire in Central Europe. The empire was never united but remained fragmented up to the Protestant Reformation, when the religious wars separated and fragmented Europe.
Hundred Years War (1337 to 1453)	The long conflict between the kingdoms of England and France over the succession of the French throne.
War of the Roses (1455 to 1487)	The Civil War in England between the House of York and the House of Lancaster. This war took place in the context of the Hundred Years War and it established the national identity for England.
Crusades (1095 to 1291)	The religious wars between Western Catholic Europe and the Islamic Turks over the holy lands in Jerusalem.
RELIGIOUS	
Term/Concept	**Brief Description**
Ali	One of the four Rightly Chosen. He became the leader of the Shiite movement. He claimed to be the next leader since he was the cousin and son-in-law of Muhammad. Ali claimed that leadership in Islam should come from the bloodline of Muhammad.
Sunni vs. Shiite	These two sects claimed different justifications for leadership in Islam. Sunni Muslims claimed that it was based on spontaneous and organic leadership from Allah. Shiite Muslims claimed it was from the bloodline of Muhammad.
Western Catholicism and Eastern Orthodox Christianity	These two sides of Christianity were united in Rome until the Great Schism in 1054 C.E. Western Rome claimed absolute authority in the papacy. Eastern Orthodoxy, located in Byzantium, claimed shared power among the bishops.
Great Schism	The break between the Western and Eastern churches in 1054 C.E.
Kaaba	The main monument or black box in Saudi Arabia that housed the statues to the Quraysh tribes. Muhammad changed this to the monument to Allah.
Quran	The main holy book or scriptures of the Islamic faith.
Hadith	The sayings of Muhammad used to develop Islamic doctrine. While some are authentic, others are falsely attributed to Muhammad.

RELIGIOUS	
Term/Concept	Brief Description
Five Pillars	The principal beliefs of Islam. They include: **Shahadah:** Sincerely reciting the Muslim profession of faith **Salat:** Performing ritual prayers in the proper way five times each day **Zakat:** Paying an alms (or charity) tax to benefit the poor and the needy **Sawm:** Fasting during the month of Ramadan **Hajj:** Pilgrimage to Mecca
Shariah	The laws of Islam. They come from the principle of Shariah in the Quran as a method for determining and interpreting legal matters based on the faith.
Imam	The priests who are the leaders of Islamic communities.
Umah	The Islamic community. The Quran calls for people to look out for the needs of the community as well as the individual.
Four Rightly Guided Caliphs	The first four caliphs after Muhammad's death. They included Uthman, Bakr, Umar, and Ali.
Abu Bakr	The father-in-law of Muhammad and the first leader of Islam following Muhammad's death.
Investiture Controversy	The Roman Catholic controversy—when kings tried to appoint their own bishops and weaken the power of the pope. The kings failed, but they created the foundations for the Protestant Reformation.
Papacy	The pope of the Catholic and Western Roman church. The papacy was viewed as the leader of the bishops and was more like a pyramid, with the pope on the top.
Patriarch	The leader of the Eastern Orthodox Church. He shares power with the other bishops.
TECHNOLOGICAL	
Term/Concept	Brief Description
Proto-industrialization	The increasing production of goods by rural households through the putting-out system and other methods. Generally regarded as the first step toward industrialization. While this primarily took place in Western Europe, there are examples of proto-industrialization in other societies, including the Grand Canal in China.
Grand Canal	The Chinese creation of a trade route or canal between Northern and Southern China. It was created during the Post-Classical Age to connect the areas conquered by China.
ECONOMICS	
Term/Concept	Brief Description
Swahili city-states	The port cities established by the Bantu tribes that moved to Eastern Africa. These cities would trade with other regions over the Indian Ocean trade route.
Manors	A large estate including a manor house and the surrounding lands where a lord provided land for production and rent of peasants' labor.
Hanseatic League	A league or confederation of Northern European states in trade.
Marco Polo (1254 to 1324)	An explorer who traveled along the Silk Roads. Marco Polo discovered the connection to Kublai Khan and the Yuan Dynasty. He brought back major navigational technologies to Europe that led to exploration.
Three-field system	A system of farming where crops were rotated between fields and one of the fields would be allowed to lie bare for a year to replenish itself.
Black Death	The microbial disease passed from China to Europe through the Indian Ocean and Silk Roads trade routes.

Chapter Review

The changes and continuities during this 850-year period provide interesting historical material. The best way to handle this long period is to focus on one region at a time, and then examine how the regions impacted one another. Some of the main topics that contributed to the collapse or rise of new empires during this time include: networking and expansion that led to new trade routes, the diffusion of cultures, the rise of Islam, and the Christian Crusades.

> **TEST TIP:** Remember to use the acronym SPRITE (social, political, religious, ideological, technological, and economic) to understand commonalities and differences among regions.

Civilizations of the Post-Classical Era

Let's start with the region that was the most dominant at the time, East Asia, and then expand our review to the Middle East, Europe, Africa, and Mesoamerica.

Eastern and Southeastern Asian Civilizations

China reigned over East and Southeast Asia during this period. The three powerful Chinese dynasties that emerged as dominant global rulers were the Sui, T'ang, and Song empires. Through the tributary system, these dynasties expanded their territories into local civilizations: Korea, Vietnam, Manchuria, and even into what is today Afghanistan. The powerful Chinese dynasties even attempted to invade and force Japan into the Chinese system.

China's Civilization

Chinese Dynasties During the Golden Age (600 to 1450 C.E.)		
Sui Dynasty	581–618 C.E.	Ruled by a progressive leader. Known for inventing porcelain. Built many Buddhist temples and meditation caves.
T'ang Dynasty	618–907 C.E.	The T'ang Dynasty is one of the greatest Chinese dynasties in world history. Known for its aggressive military and economic expansion along the Silk Roads. The dynasty collapsed when class uprisings and a group of warlords took control of the Silk Roads. The T'ang Dynasty was accomplished in philosophy, architecture, science, poetry, silk, and transportation.
Song Dynasty	960–1279 C.E.	Known for having a thriving economy, the Song Dynasty made advancements in technology (iron-working, gunpowder, compass), agriculture, and printing. The Song Dynasty was known for practicing Neo-Confucianism and advancing intellectual and scholarly practices (i.e., government officials were selected according to the civil service exam).

Heads Up: What You Need to Know

On the WHAP exam, you should remember an important political management system that China and other empires used—the tributary system.

China's Tributary System

China formed a ruling system over local populations called a **tributary system** that helped to shape East Asian foreign affairs. The tributary system was a foreign policy that required weaker regions that wanted to trade with China to submit culturally and economically to the superior China. This system guaranteed the Chinese emperor's rule of "all under heaven." For example, Korea had The Three Kingdoms: Koguryo, Silla, and Paekche vying for control over the peninsula. China allied with the neighboring Silla Kingdom, but when China tried to take direct control of Korea, Silla resisted. China decided instead to use a tributary system, in which Korea paid a tax to China and was duty-bound to a "China-centered" authority.

It's important to understand that during this period, when a tax was paid to a foreign dynasty, respect for the dynasty and its authority was implied when making the tax payment. Therefore, the tributary system maintained Chinese dominance without enforcing a direct military rule over a population. The tributary system also played a critical role in cultural exchange.

Critical Thinking Question: If China did not have direct control over Korea, then did they really have power over people in their region?

Well . . . yes, and here's why.

Key Facts about China's Regional Control

China was symbolically powerful. The nobles in Korea, Vietnam, and other countries around China began to see Chinese culture as symbolically sophisticated and having a legitimate set of values and customs.

China's political management. The nobles in Korea, Vietnam, and other countries around China incorporated the Chinese **civil service exam** for political management. The traditional Chinese government used the civil service exam to select people for Chinese government.

China's Confucianism. The nobles in Korea, Vietnam, and other countries around China blended Confucianism with their local values. As discussed in Chapter 6, Confucianism was not a religion; it was a practical system of government and social order based on filial obligations.

China's language. The nobles in Korea, Vietnam, and other countries around China used the Chinese language as the official national language and recordkeeping system.

China's sphere of influence. China was able to establish a "sphere of influence" over Southeast Asia, meaning China was able to highly influence surrounding countries through language, cultural values, and social institutions. In many ways, this "soft power" was more influential than military control because it had a greater impact on the fundamental change of Asia.

China's trade. China faced massive infrastructure challenges due to its expansion. As China expanded, its trade increased. The Chinese constructed a waterway system, called the **Grand Canal,** to help transport goods, food, and people. The Grand Canal was a human-made canal that connected Northern and Southern China. It played an important role in China's economic prosperity and is still used today. Until the Industrial Revolution, the Grand Canal was the world's largest engineering project known to mankind. As the canal was created, port cities were developed for trade and merchants created businesses along the canal.

HISTORIOGRAPHY. *Many historians today see the Grand Canal as early capitalism, called **proto-industrialization**. Historians use this term because the Chinese were creating small, competitive industries to market silk, porcelain, and utensils. But think about why this might have been a problem. China was based on the Confucian filial piety of familial intergenerational responsibilities. This new middle class and its emphasis on individual accumulation of wealth created a conflict with the Confucian's emphasis on filial obligations and piety.*

China's Neo-Confucianism. How did China maintain traditional Chinese Confucianism in a competitive market-based system? The solution was to blend Confucianism with Buddhism to legitimize their earnings. Merchants who followed their obligations and duties to their families and communities could achieve *nirvana* in the afterlife as defined by Buddhism. This new system created a rational system of Confucian teachings known as **Neo-Confucianism.**

China's class system. This still leaves the problem of the class system that existed under Confucianism. China distinguished the classes by four occupations: merchants, craftsmen, landlords, and peasants. How would China retain respect and separation among the classes with a rising merchant group? Remember that most Asian societies were suspicious of merchants because of their economic self-interests.

> **Did you know?** To distinguish between classes, the Chinese Song Dynasty (960–1279) developed a new cultural practice for women called **foot binding.** Foot binding started as a practice that upper-class women used. During the early years of infancy, a girl's feet were broken and then tightly bandaged. This procedure would cause the bones of the feet to fuse together. Later in life, girls were taught how to walk. The Song people saw this as a very graceful and feminine form of walking, but as women aged, it became very painful. Women had limited mobility and were subordinated in this patriarchy system. This ensured both a subordinate status for women and it distinguished upper-class women from middle-class women.

Now, this brings us to China's relationship with Japan.

Japan's Civilization

Japan is an island nation off the coast of Asia that consists of four main islands: Hokkaido, Honshu, Shikoku, and Kyushu. For centuries, Japan maintained a strong sense of isolation and differentiation from China because they were separated by a narrow stretch of ocean. In its early history, Japan was a decentralized nation that did not have a strong unified emperor, religion, or nation-state.

Japan resisted China's domination so as to not lose its cultural identity. However, Japan embraced many aspects of China's culture, including Confucianism, Buddhism, and the civil service exam. Japan's main spiritual tradition of *Shintoism* is a combination of its own traditional beliefs in natural gods and the Chinese practice of Buddhism.

Did you know? Although Japan was decentralized in the Post-Classical Era, after Japan survived the natural events of the kamikaze (typhoon) in 1281, the country started its unification process and formed a national unity that led to a **Bushido code** (the way of the warrior). The Bushido code stressed family obligations, chivalrous attitudes toward women, and a loyalty to the Japanese identity. This created the beginnings of a national loyalty that would eventually become much stronger under the Meiji period in the Modern Era.

Japan's Post-Classical Civilizations		
Asuka Period	538–710	Japan was fragmented into different clans for most of its history, but the clans' strength had diminished in power. Japan looked for a way to create a stronger emperor who could unify Japan. As China grew in its sphere of influence, the leaders of Japan feared being conquered by China.
		Prince Shotoku Taishi, a believer in Buddhism, allowed a Chinese influence in order to create a more centralized system. However, Taishi also wanted to remain separate from China. Taishi sent China a letter that started with "The sovereign of land where the sun rises is sending this mail to the sovereign of land where the sun sets." The implication was that Japan was growing in strength, and China was declining in strength. This was an insult to China. (Note: The sun is the official symbol of Japan even today.)
Heian Period	794–1185	When Taishi died in 622 C.E., his successor, Emperor Kotoku, initiated the **Taika reforms** that created a new tax system and nationalized all land in Japan. The new tax system took power away from the clans and gave it to a centralized government in Japan, but did not remain an official policy. Japan's central government declined throughout the Heian period. By the 11th century, the government didn't have enough revenue to pay for a national army. Local governors, or *daimyo*, took power back from the emperor.
		Eventually two powerful families, the Minamoto and Taira clans, tried to create a national military system under the *shogun* (military dictator with unquestionable power granted by the emperor of Japan). The shogun was appointed as the supreme authority over territories, but did not create a national identity. In the 12th century, local families fought for power and families hired *samurai* (warriors) to protect their individual areas of landownership. Samurai cultivated the martial arts virtues and were dedicated to serving the lives of their aristocratic masters. Japan remained largely fragmented throughout the Post-Classical Age.
Kamakura Period	1185–1333	In 1250, Japan entered a period of growth and prosperity, but in 1274 and then in 1281, Samurai armies were mobilized when China's Yuan Dynasty tried to invade Japan. By 1281, Chinese soldiers, led by the Chinese Mongol Kublai Khan, attempted to attack the small island of Japan. However, Khan and his troops were defeated, not by the Japanese, but by the divine intervention of two natural disasters—enormous typhoons! When the Chinese fleet of ships arrived in Japan, they were met with two major typhoon storms that spared the Japanese. The Japanese called these natural events the *kamikaze* (the divine wind), which destroyed the Mongol's fleet. This event provided a basis for unity around the traditional Japanese *Shinto* (action-centered religion) spiritual beliefs based on the Bushido Code.

Did you know? Today, the swastika is a powerful symbol that evokes strong negative feelings. Although the German Nazi Party used this symbol in the 20th century during World War II, this symbol did not always suggest something bad. Actually, it was a good symbol in the 12th century. The samurai warriors used the swastika as a religious Buddhist symbol on their uniforms. It means "eternal life." This shows how the consequences of historical events can symbolically change world perceptions over time periods.

Central Asia and the Middle East

The Rise of Islam

The development of the Islamic religion (the religion of Muslims) in the Middle East would fundamentally change the social, political, and religious dynamics of Central Asia and the Middle East. In order to understand how a religion dramatically changed these regions and the context of this change, it is important to learn about the Holy Prophet Muhammad and the new faith he introduced to the region in 600 C.E.

TEST TIP: On the WHAP exam, it is important to differentiate Islam and Muslim. Students tend to use these words interchangeably, but they are very different. Islam is a religion, whereas Muslim refers to the people who follow the religion of Islam. Before the Islamic religion, Arabs believed in *polytheism* (belief in many gods), but Muhammad founded a religion of *monotheism* (belief in one god) called the Islamic religion.

Key Facts about the Rise of Islam in the Middle East

Tribes in the Middle East were polytheistic. Arabs lived in tribes as sheepherders and farmers, but expanded to caravan trades to move goods from the Indian Ocean to the Mediterranean Ocean. Although most Arabs were polytheistic, many recognized *Allah* (God in Arabic) as their supreme god. Muhammad was born to a merchant family in what is known today as Saudi Arabia. The merchants lived in tribes, and the most dominant mercantile tribe was the Quraysh. The tribes competed with each other in the desert because they had scarce resources.

Tribes built a sacred monument in Mecca. In order to solve the problem of violent competition, the tribes created a monument called the sacred *Kaaba* (a stone cube building of worship) in the center of the city of Mecca. The Kaaba housed the statues of all the gods for the different tribes, about 360 shrines. The policy of the tribes was that no violence could take place in Mecca or the gods would become angry and take out their vengeance on the violators.

Muhammad's angelic revelation of the Five Pillars of Faith. Until Muhammad's revelation, there was violence, competition, and blood feuds among Arabs. Remember, Arabs believed in many gods and religion was not a source of morality. Then Muhammad received an angelic revelation. Muhammad claimed that the archangel Gabriel had appeared to him on a mountain and gave him the holy words of *Allah* (God). Muhammad wrote the holy words in the *Quran* (religious text of Islam) throughout his life. The Quran is very complicated, with many revelations from Allah, but the main message of the Quran was a criticism of the *Jahiliyyah* (Arabic for "ignorance of divine guidance"), in which the tribes focused on earthly material profit over the needs of the individual.

Muhammad's teachings identified **Five Pillars of Faith:**

Five Pillars of Faith				
Shahadah **FAITH**	Salat **PRAYER**	Zakat **CHARITY**	Sawm **FASTING**	Hajj **PILGRIMAGE**
Belief in one God (Allah). Muhammad is the messenger of Allah.	Obligatory praying five times a day.	Giving *alms* (charity) to the poor based on wealth.	Fasting during the month of Ramadan.	Making a pilgrimage to Mecca (the house of Allah).

Muhammad exiled. The principles of the Five Pillars caused a conflict between Muhammad and the leaders of the Quraysh tribe. Muhammad was exiled from the holy city of Mecca and traveled north to the city of Medina. His flight from Mecca is called the *Hegira* and is seen by Muslims as proof of Allah, since Muhammad made the trip safely. The leaders of Mecca soon attacked the Muslims at Medina and several wars ensued. By the end of these wars, the Muslims gathered enough followers to conquer and take over Mecca. However, although most of the Middle East had converted to Islam, Muhammad became ill and died in 632 C.E. before determining a new leader of the Islamic faith.

Division of Islam into Sunni and Shiite. After Muhammad's death, the first four caliphs who were seen as the "rightly guided" leaders of Allah were Umar, Bakr, Uthman, and Ali. In 656, the first major conflict between the different leaders arose when Ali claimed leadership based on his blood lineage to Muhammad (he was Muhammad's cousin and son-in-law), but Umar, Bakr, and Uthman claimed that Allah had chosen them as leaders due to their religious knowledge and charismatic personalities. This led to a war in which Ali was assassinated. The followers of Bakr, Umar, and Uthman became the **Sunni** sect of Islam. The followers of Ali became the **Shiite** sect of Islam. This led to a religious division in Islam that has remained the central conflict ever since in the Middle East.

Heads Up: What You Need to Know

The opposition between the religious Islamic Sunnis and Shiites continues to exist in the 21st century. On the WHAP exam, it's important to know the differences between these two important Islamic religious groups. The original split between the two was not over a religious doctrine, but over political leadership.

Islamic Sunnis and Shiites	
Similarities	**Differences**
Both Islamic sects believe that Allah is the supreme God. Both believe that the Prophet Muhammad was the messenger of Allah and both follow the Five Pillars of Faith: ■ Shahadah: Faith ■ Salat: Prayer ■ Zakat: Charity ■ Sawm: Fasting ■ Hajj: Pilgrimage to Mecca Both read the same scripture, the Quran. Both have secular to fundamental believers. Both believe in *Jihad* (sacred holy struggle, but the 21st-century definition often means "holy war").	*Sunni* means "followers of the Sunna, or way of the Prophet." *Shia* means "party of Ali." Shiites believe Ali is the leader who came after Muhammad, and Sunnis believe Bakr, Umar, and Uthman are the true leaders after Muhammad. Shiites believe that the Shiite leader must be a male from the lineage of Ali: "Ali is from me and I am from him." Whereas Sunnis allow any practicing Muslim who is elected by the Islamic authorities to be a leader. Shiites believe they are the only divinely guided interpreters of the Quran. Today, almost 90 percent of those practicing the Islamic religion are Sunni. Today, most Shiites live in Iran, Iraq, and Bahrain, but a sizeable number also live in Syria, Lebanon, Pakistan, Saudi Arabia, and Yemen. Although both religions pray every day, the Shiites stand with their hands at their sides, and Sunnis put their hands on their stomachs. The Shiites give human beings an exalted status that is only given to prophets in the Quran.

Expansion of Islam. The first expansion of Islam took place under religious *caliphates* (Islamic kingdoms). The Umayyads were the first Sunni kingdom. Its capital was in Damascus. Eventually, the Umayyads fell to the first Shiite caliphate, the Abbasids. Its capital was in Baghdad. Both caliphates stretched their control from the Middle East into Northern Africa and incorporated a large group of religious and ethnic minorities. They established a tradition of tolerance for these groups and allowed them to have local rule and local religious practices. However, they also placed these different people into a second-class citizenship called the *dhimmis* (people of the book). Dhimmis were not Muslim, so they could not serve in the army. They had to pay a *jizyah* tax (a replacement tax) for having someone else serve for them. Therefore, the history of the Islamic caliphates in relation to the other groups in the area (Christians and Jews) has been one of both tolerance and conflict.

Africa

Key Facts about Africa

Trans-Saharan trade route. Africa played an enormous role in the international trade routes that were forming during this period. On the western side of Africa, Sundiata led an effort to organize the city-states under one rule. **Mansa Musa** (Mansa means sultan or king) then created the empire of Mali, and Mali became Islamic under Mansa Musa.

Mansa Musa then connected Mali to the Middle East through the Trans-Saharan trade route. This caravan trade route connected the Mediterranean economies to the Sub-Saharan economies. This route made travel possible with the use of camels. Mansa Musa traveled back and forth between the Middle East and Africa, spreading Islam and exchanging gold for salt, among other supplies. In fact, he spread so much gold that he caused a massive inflation of currency.

Indian Ocean trade routes. On the east coast of Africa, the Swahili city-states connected Africa to the Indian Ocean trade routes. The Swahili city-states had been founded by the Bantu tribes, who migrated from Western Africa to the Southeast. They brought iron and the Swahili language. This led to city-states that traded along the Indian Ocean.

Ethiopia. One significant cultural exception in Africa was Ethiopia. Ethiopia became the one Christian kingdom in East Africa. This would become significant for the long term. In later years, Ethiopia would form more alliances with Europe and would become resistant to European exploration and imperialism due to their cultural similarities and being surrounded by Islamic kingdoms.

Europe

Europe was really a decentralized mess, and this was a real problem during the Post-Classical Age. In the Modern Age, the lack of a centralized Europe would be an advantage due to competition and innovation.

Critical Thinking Question: Why was Europe so divided at a time when so many kingdoms and empires were becoming centralized?

Historians continue to debate the primary reasons for the fall of the Roman Empire. To give you a broad view of the topic, here are some of the most common explanations for Rome's decline: (1) Military failures and overspending after invasions from Germanic and Barbarian tribes. (2) Political instability caused by conflict between the Roman emperor and the senate. (3) Political corruption. (4) Romans were unable to effectively manage overexpansion. (5) Excessive taxation and an economic crisis. (6) The rise of the eastern Byzantine Empire (Constantinople). (7) Natural disasters: famines, earthquakes, and plagues.

Key Facts about Europe's Dividing Nations

The collapse of the Roman Empire. The Roman Empire crumbled in 476 C.E., primarily due to Germanic and Barbarian tribal invasions. This led to a collapse of any centralized European authority.

Division in the Catholic Church. While the Roman Catholic Church remained the dominant religious leadership, there was a split in Christianity. Eastern Orthodox Christianity split with the pope about his authority. The Eastern Orthodox, located in Byzantium, followed the leadership of the *patriarch,* similar to the papacy in the Western Catholic Church. The pope in Western Europe led a hierarchy of the priestly leaders. The patriarch worked more as a facilitator with the other bishops. This *Great Schism* of 1054 C.E. would divide the leadership of Christendom into the Eastern Orthodox Church and Roman Catholic Church.

Fragmented European kingdoms. European kingdoms were fragmented and had very limited government under the leadership of Charlemagne. Although Charlemagne was instrumental in the **Treaty of Verdun** (843 C.E.), which partitioned boundaries very similar to the European continent today, it was signed by his son. Charlemagne hoped to revive a type of Roman Empire under his leadership. Charlemagne called Central Europe the Holy Roman Empire, but it was not at all what it used to be. The Holy Roman Empire was really a group of Germanic small city-states loosely led by the emperor of the kingdom. The Holy Roman Empire started in 843 with the Treaty of Verdun and lasted until 1806 during the Napoleonic Wars.

European trade. Europe did form a trading relationship with Northern Africa and the Middle East. This trading confederation, called the *Hanseatic League,* traded with the other powers in the region over the Mediterranean trade. It would become important for laying the groundwork for Europe's eventual takeoff with their exploration into Mesoamerica, Africa, and India.

The Crusades

The Crusades took place between 1095–1291 C.E., and were about to change everything. The Crusades were holy wars fought between Christians in Europe and Muslims in the Middle East, with the Christian goal of liberating the Holy Land and Jerusalem from Muslim dominance.

Causes	Consequences
The crusade wars started as a fight between migrant groups that entered into the Middle East. For many years prior, Christian pilgrims traveled from Europe to Jerusalem, but the **Turkish** invaders (Muslims) coming from the steppe regions above Afghanistan invaded the Middle East, eventually encircling the Byzantine Empire (Christians). The Byzantine emperor asked Christians in Europe to help protect his empire from the Turks. The Western Catholic Church saw an opportunity to reunite Western and Eastern Christianity. Pope Urban II called for a series of Crusades to retake Jerusalem and protect Constantinople.	After the different holy Crusades, the Middle East hardly changed in its demographics. Instead, after the violence, death, and destruction, what did happen was the opening up of new ideas brought back by the Crusaders from Islamic kingdoms into Europe. The Crusaders sparked an increase in demand for spices, fabrics, and scientific knowledge.

Key Facts about the Significant Changes after the Crusades

Investiture crisis. First, there was a dramatic struggle that began within Western Europe over political control. Kings tried to appoint bishops without the authority of the papacy. This was called the *investiture controversy*. Popes retained their power largely through religious authority, and the task of appointing local leaders was central to this authority. A king's attempt to take this power was a signal that there was a lack of trust in the papacy. The investiture controversy did not stop the pope, but it was a signal of what was to come during the Protestant Reformation in the 16th century.

Disease: The Black Death. The migrations of the *steppe people* (people from Eurasia: Central Asia and Mongolia) led to the passage of disease. The most prominent disease was the Black Death (bubonic plague) in the 14th century. The Black Death was transmitted by the Mongols from East Asia to Europe in 1347. Sicilian sailors, who had been fighting against the Mongols, unknowingly brought this horrific disease with them when they returned home. It led to the deaths of one-third of Europe's population.

New innovations in agriculture and increased merchant trade. Because of the decline in population, landowners searched long and hard to find workers for their land. The vassals (wealthy landowners) began to use new innovations to grow crops. One new innovation was the *three-field system* of crop rotation. The rotation system divided the land into three parts so that crops between three fields could be rotated in consecutive seasons. For example, one field could be planted in the winter, one field could be planted in the spring, and one field could be left fallow to regenerate. This rotation system lessened the need for *serfs* (peasant field laborers), so peasant workers began to migrate to small cities. In Western Europe, this meant a population growth in the cities and an increase of commercial merchants.

The Turks were eventually victorious in the Crusades, and they were able to eventually conquer the Byzantine Empire. This led to the development of new Muslim empires that would dominate the Middle East and India, called the gunpowder empires.

Gunpowder Empires

The **gunpowder empires** followed the caliphates in the Middle East. They were known as gunpowder empires because they implemented and used the Chinese invention of gunpowder for conquering land and maintaining leadership. These empires included the Sunni Ottoman Empire, the Shiite Safavids, and the Mughal Dynasty in India. The biggest issue for these empires was how to manage the numerous ethnicities, languages, religions, and cultural groups in their expansive empires.

Ottoman Empire (1301–1922)

The Ottoman Empire, also known as the Turkish Empire, was inspired by Islam. It stretched from the boundaries of modern-day Iraq to Northern Africa. It was one of the largest empires in history, and had a navy on the Mediterranean comprised of numerous different communities and cultural groups. To manage this, it developed a highly complex system of centralized rule with local governance. The sultan was the center of leadership and was considered a messenger from Allah. The sultan allowed *millets* (local communities) to lead themselves.

To maintain centralization, the Ottomans were known to kidnap children from local communities and recruit them into their *Janissary corps,* or military leadership. The sultan was advised by the Janissaries and the *Wazir,* or civilian leadership. The sultan's purpose was to have people from all the communities in leadership roles in order to assure loyalty. By accepting military and civilian advisement, no one group could gain too much power. In addition, girls from each community were placed into the *devshirme* (or harem). Here, the sultan would have multiple wives (*polygyny*), and produce heirs from each community. Hence, a future sultan could come from a Christian, Jewish, or Muslim background. No one knew. This discouraged rebellions among the population since the future sultan could be one of their own. The Ottoman Empire had a highly complex system of maintaining a centralized rule and motivating local cooperation among its people. This system kept the Ottoman Empire strong for over four centuries.

Safavid Empire (1501–1722)

Early in the 16th century, a new empire arose. The Safavid Empire began after the collapse of the Timurid Empire when several Muslim religious groups emerged to gain control of the Persian territory. Shah Ismail arose as the leader of the Safavid Empire in 1501 and established Shiite Islam as the practicing religion of the empire. As practicing Shiites, the Safavids continued to have many conflicts with their neighboring Turkish Sunnis in the Ottoman Empire.

The Safavids had a very different system for controlling religious minorities. At the height of the Safavid Empire's power, Shah Abbas (1587–1629), supported trade, industry, and the arts. However, he suppressed other minorities, including the original Persian religion of *Sufiism*. The Shah brought in outside advisers from other empires which created competition between the advisers and did not allow for any one faction to take control.

The Safavid Empire is responsible for establishing the strong political and religious system of Shiites in Iran and Iraq today.

Mughal Empire (1526–1748)

The Mughal Empire was a Muslim branch of the Timurid Empire which provided a third possible model for blending different minority groups. The Mughals were located in Northern India. The Mughal Empire was founded by Babur in 1526, who descended from the Mongol ruler Genghis Khan and a Turk conqueror of Timurid. Babur invaded Northern India in the 1520s, and his descendant, Akbar the Great, tried to unify Northern India by creating the *Divine Faith*. This new religion took the common beliefs of Hinduism, Islam, and Christianity and tried to merge them together. Akbar allowed for Hindu advisers to reach senior government positions and maintained both Muslim mosques and Hindu temples. He ruled by having a centralized control with local governors called *zamindars*. In 1658, Akbar's successor, his grandson Aurangzeb, became ruler. Akbar's work to bring about religious and political diffusion was undone. Aurangzeb was a devout Muslim and feared that the Divine Faith had corrupted Islam and called for a purity movement. Aurangzeb's rule eventually led to rebellions among groups that were similar to a civil war. A fragmentation and steady economic decline resulted.

Mesoamerica

In today's Mexico, the **Olmecs** (1600–200 B.C.E.) and the **Toltecs** (900–1186 C.E.) were the first two empires. They established a centralized authority and created a center of trade networks. South of these large empires were the **Mayans** (peaked c. 300–900 C.E.), a confederation of smaller kingdoms known for trade. The Mesoamerican region was vacated from 900 to 1524 C.E., possibly due to climate changes or overpopulation. The classical empires of the Olmecs and the Toltecs had disappeared. This led to a vacuum of power in Mexico and Central America. A group of migrants from North America, the **Aztecs**, filled that gap as they migrated into Mexico. According to legend, they discovered a swampy area in central Mexico and established their kingdom at Tenochtitlan. In that kingdom, they created a massive irrigation system called *chinampas*. These structures captured rainwater at a rate that would support populations larger than European cities at the time. The Aztecs then went out and conquered local tribes and established tributary systems with these tribes, creating trading relationships that sustained a large empire within the deserts of central Mexico.

In South America, a group of natives formed different small communities in the Andean Mountains. They started as a religious movement called the *Moche*. They eventually evolved into the kingdom of the **Incas.** The Incas spread out and conquered nearby lands through a rule that did not allow the emperor to inherit his father's lands. This meant that each new emperor had to go out and conquer new lands. The Incas then established a trading network throughout the Andean Mountain range. The Incas were known for their strong communal culture and established a system of *mit'a* that was socialist in nature (except for nobility who were exempt). The mit'a was a mandatory public service system that required citizens to pay a tribute to the central empire and to help with building projects (roads and bridges).

Heads Up: What You Need to Know

To summarize Period Three, look through the following major themes, commonalities, differences, and turning points that are important to remember for the WHAP exam.

- Period Three is the Post-Classical Era and is generally inclusive of large land-based empires that ruled multiple ethnic, linguistic, and religious groups.

- The social relationships throughout the world were based on *feudalism* (political decentralization), in which social obligations and duties centered on land ownership. For example, landowners (vassals) were tenants of the nobles (the king owned all land), and the landowners would grant people (serfs) parcels of land and military protection in exchange for labor, service, and a share of their crops or livestock.

- The main economy was based on increased production of agriculture and farming, and this led to traditional beliefs about *filial piety* (duty to care for one's elderly family members—parents or grandparents).

- The contacts and conflicts among empires influenced trade and the transfer of culture, ideas, religion, foods, and innovations.

- The major beliefs around the world centered on obligations and duties including Neo-Confucianism, the caste system, and the *Great Chain of Being* (a strict religious hierarchical structure where God is the highest level).

- Major differences in how these beliefs were practiced started to emerge. China and Southeast Asia saw a mixture of Confucian practicality and Buddhist spirituality to maintain obligations. India tried to merge all of its religious beliefs into a single faith system. Africa used trade to unite cities and kingdoms. The Ottomans used a shared and decentralized power system for management. The spread of Islam introduced the new concept of *caliphate* (state ruled by a Muslim ruler). Europe created a system that was fragmented, but competitive.

- The spread of the Black Death in Europe led to major demographic changes that would lead to urbanization and the rise of merchant trade.

- The Crusades launched an internal crisis for authority within European kingdoms and the Catholic Church.

Chapter Review Practice Questions

The practice questions show the types of questions that may appear on the exam. On the actual exam, the questions are grouped into sets. Each set contains one source-based prompt and two to five questions.

Multiple-Choice Questions

Questions 1–3 refer to the following passage.

The condition of these people is strange and their manners outlandish . . .
With regard to their women, they are not modest in the presence of men, they do not veil themselves in spite of their perseverance in the prayers. The women there have friends and companions amongst men outside the prohibited degrees of marriage. Likewise for the men, there are companions from amongst women outside the prohibited degrees. One of them would enter his house to find his wife with her companion and would not disapprove of that conduct . . .

—Source: Ibn Battuta, "Travels of Ibn Battuta," 1325–1354 C.E.

1. Which of the following best describes Ibn Battuta's account in the passage above?

   A. The conflict between Islamic caliphates over the leadership of the religion of Islam after Muhammad's death
   B. The differing cultural applications of Islamic doctrines in the Northern and Western African regions
   C. The spread of gold and resources over the Trans-Saharan trade route
   D. The conflict between the Muslims and other ethnic and religious minorities within the Islamic caliphates

2. What is the significance of the passage for social relationships in the religion of Islam?

   A. The passage describes the conflict between religious minorities and how the Islamic leaders resolved these differences.
   B. The main point of the argument is how Islamic leaders judged the appropriate relationships for merchants.
   C. The argument discusses how the replacement of jizyah tax ought to be applied to dhimmis.
   D. Battuta expresses the early Islamic beliefs about gender relationships and the appropriate role for women in the Muslim faith.

3. Based on your knowledge of world history, which of the following statements is most similar to Battuta's observations?

   A. Christopher Columbus' descriptions of Native Americans' social relationships during his explorations in the Caribbean
   B. Oral histories about Genghis Khan's efforts to conquer areas in Central Asia
   C. The sultan's records of taxes levied against religious minorities within the Ottoman Empire
   D. The Chinese emperor's declarations about the need to defend the Sui Dynasty against the Northern steppe invaders

Questions 4–6 refer to the following passage.

The Kamo festival was held on the birthday in the Fourth Month. The older emperor's third daughter, whose mother was Kokiden, replaced the high priestess. Because of this alteration, the processions taking place were grander than usual. Genji was among the attendants. The roads were full of people and vehicles. The Rokujo lady had also come quietly to see the procession. But a latecomer took her place: it was Aoi's carriage. Aoi's servants had broken the stools for her carriage shafts. She was filled with tears at that insult. On the following day, Genji decided to set out to view the festival with Murasaki. He went to her room in the west wing. Ladies were also preparing for the outing. He found that her hair was too long, so he summoned a doctor to check the Buddhist calendar to confirm whether the day was suitable for a haircut. Then he trimmed her hair himself. She stood on the Go plate to check the length of her hair.

> Source: Murasaki Shikibu, *The Tale of Genji*, early-11th century. The story describes the life and social ettiquette in the Japanese imperial court as portrayed by the son of the emperor, Genji.

4. Based on *The Tale of Genji* and your knowledge of world history, which statement best explains the social relationships in Japan during the 11th century C.E.?

   A.   Japan was completely isolated from all influences from China.
   B.   Japan had opened itself up to the Western influences of technological innovation.
   C.   Japanese women were tied to the court through filial obligations and familial honor customs.
   D.   Japanese women were expected to raise large families for the purposes of agricultural labor.

5. In the context of Japanese history, which of the following most likely influenced the social relationships as portrayed in the 11th-century passage?

   A.   Japan's decentralized political structure with local daimyo rule
   B.   China's influence during the Song and T'ang dynasties through the civil service exam and Confucian values
   C.   The threat of the Northern steppe invaders into China
   D.   The influence of Buddhist missionaries sent from Ashoka over the Silk Road's

6. The passage above reflected what major change that occurred in Japan during the Post-Classical Age?

   A.   The attempt by the Japanese emperor to establish a military shogunate to rule its people.
   B.   The desire to mix Japanese culture with Chinese customs such as Confucianism and the Chinese Mandarin language
   C.   The attempt by the Japanese emperor to take power away from the local daimyo leaders
   D.   The moving of Japanese farming leaders into urban areas to develop proto-industrial manufacturing

Document-Based Question

1 question

60 minutes

Reading Time: 15 minutes (brainstorm your thoughts and organize your response)

Writing Time: 45 minutes

Directions: The document-based question is based on the seven accompanying documents. The documents are for instructional purposes only. Some of the documents have been edited for the purpose of this practice exercise. Write your response on lined paper and include the following:

- **Thesis.** Present a thesis that supports a historically defensible claim, establishes a line of reasoning, and responds to all parts of the question. The thesis must consist of one or more sentences located in one place—either the introduction or the conclusion.

- **Contextualization.** Situate the argument by explaining the broader historical events, developments, or processes that occurred before, during, or after the time frame of the question.

- **Evidence from the documents.** Use the content of at least three to six of the documents to develop and support a cohesive argument that responds to the question.

- **Evidence beyond the documents.** Support or qualify your argument by explaining at least one additional piece of specific historical evidence not found in the documents. (Note: The example must be different from the evidence used to earn the point for contextualization.)

- **Analysis.** Use at least three documents that are relevant to the question to explain the documents' point of view, purpose, historical situation, and/or audience.

- **Historical reasoning.** Use historical reasoning to show relationships among the documents, the topic question, and the thesis argument. Use evidence to corroborate, qualify, or modify the argument.

Based on the documents that follow, answer the question below.

Question 1: Analyze the causes that led to a diffusion of culture and the creation of new empires during the Post-Classical Era.

Document 1

Source: The Chronicle of Novgorod, 1016–1471, written by anonymous monks near Novgorod, Russia.

[In 1238] foreigners called Tartars came in countless numbers, like locusts, into the land of the Ryazan, and on first coming they halted at the river Nukhla, and took it, and halted in camp there. And thence they sent their emissaries to the Knyazes of Ryasan, a sorceress and two men with her, demanding from them one-tenth of everything: of men and Knyazes and horses—of everything one tenth. . . . And the Knyazes said to them: "Only when none of us remain, then all will be yours." . . . And the Knyazes of Ryasan sent to Yuri of Volodimir asking for help, or himself to come. But Yuri neither went himself nor listened to the request of the Knyazes of Ryasan, but himself wished to make war separately. But it was too late to oppose the wrath of God. . . . And then the pagan foreigners surrounded Ryazan and fenced it in with a stockade. And the Tartars took the town on December 21, and they had advanced against it on the 16th of the same month. They likewise killed the Knyazes and the Knyaginya, and men, women, and children, monks, nuns and priests, some by fire, some by sword, and violated nuns, priests' wives, good women and girls in the presence of their mothers and sisters. . . . And who, brethren, would not lament over this, among those of us alive when they suffered this bitter and violent death? And we, indeed, having seen it, were terrified and wept with sighing day and night over our sins . . .

Document 2

Source: The Silk Roads, the ancient network of trade routes.

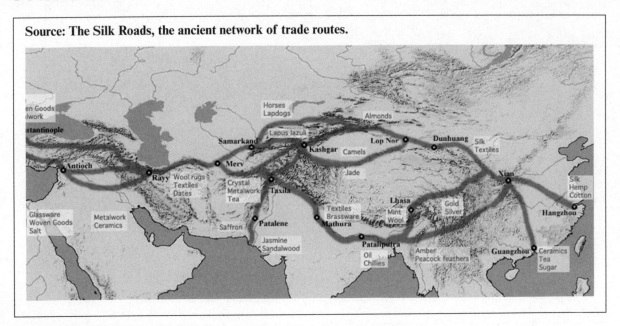

Document 3

Source: Ahmad al-Maqrizi, "The Plague in Cairo," c. 1410.

In January 1349, there appeared new symptoms that consisted of spitting up of blood. The disease caused one to experience an internal fever, followed by an uncontrollable desire to vomit; then one spat up blood and died. The inhabitants of a house were stricken one after the other, and in one night or two, the dwelling became deserted. Each individual lived with this fixed idea that he was going to die in this way. He prepared for himself a good death by distributing alms; he arranged for scenes of reconciliation and his acts of devotion multiplied . . .

One began to have to search for readers of the Koran for funeral ceremonies, and a number of individuals quit their usual occupations in order to recite prayers at the head of funeral processions. In the same way, some people devoted themselves to smearing crypts with plaster; others presented themselves as volunteers to wash the dead or carry them . . .

Family festivals and weddings had no place [in life]. No one issued an invitation to a feast during the whole time of the epidemic, and one did not hear a concert.

Document 4

Source: Indian Ocean trade route between Asia and Africa.

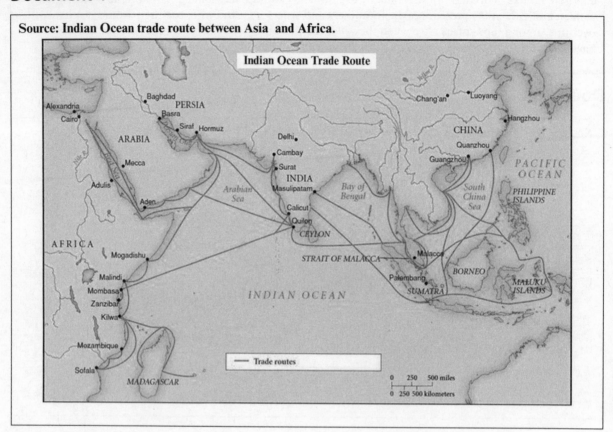

Document 5

Source: "The Travels of Marco Polo," 1299. An account of Polo's adventures along the Silk Roads through Asia from 1276 to 1291 that inspired other European explorers.

In this part are the ten principal markets, though besides these there are a vast number of others in the different parts of the town. . . . Toward the market squares are built great houses of stone, in which the merchants from India and other foreign parts store their wares, to be handy for the markets. In each of the squares is held a market three days in the week, frequented by 30,000 or 50,000 personnel, who bring thither for sale every possible necessity of life, so that there is always an ample supply of every kind of meat and game. . . . Those markets make a daily display of every kind of vegetables and fruits. . . . Very good raisins are brought from abroad, and wine likewise. . . . From the Ocean Sea also come daily supplies of fish in great quantity, brought 25 miles up the river . . .

Document 6

Source: Ibn Battuta, "Travels of Ibn Battuta," 1325–1354 C.E. A vast account of the journey into the kingdoms of Islam in the 14th century.

This is a village with nothing good about it. One of its marvels is that its houses and its mosque are of rock salt and its roofs of camel skins. It has no trees, but is nothing but sand with a salt mine. They dig in the earth for the salt, which is found in great slabs lying one upon the other as though they have been shaped and placed underground. A camel caries two slabs of it. Nobody lives there except the slaves of the Masufa who dig for the salt. They live on the dates imported to them from Morocco and on camel meat. . . . The Sudan peoples from the gold-producing forest lands to the south come to them from their land and carry the salt away. One load of it is sold at the city of Niami for 30 or 20 mithqals of gold.

Document 7

Source: Trans-Saharan land-based trade route that connected Africa to the Mediterranean.

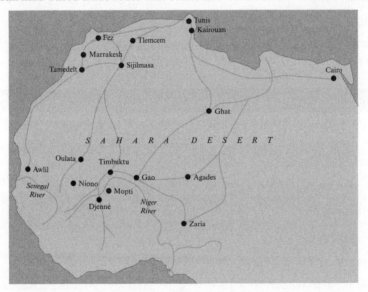

Answers and Explanations

Multiple-Choice Questions

1. **B.** Ibn Battuta was a Muslim traveler throughout the Islamic world. He expressed concerns about what he saw as the loose application of Muslim religious principles and laws in Africa. His writings show how Islamic doctrine was applied in different cultural contexts.

2. **D.** The passage demonstrates the gender norms in Islam and how they were interpreted in different cultural settings. Battuta comes from a more patriarchal interpretation that saw a need for feminine subordination and modesty.

3. **A.** Columbus and other Spaniards justified the enslavement, conquering, and domination of the natives in Hispaniola and Mesoamerica based on religious needs for reform because of supposed immoral and uncivilized behaviors.

4. **C.** *The Tale of Genji* is about the relationships in the Japanese court. The cultural difference is how women were expected to create relationships either for marriage or courtship to gain alliances for power.

5. **A.** The question asks you to analyze the context of the Japanese *Tale of Genji*. Japan had a decentralized system, and the tale demonstrates how local daimyo or governors competed for power and influence. Emperors would use their wives for political gain and competition.

6. **C.** The Japanese emperor lacked power throughout Japanese history until the 1800s and the Meiji restoration. This passage shows how the emperor was trying to gain power by having local daimyos and families create alliances in his court.

Document-Based Question

DBQ Scoring Guide

To achieve the maximum score of 7, your response must address the scoring criteria components in the table below.

Scoring Criteria for a Good Essay	
Question 1: Analyze the causes that led to a diffusion of culture and the creation of new empires during the Post-Classical Era.	
Scoring Criteria	**Examples**
A. THESIS/CLAIM	
(1 point) Presents a historically defensible thesis that establishes a line of reasoning. (Note: The thesis must make a claim that responds to *all* parts of the question and must *not* just restate the question. The thesis must consist of at least one sentence, either in the introduction or the conclusion.)	This essay provides a strong thesis that shows clear causes about the changes to culture and the creation of new empires in the Post-Classical Era. The sample response argues that the main cause was the creation of a variety of trade routes that led to a significant exchange of new ideas, culture, goods, and diseases. Remember not to just restate the question in the thesis statement, and remember to stay on topic so that you can show a line of reasoning.
B. CONTEXTUALIZATION	
(1 point) Explains the broader historical context of events, developments, or processes that occurred before, during, or after the time frame of the question. (Note: Must be more than a phrase or reference.)	The essay starts by discussing the broader general context of when humans started trade. It outlines how people migrated out of Africa and formed trade routes for small villages and city-states. Then, it shows how small political organizations became large land-based empires. This leads up to the essay's discussion about the creation of multiple trade routes in the Post-Classical Era.

Scoring Criteria	Examples
C. EVIDENCE	
Evidence from the Documents **(2 points)** Uses at least *six* documents to support the argument in response to the prompt. OR **(1 point)** Uses the content of at least *three* documents to address the topic prompt. (Note: Examples must describe, rather than simply quote, the content of the documents.)	Before you can analyze the documents to provide evidence, you first need to look through each document to get a general idea of the context of each document. Look at the author, title, subject, date, and intended audience (if known). You will not be meticulously reading each document for specific details during this step. Instead, you should first get an overall understanding of each document. Then you can determine which documents to include for evidence. To receive the highest score of 2 points, the response must include at least six documents. The sample response uses all seven of the documents and utilizes some element of analysis. Documents 2, 4, and 7 show the trading routes that helped to expand empires and transfer beliefs and ideas. Documents 1, 5, and 6 show the benefits and misfortunes of world exchanges.
Evidence Beyond the Documents **(1 point)** Uses at least one additional piece of specific historical evidence beyond those found in the documents that is relevant to the argument. (Note: Evidence must be different from the evidence used in contextualization.)	The argument needs to provide at least one specific example of outside evidence that relates to the topic question of reasons for cultural diffusion. The essay does this by discussing the Mongol invasions, port cities, and new navigational techniques gained from the Yuan Dynasty by the Polo family.
D. ANALYSIS AND REASONING	
(1 point) Uses at least *three* documents to explain how each document's point of view, purpose, historical situation, and/or audience is relevant to the argument. (Note: References must explain how or why, rather than simply identifying.)	Most of the documents are analyzed using purpose; however, Documents 1, 3, 5, and 6 explain the historical situation of the benefits and problems with expansion and trade by presenting the author's point of view.
(1 point) Uses historical reasoning and development that focuses on the question while using evidence to corroborate, qualify, or modify the argument. (Examples: Explain what is similar and different; explain the cause and effect; explain multiple causes; explain connections within and across periods of time; corroborate multiple perspectives across themes; or consider alternative views.)	The essay provides coherency throughout the argument and presents explicit historical evidence to modify the main thesis. The evidence modifies the thesis by opposing the idea of ideological views as the cause for change. The essay argues that new trade routes led to more diffusion of ideologies. In addition, the essay ends with a different time period. The comparison is made between the multiple trade routes of the Post-Classical Era and the Internet as a trade route in the era of globalization.

DBQ Sample Response

The creations of new empires started with trade. Humans created trade routes as soon as they migrated out of Africa into Central Asia. Small villages and city-states were a part of trade routes along the Tigris, Euphrates, and Nile river systems. These small villages created political organizations that eventually consolidated into land-based empires. And, by the Post-Classical Era, these empires conquered smaller tribes and city-states and placed them into tributary relationships for power.

The Post-Classical Era was unique in the historical context of expanding multiple trading routes that connected land-based empires (Documents 2, 4, and 7). This myriad of trade routes allowed for the spread of food, spices, and goods, but also spread new ideas, religions, languages, diseases, and natural resources (Documents 1, 5, and 6). The effect of these dynamic changes was the rise of new mixtures of political ideologies.

Some historians would argue that the creation of empires during the Post-Classical Era was unique due to the rise of new religious ideologies like monotheism (the belief in one god). However, these new ideologies only had a vast impact because of the varied interconnections of trade routes that allowed for the diffusion of cultures.

Trading had always existed in human interactions, but the Post-Classical Era established a number of trade routes that created a diverse set of communications and exchanges between civilizations. Document 2 charts the multiple Silk Roads that were re-established by the Mongol Empire. The Silk Roads had arisen during the Han Dynasty, but the empire collapsed around 200 C.E. The Mongolian expansion from East Asia to Eastern Europe led to a new revitalization of these routes. The routes were connected with the Indian Ocean trade route that connected East Africa, the Middle East, and India. Document 4 maps out the significance of this large Indian Ocean trade route in the Post-Classical Era since it connected port cities from a variety of different cultures, including Islam in the Middle East, Hinduism in India, and Judaism, which was located in multiple locations. Villages along these trade routes were peaceful and people shared a variety of produce, goods, and cultures. Trade networks were even further expanded with the use of the camel across the Trans-Saharan trade route because the camel was able to store water in its humps. Document 7 shows how the Trans-Saharan route connected West Africa to the Middle East. This connected Western Africa to the other trade routes and the Islamic culture.

Trade routes had an enormous impact on spreading new ideas across major land-based empires. The interactions among civilizations changed political relationships, introduced new religious beliefs, and shared technological innovations. Document 5 was written from the point of view of Marco Polo, a European, who documented innovations from the Mongol Yuan Dynasty which had a technologically advanced society. Polo and his family would bring back new innovations from the Yuan Dynasty, led by Kublai Khan. These new technologies, like the compass and astrolabe, would enable European nations to centralize and invest in large-scale exploration. Document 7 charts the Trans-Saharan trade route that led to the development of the Western kingdom of Mali under Mansa Musa, who brought Islam to Northern Africa. This connects to Document 6, which was written by the religious Islamic scholar and explorer Ibn Battuta, who wanted a more pure form of Islam throughout the caliphates and an expansion of his faith. This document is significant because it shows how religious ideas had spread, leading to a diffusion of ideas and a syncretism of the principles of faith in different cultures.

New trade routes often led to dramatic changes in political structures as empires conquered regions and expanded using tributary relationships. Document 1 was written from the point of view of Russian monks who were appealing to the Russian king for protection. The document demonstrated the fears that many people had of interactions with foreign peoples. The monks depicted these conquerors as pagans and threats to the Russian culture. This would justify the Russian need for expansion and consolidation of foreign tribes into the Russian kingdom. New trade routes also meant the blending of people, leading to disease. Document 3 was written from the point of view of an upper-class Egyptian who was observing and documenting the effects of the bubonic plague. This is especially noteworthy, given that the writer would have benefitted from international trade through the Silk Roads and Trans-Saharan route. But he was also a witness to the deadly disease. This disease was passed through the Silk Roads and Indian Ocean as merchants traveled from China to Western Europe. The author would not have understood how the disease passed during this time, but his observations were witness to the disadvantages of the transfer of such a deadly biological infection.

This intermixing of political, social, and cultural ideologies due to new widespread trade routes is similar to the process of globalization. In the 20th and 21st centuries, the creation of virtual trade routes along the Internet has allowed for new social media to share ideas. Globalization has allowed Eastern ideas of Buddhism and Daoism to influence Westerns ideals. Islam has utilized the Internet to share ideas with people in the West. The nature of the Internet alone has been one of sharing information for the purposes of education and competition. This varied and international informational trade has led to increased competition of goods and services, but it has also influenced a massive new change in the distribution of power. No longer can established media sources be the only information centers. Instead, people are sharing ideas much more freely due to this new avenue of trade.

Societies evolved during the Classical and Post-Classical eras from small city-states into large land-based empires. This was largely due to the diffusion of political, cultural, and technological trading relationships between these societies and the expansion of empires into tributary relationships with conquered regions.

Period Four examines the vast global interconnections made possible through transoceanic expeditions, explorations, and discoveries.

- Europe's Reformation (c. 1515 to c. 1650)
- The Age of Exploration
  - China's Exploration
  - European Exploration: Phase I
  - European Exploration: Phase II
- The Scientific Revolution (c. 1543 to c. 1700)
- The Enlightenment (c. 1685 to c. 1789)
- Powerful Empires: China and the Middle East

Overview of AP World History Period Four

As networks of communication and exchange began to spread across the world, new forms of political centralization, economic expansion, and scientific achievements changed the relationships among nations throughout the world. When I was in school, studying the facts of this period was tough for me because I had to memorize so many names of explorers, scientists, and philosophers. Here is the good news—you don't have to memorize a lot of names, and the ones that you do need to memorize are easy to remember if you see this period as a chain of exciting stories about the people of civilizations meeting and opposing one another.

Before we go through the important world explorations and scientific achievements, let's review the WHAP curriculum framework and key concepts. Use the chart that follows as a guide to help you make mental connections between the key concepts and the topics covered in this chapter.

The information contained in this chart is an abridged version of the concept outline with topic examples. Visit https://apstudent.collegeboard.org/apcourse/ap-world-history/ for the complete WHAP course curriculum descriptions and key concepts.

AP World History Key Concepts (c. 1450 to c. 1750)	
KEY CONCEPT 4.1: GLOBALIZING NETWORKS OF COMMUNICATION AND EXCHANGE **The interconnection of the Eastern and Western Hemispheres, made possible by transoceanic voyaging, transformed trade and religion and had a significant economic, cultural, social, and demographic impact on the world.**	Existing regional patterns of trade intensified in the context of the new global circulation of goods. The intensification of trade brought prosperity and economic disruption to the merchants and governments in the trading regions of the Indian Ocean, Mediterranean, Sahara, and overland Eurasia. European technological developments in cartography and navigation built on previous knowledge developed in the Classical, Islamic, and Asian worlds. The developments included the production of new tools, innovations in ship designs, and an improved understanding of global wind and current patterns—all of which made transoceanic travel and trade possible. Remarkable new transoceanic maritime reconnaissance occurred in this period. For example, Portuguese development of maritime technology led to increased travel and trade with West Africa; Spanish sponsorship of the first Columbian and subsequent voyages across the Atlantic and Pacific Oceans increased European interest in transoceanic travel and trade; and Northern Atlantic crossing for fishing and settlement continued and spurred European searches for multiple routes to Asia. The new global circulation of goods was facilitated by chartered European monopoly companies and the flow of silver from Spanish colonies in the Americas to purchase Asian goods for the Atlantic markets. Regional markets continued to flourish in Afro-Eurasia by using established commercial practices and new transoceanic shipping services developed by European merchants. The new connections between the Eastern and Western hemispheres resulted in the Columbian Exchange. The increase in interactions between the newly connected hemispheres and intensification of connections within hemispheres expanded the spread and reform of existing religions and created syncretic belief systems and practices. As merchants' profits increased and governments collected more taxes, funding for the visual and performing arts, even for popular audiences, increased, along with an expansion of literacy and increased focus on innovation and scientific inquiry.
KEY CONCEPT 4.2: NEW FORMS OF SOCIAL ORGANIZATION **Although the world's productive systems continued to be heavily centered on agriculture, major changes occurred in agricultural labor, the systems and locations of manufacturing, gender and social structures, and environmental processes.**	Beginning in the 14th century, there was a decrease in average temperatures around the world, often referred to as the Little Ice Age, which lasted until the 19th century, contributing to changes in agricultural practices and the contraction of settlement in parts of the Northern Hemisphere. Traditional peasant agriculture increased and changed, plantations expanded, and demand for labor increased. These changes both fed and responded to growing global demand for raw materials and finished products. As social and political elites changed, they also restructured ethnic, racial, and gender hierarchies.

KEY CONCEPT 4.3: STATE CONSOLIDATION AND IMPERIAL EXPANSION	Rulers used a variety of methods to legitimize and consolidate their power. Rulers continued to use religious ideas, art, and monumental architecture to legitimize their rule.
Empires expanded around the world, presenting new challenges in the incorporation of diverse populations and in the effective administration of new coerced labor systems.	Imperial expansion relied on the increased use of gunpowder, cannons, and armed trade to establish large empires in both hemispheres.

Competition over trade routes, state rivalries, and local resistance all provided significant challenges to state consolidation and expansion. |

Important Themes, Terms, and Concepts

The list below shows important themes, terms, and concepts that you should be familiar with on the WHAP exam. Please don't memorize each concept now. Place a check mark next to each topic as it is studied and refer to this list as often as necessary. After you finish the review section, reinforce what you have learned by working the practice questions at the end of this chapter. The answers and explanations provide further clarification into the people who lived in the 15th to the 18th centuries.

Themes, Terms, and Concepts You Should Know	
SOCIAL	
Term/Concept	**Brief Description**
Disease and Native Americans	Native Americans experienced a dying off when they encountered Europeans. This was due to a lack of immunities to European diseases.
Smallpox	Smallpox was one of the key European diseases to cause a massive death rate of Natives.
Primogeniture	A system of land distribution. The eldest son of each family would inherit the family land.
Indentured servitude	Immigrants from European countries would work for families for 7 years to pay for their passage across the Atlantic.
Slavery (African)	Europeans used African labor in Brazil, the Caribbean, and North America to farm sugar, cotton, and tobacco. Africans were defined as property to exploit their labor.
Middle Passage	The passage transporting African slaves from Western Africa to the Caribbean for sale to slave owners.

Continued

POLITICAL	
Term/Concept	**Brief Description**
Religious tolerance	The principle developed after the Thirty Years' War to stop future religious wars. The principle respected each kingdom's, nation's, or province's choice of a sovereign faith.
Edict of Nantes (1598)	France's principle of religious tolerance passed after its civil war respecting both the practice of the Catholics and the Hugenots' Calvinist faith.
Peace of Augsburg (1555)	The treaty after the Thirty Years' War that established the principle of religious tolerance between nations, kingdoms, and provinces.
Peace of Westphalia (1648)	An agreement between the European nations to respect national sovereignty. This institutionalized the rise of nation-states.
Nation-states	A form of political and social organization that was developed after the 1600s. Societies would be organized around a common government, language, and marketplace.
American Revolution (1775 to 1783)	A revolution started by English colonists. It was based on a belief that they were not represented on issues of taxation and land rights.
French Revolution (1789 to 1799)	A radical revolution against the French monarchy and nobility. Its adherents argued for a new society based on the ideals of egalitarianism, brotherhood, and freedom.
Haitian Revolution (1791 to 1804)	The only successful black slave rebellion against the slave holders and the French empire.
Portugal versus Spain	The two European countries that started European explorations. Portugal discovered areas in Africa, Asia, and Brazil. Spain discovered areas in the Caribbean, Mesoamerica, and North America.
Treaty of Tordesillas (1494)	The treaty made between Catholic Spain and Portugal to divide colonial possessions. The pope made the agreement between the countries to avoid war between Catholic countries.
England versus France	England and France competed over areas in North America. England colonized the coastal areas next to the Atlantic with family settlements. France colonized Canada and the Louisiana territory.
RELIGIOUS	
Term/Concept	**Brief Description**
Protestant Reformation (1515 to 1650)	A European religious reform movement that criticized the Catholic Church for abuses and hierarchical corruption.
Lutheranism	A Protestant reform movement started by Martin Luther. It stressed the principles of sola scriptura (only the Bible) and sola fide (faith only).
Calvinism	A Protestant reform movement started by Jean Calvin. He argued that God chooses or predestines people to be saved or damned.
Anglicanism	In 1521, a Protestant reform movement started by Henry VIII. Henry broke with the Catholic Church over his marriage. In 1562, Queen Elizabeth I formally established Anglicanism as the national church of England.
Counter-Reformation	The Catholic Church's response to the Protestant Reformation. The Catholic Church provided new justifications for the Church's authority, sacraments, and priesthood.
Thirty Years' War (1618 to 1648)	The war between the Catholics and the Protestants in the Holy Roman Empire.

IDEOLOGICAL

Term/Concept	Brief Description
Scientific Revolution (1543 to 1700)	An age when European thinkers used scientific thinking and empirical methods to discover laws of nature.
Ptolemaic System	The initial cosmological explanation for the ordering of the universe. It was developed by Aristotle and Ptolemy. It argued for a universe in which the earth was at the center of eight circles.
Geocentric	The belief that Earth was at the center of the universe.
Heliocentric	The scientific argument by Copernicus that the sun was at the center of the universe.
Enlightenment (1685 to 1789)	A philosophical movement in the 1700s that argued that methods of reason should be used to seek truth.
Rene Descartes (1596 to 1650)	A philosopher of rationalism who advocated for doubting all sources of truth in order to develop a more rational understanding of reality.
John Locke (1632 to 1704)	A philosopher and advocate of empiricism who argued for the natural rights of people.
Jean-Jacques Rousseau (1712 to 1778)	A French philosopher who wrote "The Social Contract."

TECHNOLOGICAL

Term/Concept	Brief Description
Rudder	The Chinese development of a way to steer ships for trade routes.
Lateen sail	A new form of triangular sail that allowed for more efficient capture of winds for travel.
Astrolabe	A Chinese navigational tool that could use the stars for trade routes on the seas.
Gunpowder	A Chinese invention that was used for military purposes.
Compass	A Chinese innovation that used the earth's magnetism for navigation.
Wood block printing	A technology that allowed for the printing and stamping of words for writing. This allowed for the creation and mass production of books. It was first created in China and then was sent to Europe, where Johannes Gutenberg popularized the idea of the printing press in 1439.

ECONOMICS

Term/Concept	Brief Description
Atlantic Ocean Trade Route	The ocean trade route that replaced the Silk Roads. Europeans created a trade route connecting Europe to India through the Atlantic Ocean.
Prince Henry the Navigator	The Prince of Portugal who started a school to train sailors to find new trade routes over the seas.
Columbian Exchange	The exchange of plants, animals, and diseases between Europe and civilizations in Mesoamerica and North America.
Encomienda	Spain established a legal system to grant colonists the right to demand forced Native labor for farming and mining plantations.
Sugar and silver	The two main goods that were exploited from the Caribbean and Mesoamerica by Europeans.
Mercantilism	An economic system developed in the 1700s. Nation-states would use colonies to gain raw resources for manufacturing and as markets for manufactured goods. The relationship between colonies and nations was meant to create a balance of trade.
Atlantic slavery	The system of coerced labor used by Europeans to exploit sugar from the Caribbean and Mesoamerica. African slaves were defined as property, which meant that their future generations would also be considered slaves.

Chapter Review

Period Four marks the first significant time in history when the global relations among civilizations, regions, and cultures were becoming increasingly connected with worldwide networks of discovery, trade, and colonization. Before we discuss these global interactions among regions and empires, let's begin with a major European development that influenced world history—the European Reformation.

Europe's Reformation (c. 1515 to c. 1650)

Europe's Reformation, known as the **Protestant Reformation,** was a religious and cultural movement that altered Europeans' traditional ways of thinking about religion and politics. The Reformation challenged the powerful Roman Catholic authority and caused government rulers to wage religious warfare throughout Europe. As a result, new branches of Christianity surfaced: Lutheranism, Calvinism, and Anglicanism.

The Rise of Competing City-States

Since the fall of Rome in 496 C.E., Europe had collapsed into numerous small city-states and kingdoms. The emperor of Western Europe, Charlemagne (768–814), hoped to reunite Europe under a new Roman empire, but the new Holy Roman Empire in Central Europe existed in name only. The reality was a group of competing kingdoms loosely held together under the authority of the Roman Catholic Church. Then, with the Protestant Reformation, Europe exploded into numerous competing and individual states. In fact, Central Europe, Northern Europe, and Southern Europe would fight a **Thirty Years' War** (1618–1648) based on religious and national differences. The result was the **Peace of Westphalia** (1648), which recognized the sovereignty of nation-states. This meant there was no central ruling power.

The Rise of Lutheranism

In the early 1500s, a highly intelligent and morally conscientious young man named **Martin Luther** said that one night when he was walking outside and a horrible storm surrounded him, he promised God that if he survived, he would dedicate his life to the service of God. Luther became a devout monk and began to question the integrity and doctrine of the Catholic Church. Luther eventually published and posted *95 Theses,* criticizing Church practices. Luther was called to the *Council of Worms* by King Charles V to renounce his criticisms. When Luther rejected the authority of the Church and its papacy, the pope excommunicated him. Drawing from the teachings of St. Paul the Apostle, Luther broke from the Catholic Church and formed Lutheranism with these main principles:

- **Sola Scriptura:** Only the Bible should be the guide for Christian life.
- **Sola Fide:** Only faith, not deeds, saves people.
- **Priesthood of All Believers:** All Christians are equal and could communicate directly with God; no priests are necessary to be a worshiper of God.

Critical Thinking Question: Why did Lutheranism become so popular?

Luther's ideas quickly spread in Europe and he created a following of people.

The Rise of Lutheranism	
Reasons that Luther's Ideas Became Popular	**Results of Lutheranism**
Protestants like Luther broke away from the Church because of their criticisms of both the Church doctrine and Church practices. Up until the Reformation, the Catholic Church had authority with monarchies, but many local princes and kings were looking for a way to split from the Catholic Church and establish their own political power. The Catholic Church was the only religious authority, and many believers had lost faith during the Black Death. Church scandals, such as the sale of indulgences for salvation, caused people to question whether the papacy and the Church were as holy as they should have been.	Nation-states started to form around a national religion. For example, Henry VIII broke from the Catholic Church and created the English national religion of Anglicanism. These movements allowed for a fragmenting of Europe into nation-states that followed a national religion. Luther's movement fueled other religious movements like Calvinism. The *Calvinists* believed that God had predestined selected people to be saved. Other religious movements were the *Puritans* in England and the *Huguenots* in France. Luther's views helped to establish ideas about the separation of church from political power. Luther's revolutionary ideas had unforeseen consequences. Armed with his radical beliefs, German peasants began to question their repressed social status. If the mighty Catholic Church, 1,500 years old, could be challenged, why not the power of the German princes? German peasants in the south of the region, began to denounce the clergy and aristocracy for persecuting and oppressing the people.

The Peace of Augsburg (1555)

With the spread of Protestantism, religious differences sparked conflicts and war throughout Europe. The Peace of Augsburg set up a new system of political and religious governance in the Holy Roman Empire based upon the axiom, *cuius regio, eius religio* ("his realm, his religion"). The treaty allowed princes throughout the Europe to adopt Lutheranism or Catholicism and enforce religious unity within their territories.

The Thirty Years' War (1618–1648)

In the decades after the Peace of Augsburg, tensions between Catholics and Protestants across central Europe reduced, but the rivalries among different faiths and polities never disappeared. Augsburg represented the acknowledgment by the Holy Roman Empire and its Protestant princes that neither side could achieve a complete religious and political victory over the other.

The Thirty Years' War (1618–1648)	
Cause	Consequence
Eventually, this political and religious conflict resolved through the Thirty Year's War in central Europe. This war split the Holy Roman Empire between the Protestants in the North and the Catholics in the South.	The Thirty Years' War is often remembered for beginning as a war of religious differences between Catholics and Protestants in the Holy Roman Empire, and ending as a secular war fought over the balance of power in Europe. It has been called "the first secular war in Christian Europe." The end of the war produced two main principles for European religion and politics: ■ *Peace of Augsburg:* Religious tolerance would be centered on nations choosing their own religion. ■ *Peace of Westphalia:* Nation-states would be allowed to pursue their own national sovereignty or cultural identity.

Heads Up: What You Need to Know

On the WHAP exam, the 1648 **Peace of Westphalia** is considered one of the most important treaties in world history. Be prepared for questions on this treaty (its winners and losers), as well as its long-term effects and consequences for the continent of Europe. This treaty played an important role in the shift in the balance of power and reasons for world wars in the 20th century.

The Peace of Westphalia officially established the nation-state (rather than churches, multinational empires, or multistate leagues) as the center of international politics. It also enshrined the concept of the European balance of power, a system in which smaller powers would unite in coalitions to prevent one *hegemon* (a leading power) from dominating the continent.

So, how does the information about nation-states and religious conflict connect to exploration? Well, the development of nation-states meant the need for national competition to find resources and develop power. This meant finding new trade routes for resources and colonization. The following section will discuss European exploration in two parts: European Exploration Phase I and European Exploration Phase II.

The Age of Exploration

Although the principal reasons for global interrelations were driven by European exploration, this section will start our discussion about exploration in another part of the world, probably the one place you would not identify as the starting point of European exploration—China.

China's Exploration

Did you know? The first explorer was not from Europe but from China. Chinese admiral Zheng He commanded over 300 ships and 20,000 men from 1405 to 1433. Zheng He explored regions from India to Eastern Africa. This first major exploration helped to connect China to Africa and led to a massive exchange of goods and animals. The Chinese emperor **Yongle** of the **Yuan Dynasty** was initially interested in establishing a Chinese presence and imposing imperialism in foreign territories. However, over time, the Confucian leaders became skeptical about opening China to so many foreign cultures and exchanges, so eventually Yongle shut down the exploration schedule.

Chinese Inventions Led to European Exploration

During the Yuan Dynasty, the emperor of China, **Kublai Khan,** presided over a period of incredible innovation. Until the Age of Exploration, China was independent from other regions of the world, but many of its inventions directly led to Europeans being able to develop their means of exploration.

Chinese inventors created gunpowder, navigation tools (**astrolabe and compass**), recording tools (**block printing**), and new **lateen sails** for shipping. China could have used all of these innovations to develop a strong navy and merchant system for exploration. However, due to the Chinese beliefs in Confucianism, Buddhism, and Daoism, the focus was more on the need for harmony and balance between the social classes. Plus, with an agricultural economic system, the leadership of China wanted to keep strong filial systems of obligations and relationships. In addition, since China was the dominant empire in East and Southeast Asia, there was no competition to push China outward to explore the rest of the world.

HISTORIOGRAPHY. *World historians raise a significant question about what the globe would look like today had the Confucian elders of the time chosen differently. Would China have created a global system of trade? Would China have remained the dominant leader in the world? Would China have defined global relationships based on its main ideologies of Confucianism and Buddhism? The question becomes even more thought-provoking when we consider how Europeans were able to develop their means of exploration. This again starts with Chinese innovations.*

Europe was just the opposite of China. To understand these trends in Europe, it's important to understand the social, political, and religious climate of Europe during the Age of Exploration.

European Exploration: Phase I

Italy's Exploration

Italian merchant Marco Polo and his family used the Silk Roads to explore civilizations in Central Asia and East Asia. They ended up discovering the powerful Mongol ruler, Kublai Khan, and the Yuan Dynasty with all of the incredible innovations produced in the region. The Polos brought silk, gems, and spices back to Europe, creating intrigue and the foundation for competition.

Portugal's Exploration

The European desire for new trade routes led to the explosion of kingdoms looking for leverage. The first was Portugal. Why Portugal? Well, it's located north of the Mediterranean right along the Atlantic Ocean, and its biggest neighbor was Spain, which had just consolidated its two biggest kingdoms under **Isabella and Ferdinand.** In addition, Portugal and Spain had to compete with the large Ottoman Empire in Northern Africa. Most importantly, Portugal had a chance to increase its trade without having to worry about either its European or Muslim competitors, but it needed to have a new trade route to do this. The king's son, **Prince Henry the Navigator,** found a way.

Heads Up: What You Need to Know

Prince Henry the Navigator created a school at the city of Sagres in Portugal for training explorers based on his discoveries at the Yuan Dynasty. The first important explorer was **Bartholomew Diaz.** Diaz used the new navigational techniques to find a route along the African coast down to the Cape of South Africa. Unfortunately for him, his men were not too happy with the length of the trip and the resulting deaths among the crew from diseases. They forced him to turn the boat around. But the next explorer, **Vasco da Gama,** followed that same path and found a way around Africa to India. This changed everything!

Vasco da Gama

How did Vasco da Gama's explorations in India change the course of history? New trade routes, weaponry, and trade expansion.

Developments from Vasco da Gama's Exploration	
Atlantic Trade Route	Exploration created a new **Atlantic trade route** that did not require Europeans to go over the land occupied by the Ottoman Empire.
Weaponry	The Portuguese introduced cannons to the new trade route. This resulted in trade intersecting with power and war.
Trade Expansion	Other European kingdoms decided to invest in their own trade routes.

Christopher Columbus

And now we arrive at the voyages of Christopher Columbus.

Key Facts about Christopher Columbus

Columbus was commissioned by Spain to explore the West. Many people think the big issue with Columbus was whether or not the world was round. Well, actually, that's not the case. Most educated people knew that the world was round. The real question was what was on the other side of the horizon. Columbus believed it was a quicker route to China, which would mean better competition with Portugal. He asked the kingdoms and cities in his homeland of Italy to fund his expedition, but they were not interested. So Columbus went to Spain, where Isabella and Ferdinand did want to invest in the quest. Columbus took their money and sailed west.

Columbus discovered the West Indies. Columbus was correct that the world was round and that there was a good trade route to the West, but he was wrong about what was on the other side. Columbus thought it was China and India. Thus, the area he "discovered" was later named the **West Indies.** Actually, what he discovered were islands near two huge continents that had been the home of 30 million to 70 million people for centuries.

Did you know? Do you know where the term *Indian* originated? One version of the story is that Columbus called the natives Indians because he purportedly believed that he discovered the trade route to the Indies. What he really discovered were a group of indigenous civilizations spread out between North America and Mesoamerica. The term *Native American* was popularized in the 1970s as an alternative to *Indian* because it more accurately describes indigenous people who were born in the Americas. Indigenous people prefer to be referred to by their specific nation or tribe name. *Native American* is the official legal term used in the United States.

Columbus and the New World (1492). This gets us into the big controversy about the "New World" in the Americas. From the European perspective, this was a New World, which had serious implications. For one, nothing in the European philosophies, religious texts, or experiences had foretold of entirely new civilizations that had existed for centuries before European contact. Also, the civilizations they encountered had a different way of living. Some, like the Northeastern American natives, lived in a farming confederation that included trade zones throughout the Ohio River Valley. Others, living in the Southwest of North America, were nomadic and created whole cities out of rock. Still others in Mesoamerica, such as the Aztecs and Incas, had created cities and kingdoms that dwarfed the European cities of the time.

Portugal and Spain conflict. The two superpowers of the time, Portugal and Spain, wanted land and resources. To make matters worse, they were both Catholic countries. This predicament threatened to split apart the Catholic Church, but Pope Alexander VI negotiated an agreement, the **Treaty of Tordesillas (1494),** between Portugal and Spain. All areas east of Europe would go to Portugal, and all areas west of Europe would go to Spain. The one exception was Brazil, which had already been settled by the Portuguese.

Spain's economic failure. After **Hernan Cortez** conquered the Aztecs (1519) and **Francisco Pizarro** conquered the Incas (1532), the Spanish discovered vast amounts of silver. This promised to be a new form of currency that would give Spain a huge economic boost. However, the great empire struggled to manage its economic prosperity gained from the "Golden Age" of colonial conquests. Spain made poor overseas investments, had huge loans to finance religious wars, had high taxes, and had internal political rebellions. By 1648, Spain suffered a devastating economic decline and was no longer a world power. This was bad news for Spain, but excellent news for the two new superpowers in the Western world: Britain and France.

TEST TIP: The Columbian Exchange starting in the 16th century frequently appears on the WHAP. The exchange of people, animals, plants, goods, and diseases across the Atlantic Ocean fundamentally transformed both Natives and Europeans.

European Exploration: Phase II

Britain's and France's Explorations

Britain and France realized that the true key to a nation's success was economic stability and wealth. To achieve economic success, a nation must first invest its newfound riches from imports in a strong military. By doing so, some of the currency is removed from the national reserves so that the nation's economy doesn't appear inflated. In order to preserve a healthy economy, the nation must not send the nation's wealth to competing nations. Lastly, the nation's strong military should be able conquer new lands, establish colonies, and profit from new resources. France accomplished this by seizing Canada, the Ohio River Valley, the Mississippi River, and New Orleans. Britain accomplished this by controlling the east coast of North America—a new economic system was born called mercantilism.

Mercantilism

Mercantilism dominated major nations and motivated colonial expansion in Europe during the 15th to the mid-18th centuries. It was the relationship between nations trying to seize each other's wealth. Here is how mercantilism works in a five-step process.

1. A nation explores and acquires colonies in a territory such as the Americas or India.
2. The nation acquires raw resources from the colonies such as cotton, sugar, or wood.
3. The nation appropriates the raw resources to manufacture goods such as textiles, finished sugar, or ships.
4. The nation sells these goods to the colonies and foreign countries in exchange for currency and economic gain.
5. The nation uses the currency to build up an army to acquire more colonies, and then the whole process starts again.

Heads Up: What You Need to Know

Mercantilism is a key concept on the WHAP exam. It resulted in a number of different changes during the period of exploration. One of the major consequences of mercantilism is that it led to the territorial dominance after the exploration and development of colonies. Think of all the areas that you have studied in the past like the American colonies, the British colonization of India, and the Scramble for Africa. All of these colonies were driven by mercantilism.

There are two main types of mercantile trade policies: **free trade** that is closely associated with capitalism (commercial manufacturers freely trade and sell to foreign nations) and **protectionism** (the government regulates trade to benefit its nation by imposing tariffs on imported or exported goods). Mercantilist regulations are similar to modern governments' attempts to protet local markets from international competition.

Labor Systems: Voluntary, Forced, and Coercive

As Europeans established colonies, the demand for labor systems to extract raw natural resources increased. Natural resources were important for supporting the wealth of European economies. The cultivation of these natural resources (timber, cotton, sugarcane, spices, coffee, and tobacco) required "labor-intensive" efforts that rested on voluntary, forced, or coerced labor systems.

Key Facts about Solutions to Labor Systems

Enclosure movement. Europeans developed a large-scale production of agriculture that was aimed at increasing profits. The new system of crop rotation was used to maximize efficiency. Wealthy landowners seized land for themselves, enclosed their land, and posted guards. Lower-class peasants were kicked off the farmlands and forced into the new urban centers.

Poor farmers fled to the Americas. Poor farmers operating common lands could not afford to implement such large-scale practices in Europe so the solution was the **Headright System.** Many of the poor farmers could not find work in Europe, so they fled to the Americas seeking land. Those who could not afford the journey would have a settled European family in the Americas pay for their trip. Wealthy Europeans paid for the boat voyage of lower-class laborers, called *indentured servants,* to the New World. In exchange, indentured servants worked for a fixed number of years before getting their freedom and lands.

Transcontinental slave system. As more indentured servants came to the Americas, available land became scarce. Fights between settlers and Native Americans arose over the use of land, and this led to African laborers being used against their will to harvest sugar, cotton, and eventually tobacco. Tragically, slavery became a form of reliable labor at no monetary cost to the landowner.

African slave trade. Europeans found that they could manipulate the African kingdoms in Western and Central Africa to force people to migrate to the Americas. Europeans would provide African kings with guns if the African kingdoms provided slaves. African kingdoms began capturing and transporting slaves to the Middle East over the Trans-Saharan slave route. With European weapons, African kingdoms began conquering the stateless tribe societies of Central Africa and selling people into slavery. Europeans then transported these African slaves to the Caribbean over a route called the **Middle Passage.** Profits from slaves were taken back to the European continent. This three-legged journey from Europe to Africa to the Caribbean was called the **Triangle Trade.** The system was a massive transcontinental slave system, and was unique because it defined African slaves as "objects" and "property," not as human beings. Those who survived the life-threatening voyage across the Middle Passage were forced to work in the fields as slaves. Slaves and their descendants could never gain freedom.

Critical Thinking Question: Why did such a widespread global slave-trading system take place?

The answer is mercantilism. The mercantile economic system created the need for mass productivity based on manual labor. Britain, France, Prussia, Austria, and Russia all competed to gain resources for military investments and expansions. This led to mercantile wars over colonies.

Mercantile Revolutionary Wars

Throughout the 1700s, Britain and France fought each other in a series of wars over the colonies. The most famous was the **French and Indian War** (also known as the **Seven Years' War**).

The French and Indian War (1756 to 1763)

The French and Indian War initially started in Europe over the Prussian-Austrian competition for German territories, but it soon became a global war that reached North America and Asia.

The French and Indian War paved the way for the American Revolution (1775–1783) and the French Revolution (1789–1799). Both the American and French Revolutions were initially caused by tremendous economic debts incurred from mercantile wars. Britain had to tax the Americans to pay off its debt, and the French king overtaxed his peasants to try to pay off the French war debt. In the case of the Americans, the result was a revolution that led to a constitutional government. For the French, the result was a revolution that led to the terror of the guillotine and the high idealism of universal equality for all people. This led to a revolution in Haiti against slavery itself. In other words, democracy and social equality would not have come about without the context of mercantile economics. The mercantile wars formed the basis for setting the course for revolutions that would change the course of world history.

In order to fully understand these revolutions, we have to look at economic and ideological changes during this time period. There were two major European revolutionary ideological movements that introduced new ways of thinking. Both were closely intertwined: the Scientific Revolution and the Enlightenment.

The Scientific Revolution (c. 1543 to c. 1700)

New scientific views about the understanding of the cosmos and the earth had arisen by the 1500s, and scientists began to reexamine the blindly accepted theories of ancient scientists. Scientists before the Scientific Revolution followed the *dogma* (doctrine) of the Catholic Church, but by the 1500s scientists were forced to differentiate their scientific methods from the Catholic Church. The Church did not oppose scientific study, but ruled that scientific findings of the natural world must be explained within a biblical context.

To understand how these contributions led to the rise of scientific thinking in the 16th and 17th centuries, review the following table, which summarizes the original thoughts of scientists on these matters.

Important Scientific Contributions		
Scientist	Famous For	Description
Aristotle (384–322 B.C.E.) and Ptolemy (100–170 C.E.)	First cosmologies: **geocentric** model (Earth-centered universe).	Ancient scientists like Aristotle and Ptolemy established the first cosmologies, or understandings of the universe. According to the Ptolemaic system, the following was observable about nature: ■ The cosmos was made up of eight circular and perfect crystalline orbits around Earth. ■ The earth was at the center of the universe (geocentric theory). ■ All bodies in space were perfect. ■ This theory on the universe's order represented an unmoved mover, who had intelligently created what we see around us.

Scientist	Famous For	Description
Nicolaus Copernicus (1473–1543)	**Heliocentric** model (sun-centered universe).	The geocentric viewpoint would be challenged by Nicolaus Copernicus. The Catholic Church tasked Copernicus with creating a Church calendar. However, every time that Copernicus tried to accomplish this, he ended up with the wrong number of days. Why? Because the changes in the orbits did not line up with the right number of days. Finally, he changed the focus. Copernicus no longer used the *geocentric* model with the earth at the center, but instead used the *heliocentric* model with the sun at the center of the universe. Then, the calendar worked.
Galileo Galilei (1564–1642)	Invented the first telescope to observe planetary motion. Law of planetary motion.	The Ptolemaic viewpoint was challenged again by Galileo Galilei. Galileo provided evidence to support Copernicus' heliocentric theory when he created a telescope and looked into the heavens. He found that the moon had craters all over its surface. So, bodies in space were not perfect. This scientific observation caused the Catholic Church to charge Galileo with heresy.
Johannes Kepler (1571–1630)	Planets follow elliptical paths (not circular paths).	Kepler argued that mathematical formulas disproved the perfect circular orbit of the planets. Rather, planets orbit in ellipses (ovals) around objects.
Sir Isaac Newton (1642–1727)	Laws of gravity prove the force of Earth's gravity on the orbit of the moon. Laws of motion.	Isaac Newton was probably the most famous scientist during this period who changed everything when he argued in favor of a natural force that guided everything: gravity. Newton's argument was extremely important. It changed the model from one that stressed the importance of a divine creator to one that focused on natural scientific laws. In other words, the universe was now seen as a large machine running on natural laws. This model would both support and reinforce the Enlightenment.

The Enlightenment (c. 1685 to c. 1789)

The Enlightenment, also known as the **Age of Reason** or the **Age of Enlightenment,** was an ideological movement that challenged the European traditions of thought and faith. Much of the Enlightenment was based on *epistemology* (new models of finding information) to change the world.

Pre-Enlightenment Thinking

The Enlightenment followed the Medieval Era's (Middle Ages) worldview. The Medieval Era was defined by the unquestionable religious ideas of the Catholic Church in the West and the traditions of Buddhism and Confucianism in the East.

Heads Up: What You Need to Know

The WHAP exam requires that you compare the differences between ideological thinking during different time periods. Use the chart below to compare and contrast the worldview of the Medieval Era and Enlightenment Era.

Medieval Era (Post-Classical Period)	Enlightenment Era (Early-Modern Period)
Reflected the religious wisdom of the Church's authority. Religious and monarchical authorities were necessary to maintain political and religious order. The Medieval Era's worldview was expressed by priests and bishops who had fundamental interests in protecting their position in the Church's hierarchy and the social hierarchy. The wisdom of Augustine, St. Thomas Aquinas, and Confucius, while all different, argued that their world was flawed and should be approached through a duty-based value system.	Reflected the economic self-interest and need for freedom of the merchant class. New Enlightenment thinkers needed the freedom to pursue innovative avenues for business and trade. They were attempting to free themselves from the rules and constraints of the Church's authority.

Enlightenment Philosophies

There are three enlightened schools of thought that you should remember: **humanism, rationalism,** and **empiricism.**

Heads Up: What You Need to Know

The WHAP exam requires that you know the three revolutionary schools of thought that changed the face of Europe during the Enlightenment.

Humanism: Although the concept of humanism started in the Middle Ages, humanism was a form of individualism that inspired enlightened thinkers. Humanism was movement toward thinking critically and gaining knowledge, rather than blindly following religious orthodoxy.

Rationalism: Intellectual thinkers who pointed to philosophy and abstract reasoning to form the basis for new thinking.

Empiricism: Intellectual thinkers who believed that, like science, all truth could be determined by gathering and examining concrete and observable facts.

Enlightenment Philosophers

During the Enlightenment, great thinkers were aware that they were living in revolutionary times with radical new ideas. So, who were these rebels who started up this revolution, and why did their status matter? Most of the revolutionaries were intellectual thinkers (philosophers). These thinkers received a formal education in European universities. They came out of the new rising middle class of merchants and business people. Why does this matter? Because both groups had an agenda for their ideas.

Keep in mind that some overbearing governments considered these new thoughts dangerous. These thinkers exchanged their philosophies through written communications called the **Republic of Letters.** It was through these letters that great thinkers could debate one another, inform one another, and craft blueprints for the future of enlightened republics.

Let's go through some of the key philosophies of each of these great thinkers. On the WHAP exam, you should be familiar with the three key philosophers who made important political, social, and philosophical contributions during the Enlightenment: Descartes, Locke, and Rousseau.

Important Enlightenment Philosophers		
Philosopher	Famous For	Description
Rene Descartes (1596–1650)	Father of Enlightenment Method of Doubt "I think, therefore I am."	The father of the Enlightenment was Rene Descartes. Descartes argued that people should apply logic to follow the **Method of Doubt.** People needed to challenge all of their beliefs given by leaders and authorities. Then they should find the one truth they could accept and build off of that truth. The one truth for Descartes was his statement, "I think, therefore I am." What he meant was that humans have the potential for abstract thought, questions, and consciousness. Playing off of this foundational concept, he would create conclusions or deductions about everything else.
Thomas Hobbes (1588–1679)	Humans are born selfish and nasty. Government must be powerful to control society; Leviathan.	Hobbes believed that humans were really nasty and self-interested. He called for a social contract in which citizens were willing to create a strong government to keep them under control. Through security, people could be free. Hobbes called this government the Leviathan. *Leviathan* was both the title of his book and the analogy he made with the government. The Leviathan would have the power to control society and protect its people, not through religious law, but through the rational regulation of self-interest.
John Locke (1632–1704)	Humans are born in a blank state (tabula rasa). Government's purpose is to protect the natural rights of people.	On the opposite side were the empiricists like John Locke. Locke argued that we could determine truth by gathering real, concrete evidence about humans. He claimed that we could observe humans and determine that we are all born with **natural rights,** including life, liberty, and the pursuit of private property. These natural entitlements meant that we had a right to have these protected. Governments are elected to protect these natural rights. Therefore, governments come from the people, not the other way around. (Note: Locke's ideas influenced the Declaration of Independence.)
Jean-Jacques Rousseau (1712–1778)	Humans are born pure and good. The Social Contract—the general will of the people guides democracy.	Jean-Jacques Rousseau would take this argument a little further, giving rise to the **social contract** between the people and the government, or democracy. The social contract was an agreement between the people and government for management of the society. He argued that humans formed social contracts out of their innate goodness. However, somewhere along the way, this had led to authorities becoming corrupt and using their power to oppress. The only solution was a radical revolution of the common people to establish direct democracies. This would mean a tearing down of the monarchy and traditional authority altogether.
Denis Diderot (1713–1784)	Published first encyclopedia.	Diderot published the first encyclopedia (*Encyclopédie*); it contained articles that classified both natural and social aspects of societies. Diderot's point was to show that people could use science and reason to understand the world without resorting to faith or institutional religion.

Continued

Philosopher	Famous For	Description
Voltaire (1694–1778)	Freedom of conscious and freedom of religion. Separation of Church and state.	Voltaire was a vigorous critic of organized religion, especially the Catholic Church. Voltaire was originally trained by the Jesuits, a Catholic order, but he came to believe that the priestly class (a term for all people in religious authority) had created spiritual stories based on mystery. These were used to justify religious leaders, and any attempt to criticize these authorities only led to social or legal punishments. Voltaire hoped to use reason and science to disprove the reasons for these stories and free individuals for their true natural essence.
Immanuel Kant (1724–1804)	Universal principles of human reason give moral law. Synthesized early modern rationalism and empiricism.	Kant examined all of the different ideas of the Enlightenment thinkers and tried to organize them under a principle of rationality. He asked what all humans could agree on if they used their reason. Kant concluded that all humans agreed on the desire to be free. And that humans desired to establish universal rules that would make sense to all of us without allowing any one individual to violate these rules. Kant called the first principle *autonomy*. All individuals should be able to think freely without undue interference from authority. The second part was called the *categorical imperative*. All individuals should be able to agree on rules that are rational and universal. No one should be able to violate a universal rule, but the rule itself should be based on rationality, not faith or mystery.

Key Facts about the Enlightenment

The Enlightenment had a significant impact on world history, governments, and religion. Listed below are some of the noteworthy viewpoints expressed by enlightened thinkers.

Humans are self-interested. Humans are not really good or bad. Rather, humans are self-interested due to their innate biological nature. Since humans are self-interested, they are individualistic (humanistic) and only participate in the societies they inhabit for mutual interest. The goal of each society is to free individuals to pursue their own self-interests. If everyone pursues their own self-interests, the results will be mutually beneficial to the individual and society.

Sources of knowledge must be challenged. The best source of knowledge is science because science is based on actual evidence that can be observed and quantified. Government authorities should always be questioned and distrusted because they tend to abuse their power.

Traditions and authority must be challenged. The Enlightenment thinkers challenged the idea that Church traditions and monarchical authorities were the best sources of truth. Rather, science, philosophy, and rational thought became more trusted. From politics and religion to economics and culture, the philosophers of the Enlightenment believed that rational thought, reason, and evidence-based knowledge could fix the problems of society.

Citizens must have legal rights. Government leaders were now challenged and asked to represent the people in order to prevent corruption and the abuses of power in the ruling government. One of the most important political views of philosopher Jean-Jacques Rousseau, and almost all Enlightenment philosophers, was that citizens deserved inalienable rights; for example, the **social contract** (an agreement between rulers and ruled, in which there were mutual obligations and promises). Voltaire and many others contended that a free society could not truly exist if ordinary citizens did not possess the right to freedom of speech, press, assembly, and petition. Moreover, many of the Enlightenment thinkers wanted to guarantee a citizen's right to a fair trial, a jury of his peers, and the right to defend himself in a speedy trial against whatever charges had been brought against him.

Government powers must have checks and balances. Philosopher Baron Montesquieu sought to diminish the problems of society by proposing the separation of governmental powers into three branches: legislative, judicial, and executive. Rather than a government ruled by a monarchy (king or queen) or ruled by despotism (dictator), Montesquieu believed that elected leaders must have government checks and balances in order to prevent corruption and the abuse of power. This gave rise to revolutions calling for democracies and republics.

The church and state must be separate. In line with sensible thinking, many philosophers criticized what they viewed as irrational or illogical. For example, Voltaire wrote articles, pamphlets, and books that satirized irrational religion, inefficient monarchical government, and general ignorance. Religion did not disappear, but there was a call for criticizing organized religion. A new rationalist religion of **Deism** arose (people who believed that God had created the natural laws of the universe and then left the universe to run on its own).

Governments must apply new capitalistic economics. Great thinkers, like economics founder Adam Smith, applied the rationalism of the Scientific Revolution and Enlightenment principles to capitalism. Prior to Smith's revolutionary ideas, the success of a nation's economy was measured by its storage of gold and silver. When most governments were practicing heavy-handed forms of mercantilism, Smith argued for **laissez-faire capitalism** (a system of economics in which the government did not interfere in the economy). Smith wrote about an "invisible hand" of the market, whereby the element of unseen economics starting with self-interest would achieve the greatest good for everyone. If a government did not interfere, the market would self-regulate and provide benefits for everyone. It may have seemed greedy for wealthy individuals to pursue their own self-interest, Smith admitted, but when they did, they inadvertently created wealth for everyone, not just themselves.

Critical Thinking Question: What was the result regarding the conflict between the great Enlightenment thinkers and the Post-Classical Era traditionalists?

Things did not really go the way that the great thinkers had envisioned. Let me ask you this: What types of societies do you think would arise out of the Enlightenment? My guess is that you would say democracies, republics, and revolutionary societies. Are you right? Well, the enlightened thinkers actually inspired better monarchies.

Enlightened Despotism

What ended up happening was that the monarchs of Europe used the ideas of the Enlightenment thinkers to create more efficient monarchies. Many people are confused by this idea. After all, the enlightened thinkers seemed to undermine absolute monarchy. How could kings embrace their ideas? Monarchs who supported the ideals of the Enlightenment, yet remained powerful rulers, were called *enlightened despots* (tyrannical monarchs who accepted certain ideas of the Enlightenment). Some of the best known enlightened despots include: Frederick II of Prussia, Peter the Great of Russia, Maria Theresa of Austria, Joseph II of Austria, and Leopold II of Austria. These enlightened despot monarchs accepted what they liked about the Enlightenment and ignored ideas that threatened their interests. Most of all, monarchs emphasized the public use of reason to enhance the power and efficiency of the state. In exchange for reforms and changes, monarchs demanded absolute loyalty and obedience from their people. German philosopher Immanuel Kant proclaimed that these rulers said to their subjects, "Question what you like, and when you like, but obey!"

Powerful Empires: China and the Middle East

Most students tend to think that this time period was the rise of the Western European and North American states. You might walk away from this period thinking that the rest of the world was taking a backseat to Britain, France, and America. But this was hardly the case. While it is true that Europe and North America were on the rise at this time, China was still in control because it had amassed silver in trade from the Mesoamerican region. Also, the Middle East saw the rise of three great gunpowder empires dominated by different sects of Islam. As discussed in Chapter 7 (pp. 121–122), these empires were very powerful. Let's take a quick look at each empire.

Ottoman Empire

The Ottoman Empire was ruled by a Sunni theocracy. It expanded from North Africa to today's Turkey. Its leader was the sultan, who was considered to be Allah's messenger. The empire was expansive and included many ethnicities and religious minorities. The Ottomans found a way to incorporate the different groups. They would take sons from the different religious groups and place them in military advisory roles called the *Janissaries*. The sultan was also advised by a civilian group called the *Wazir*. Local religious communities were allowed to practice their own religious faiths as long as they pledged political loyalty to the sultan. This kept all the different religious communities pledging loyalty to the sultan while still making it possible for them to practice their own faiths. For centuries, the result was a united Muslim empire with a strong and expansive navy.

Safavid Empire

The Safavid Empire was more like a singular state located in Iran. It was ruled by a Shiite theocracy. Its leader was the Shah, and the Shah maintained order through two techniques. The Shah of Iran kept the national identity through an enforcement of the Shiite faith and a suppression of the Muslim minority of Sufis. He also brought in foreign advisers to keep a competition between the Safavid nobles and the foreign advisers. This maintained peace within the state. The Shah also created a military to stop the Ottomans from conquering their Safavid neighbors.

Mughal Empire

This empire was also Sunni, but it was more of a complex mix of ethnic identities due to its location in the Northern Indian region along the Silk Roads. It was regularly invaded due to its location next to the steppe plateau region. The Mughal Empire was faced with the question of how to unite the Muslim minority and the Hindu majority. Its two key leaders had very different approaches. Akbar the Great attempted to unite the groups through tolerance, but his tolerance was to embrace both faiths as representative of a larger new belief system he called the Divine Faith. As a result he angered both purist Hindus and Muslims, who believed the two faiths were different. Akbar's grandson, Aurangzeb, a devout Muslim, saw this as a corruption of the true Islamic religion, so he ended the new faith, pushed any

Hindu advisers out of the royal court, and burned down Hindu temples. The result of his efforts was a civil war between Hindus and Muslims that would lead to their vulnerability and eventually to the British takeover of India.

Heads Up: What You Need to Know

Here is a summary of the common themes and issues for Period Four.

- The early modern explorations created networks of global interrelations between the East and West, and a demand for global transoceanic exchange.
- The early modern imperialistic conquests redefined geographic territories and brought about shifts in dominant world powers.
- The early modern expansions restructured social, racial, ethnic, and gender hierarchies.
- The early modern economic system of mercantilism motivated world expansion and trade, but it also led to forced labor systems of slavery.
- The early modern revolutionary movements ignited progressive ideas, scientific innovations, and technological achievements throughout the world.
- The early modern religious reformations caused political wars and divisions among competing nations.

Chapter Review Practice Questions

The practice questions that follow show the types of questions that may appear on the exam. On the actual exam, the questions are grouped into sets. Each set contains one source-based prompt and two to five questions.

Multiple-Choice Questions

Questions 1–3 refer to the following passage.

After the wars and the killings had ended, when usually there survived only some boys, some women, and children, these survivors were distributed among the Christians to be slaves. The *repartimiento* or distribution was made according to the rank and importance of the Christian to whom the Indians were allocated, one of them being given thirty, another forty, still another, one or two hundred, and besides the rank of the Christian there was also to be considered in what favor he stood with the tyrant they called Governor. The pretext was that these allocated Indians were to be instructed in the articles of the Christian Faith. As if those Christians who were as a rule foolish and cruel and greedy and vicious could be caretakers of souls! And the care they took was to send the men to the mines to dig for gold, which is intolerable labor, and to send the women into the fields of the big ranches to hoe and till the land, work suitable for strong men. Nor to either the men or the women did they give any food except herbs and legumes, things of little substance. The milk in the breasts of the women with infants dried up and thus in a short while the infants perished. And since men and women were separated, there could be no marital relations. And the men died in the mines and the women died on the ranches from the same causes, exhaustion and hunger. And thus was depopulated that island which had been densely populated.

—Source: Bartolome de Las Casas, "Brief Account of the Destruction of the Indies," 1542.

1. Which of the following provides the best explanation for de Las Casas' account of the *repartimiento*?

    A. Vasco da Gama's attempt to create a new trade route around the southern tip of Africa to India
    B. The Confucian rejection of Zheng He's expeditions to Eastern Africa and the Indian Ocean
    C. Ibn Battuta's chronicles of the different Islamic societies along the Trans-Saharan trade route
    D. The Spaniards' use of conquered Aztec labor for the extraction of silver

2. De Las Casas' view of the *repartimiento* was most likely an appeal to influence which of the following groups?

    A. De Las Casas wanted merchants to explore new territories to establish alternative trade routes.
    B. De Las Casas was appealing to Catholic authorities to place moral teachings above resource extraction.
    C. De Las Casas wanted the leaders of kingdoms to consolidate their regions for future investment in exploration.
    D. De Las Casas wanted more exploration into the continent to find trade routes.

3. As a result of the Spanish actions described in the passage, which of the following most affected the global economic system?

    A. Silver from Mesoamerica flowed to Europe and China, creating the basis for mercantile markets.
    B. Spanish settlements in Mesoamerica conflicted with the Portuguese, leading to mercantile wars.
    C. Spanish use of silver led to an expansion of its military power in Central Europe.
    D. Spain expanded into Northern America and began to take control of trade routes along the Mississippi River.

Questions 4–6 refer to the following map.

Primary Flow of Silver. 1570–1750

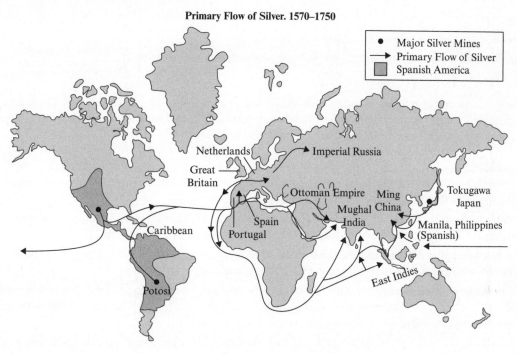

4. Which of the following best explains the primary reason for the flow of silver shown in the map above?

   A. The expansion of the Russian government into Siberia in order to create a national empire

   B. The Portuguese attempt to create an alternative trade route to the Silk Roads by exploring Western Africa

   C. The Spanish use of conquered Aztec labor for mining in Mesoamerica

   D. The French settlement along the Mississippi River in the Louisiana territory

5. Which of the following most accurately represents the impact of the silver market on the global economy?

   A. Northern Europe was able to use the new currency to its advantage for trading dominance.

   B. Spain benefitted from the new currency through proper international investments.

   C. China gained from the currency, leading to China's dominance in the trades of porcelain and silk.

   D. India benefitted from the trade due to its internal political stability.

6. Based on the map and your knowledge of world history, which of the following likely accounts for the key turning point from the Post-Classical Era to the Age of Exploration that changed the global economic system?

   A. Zheng He's effort to open the Chinese Ming Empire through his expeditions to Africa and India

   B. European efforts to replace the Silk Roads with new trade routes to India

   C. Ibn Battuta's travels to African Muslim societies to record the different cultural responses to the religion of Islam

   D. The Mongols' protection of the Silk Roads from bandits

Document-Based Question

1 question

60 minutes

Reading Time: 15 minutes (brainstorm your thoughts and organize your response)

Writing Time: 45 minutes

Directions: The document-based question is based on the seven accompanying documents. The documents are for instructional purposes only. Some of the documents have been edited for the purpose of this practice exercise. Write your response on lined paper and include the following:

- **Thesis.** Present a thesis that supports a historically defensible claim, establishes a line of reasoning, and responds to all parts of the question. The thesis must consist of one or more sentences located in one place—either the introduction or the conclusion.

- **Contextualization.** Situate the argument by explaining the broader historical events, developments, or processes that occurred before, during, or after the time frame of the question.

- **Evidence from the documents.** Use the content of at least three to six of the documents to develop and support a cohesive argument that responds to the question.

- **Evidence beyond the documents.** Support or qualify your argument by explaining at least one additional piece of specific historical evidence not found in the documents. (Note: The example must be different from the evidence used to earn the point for contextualization.)

- **Analysis.** Use at least three documents that are relevant to the question to explain the documents' point of view, purpose, historical situation, and/or audience.

- **Historical reasoning.** Use historical reasoning to show relationships among the documents, the topic question, and the thesis argument. Use evidence to corroborate, qualify, or modify the argument.

Based on the documents that follow, answer the question below.

Question 1: Based on your knowledge of world history, compare and contrast the effects of exploration on the organization of regions.

Document 1

> **Source: Ma Huan, "Ying-Yai Sheng-lan," (The Overall Survey of the Ocean's Shores), circa 1433 C.E.**
>
> The king of the country is a Nankun man; he is a firm believer in the Buddhist religion and he venerates the elephant and the ox. . . . The king of the country and the people of the country all refrain from eating the flesh of the ox. The great chiefs are Muslim people; they all refrain from eating the flesh of the pig. Formerly there was a king who made a sworn compact with the Muslim people, "You do not eat the ox; I do not eat the pig; we will reciprocally respect the taboo"; and this compact has been honored right down to the present day.

Document 2

Source: Columbian Exchange, 15th century, C.E.

From the Americas to Europe, Africa, and Asia:

- Beans
- Cocoa
- Corn
- Pineapples
- Peanuts
- Peppers
- Potatoes
- Pumpkins
- Squash
- Sweet potatoes
- Tobacco
- Tomatoes
- Turkeys
- Vanilla

Americas to Europe, Africa, and Asia

EUROPE

AFRICA

Europe, Africa, and Asia to Americas

From Europe, Africa, and Asia to the Americas:

- Bananas
- Citrus fruits
- Coffee beans
- Disease (smallpox, influenza, typhus, measles, malaria, diphtheria, pertussis)
- Grains (barley, oats, rice, wheat)
- Grapes
- Honeybees
- Livestock (cows, horses, pigs, sheep)
- Olives
- Onions
- Peaches
- Pears
- Sugarcane
- Turnips

Document 3

Source: Qiaoyuan He, Ming Dynasty court official, report to the emperor on the possibility of repealing the 1626 ban on foreign trade, 1630.

The Spanish have silver mountains, which they mint into silver coins. When Chinese merchants trade in Southeast Asia and the Indian Ocean, they trade the goods we produce for the goods of others. But when they go to Luzon (Philippines) they only return with silver coins. Chinese silk yarn worth 100 bars of silver can be sold in the Philippines at a price of 200 to 300 bars of silver there. Moreover, porcelain from the official pottery works, as well as sugar and fruit from my native province, are currently desired by the foreigners.

Document 4

Source: The Travels of Zheng He.

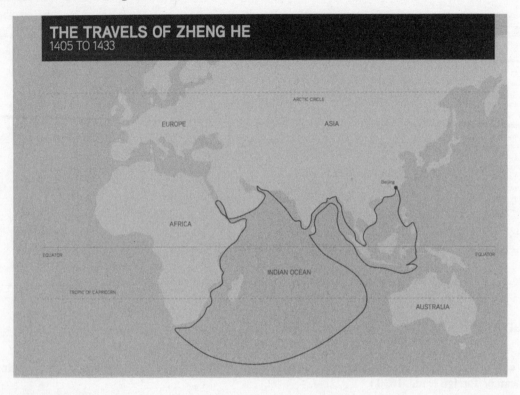

THE TRAVELS OF ZHENG HE
1405 TO 1433

Document 5

Source: Christopher Columbus, "The Writings of Christopher Columbus: Descriptive of the Discovery and Occupation of the New World, 1490," 1490 C.E.

Your Highnesses, as Catholic Christians, and princes who love and promote the holy Christian faith, and are enemies of the doctrine of Mahomet (Mohammed), and of all idolatry and heresy, determined to send me, Christopher Columbus, to the above-mentioned countries of India, to see the said princes, people, and territories, and to learn their disposition and the proper method of converting them to our holy faith; and furthermore directed that I should not proceed by land to the East, as is customary, but by a Westerly route, in which direction we have hitherto no certain evidence that any one has gone.

So after having expelled the Jews from your dominions, your Highnesses, in the same month of January, ordered me to proceed with a sufficient armament to the said regions of India, and for that purpose granted me great favors, and ennobled me that thenceforth I might call myself Don, and be High Admiral of the Sea, and perpetual Viceroy and Governor in all the islands and continents which I might discover and acquire, or which may hereafter be discovered and acquired in the ocean. . . .

Document 6

> **Source: Bernardino de Sahagun, "Florentine Codex: Book 12, The Conquest of Mexico,"16th century C.E.**
>
> And when Moctezuma went to meet them at Huitzillan, he bestowed gifts on Cortés; he gave him flowers, he put necklaces on him; he hung garlands around him and put wreaths on his head. Then he laid out before him the golden necklaces, all of his gifts [for the Spaniards]. He ended by putting some of the necklaces on him.
>
> Then Cortés asked him: "Is it not you? Are you not he? Are you Moctezuma?"
>
> And Moctezuma responded: "Yes, I am Moctezuma." Then he stood up to welcome Cortés, to meet him face to face. He bowed his head low, stretched as far as he could, and stood firm.
>
> Then he addressed him in these words: "Our lord, you are very welcome in your arrival in this land. You have come to satisfy your curiosity about your noble city of Mexico. You have come here to sit on your throne, to sit under its canopy, which I have kept for awhile for you. For the rulers and governors [of past times] have gone: Itzcoatl, Moctezuma I, Axayacatl, Tiçocic, and Ahuitzol. [Since they are gone], your poor vassal has been in charge for you, to govern the city of Mexico. Will they come back to the place of their absence?

Document 7

> **Source: Al-Umari, Arab Scholar, "Mali's King Mansa Musa's Visit to Egypt in 1324."**
>
> From the beginning of my coming to stay in Egypt I heard talk of the arrival of this sultan Musa on his Pilgrimage and found the people of Cairo eager to recount what they had seen of the Africans' prodigal spending. I asked the emir Abu ... and he told me of the opulence, manly virtues, and piety of his sultan. When I went out to meet him, that is on behalf of the mighty Egyptian sultan Al-Malik al-Nasir, he did me extreme honor and treated me with the greatest courtesy. . . . Then he forwarded to the royal treasury many loads of unworked native gold and other valuables. I tried to persuade him to go up to the Citadel to meet the sultan, but he refuses, persistently saying: "I came for the Pilgrimage and nothing else. I do not wish to mix anything else with my Pilgrimage." He had begun to use this argument but I realized that [meeting the sultan] was repugnant to him because he would be obliged to kiss the ground and the sultan's hand.

Answers and Explanations

Multiple-Choice Questions

1. **D.** De Las Casas was referring to the treatment of conquered Aztec labor on haciendas and encomiendas. He was criticizing the use of their labor for the purpose of silver mining. The Catholic Church had justified the conquering as a way to proselytize the Aztecs. De Las Casas said that the local Spaniards were using the Aztecs for hard labor.

2. **B.** De Las Casas was debating with Juan de Sepulveda. Sepulveda argued that the Aztecs needed to be conquered in order to be civilized and to stop their practices, such as human sacrifice. De Las Casas argued that the Aztecs were being exploited for labor, not trained in Catholic beliefs. All of these arguments were made in Europe to appeal to the authority of the pope to provide guidance on this issue.

3. **A.** The Aztecs worked on haciendas in the encomienda system. This system exploited Aztec labor to mine silver. The Spaniards used the silver to buy luxury goods. Most of these goods, such as silk, spices, and porcelain, came from China. So China ended up having a massive influx of silver.

4. **C.** This map depicts the movement of silver across the globe to China. The silver was mined in Mesoamerica in Mexico. The Spaniards then used it to buy luxury goods from China.

5. **C.** Most of the silver flowed to China due to the international trading market in luxury goods like porcelain, spices, and silk. China was inundated with the silver, leading to an inflation of its currency.

6. **B.** This map is the end result of the European desire to stop using the Silk Roads as their main trading route. Portugal and Spain no longer wanted to pay fees to the Ottoman Empire, so they sought out new sea-based routes for trade. Vasco da Gama would connect with India over the Atlantic Ocean. Christopher Columbus opened up the trade to the West over the Atlantic Ocean to the Caribbean.

Document-Based Question

DBQ Scoring Guide

To achieve the maximum score of 7, your response must address the scoring criteria components in the table below.

Scoring Criteria for a Good Essay	
Question: Based on your knowledge of world history, compare and contrast the effects of exploration on the organization of regions.	
Scoring Criteria	**Examples**
A. THESIS/CLAIM	
(1 point) Presents a historically defensible thesis that establishes a line of reasoning. (Note: The thesis must make a claim that responds to *all* parts of the question and must *not* just restate the question. The thesis must consist of *at least* one sentence, either in the introduction or the conclusion.)	A well-developed thesis needs to provide both comparison and contrast while following a line of reasoning about the changes that exploration brought to the development of regions. This includes cultural, social, religious, economic, or technological contributions. This thesis argues that there is a comparison between existing views and the transfer of new ideas from surrounding regions. A contrast between European versus Native hierarchies is illustrated in the essay and shows how the diffusion upheld hierarchical systems in Europe while undermining the systems in the native areas.

Scoring Criteria	Examples
B. CONTEXTUALIZATION	
(1 point) Explains the broader historical context of events, developments, or processes that occurred before, during, or after the time frame of the question. (Note: Must be more than a phrase or reference.)	The essay starts by contextualizing the time period and geographic territories of major trade routes. The essay explains the transition from the major trade routes of the Classical and Post-Classical eras into the new trade routes. It explains how these new routes were discovered in order to give Europe more independence from the trading fees of the Ottoman Empire. This sets up the essay to provide reasons for further European exploration and discovery.
C. EVIDENCE	
Evidence from the Documents **(2 points)** Uses at least *six* documents to support the argument in response to the prompt. OR **(1 point)** Uses the content of at least *three* documents to address the topic prompt. (Note: Examples must describe, rather than simply quote, the content of the documents.)	Remember to aim for the most possible points. To accomplish this, you must address at least six documents. Look through each document to get a general idea of the context of each document, then look at the author, title, subject, date, and intended audience (if known). The response addresses all seven of the documents and uses them to provide evidence for the comparisons and contrasts. Documents 2 and 4 compare the trade routes of competing regions, and Documents 3, 6, and 7 compare the economic and monetary gains made by world explorations. Documents 1 and 5 describe first-hand accounts from the explorers' viewpoints.
Evidence Beyond the Documents **(1 point)** Uses at least one additional piece of specific historical evidence beyond those found in the documents relevant to the argument. (Note: Evidence must be different from the evidence used in contextualization.)	The essay needs to provide specific details about at least one specific outside example that influenced the argument. The essay does this by providing specific historical details about the rise of Mali through Sundiata and Mansa Musa. It also discusses how Christopher Columbus addressed a Catholic audience fearful of the influence of the Ottoman Empire. And it explains the context for Hernan Cortez's conquering of the Aztecs based on old myths about the return of the gods to save the Aztecs.
D. ANALYSIS AND REASONING	
(1 point) Uses at least *three* documents to explain how each document's point of view, purpose, historical situation, and/or audience is relevant to the argument. (Note: References must explain how or why, rather than simply identifying.)	Most of the documents are used to show purpose. Document 5 uses audience by showing how Columbus addressed the Catholic hierarchy to justify exploration for cultural and religious reasons. Document 7 uses point of view to show how a Muslim scholar would see the diffusion of Islamic beliefs as necessary to counteract the lack of purity in Islamic countries. Document 1 shows how nations were able to maintain religious traditions in the face of new trading partners.
(1 point) Uses historical reasoning and development that focuses on the question while using evidence to corroborate, qualify, or modify the argument. (Examples: Explain what is similar and different; explain the cause and effect; explain multiple causes; explain connections within and across periods of time; corroborate multiple perspectives across themes; or consider alternative views.)	Essays must provide a supporting or dissenting viewpoint in order to show a coherency to the overall argument. The sample-response essay provides a brief paragraph on how some people might argue that discovery undermined all authority. The essay outweighs this argument by differentiating between European and colonial hierarchies. In addition, the essay makes a historical connection across time periods to the Mongols' invasion during the Post-Classical Era. The essay argues that the Mongols brought new culture by syncretizing the ideas of empires from Southeast and Central Asia. The essay compares how this affected the new empires by creating new social hierarchies based on these ideas.

DBQ Sample Response

Exploration had a tremendous impact on the social, cultural, religious, technological, and economic systems of world regions. The main trade routes in the Post-Classical world connected China to India, Central Asia, Africa, and Europe (Documents 2 and 4). The Silk Roads and Indian Ocean trade routes created peaceful trade between the large land empires for centuries. However, Europeans began to challenge these trade routes due to the desire to find a way around the Ottoman Empire's control of the Silk Roads and merchants' charging fees. Europeans also received new navigational technologies that allowed for the kingdoms next to the Atlantic Ocean to discover new trade routes to India and China for trade. The new explorations led to a similar diffusion of cultures that challenged the perceived purity of religious faiths. While exploration and discovery served to strengthen the new European leadership of nation-states, in contrast, the new trade routes also undermined the traditional leadership of native cultures.

Some historians would argue that the new exploration trade routes only caused the end to traditional leadership. However, this does not account for the difference between the effects of the new European monarchs who prospered from the investments that their nations could make into the discoveries (Documents 3, 6, and 7).

The exploration for new trade routes led to the expansion of traditional, religious beliefs into new regions. Islamic beliefs spread as new trade routes were created across the Middle East and Africa. For example, Sundiata and Mansa Musa created a centralized Mali Empire on the west coast of Africa. Mansa Musa then extended the influence of Mali by reinforcing the Trans-Saharan trade route. Document 1 was written by Ma Huan, a Chinese scholar who was advising the emperor on how to trade with countries whose leaders wanted to maintain their religious traditions in the face of new trading partners. The purpose of his descriptions was to call attention to honoring different beliefs throughout these regions. Similarly, Christopher Columbus called for the expansion of Spanish Christianity in Document 5. Columbus' audience was the Spanish Catholic court and religious authority. He was appealing for national investment into his discovery of a trade route to the west. He justified this by appealing to the Catholic fears of the Ottoman Muslim Empire to the South. Columbus' document was an example of the Spanish authority's desire to find a way to weaken the influence of the Islamic empires in the South by spreading Christian culture through the new trade routes.

The exploration of new trade routes led to the expansion of traditional, cultural, and religious beliefs into new regions. Islamic beliefs spread as new trade routes were created across the Middle East and Africa. For example, Sundiata and Mansa Musa created a centralized Mali Empire on the west coast of Africa. Mansa Musa then extended the influence of Mali by reinforcing the Trans-Saharan trade route. Document 1 was written by Ibn Battuta, an Islamic scholar, who traveled across the new trade routes and documented the intersection of Islamic beliefs with other cultures. The purpose of his descriptions was to call for the purity and validity of Islamic beliefs throughout these new regions. Similarly, Christopher Columbus called for the expansion of Spanish Christianity in Document 5. Columbus' audience was the Spanish Catholic court and religious authority. He was appealing for national investment into his discovery of a trade route to the west. He justified this by appealing to the Catholic fears of the Ottoman Muslim Empire to the South. Columbus' document was an example of the Spanish authority's desire to find a way to weaken the influence of the Islamic empires in the South by spreading Christian culture through the new trade routes.

The new trade routes served to undermine or isolate some traditional authorities while providing resources to justify other traditional hierarchies. The Chinese Ming Empire provided the first significant investment into exploration. Document 4 documents how Zheng He, a Chinese explorer, sought out new trade routes for China from India to the east coast of Africa. He was known to have brought back to China new discoveries in resources, culture, and animal life. However, the Chinese Confucian rulers feared the foreign influence from Eastern Africa would undermine the filial relationships in traditional China. To reinforce their hierarchy, these traditional rulers stopped his explorations and isolated China. However, the European kings were strengthened by the new investments into discoveries. In the 1600s, European regions were consolidating into empires like the new Spanish monarchy. Ferdinand and Isabella combined Spain and then invested into new trade routes. This led to Columbus' trip. Document 2 maps out how the Europeans brought new animals to Mesoamerica such as cattle and pigs. Spain received new crops like coffee, sugar, and potatoes. The Spanish also conquered significant civilizations and placed them in a dependent economic relationship. Document 6 was written by a Spanish observer who justified the Spanish explorer Hernan Cortez' conquering of the Aztecs. The Aztecs saw the Spanish as the return of the ancient gods who would save the Aztecs. Instead, the Spanish conquered the Aztecs and placed them under their control for Spanish extraction of silver.

Still, all empires had to eventually recognize the influence of new ideas on the organization of societies due to the spread of trade routes. For Muslims, the fear of new trade routes was that there would be a dilution of pure Islamic beliefs. Document 7 demonstrates that cultures did mix together within the Islamic world, leading to a syncretism of African and Middle Eastern viewpoints on Islam. Similarly, the Chinese tried to isolate themselves from the impacts of trade. However, the influx of silver documented in Document 3 demonstrates how trade led to the rise of a new merchant class in China that gave it dominance in Southeast Asia. Silver was used by the Chinese government to inflate its currency and create a new market for merchants in luxury goods like porcelain, silk, and spices.

New European trade routes helped nations in Southern and Northern Europe to consolidate and create a mercantile exchange of goods with newly encountered colonies. But the native cultures in these communities found that their traditional social relationships were dramatically changed.

Chapter 9

Period Five: Industrialization and Global Integration (c. 1750 to c. 1900)

Period Five examines the far-reaching ideas and advancements of global commerce, innovations, and cultures of the modern world.

- The Enlightenment (c. 1685 to c. 1789)
- The Industrial Revolution (1840 to 1870)
- Capitalism
- Socialism
- The Second Industrial Revolution (1870 to 1914)
- New Imperialism (1870 to 1914)

Overview of AP World History Period Five

New ideas began to spread across Europe by the end of the 18th century that modernized the entire world. These ideas changed the way that people around the world thought and responded to social, economic, and political traditions. Why are the ideas of over 300 years ago so central to the world today? Because it was more than a historical moment in time. The new ideas, inventions, and social reforms changed how humans lived, worked, and perceived everything in the world. It was the beginning of our modern-day world.

Use the curriculum framework and key concepts chart that follows as a guide to help you make mental connections between the key concepts and the topics covered in this chapter.

The information contained in this chart is an abridged version of the concept outline with topic examples. Visit https://apstudent.collegeboard.org/apcourse/ap-world-history/ for the complete WHAP course curriculum descriptions.

AP World History Key Concepts (c. 1750 to c. 1900)	
KEY CONCEPT 5.1: INDUSTRIALIZATION AND GLOBAL CAPITALISM **The process of industrialization changed the way in which goods were produced and consumed, with far-reaching effects on the global economy, social relations, and culture.**	Industrialization fundamentally changed how goods were produced. A variety of factors led to the rise of industrial production including Europe's location on the Atlantic Ocean; the geographical distribution of coal, iron, and timber; European demographic changes; urbanization; improved agricultural productivity; legal protection of property; an abundance of rivers and canals; access to foreign resources; and the accumulation of capital. New patterns of global trade and production developed and further integrated the global economy as industrialists sought raw materials and new markets for the increasing amount and array of goods produced in their factories. To facilitate investments at all levels of industrial production, financiers developed and expanded various financial institutions. There were major developments in transportation and communication, including railroads, steamships, telegraphs, and canals. The development and spread of global capitalism led to a variety of social responses (labor movements, socialism/Marxism, anarchism, Tanzimat reform movement in the Ottoman Empire, the Self-Strengthening Movement in China, the Meiji Restoration in Japan, suffrage in Britain, etc.). The ways in which people organized themselves into societies also underwent significant transformations in industrialized states due to the fundamental restructuring of the global economy (new social middle class, gender roles, and rapid urbanization).
KEY CONCEPT 5.2: IMPERIALISM AND NATION-STATE FORMATION **As states industrialized, they also expanded existing overseas empires and established new colonies and transoceanic relationships.**	Industrializing powers established transoceanic empires. European states, as well as the United States and Japan, established empires throughout Asia and the Pacific, while Spanish and Portuguese influence declined. Imperialism influenced state formation and contraction around the world. In some imperial societies, emerging cultural, religious, and racial ideologies, including social Darwinism, were used to justify imperialism.
KEY CONCEPT 5.3: NATIONALISM, REVOLUTION, AND REFORM **The 18th century marked the beginning of an intense period of revolution and rebellion against existing governments, leading to the establishment of new nation-states around the world.**	The rise and diffusion of enlightened thought that questioned established traditions in all areas of life often preceded revolutions and rebellions against existing governments. Beginning in the 18th century, people around the world developed a new sense of commonality based on language, religion, social customs, and territory. These newly imagined national communities linked this identity with the borders of the state, while governments used this idea of nationalism to unite diverse populations. In some cases, nationalists challenged boundaries or sought unification of fragmented regions (German nationalism, Italian nationalism, Filipino nationalism, and Argentinian nationalism). Increasing discontent with imperial rule propelled reformist and revolutionary movements. The global spread of European political and social thought and the increasing number of rebellions stimulated new transnational ideologies and solidarities.

KEY CONCEPT 5.4: GLOBAL MIGRATION	Migration in many cases was influenced by changes in demographics in both industrialized and unindustrialized societies that presented challenges to existing patterns of living.
As a result of the emergence of transoceanic empires and a global capitalist economy, migration patterns changed dramatically, and the numbers of migrants increased significantly.	Migrants relocated for a variety of reasons (manual laborers, specialized professions, etc.). The new global capitalist economy continued to rely on coerced and semi-coerced labor migration, including slavery, Chinese and Indian indentured servitude, and convict labor. The large-scale nature of migration, especially in the 19th century, produced a variety of consequences and reactions to the increasingly diverse societies on the part of migrants and the existing populations.

Important Themes, Terms, and Concepts

The list below shows important themes, terms, and concepts that you should be familiar with on the WHAP exam. Please don't memorize each concept now. Place a check mark next to each topic as it is studied and refer to this list as often as necessary. After you finish the review section, reinforce what you have learned by working the practice questions at the end of this chapter. The answers and explanations provide further clarification into the perspectives that shaped new thoughts and technological innovations of the modern world.

Themes, Terms, and Concepts You Should Know	
SOCIAL	
Term/Concept	**Brief Description**
Middle class	A position in the economic hierarchy between those considered wealthy and those considered poor. In the Modern Era, this tended to be merchants that arose through trade.
Urbanization	A demographic movement from rural to city centers.
Suffragette criticism of patriarchy	Suffragettes criticized patriarchy, arguing that men and women had similar intellectual abilities. Suffragettes also argued for women's rights to vote, inherit property, and be able to divorce.
Seneca Falls Convention (1848)	A convention run by suffragettes in the 1830s. It called for women's rights to vote, inherit property, and be able to divorce. The document they provided was the Declaration of Sentiments and was modeled after the Declaration of Independence.
POLITICAL	
Term/Concept	**Brief Description**
Parliamentary democracy	A form of government based on representation through voting from the general public.
Women's suffrage	A movement for women to get the right to vote in national and local elections.
Unions	A voluntary group of workers joined together to collectively bargain for higher wages, fewer working hours, and better working conditions.

Continued

POLITICAL	
Term/Concept	Brief Description
Bureaucracy	The offices created in government in order to manage different activities in society such as irrigation.
Radicalism: socialism, Marxism, anarchism	Movements that aimed to change the society by uprooting basic conventions and structures. **Socialism** called for the government to narrow the gap between rich and poor. **Marxism** called for a utopia of egalitarianism. **Anarchism** expressed a distrust of all authority and called for a "collective peer governance" for farming communities.
Open Door Policy	Policy made by the U.S. and European powers to divide up China into trade regions in the 1890s.
Taiping Rebellion (1850 to 1864)	A rebellion in China led by Hong Xiuquan to topple the Qing Dynasty and replace it with a Christian government. He claimed to be the long-lost brother of Jesus.
Boxer Rebellion (1899 to 1901)	A rebellion in China of traditional Confucian farmers against the Qing Dynasty and western incursions into China.
Matthew Perry and the Opening of Japan	Matthew Perry came to Japan and forced the Tokugawa Dynasty to open up to trade with the West through naval superiority.
English "Raj" over India	The English East India Tea Company established itself in India. Then its military under John Clive used the company's military to take over regions. This led to the British imperialism of India or the "Raj."
Sepoy Rebellion (Indian Rebellion) (1857)	An uprising in India. The English used local Indians in the military. When they tried to encase their shells in pork casing, the Muslim Indians rebelled against the cultural imperialism.
Boer Wars (1899 to 1902)	The wars in South Africa between the British, Dutch settlers, and Zulu tribes. The British won the rights to the gold mines, but they allowed the Dutch to establish racial control over the natives.
Opium Wars (1839 to 1842; 1856 to 1860)	The wars between China and Britain. Britain faced an imbalance of trade with China over silk and tea, so Britain sold opium to the Chinese. The Chinese foreign minister Lin Xezu closed the ports. This led to Britain attacking the Chinese fleet for access. The result was the Treaty of Nanking, in which Britain got access to Chinese ports.
Dutch East India Company	A mercantile company under the Dutch. They would buy and sell goods in Eastern Africa and India for the Netherlands.
British East India Company	British mercantile company that bought and sold goods in the Indian Ocean and the Chinese region. The British East India Company established a base in India. Under John Clive, it would expand outward to colonized India.
Latin American nationalism and Simon Bolivar	Simon Bolivar led a nationalist movement in South America to free the Creoles from Spanish control. He advocated for a Gran Columbia that would unite the countries into a federal union.
Berlin Conference (1884)	A conference headed by Germany and its chancellor, Otto von Bismarck. He divided up the colonial possessions in Africa.
Otto von Bismarck	The chancellor of Germany in the 1870s. He advocated for European imperialism in Africa, but he wanted an orderly division of the land to avoid a European war.
"White dominions"	Areas ruled by settlers from Europe in the colonized world. Examples included Australia and New Zealand.

POLITICAL	
Term/Concept	Brief Description
Meiji Restoration (1868)	The Japanese dynasty after the 1850s. In response to the Americans forcibly opening up Japan to international trade, the Meiji created an industrial state with centralized power.
Sino-Japanese War (1894 to 1895)	The war between Japan and China in the 1890s over Korea and Sakhalin Island. The Japanese won, showing that they had grown in industrial power.
Russo-Japanese War (1904 to 1905)	The war between Japan and Russia in 1906 over Manchuria. Japan won the war, gaining areas for oil.
Collapse of Ottoman Empire	The Ottoman Empire started to decline during the late 1800s when the Egyptians, Greeks, and Bosnians broke away due to nationalism. The empire collapsed after World War I.
Crimean War (1853 to 1856)	A war in the 1850s between the Russians, British, and French over control of the Turkish peninsula and the Dardanelles.
Egyptian, Bosnian, and Greek nationalist movements	Three nationalist movements that caused a fragmentation of the Ottoman Empire.
Tanzimat reforms (1839 to 1876)	The Turkish attempts to reform the Ottoman Empire. The purpose was to modernize the Ottoman Empire with new forms of science and industrialization.
Young Turks	A group of leaders in the Ottoman Empire in the late 1800s. They wanted to modernize the Ottoman Empire by advocating for science, industrialization, and separation of church and state.
IDEOLOGICAL	
Term/Concept	Brief Description
The Enlightenment (1685 to 1789)	An intellectual and philosophical movement in Europe that stressed rationalism. Its end result was to stress the need for a social contract between the government and the people promising to protect individual natural rights.
American Revolution and natural rights (1765 to 1783)	The American Revolution against the British was justified as a rebellion to protect the natural rights of people entitled by birth. These included the rights to life, liberty, and pursuit of happiness.
The Declaration of the Rights of Man (1789)	France's Declaration of the Rights of Man was similar to the Declaration of Independence. It stressed natural rights and universal rights to all people in and outside of France.
Romanticism	An artistic and poetic movement that stressed the identity of people being rooted in their ethnicity and nationality. This movement justified many of the rebellions against outside powers in the 1800s and 1900s.
Utilitarianism	A philosophical belief system developed in the 1700s by Jeremy Bentham and John Stuart Mill. They argued that good and bad behavior can be determined by weighing the consequences of pleasure and pain.
Realism	A philosophical school that stressed the need to look at the realistic consequences of decisions.
Pragmatism	A philosophical school of thought in late-1800s America that stressed that we should do what logically works best.
Nationalism	A social belief system that stresses a person's identity as rooted in the nation-state. This leads to extreme pride in one's identity as based on national identity.
"White Man's Burden"	A poem written by Rudyard Kipling used to justify the American colonization of the Philippines. He argued that Americans had a responsibility to civilize people in the developing world.

Continued

TECHNOLOGICAL	
Term/Concept	Brief Description
Steam engine	A technology for transportation based on the use of coal and steam.
Coal	A mineral that can be used for creating extreme heat. This was used to create steam, which was used to cause movement in machines.
Gas	An energy created from fossil fuels that allowed for increased transportation.
Electricity	An energy that is created from the use of coal. This allows for the increased heating of water and the use of steam for movement.
Fossil fuels	The use of coal and oil for energy. Fossil fuels are natural energies based on the remains of living organisms.
Internal combustion engine	A heat engine that uses gas to produce heat to move an object.
Steel and the Bessemer process	A British process of taking minerals and melting them down together. Cold air would then be blown onto the molten material to cool into steel.
Transcontinental railroad	A transportation system that would stretch over an entire continent or nation. This was used by governments to create a national transportation system for markets.
Russia's Trans-Siberian Railway	Russia created a railroad system that connects from Southeast Asia to Moscow through Mongolia.
ECONOMIC	
Term/Concept	Brief Description
Cottage industry	The model of investment and production before the Industrial Revolution. The principle was that an individual would produce a high-quality item over a period of time.
Adam Smith	The economic philosopher and founder of capitalism, Adam Smith wrote *The Wealth of Nations*, which advocated for a competitive economic system based on laissez-faire government (minimal government).
Laissez-faire economics	The economic philosophy that the government should have a minimal role or intervention in the economy. The majority of economic activity should be based on free-market competition.
David Ricardo and comparative economics theory	An economic philosopher who supported a competitive market system between nation-states, David Ricardo argued to lower tariffs to increase competition in order to raise the supply of goods and choices for consumers.
Natural resources from Latin America and South America	Latin American countries provided coffee, bananas, wheat, beef, and sugar to the international market in the 1800s. South American countries provided gold and diamonds.
First Industrial Revolution—coal (1840 to 1870)	Coal was the fuel used to drive the First Industrial Revolution.
Second Industrial Revolution—from steam to gas (1870 to 1914)	The Second Industrial Revolution used gas and electricity for fuel.
Irish potato famine (1845 to 1851)	The main crop in Ireland was the potato. The natural blight of the potato caused a massive number of deaths in Ireland. This led to a mass immigration to the U.S.

Chapter Review

WHAP Period Five covers c. 1750 to c. 1900, when humans entered a period of forming new attitudes, ideas, and values about themselves, others, and their surrounding world. It was the start of the modern world as we know it today. So what changed? Before we discuss this important turning point in history, let's begin by reviewing a concept that we discussed in Chapter 6: worldview.

Expanding Your Understanding of Worldview

The Age of Enlightenment changed how humans perceived the world, known as *worldview* or point of view. What do I mean? Well, a worldview is simply a set of values that people believe about how the world operates. It usually challenges human perspectives from their previous understandings about the world. Points of view are often opinions of a person or group of people with a social status who frequently have an agenda (political, social, or religious). For the purpose of the WHAP exam, the worldview of the people who lived during this time period is critical to understanding the mindset of the people who were inspired by the rise of new political philosophies of the Enlightenment.

TEST TIP: When studying for the WHAP exam, it's important to understand the worldview for particular time periods. If you understand the point of view of people in the context of a specific time period, you will understand why certain events took place.

Ask yourself the following questions as you work through the material in this chapter.

- <u>Who</u> is making the statements and why?
- Who is the <u>audience</u> for these statements? (Keep in mind that part of the audience will be people with opposing perspectives.)
- What is the <u>purpose</u> of giving this point of view?
- What is the <u>effect</u>, or bigger significance, about what this point of view did?

Now, let's review the worldview during the Age of Enlightenment that was discussed in Chapter 8 (pp. 149–154).

The Enlightenment (c. 1685 to c. 1789)

As discussed in Chapter 8, the Enlightenment was an intellectual movement that was sparked by the Scientific Revolution and humanism. Prior to enlightened thinking, people believed that authorities were necessary to maintain social and political order. In the Middle Ages, scientists, philosophers, and ordinary citizens believed that the best source of knowledge was through religious and monarchical authorities.

Then 17th-century thinkers, philosophers, and writers began to question some of the social and political problems of the time and developed the theories of the Enlightenment based on reason, logic, and humanism. Enlightenment thinkers believed that reason, logic, and knowledge could change the world. The enlightened ideas led to European revolutions in Prussia, Austria, and France, where monarchies had more efficient militaries and stronger trade systems, but the conflicts of enlightened ideas later impacted America, France, Haiti, and Russia.

How did the Enlightenment change the way that the world would act? It started with a revolution. An economic revolution—industrialization!

The Industrial Revolution (c. 1840 to c. 1870)

The Industrial Revolution was a major economic revolutionary turning point in world history.

Critical Thinking Question: Why was the Industrial Revolution so groundbreaking?

Most people tend to think of the Industrial Revolution as a series of inventions that were created by brilliant individuals. And although this is true, it was not the underlying reason why the Industrial Revolution was so significant. Rather, the Industrial Revolution was important because it created a massive change in how humans discovered and used energy to make life easier and more efficient.

Heads Up: What You Need to Know

On the WHAP exam, you must be familiar with the significance of the Industrial Revolution—its causes and consequences. Some of the reasons that led to the rise in industrialization include: Europe's demographic changes including urbanization with factories; improved agricultural production; scientific innovations; the distribution of natural and other resources (coal, iron, and wood); trade with foreign resources; wealthy economies; and improved water transportation.

Industrialization spurred new innovations to increase human efficiency and gave rise to mechanized and commercial productivity. Although industrialization emerged during the 19th century, it did not happen all at once. As new innovations were invented, industrialization expanded in phases. For the purpose of the WHAP exam, we will discuss the Industrial Revolution in two separate phases: the First Industrial Revolution (1840–1870) and the Second Industrial Revolution (1870–1914).

Key Facts about the First Industrial Revolution

Agricultural revolution. The story does not start in the urban centers, as most people think. Rather, the Industrial Revolution really started as an agricultural revolution. As discussed in Chapter 8, 18th-century landowners in Britain and Northern Europe realized that they could produce high-yield crops by using a new system of crop rotation to maximize harvests. First, they started with a three-field rotation and then moved to a four-field rotation. Landowners would grow different crops on each of the different fields, and rotate crops so that one field would lie fallow, or unused. This process allowed the soil to become replenished with nutrients. Landowners benefitted from the increased productivity, and cities benefitted from the increased supply of food.

Displacement. Up until this time, landowners and peasants had an implicit agreement using the *open-field system.* Peasants (and *serfs*) would "squat" on the land (live on the land), and help to maintain the landowner's property (and were allowed to consume the excess agricultural food products). The emphasis was not on who owned the land, but rather on the common benefit to all. Wealthy landowners wanted to use every square inch of land for production, so they would enclose the land and keep peasants out—called the *enclosure movement.* Where would these individuals relocate to make a living? Simple. People started the process of **urbanization,** or movement into the cities. This meant a huge increase in the labor force in cities like London.

But, now comes the next question: What were all these people going to do? The answer is that landless people searched for work in city factories. Cities had just become the centers of a booming 19th-century industrialization movement.

Did you know? A central historical question in this time period is why did the Industrial Revolution first start in Britain? One of the primary reasons that Britain was the first to industrialize may have been accidental. In the Northern part of Britain, huge natural deposits of worthless, ugly, and dirty black rocks were discovered. Well, at least that was the case up until the 1600s. Those horrible-looking rocks were actually coal, a combustible natural resource. The English discovered that if you heat up these rocks, a substantial amount could generate enough fuel to power iron machines. This connection between coal, heat, and the English inventions of machinery replaced wooden hand tools. More and more commercial factories began using coal and iron machines to increase productivity.

Inventions

The following table details important technological inventions that helped to start the Industrial Revolution.

Invention	Inventor	Importance
Spinning jenny	James Hargreaves (1760)	Allowed for spinning multiple threads together, thus reducing the amount of work needed to produce cloth.
Steam engine	James Watt (1765)	The steam engine was the first type of engine to power early locomotives and machinery in factories. It changed the world from manual and animal-pulled power to high-pressure steam for engine power to transport people and goods throughout the world. The steam engine used coal to create steam and drive movement.
Steamships		Steamships ran on the same principle as steam engines, using coal to create steam for faster and more efficient transportation over long distances.
Cotton gin	Eli Whitney (1793)	The cotton gin, invented by Eli Whitney, one of the most famous of the industrial inventors, sped up the process of weaving cotton to make clothing. This reduced the cost of clothing so that even the poorest populations could afford to wear cloth.

Key Facts about the Impact of the Industrial Revolution

Increased productivity. The result of industrialization showed a dramatic increase in the production of modernized goods, particularly textiles (clothing and rugs), and a rise of factory manufacturing. In addition, the British discovered that coal could be used to generate heat and other innovations. In major cities, inventors discovered that they could use water to power machines for producing textiles. Factories were built using the spinning jenny to produce mass quantities of textiles.

Inventions dramatically changed the economic model for producing merchandise. During the Post-Classical Age, the model for creating goods was the **cottage industry,** or "putting out system." Typically, an investor would provide money to a single individual to make one quality product. For example, factory owners would manufacture sweaters made from farm textiles like wool or cotton. The result of the Industrial Revolution was a dramatic increase in the interest of mass-producing goods and items. Hundreds of goods that previously required using human labor from the farmlands had moved into factories in the cities.

Improved transportation. Britain was a world colonial and maritime power that could easily manufacture, market, and ship raw and finished products. The island nation had access to ports and waterways through which products could be shipped more cheaply than using land transportation. Steamships were used to transport these goods to the rest of the world for trade. Remember that the British had limited space on an island. The British created a system whereby railroads would run on steam to transport coal to other cities. By using the railroad for transportation, laborers could travel to cities for jobs.

Demographic changes. The first years of the Industrial Revolution resulted in hardship for millions of people who were forced to change their lifestyles when they moved from rural communities to urban centers. For example, the population of London more than doubled from c. 1800 to c. 1850, but birth rates fell as people moved from rural to urban centers.

Note: The negative impact of the First Industrial Revolution is discussed on pp. 178–179.

Capitalism

Let's take a look at the new ideologies of economics during the Industrial Revolution: **laissez-faire capitalism**, **comparative advantage**, and the negative consequences of industrialization. But before we start, let's recap our discussion of the mercantile theory examined in Chapter 8.

Mercantilism—Pre-Capitalism

1. Nations are built upon national economic interest.
2. Nations should seek out raw resources.
3. Nations should use the raw resources for manufacturing finished goods for trade.
4. Nations should sell these goods to foreign nations to acquire economic wealth.
5. Nations should use their new wealth to invest in militaries and start the process all over again.

Capitalism—A New Economic Theory

A revolution was about to happen in 1776. I am not referring to the violent American Revolution against the British taxation and lack of American representation. This next revolution was started by

Adam Smith, an older gentleman in an English cottage picking up a quill and writing a book called *The Wealth of Nations*. Smith was a social philosopher who truly revolutionized the world with his theory of capitalism.

Heads Up: What You Need to Know

Adam's Smith's theory of capitalism is an important economic concept on the WHAP exam. Smith wrote the first book of political and capitalistic economics, *The Wealth of Nations*. Some say his work on capitalism is one of the most groundbreaking contributions to political economics. Smith argued that mercantilism (the prevailing economic theory prior to the Enlightenment) was based on a flawed understanding of the natural laws of human nature—humans were self-interested individuals. Therefore, mercantilism could never produce real economic progress.

Key Facts about the Laissez-Faire Capitalism Theory

Smith argued the following five counterpoints to mercantilism.

1. Individuals seek out goods and services that should only be governed by the natural forces of supply and demand.
2. Individuals should be allowed to compete at every level of economics in society.
3. This competition should create better quality, lower prices, and new innovations.
4. Individuals should sell to each other both within and outside of their residing nations.
5. Individuals should invest in growing businesses in order to create new innovations instead of wars.

Smith's theory changed the way that people understood economics, the role of government, and the interaction among business owners and their employees. Smith argued for a society that was based on individual competition. This meant a dynamic economic society of individuals creating machines, businesses, and new ideas. The old ideas and traditional institutions soon failed due to competition.

TEST TIP: For the WHAP exam, you should be familiar with Smith's two important economic concepts: the *invisible hand* and *laissez-faire capitalism*.

The invisible hand. Most importantly, Smith wrote about a system of competition built upon an invisible set of natural laws. He referred to them as a sort of invisible hand that organized the economics of society without a controlling organizing agent. An invisible hand means that there are unseen factors in economics, starting with self-interest, that help the economic climate of a nation reach the greatest good for everyone. It may have seemed greedy for wealthy individuals to pursue their own self-interest, Smith admitted. But when they did, the unintentional effect was economic wealth for everyone.

Laissez-faire capitalism. Smith argued for laissez-faire capitalism, an economic theory in which the government did not interfere in the natural system of the economy. If the government did not interfere, the economy would self-regulate and everyone would benefit. In this mindset, the government was more like a referee upholding the rules of the competitive economic game.

Comparative Advantage Theory

Now, let's discuss an important outgrowth of Smith's economic theory. **David Ricardo,** a disciple of Adam Smith, applied Smith's ideas to international trade. Britain had done what all mercantile governments did with international trade—Britain established *tariffs* (taxes) on foreign imported goods. The British did this to protect their local businesses. The tariffs would protect British merchants from foreign competition. Ricardo disagreed; he developed the **comparative advantage theory** in support of free trade
(Note: Comparative advantage is also covered in Chapter 10, p. 239).

Key Facts about the Comparative Advantage Economic Theory

Free trade. Ricardo said that lower tariffs and free trade should create a comparative advantage for each nation. The main point of the comparative advantage was that both nations would benefit from free trade. Free trade was a voluntary interplay among nations that specialized in what they were best at: manufacturing. (As a side note, Ricardo also opposed the *Corn Laws,* which restricted the import of wheat. He said the Corn Laws would be a burden to the agricultural economy.)

Politicians were biased. Britain had established laws to protect its farmers. Politicians during this time period wanted to uphold these laws; otherwise, farmers would vote them out of office. Ricardo argued this was precisely the problem. Politicians were incentivized to make poor economic decisions based on their own political self-interests and not what was best for individuals.

Benefits of free trade. What if free trade opened up among countries? Would it be disastrous? Ricardo argued that there would be no disaster; instead, everyone would benefit. The consumers would benefit from increased competition and the competition would force British farmers to produce mass quantities of crops, or the consequence would be that they might go out of business.

Foreign benefits of free trade. Foreign countries would benefit from free trade because they would have another market in which to sell their goods. Therefore, free trade would eliminate debt problems. As you may remember from the American Revolution and French Revolution, their nations' extreme debt forced them into war. The domestic British market would benefit since farmers who could not keep up with the competition could simply modify what they grew to contend with foreign competition. In other words, competition would benefit everyone and create new, harmonious markets among countries. Hence, free trade had the ability to end wars.

As you can see, the Industrial Revolution led to massive changes in everything from technology to productivity, to demographic movements, to the role of governments, and to new points of view. You might be thinking that the Industrial Revolution was simply a great advantage for societies, and that it created a new sense of stability and peace. Well, not completely.

Negative Impact of Industrialization

Smith's capitalism theory has largely been proven to be true over the last 300 years, but in the 18th century, industrialization had several disadvantages. Although industrialization created increased productivity and extraordinary wealth for business owners, it also divided social classes between the rich and the poor. Socialist movements began to emerge after the following negative effects of industrialization.

Key Facts about the Negative Impact of Industrialization

Division of classes. The Industrial Revolution created enormous and unprecedented amounts of wealth for elite classes, but divided social classes between the rich and the poor. Other social classes were beginning to take shape during this period: the working class and the middle class.

Poor living and working conditions. Little was done to improve conditions for the working class and poor populations. Some workers and supporters began to protest poor working conditions:

- Factory workers had no government legal protections.
- People working in industrial cities witnessed horrible, unsanitary working conditions.
- Laborers were being injured due to unsafe working conditions in factories.
- Laborers were overworked and forced to work 12–14 hour shifts, 6 days a week. The work tended to be repetitive and monotonous.
- Children were exploited working as young as 8 years old for what is equivalent to about $1.50 per week.
- Laborers were underpaid. Men were paid what is equivalent to about $6.00 per week, and women were paid half that amount.
- The housing for the families of wage-earners consisted of dark, crowded, and unsanitary tenements.

Unhealthy conditions caused black lung disease. One of the most famous examples of the poor working conditions was that of a coal miner. Miners seeking coal would go deep into the earth. Children were usually sent first since they were small and could fit into the holes in the ground. Mine caverns were known to easily collapse, and stored methane in the earth could easily lead to mine explosions. But the worst part of the work was the accumulation of dust in the tight spaces. This dust would get into the miners' lungs. The resulting *black lung disease* would literally suffocate a miner over several years.

Socialism. The greatest and longest-lasting impact of industrialization was socialism (see below). While historical precedents exist for socialism from the early Christians, socialism was a response to industrial capitalism that emerged in the second half of the 19th century.

Socialism

The negative working conditions led to several responses by society starting with labor unions and socialist radicals, but the greatest response to industrial capitalism that emerged in the mid-19th century was **socialism.** Social and political movements were gaining momentum in every nation.

Labor unions arose as a way for workers to negotiate with the owners of businesses. Workers organized and used their labor power to stop productivity. The "strike" stopped the owners' ability to produce mass quantities of goods, and profits plummeted. The labor unions hoped to eventually force business owners to raise wages, limit workers' hours, and improve working conditions. Unions also organized to persuade politicians to create laws favorable to the workers. These efforts eventually led to reforms for greater expansion of suffrage and voting for the common person.

Socialist radicals. Radicals argued that the political system and unions could not cure the underlying problem in a society of economic competition. For socialist radicals, every temporary solution simply steered owners to use their self-interests and powers to find another way to oppress workers and exploit laborers.

Socialist Movements

The following radical socialist movements responded to industrial capitalism.

Group	Known For	Description
Utopian socialists	A movement to form new societies.	**Utopian socialists** argued that the only solution was to create a new society. Typically, they formed cooperative "model societies" that emphasized socialist cooperation instead of capitalist competition. These included New Harmony and Brooks Farm in the United States. These societies attempted to create small communities based on principles of cooperation, sharing, and complete equality (similar to the hippies who built communes in the wilderness in the 1960s).
Marxist socialists	A movement to overthrow capitalism. The beginning of communism.	**Marxist socialism** was founded by Karl Marx, a scientific socialist who wanted to overthrow capitalism. He asserted that utopian socialists were simply too naïve and idealistic. According to Marx, to achieve real change, one had to understand the laws of society and that society developed through competitive groups of people. Marx identified two major groups: the **bourgeoisie** and the **proletariat.** The bourgeoisie owned factories and businesses or the means of production. The proletariat were the workers. The bourgeoisie would pursue their self-interests by exploiting the labor of workers and using that surplus profit to make more wealth. Eventually, the only way for the bourgeoisie to maximize their profit would be to replace workers with technology and machines. Without a way to support themselves, workers would have to resort to a revolution to change society. Once they rebelled against such an oppressive system, the workers would want to find an alternative to the competitive economy that led to their disaster. So they would turn to a system that was not dependent on money, wealth, competition, or the use of other people's labor. This new system would be the perfect sharing community or **communism.** Karl Marx and Friedrich Engels wrote *The Communist Manifesto* (1848), which outlined modern scientific socialism.
Anarchists	A movement to dismantle an industrial society.	**Anarchists** were another form of radicalism. Anarchists agreed with socialists and communists that the competitive economic system was a disaster for workers, but they claimed that the reason for this problem was not economic competition. Rather, anarchists believed that the problem was all forms of authority over people. Capitalism was inherently flawed for producing economic robber barons. But socialists and communists only ended up creating their own oppressive authorities to solve the economic problems. Anarchists argued for a deconstruction of an industrial society. They wanted to return to small farming communities and wanted these communities to be governed by citizens of equal authority who could debate issues and make decisions in local town halls.

Group	Known For	Description
Women suffragists	A movement to demand equal rights for women.	**Suffragists** began to demand a greater role for women in the public sphere. Men had defined women's roles as mothers and child caregivers ever since the sedentary societies. During the Industrial Revolution, gender roles became defined, similar to the division of labor. A man was defined as a public person who had an aggressive nature and was best suited for industrial competition. A woman was defined as a private person who had a nurturing disposition that made her suitable to perform duties at home for her children and her husband. At first, the suffrage participants were radicals and extremists, but as the movement gained momentum, there were two groups of suffragists: radical suffragists and moderate suffragists. This gender role did not necessarily apply to all women, and the overall division of the gender roles was distinctly defined. For example, poor women were expected to go into the factories to work. This was challenged by suffragists, who argued that women were equal to men intellectually and deserved a participating role in society. In Britain, this meant a militant movement of suffragists who demanded the right to vote. In the United States, women leaders joined together in the 1830s at Seneca Falls. They wrote a **Declaration of Sentiments,** which was modeled after the Declaration of Independence. Women demanded the rights to vote, inherit property, divorce, and receive higher education. Suffragists eventually won the vote. But it would be the **feminist movement** in post WWII who would challenge gender roles as social constructs.

TEST TIP: On the WHAP exam, you should be familiar with Marxism and the women's suffragist movement. These are key social concepts of the 19th century.

The Second Industrial Revolution

The Second Industrial Revolution spread out from Britain to Central Europe and the United States, and then to the globe. New technologies in energy (electricity), communication (telephones), and transportation (automobiles, railroads, and airplanes) changed the way humans looked at their role in the world.

Britain. The first Industrial Revolution formed in Britain through the rise of urbanization, use of coal, and new industries.

Germany. The German kaiser pursued industrialization by building up the military and investing in public programs. This allowed the kaiser to maintain public power while protecting the conservative interests of the Junker landowning class.

United States. In the U.S., the federal government used its investment power to build up a transcontinental railroad and incentivize immigrants to settle the western part of North America.

Key Facts about Important Scientific Innovations

Transportation and communication. By the late 1800s, there were some common patterns in how countries became industrialized. Most countries invested in national transportation and communication systems, like trains and telegrams. Many nations incentivized or moved people into urban centers for high-volume labor production. Nations created environments to build their innovations, or those of other nations.

Electricity. In the late 1800s, a second Industrial Revolution was sparked through the increased and innovative use of electricity. Electricity was now used to power mass production, and thanks to Thomas Edison's light bulb, it was possible to provide light for longer days of production. New business organization models were created. Henry Ford created the assembly line, which organized workers through specialized labor. This meant that individual workers would become skilled in one task and then repeated it over and over again. This was so successful that workers in Ford's factories produced a car every 90 seconds on average. The combination of both a new energy and new labor organization led to an economic takeoff in industrial productivity.

Medical science. New innovations influenced other significant areas of life, such as medical science. Before the industrial era, doctors were typically not held in high esteem. Why? Doctors operated under what was called the *fluids theory*. This assumption was that the human body was held in balance through four basic fluids: phlegm, black bile, yellow bile, and blood. If a person was sick, the solution was to put the fluids back in balance. The way to do this was by cutting a slit in a person's arm and allowing the poisoned fluid to drain. However, this theory was both flawed and dangerous. It would dehydrate individuals, causing them to become more ill. But the Industrial Revolution led to new scientific approaches to medicine, and by the early-20th century a new model of medical science arose called *germ theory*. The germ theory claimed that diseases were caused by the spread of bad germs. This meant that there was a need for new medicines and for clean environments such as medical centers and hospitals.

Did you know? In the 19th century, many people died from unsanitary hospitals and disease. **Florence Nightingale**, from Italy, was the driving force to improve unsanitary conditions in hospitals. During the Crimean War (1853–1856), Nightingale's efforts to sanitize the hospital (bedding, clothing, water, etc.) dramatically improved soldiers' survival rate.

Europe's New Imperialism (1870 to 1914)

As you can see, the issues and events that took place during Period Five built on each other, or were a consequence of each other. This is definitely the case with European imperialism. So what is imperialism?

Imperialism is when a stronger country uses power and control to take over foreign territories by way of military force or economic control. Imperialism has been a form of political control since ancient times. The term *imperialism* was first used to describe when nations took over land, roughly between c. 1500 to c. 1800. In the late 1800s, a new wave of imperialism emerged as the great European powers turned their sights to other continents of the world. The leading great powers of this period, Britain and France, made the largest additions to their colonial domains, but Belgium, Germany, Austria-Hungary, Russia, and Italy also turned their sights to other continents of the world in Africa and Asia. This new wave of imperialism involved some of the same powers (Portugal, Spain, Holland, Britain, and France), but Spain and Portugal were minor powers in the new wave of imperialism. Even the United States was not immune to imperialistic fever and moved across the Pacific to seize the territories of Hawaii and the Philippines.

The new imperialism was a continuation of the changes that took place during the period of industrialization.

Heads Up: What You Need to Know

Industrialization led to a few major results that you should remember for the WHAP exam.

- Nation-states centralized power as governments formed rules and regulations for economic market transactions.
- New technologies and innovations led to mass production and the need for more raw resources.
- Europeans developed a sense of cultural superiority based on their new ideas and innovations.

New developments from imperialism and industrialization led to Europe's ability to expand into different parts of the world. It is important to remember this because students often make the mistake of believing that Europeans dominated places like Africa and Asia ever since the Age of Exploration, but they didn't. In fact, it was unclear if Europeans would be able to control major parts of the world until about the 1800s. So what changed?

TEST TIP: Keep the following major changes in mind when thinking about what made it possible for Europeans to expand and control parts of Africa and India at the end of the 19th century.

- Weaponry: Industrialization led to the mechanization of weapons and the introduction of fully automatic weaponry such as the Gatling gun and the Maxim gun.
- Medical science: Industrialization led to changes in medical science that allowed for the discovery of medicines such as quinine, which slowed the effects of malaria.
- Transportation: Industrialization led to both the innovation of and the desire for new forms of transportation such as steamboats and railroads. This made it possible to transport the military much more quickly into remote areas.

Key Facts about New Imperialism

Conflict over Africa. The result of these major changes in weaponry, medical science, and transportation was a rapid European expansion into Africa. In fact, it was so rapid that the European powers feared that they would end up in a global war, not with the African kingdoms, but with each other. This struggle for control of Africa led to the famous **Berlin Conference.** The chancellor of Germany, **Otto von Bismarck,** organized all of the European leaders to agree to a partitioning or separating of Africa that would draw distinct boundaries for European conquests. However, one group of leaders was missing from the conference—the Africans.

China's resistance. You might think that Europeans were able to conquer all parts of the world. Actually, they had a very difficult time getting into Asia, especially China. In the late 1790s, the British sent Ambassador **Lord Macartney** to the Chinese court of **Qianlong** to open up trade between the English and the Qing Dynasty. Macartney came to the court and entered walking backward (a traditional way to approach the emperor). Macartney then performed the *kowtow* (a bow signifying the emperor's superiority). He then asked for trade between Britain and China, and he was promptly thrown out of the court. For most of this period, the English continued to have a very difficult time expanding into China.

Did you know? Until this time, China was known around the world as a superior civilization. After the presence of the British in China during the Opium Wars, the global perception of China changed, and the world realized that China's government, economy, and military were weak.

China's resistance to trade. In the 1830s, the British sold **opium** to the Chinese. Chinese ports started to have multiple opium dens spring up along the coastline, and the Chinese leaders started to fear that their local population was being corrupted by English influence. China was faced with a choice: It could allow the trade in opium (with regulations) or it could stop the trade of opium. China's foreign minister decided to cut off all trade and forbid the sale of opium. Britain used this as a pretext for what it really wanted, and the **Opium Wars** (1839–1842) erupted. English papers claimed that the Chinese were barbaric and would not allow for free trade, and Britain sent its industrialized navy to destroy the Chinese navy. The end result was that China was forced to sign the **Treaty of Nanjing.** While Britain did force China to open up its ports to English trade, the British could not conquer China or force the Chinese into submission.

Japan's resistance to trade. A similar event took place just outside of China in Japan. For centuries, the Japanese had been isolated under the **Tokugawa Dynasty,** but in 1853 **Commodore Matthew Perry** from the United States used the U.S. Navy to force the Japanese to open up their markets to trade. The United States could not control Japan, but it did influence Japan to enter into the global marketplace of trade.

Open Door Policy. Eventually, this led to a global agreement, more about trade than about territorial acquisition. The U.S. and the European powers wanted to open up China to trade. China's population was about 100 million at the time. This was a huge consumer market for Western goods, but the Western powers had difficulty influencing China. Instead, U.S. Secretary of State **John Hay** created an agreement with China called the **Open Door Policy,** which allowed for equal trading privileges among countries. Even today, this policy is the foundation of foreign policies in Asia. The policy called for trade zones in China whereby each Western power would have access to ports open for trade in China.

Heads Up: What You Need to Know

For the WHAP exam, what do you need to remember about the new imperialism? Remember that the techniques of imperialism were not the same during this time period, and imperialism was different in every part of the world. Previously, the main purpose of imperialism was domination and control of new territories. But during this new wave of imperialism, the focus was on economics. For example, in Africa and India, the Europeans established more direct control over their conquered territories and utilized raw materials and land. In Asia, Europeans and Americans influenced the regions through global trade and military force.

Global Reactions to Imperialism

Just as European imperialism was different in different parts of the world, the reactions to European imperialism also varied. In some parts of the world, the reaction was to embrace new Western ideas. Other parts of the world tried to block themselves from Western ideas in the hopes of retaining their traditions. Still, there were those who initiated rebellions. In the end, the territories with the greatest success attempted to integrate new ideas into the traditions of the past.

Use the following table to help you remember some of the key ideas about new imperialism.

New Imperialism (1870–1914)		
Types of New Imperialism	**Key Facts about New Imperialism**	**Consequences of New Imperialism**
Sphere of influence—The new imperialist nation gained economic power in a region and acquired all economic rights to trade (i.e., China). **Colonial**—The nation took control over a territory, but made it part of its empire (i.e., Britain in India and France in Indochina). **Protectorate**—The colonial nation allowed the native ruler to remain in power, but the ruling nation made all major decisions (i.e., Eastern European nations controlled by Russia during World War II). **Concession**—The foreign nation was granted permission to make economic gains within the new nation (i.e., Britain built a railroad in the Middle East).	Imperialist leaders were Britain, France, Germany, Italy, Belgium, Russia, and the U.S. Geographic territories that were defeated by foreign nations include: South and Southeast Asia; Sub-Saharan Africa; Latin America. The New Imperialism was more hostile than the first imperialism. It had more bloodshed, racism, and oppression. The focus was on economic gains, large profits with minimum risks. The primary missionaries were Catholic and Protestant.	Negative consequences: economic exploitation, death of Natives from diseases, political divisions, loss of traditions and culture. The new imperialism was focused on exploitation of Africa's raw materials. Africans responded to European imperialism by either trying to work with Europeans (Ethiopians) or rebellion (Herrero). Latin American countries tried to use new "liberal" governments that centralized power and opened their economies for foreign investment. China tried to retain its traditional Confucian hierarchy with limited European access to trade. Japan centralized its empire, accepted Western industrialization, and developed a strong professional navy.

China

China was a good example of attempting to block Europeans' interventions. Chinese philosophers saw the need for a **Self-Strengthening Movement** (1861–1895). During the Qing Dynasty, this movement attempted to modernize China by merging together Western technology with the wisdom of Eastern ideologies. However, the Confucian leaders of the Qing Dynasty feared the possible undermining of the social hierarchy and family (*filial piety*), so the leaders of the movement were imprisoned, but they tried to retain their agricultural empire. Trust me . . . this was not a good idea! Unlike Japan, China remained traditional in its practices of agriculture. This left it behind in the expansion of industrial trade, and it left its military underdeveloped in contrast to Japan's. China's weak military would become a disaster for China when it lost the Sino-Japanese War in 1894–1895.

Japan

The **Meiji Restoration** (1868–1912) was a revolutionary movement that was named after a strong emperor, Meiji. He transformed Japan from a Tokugawa *shogun* (military government) to a nation that adopted Western doctrines (technologies, weapons, etc.). The emperor heavily taxed the daimyo in the farmlands. This forced these leaders to move to the cities. The emperor then rewarded these leaders with positions in the new Japanese parliament. The parliament, in conjunction with the emperor, used Western ideas to build up Japanese industry, but retained the social hierarchy of the emperor, social leaders, and local families. The parliament then used this loyalty to fund investments in factories, mass production, and a new navy. In addition, they used the new navy to expand into China, Korea, and the Eastern Russian region. In winning both the **Sino-Japanese War** (1894–1895) between Japan and China for control of Korea, and the **Russo-Japanese War** (1904–1905) between Japan and Russia, Japan established itself as the dominant imperialistic leader in Southeast Asia.

Latin America

Latin American leaders also tried to intermingle the new industrial ideas with local culture, but their successes were not as evident. **Porfirio Diaz** of Mexico emphasized the philosophy of *positivism* (a philosophical theory stating that true knowledge is only found through derived knowledge free of values). This social, political, and economic point of view stressed science, progress, modernity, and democracy as approaches to build up Latin America. The hope was to eventually create a unified Central and Southern America similar to the United States' system. However, Latin American countries had never progressed beyond their ethnic/class hierarchy inherited from Spanish colonization. Military families retained control over the land and the national armies. This led to a series of military dictators in Latin America who used a combination of science, traditional religious beliefs, and their economic power to build up nationalism and their political power, but they did not further the Latin American countries into successful industrial nation-states.

India

One last movement would become very powerful in the next century—ethnic revolutions. In 1885, India's middle-class population established the **Indian National Congress.** Its stated goal was to create a self-governing, independent India with equal treatment for all citizens. It hoped that one day it could force the British to leave India and free it to enter into the international trading system.

However, the Indian National Congress was divided by internal conflicts. Muslims from India feared a dominant Hindu majority. Some Indian nationals wanted to see India become an industrial power, while others believed it should remain a traditional agricultural nation. Some believed that the Indian nation could not become modernized until it gave up some of its traditional practices, such as child marriage, *saty* (when a widow commits suicide to join her deceased husband), and *thugee* (the legalization of bandits in the northern part of India). Another issue that intensified this division was that there were those in India's middle class who believed that the British presence in India was necessary to maintain social order. Still, it was from this new revolutionary movement that a great leader would emerge, **Mahatma Gandhi,** the well-known 20th-century leader of India's independence movement.

Ottoman Empire

Similarly, ethnic revolutions tore apart one of the longest-lasting empires in global history, the Ottoman Empire. The Ottoman Empire had been formed during the Crusades in the 1500s. It incorporated regions from Northern Africa to the boundaries of modern-day Iraq. By the late 1800s, several ethnic movements struggled to have national sovereignty. The Greeks, Egyptians, and Bosnians all broke away from the Ottoman Empire. By the beginning of the 20th century, the Ottoman Empire was limited to the Anatolian peninsula. European powers saw this as an opportunity to gain control over the important trade waters of the Dardanelles Straits, but the British and the French agreed to hold off for fear of a major war. The Russians, however, saw this area as their sphere of influence and rushed to fill the void so that they could have access to the Mediterranean. This caused a war between the Russians and the British-French alliance, the **Crimean War** (1853–1856). The Crimean War was the first major European war since the Congress of Vienna in 1815. Britain and France felt that Russia was threatening the balance of power in the Turkish-ruled Jerusalem Holy Land. Although Russia had enormous potential in size, it had fallen behind in industrialization and modernization matters compared to other European powers. Russia did not become modernized until 1861 under Tsar Alexander II. The Crimean War quickly led to a Russian defeat and a short lease on life for the Ottoman Turks.

Ottoman Turks

The Ottoman Turks (later known as the Republic of Turkey) tried to reform and modernize. A group of reformers, the **Young Turks,** took power from the sultan. Influenced by Western thinking, these reformers stressed science, a secular government, and minority rights. The Young Turks passed a series of *Tanzimat* laws (reforms) that promised the protection of religious minorities. It appeared that the Young Turks wanted to follow the Western model in economics and government. However, this changed during World War I. The Turks joined the Germans to fight in the First World War. When the Turks were threatened by a possible Russian invasion during the war, the Turks needed a scapegoat. They turned against an ethnic minority in Turkey, the **Armenians.** The Turks feared that the Christian Armenians would betray Turkey and form alliances with the Russians. The Turks instituted a genocidal removal policy of the Armenians that ended with the deaths of over 1.5 million Armenians, called the **Armenian Genocide.** In 1915, almost 2 million Armenians were expelled from the Ottoman Empire through forced deportation.

Heads Up: What You Need to Know

The following is a summary of the common themes and issues for Period Five:

- Industrialization revolutionized the world in the 18th and 19th centuries with new forms of transportation, communication, medicine, weaponry, and power (electricity).
- Economic systems changed from agricultural-based mercantilism to industrial-based capitalism with manufacturing, trade, and commerce.
- New imperialism caused underdeveloped foreign lands to be conquered, leading to transoceanic empires. Carnage and oppression were negative consequences of new empires.
- Socialist movements began to emerge: utopian and Marxist. Anti-imperialist and ethnic movements emerged during this time period.
- Gender roles started to shift as more women worked in industrial factories and started to demand equality.

Chapter Review Practice Questions

The practice questions show the types of questions that may appear on the exam. On the actual exam, the questions are grouped into sets. Each set contains one source-based prompt and two to five questions.

Multiple-Choice Questions

Questions 1–3 refer to the following passage.

Article V The Government of China having compelled the British Merchants trading at Canton to deal exclusively with certain Chinese Merchants called Hong Merchants (or Cohong) who had been licensed by the Chinese Government for that purpose, the Emperor of China agrees to abolish that practice in the future at all Ports where British Merchants may reside, and to permit them to carry on their mercantile transactions with whatever persons they please, and His Imperial Majesty further agrees to pay to the British Government the sum of Three Millions of Dollars, on account of Debts due to British Subjects by some of the said Hong merchants (or Cohong) who have become insolvent, and who owe very large sums of money to Subjects of Her Britannic Majesty.

—Source: The Treaty of Nanjing, Article V, August 1842.

1. Which of the following historical developments best explains the context for the treaty above?
    A. The British colonization and Raj in India during the mid-1800s
    B. The British ambassador, Lord Macartney's, appeal to the Qing Emperor Qianlong to open trade
    C. The British use of its navy to force China to open up to the opium trade in the early 1800s
    D. The British use of mechanized weaponry and railroad transportation to gain successes in imperialism

2. Based on the passage, which of the following best summarizes the result of the Treaty of Nanjing?

   A. China was forced by the Western powers to open to international trade through its port cities.
   B. China remained isolated from Western influence.
   C. China developed an openness to Western technology and values.
   D. China began to expand outward in Southeast Asia to become the predominant leader in that region.

3. Based on the passage and your knowledge of world history, which of the following most accurately expresses the internal Chinese response to British actions?

   A. China opened up to Western ideologies and political democracy.
   B. China expanded into Korea and Southern Russia to establish a national market.
   C. China initiated a self-strengthening reform movement based on openness to ideas in the West but then chose to remain culturally isolated.
   D. Chinese leaders initiated policies that took away power from local agricultural leaders and moved the country toward industrialization.

Questions 4–6 refer to the following passage.

In England, exclusive of Wales, it is only in some of the colliery districts of Yorkshire and Lancashire that female Children of tender age and young and adult women are allowed to descend into the coal mines and regularly to perform the same kinds of underground work, and to work for the same number of hours, as boys and men; but in the East of Scotland their employment in the pits is general; and in South Wales it is not uncommon.

West Riding of Yorkshire: Southern Part — In many of the collieries in this district, as far as relates to the underground employment, there is no distinction of sex, but the labour is distributed indifferently among both sexes, except that it is comparatively rare for the women to hew or get the coals, although there are numerous instances in which they regularly perform even this work. In great numbers of the coalpits in this district the men work in a state of perfect nakedness, and are in this state assisted in their labour by females of all ages, from girls of six years old to women of twenty-one, these females being themselves quite naked down to the waist.

—Source: Excerpt from Great Britain Parliamentary Papers, Vol. XVI, 1842.

4. Which of the following best explains the consequences of the problems illuminated in the passage above?

   A. British workers joined radical movements like communism and anarchism.
   B. British workers believed that the laissez-faire marketplace would solve the problems of workers.
   C. British workers joined unions to collectively bargain for better wages and working conditions.
   D. British economists advocated for the lowering of tariffs to increase trade.

5. Which of the following conditions best explains the reason for the development of economic problems in Britain?

    A. Britain faced a dramatic war debt after engagements with the French over territories in North America.

    B. Britain had a large urbanization of former farmers who were seeking factory jobs in cities.

    C. British developments in diesel engines and mechanical reapers led to small farmers immigrating to the Western Hemisphere in search of new opportunities.

    D. The British middle class demanded more representation through the British parliament in the House of Commons.

6. Which of the following is most similar to the example in the passage above?

    A. The Mongols' conquest and protection of the Silk Roads trade routes for international trading of goods and services

    B. The use of silver for trade of silk between China and Britain during the 1800s

    C. The use of irrigation to create food surpluses in sedentary societies

    D. Transnational companies using cheap labor in the developing world in the 21st century for international trade

Document-Based Question

1 question
60 minutes

Reading Time: 15 minutes (brainstorm your thoughts and organize your response)
Writing Time: 45 minutes

Directions: The document-based question is based on the seven accompanying documents. The documents are for instructional purposes only. Some of the documents have been edited for the purpose of this practice exercise. Write your response on lined paper and include the following:

- **Thesis.** Present a thesis that supports a historically defensible claim, establishes a line of reasoning, and responds to all parts of the question. The thesis must consist of one or more sentences located in one place—either the introduction or the conclusion.

- **Contextualization.** Situate the argument by explaining the broader historical events, developments, or processes that occurred before, during, or after the time frame of the question.

- **Evidence from the documents.** Use the content of at least three to six of the documents to develop and support a cohesive argument that responds to the question.

- **Evidence beyond the documents.** Support or qualify your argument by explaining at least one additional piece of specific historical evidence not found in the documents. (Note: The example must be different from the evidence used to earn the point for contextualization.)

- **Analysis.** Use at least three documents that are relevant to the question to explain the documents' point of view, purpose, historical situation, and/or audience.

- **Historical reasoning.** Use historical reasoning to show relationships among the documents, the topic question, and the thesis argument. Use evidence to corroborate, qualify, or modify the argument.

Based on the documents that follow, answer the question below.

Question 1: Evaluate the causes and effects of European imperialism on the developing world.

Document 1

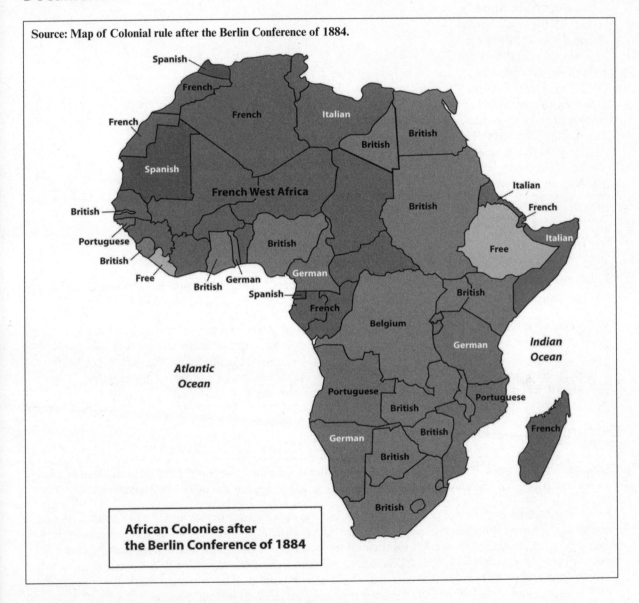

Source: Map of Colonial rule after the Berlin Conference of 1884.

African Colonies after the Berlin Conference of 1884

Document 2

Source: Rudyard Kipling, "White Man's Burden," 1899. A poem about America's moral responsibility to civilize colonized nations of the world.

Take up the White Man's burden—
Send forth the best ye breed—
Go bind your sons to exile
To serve your captives' need
To wait in heavy harness,
On fluttered folk and wild—
Your new-caught, sullen peoples,
Half-devil and half-child . . .
Take up the White Man's burden—
And reap his old reward;
The blame of those ye better,
The hate of those ye guard

Document 3

Source: "Papers of the Royal Niger Company: Standard Treaty," 1886. The British Royal Niger Company was instrumental in the formation of colonial Nigeria.

We understand that the said Royal Niger Company have full power to mine, farm, and build in any portion of our country. We bind ourselves not to have any intercourse with any strangers or foreigners except through the said Royal Niger Company. In consideration of the foregoing, the said Royal Niger Company bind themselves not to interfere with any of the native laws or customs of the country, consistently with the maintenance of order and good government.

Document 4

Source: Ndansi Kumalo, "The Fate of the Ndebele: Ndansi Kumalo, His Story," 1932. Ndansi Kumalo was an African tribesman who played a role in the Ndebele rebellion against the British in Zimbabwe.

So we surrendered to the white people and were told to go back to our homes and live our usual lives and attend to our crops. But the white men sent native police who did abominable things; they were cruel and assaulted a lot of our people and helped themselves to our cattle and goats. Those policemen were not our own people; anybody was made a policeman. We were treated like slaves. They came and were overbearing and we were ordered to carry their clothes and bundles. They interfered with our wives and our daughters and molested them. In fact, the treatment we received was unbearable.

Document 5

> **Source: "Recollection of Nduli Concerning Work on a Plantation Owned by a German Settler," 1897.**
>
> During the cultivation there was much suffering. We, the labor conscripts, stayed in the front line cultivating. Then behind us was an overseer whose work it was to whip us. Behind the overseer there was a jumbe, and every jumbe stood behind his fifty men. Behind the line of jumbes stood Bwana Kinoo himself. . . . The overseer had a whip and he was extremely cruel. His work was to whip the conscripts if they rose up or tried to rest, or if they left a trail of their footprints behind them.

Document 6

> **Source: Sayyid Jamal ad-Din, "Letter to Hasan Shirazi," 1838. Sayyid Jamal ad-Din was a political activist, Islamic ideologist, and founder of Islamic modernism in the Muslim world during the 19th century.**
>
> After this the ignorant traitor, desiring to pacify the people by his futile arguments, pretended that these agreements were temporary, and these compacts were only for a limited period which would not exceed a hundred years! God! What an argument, the weakness of which amazed even the traitors! In short this criminal has offered the provinces of Persia to auction among the Powers of Europe, and is selling the realms of Islam and the abodes of Muhammad and his household to foreigners. But by reason of the vileness of his nature and meanness of his understanding he sells them for a paltry sum and at a wretched price.

Document 7

> **Source: Dadabhai Naoroji, London speech, 1871. Dadabhai Naoroji was an intellectual, educator, cotton trader, and early Indian political thinker.**
>
> *Generally:* A slowly growing desire of late to treat India inequitably, and as a country held in trust. Good intentions. No nation on the face of the earth has ever had the opportunity of achieving such a glorious work as this. I hope in this credit side of the account I have done no injustice, and if I have omitted any item which anyone may think of importance, I shall have the greatest pleasure in inserting it. I appreciate, and so do my countrymen, what Britain has done for India, and I know that it is only in British hands that her regeneration can be accomplished.
>
> *Financially:* All attention is engrossed in devising new modes of taxation, without any adequate effort to increase the means of the people to pay: and the consequent vexation and oppressiveness of the taxes imposed, imperial and local. Inequitable financial relations between Britain and India, i.e., the political debt of 100 million pounds clapped on India's shoulders, and all home charges also, though the British exchequer contributes nearly 3 million pounds to the expenses of the colonies.

Answers and Explanations

Multiple-Choice Questions

1. **C.** The Treaty of Nanjing was signed after the Opium Wars. The British forced the Chinese to open up their ports to international trade. The British had been selling opium to the Chinese. The foreign minister Lin Zexu closed the ports. This incited the British to use their navy to force the Chinese to open up to their trade. The justification given was due to international free trade, but it was more likely due to the imbalance of trade between China and Britain that favored Chinese silk at the time.

2. **A.** China lost the Opium Wars, and the Treaty of Nanjing obligated China to open its ports to British trade.

3. **C.** After the Opium Wars, the Chinese created a reform movement called the Self-Strengthening Movement that pursued Western technology for modernization. But the Chinese leadership feared this would undermine the traditional Confucian beliefs and ended the reforms.

4. **C.** British workers chose a moderate route for reforms of the Industrial Revolution. Unlike many continental countries that chose radical movements, British workers formed unions. The unions used collective bargaining to advocate for workers' higher wages, fewer hours, and better working conditions. The success was in laws that protected women and children workers.

5. **B.** The British Industrial Revolution began with the discovery of coal and the creation of new technological innovations that led to mass production. The movement of small farmers and serfs from rural areas into urban centers provided the labor needed for the new factory work.

6. **D.** The passage is about the use of cheap labor and the effect on women and children. Women and children faced long hours, dangerous conditions, and low pay. The similarity is to the use of cheap labor by transnational companies in the developing world. The use of sweatshop labor has led to the use of female and child labor to create cheap exports to the developed world.

Document-Based Question

DBQ Scoring Guide

To achieve the maximum score of 7, your response must address the scoring criteria components in the table that follows.

Scoring Criteria for a Good Essay	
Question 1: Evaluate the causes and effects of European imperialism on the developing world.	
Scoring Criteria	**Examples**
A. THESIS/CLAIM	
(1 point) Presents a historically defensible thesis that establishes a line of reasoning. (Note: The thesis must make a claim that responds to *all* parts of the question and must *not* just restate the question. The thesis must consist of *at least* one sentence, either in the introduction or the conclusion.)	The thesis must answer all parts of the question while following a line of reasoning. In this question, the thesis has to address BOTH the causes and effects of European imperialism. You must give at least two causes and two effects since the question specifically asked for more than one each. The thesis in the sample response argues that the causes were the European desires for both civilizing developing countries and raw resources. The effects were the subjugation and the dependency that was created for the developing world.

Scoring Criteria	Examples
B. CONTEXTUALIZATION	
(1 point) Explains the broader historical context of events, developments, or processes that occurred before, during, or after the time frame of the question. (Note: Must be more than a phrase or reference.)	The essay begins by discussing the broader context of change in global power since the Classical and Post-Classical eras. The writer lays out how the Europeans gained new navigational technologies from the Yuan Dynasty and argues that the Industrial Revolution also provided a driving force for Europeans to look for natural resources for mass production.
C. EVIDENCE	
Evidence from the Documents **(2 points)** Uses at least *six* documents to support the argument in response to the prompt. OR **(1 point)** Uses the content of at least *three* documents to address the topic prompt. (Note: Examples must describe, rather than simply quote, the content of the documents.)	To receive the highest possible points, the response addresses all seven of the documents and relates the documents back to the thesis. The essay provides a number of specific examples that influenced the documents and uses the indirect rule of management to explain how the British had the intention of civilizing people in the colonies (Documents 2 and 3). The writer also uses the examples of India, tariffs, and salt laws to show how the British created economic dependency in the colony of India. However, the contrasting colonists' point of view was evidenced in Documents 4, 5, 6, and 7 shows that the desire for colonization was not mutual among the local natives.
Evidence Beyond the Documents **(1 point)** Uses at least one additional piece of specific historical evidence beyond those found in the documents relevant to the argument. (Note: Evidence must be different from the evidence used in contextualization.)	To bring the essay together with outside evidence, the writer compares the European imperialism of the 1800s to the motives of the British and the French in the mandate system after World War I. The comparison claims that the British and French were trying to extract oil in the Middle East after World War I, just as they extracted resources from the developing world in the 1800s. Plus, the writer argues that this is a continuous pattern from the 1800s into the 1900s.
D. ANALYSIS AND REASONING	
(1 point) Uses at least *three* documents to explain how each document's point of view, purpose, historical situation, and/or audience is relevant to the argument. (Note: References must explain how or why, rather than simply identifying.)	The essay provides a purpose for most of the documents, and provides a point of view for at least three documents. For example, Kipling's justification for colonization (Document 2), Kumalo's appeal to the public (Document 4), and Jamal al-Din's outrage over colonization (Document 6).
(1 point) Uses historical reasoning and development that focuses on the question while using evidence to corroborate, qualify, or modify the argument. (Examples: Explain what is similar and different; explain the cause and effect; explain multiple causes; explain connections within and across periods of time; corroborate multiple perspectives across themes; or consider alternative views.)	The essay provides a coherent and well-organized argument and uses the historical reasoning of causation throughout the response. The writer also provides a possible counterargument in the second paragraph to provide a modification to the essay. The writer argues that some historians could prioritize the civilization or ideological motive, but also argues that the primary driving force was the desire for extraction of resources for mass manufacturing.

DBQ Sample Response

Europeans had been behind the developments of China and Central Asia throughout the Classical and Post-Classical periods. The sharing of navigational technologies from the Yuan Dynasty in China to Italy and Spain led to European exploration. As European markets grew, the discovery of coal in Britain would lead to the Industrial Revolution and an even greater need for raw resources. Britain, Germany, France, and Russia then used mechanized weapons like the Maxim gun and more efficient transportation like the railroad to create imperial colonies in most of the developing world. For example, see the European colonial divisions in Africa (Document1). The need for resources for mass production led to the European mandate to "civilize" the developing world and utilize their economies in a manner that created dependence through subjugation.

Some historians would argue that the Europeans' primary drive in imperialism was based on the need to civilize the developing world to the Christian, parliamentary, and modern market values of the West. However, this was only the justification for the real purpose of providing raw resources from the developing countries to Europe for mass production.

Europeans did claim that their main purpose in developing colonies in the developing world was for the purpose of creating modern nation-states that could compete in trade markets while establishing orderly governments. Document 2 was written from the point of view of a British poet who tried to justify American and British colonial acquisitions as a way to spread Christian modernism. Kipling argued that the natives in the developing world would one day come to understand that the Europeans and Americans had the best of intentions for the people in the developing world. Document 1 shows how the Europeans attempted to create an orderly system of imperialism in the Berlin Conference under the leadership of the German chancellor Otto Von Bismarck. And, the Europeans could point to their system of management as further proof that they wanted to help local natives. The British would rule their colonies through indirect rule. For example, in India, the British used middle-class Hindus and Muslims to run the daily affairs. There was a military viceroy who was ultimately in charge. The explanation was that the British were in India to build roads, schools, and a modern nation-state ready for trade with the rest of the world.

However, if one were to look to the historical perspective of the local population, you can see that the treatment of the labor force did not show a desire for mutual benefits (Documents 4, 6, and 7). Document 3 was written from the point of view of the company leaders of the Royal Niger Company and used to present a public image of protecting local sovereignty. However, Document 4, written by a local African worker, appeals to the public to understand that the actual European method was to extract labor from the Africans through force. This can be seen in the example of Belgium's use of the Congo. Belgium had Africans work in the mines in dangerous labor conditions. Any complaints by the local population would lead to harsh treatment to force them back into extracting diamonds for the Belgian economy. This is further seen in Document 5, where Africans on German plantations were depicted as suffering from violence through the overseers. This could explain why the African native group the Herero rebelled against the Germans in order to achieve their freedom. These documents and examples demonstrate how the European depiction was contradicted by the native depiction of everyday life.

This then raises the question of what was really causing the European drive for controlling local developing nations. The answer appears to be the need to create dependent markets of raw resources for the European Industrial Revolution. The advent of the Industrial Revolution created newly mechanized forms of production that allowed for mass production of goods. This also allowed Europeans to create automatic weaponry like the Maxim gun. With these new weapons, the Europeans could seek out and exploit areas for resources. Document 6 was written from the point of view of a Muslim from the areas of Iraq and Iran.

He was expressing outrage at the local population for giving up their land and resources to the growing European powers. Document 7 further shows what the Europeans did once they had attained the resources. Document 7 expressed to a British audience that the real reason for the colonial acquisition of India was about using their resources. This can be defended by the example of how Britain used cotton and salt from India for mass production. Britain created tariffs against local Indian farmers' production of cotton. Britain would pass the Salt Laws, stopping Indians from farming and selling salt. These laws created a permanent dependency of the Indian farmer on the British manufacturing system.

Europeans utilized a so called mandate to bring Western culture to the developing world as a justification for extracting resources used for industrialized mass production.

Chapter 10

Period Six: Accelerating Global Change and Realignments (c. 1900 to the Present)

Period Six investigates the turbulent wars of the 20th century and the shift in the balance of world powers.

- World War I (1914 to 1918)
- The Russian Revolutions and the Rise of Communism
- The Post-War Era
- The Road to World War II
- World War II (1939 to 1948)
- Post–World War II
    - The Establishment of Global Organizations
    - The Cold War
    - The 1950s and 1960s
    - The 1970s, 1980s, and 1990s
- Decolonization
- Globalization

Overview of AP World History Period Six

The 20th century opened with amazing hope and inspiration for human progress. Societies had evolved from the Biological Old Regime sources of wind and water to the industrialized sources of coal and electrical power, but the underlying world conflicts that threatened a crisis of war were intensifying.

Before we analyze the threats that led to global wars, let's examine the WHAP curriculum framework and key concepts for Period Six. Use the chart that follows as a guide to help you make mental connections between the key concepts and the topics covered in this chapter.

The information contained in this chart is an abridged version of the concept outline with topic examples. Visit https://apstudent.collegeboard.org/apcourse/ap-world-history/ for the complete WHAP course curriculum descriptions.

AP World History Key Concepts (c. 1900 to the Present)	
KEY CONCEPT 6.1: SCIENCE AND THE ENVIRONMENT **Rapid advances in science and technology altered the understanding of the universe and the natural world and led to advances in communication, transportation, industry, agriculture, and medicine.**	Researchers made rapid advances in science that spread throughout the world, assisted by the development of new technology. There were new modes of communication, including the Internet, radio communication, and cellular communication. New modes of transportation reduced the problem of geographic distance. The Green Revolution and commercial agriculture increased productivity and sustained the earth's growing population, but also spread chemically and genetically modified forms of agriculture. During a period of unprecedented global population expansion, humans fundamentally changed their interactions with the environment. As human activity contributed to deforestation, desertification, and increased consumption of the world's supply of fresh water and clear air, humans competed over these and other resources more intensely. The release of greenhouse gases and other pollutants into the atmosphere contributed to debates about the nature and causes of climate change. Disease, scientific innovations, and conflict led to demographic shifts. Diseases associated with poverty persisted, while other diseases emerged as new epidemics and threats to human survival (**poverty:** malaria, tuberculosis, cholera; **epidemics:** 1918 influenza pandemic, Ebola, HIV/AIDS; **lifestyles:** diabetes, heart disease, Alzheimer's).
KEY CONCEPT 6.2: GLOBAL CONFLICTS AND THEIR CONSEQUENCES **Peoples and states around the world challenged the existing political and social order in varying ways, leading to unprecedented worldwide conflicts.**	Europe dominated the global political order at the beginning of the 20th century, but both land-based and transoceanic empires gave way to new states by the century's end. Emerging ideologies of anti-imperialism contributed to the dissolution of empires and the restructuring of states. Political changes were accompanied by major demographic and social consequences. Military conflicts occurred on an unprecedented global scale. Although conflict dominated much of the 20th century, many individuals and groups—including states—opposed this trend. Some individuals and groups, however, intensified the conflicts. Groups and individuals challenged the many wars, and some, such as Mohandas Gandhi, Martin Luther King, Jr., and Nelson Mandela, promoted the practice of nonviolence as a way to bring about political change.
KEY CONCEPT 6.3: NEW CONCEPTUALIZATIONS OF GLOBAL ECONOMY, SOCIETY, AND CULTURE **The role of the state in the domestic economy varied, and new institutions of global association emerged and continued to develop throughout the century.**	States responded in a variety of ways to the economic challenges of the 20th century. States, communities, and individuals became increasingly interdependent, a process facilitated by the growth of institutions of global governance. New international organizations formed to maintain world peace and to facilitate international cooperation. People conceptualized society and culture in new ways; rights-based discourses challenged old assumptions about race, class, gender, and religion. In much of the world, access to education, as well as participation in new political and professional roles, became more inclusive in terms of race, class, and gender. Political and social changes of the 20th century led to changes in the arts and literature. In the second half of the century, popular and consumer culture became more global.

Important Themes, Terms, and Concepts

The list below shows important themes, terms, and concepts that you should be familiar with on the WHAP exam. Please don't memorize each concept now. Place a check mark next to each topic as it is studied and refer to this list as often as necessary. After you finish the review section, reinforce what you have learned by working the practice questions at the end of this chapter. The answers and explanations provide further clarification into world conflicts and consequences of globalization.

Themes, Terms, and Concepts You Should Know	
SOCIAL	
Term/Concept	**Brief Description**
Suburbanization	A demographic movement of people from urban areas into suburbs. It is usually associated with the growth of the middle class and increasing economic progress.
POLITICAL	
Term/Concept	**Brief Description**
Alliance systems: Triple Alliance and Triple Entente	The two alliance systems in Europe that led up to World War I. The **Triple Alliance** included the Germans, Austro-Hungarians, and Italians. The **Triple Entente** included the Russians, French, and Serbians.
Zimmermann Telegram	A coded telegram dispatched by Germany's foreign secretary that was intercepted by the British. The message was from the German ambassador Zimmermann to the German ambassador to Mexico promising that Mexico would get back land in the southwest U.S. if it entered World War I against the U.S.
Bolsheviks	The leaders of the Russian Communist Revolution led by Vladimir Lenin.
Vladimir Lenin (Russia) (ruled 1917 to 1924)	The leader of the Russian Revolution. He advocated for a communist intelligentsia to lead the poor farmers into the communist revolution.
Joseph Stalin (Russia) (ruled 1929 to 1953)	A leader in the communist revolution. He exploited the differences between Leon Trotsky and Nicolai Bukharin to take power.
Collectivization	A government policy in communist governments to pursue rapid industrialization. Farmers would farm common land and would then be taxed on their produce, and the produce would be sold on the international market to get money for building industrial cities.
Totalitarianism	A type of government that controls all aspects of individual life in order to create social order. It was most used by communist governments in Russia, China, Vietnam, North Korea, and Cuba.
Armenian genocide	The Young Turks during World War I saw the Armenian Christians as an internal threat. The Young Turks argued that the Armenians would join up with the Russians in World War I. The Young Turks tried to eliminate Armenians through exile or murder.
The Fourteen Points	Woodrow Wilson developed a plan after World War I to ensure long-term peace. It included 14 points but is best summarized as follows: ■ Freedom of the seas for trade ■ Open diplomacy ■ No secret alliances ■ Limited production of arms ■ Creation of the League of Nations

Continued

POLITICAL	
Term/Concept	Brief Description
Treaty of Versailles (1919)	The treaty ending World War I. The British and French humiliated the Germans by blaming them for World War I and demanding they pay for all of the war damages.
League of Nations and United Nations	Both were international institutions created after the World Wars. The **League of Nations** was created for collective security. The idea was to stop countries from starting wars by forcing them to follow international laws. The **United Nations** was created as a place for international diplomacy.
Russian communism vs. Chinese communism	Both Russian and Chinese communism attempted to form collectives of farmers. Russians attempted to accomplish this through the rapid industrialization of collective farms. The Chinese tried to maintain traditional farming practices through government-mandated collectivized farming.
Fascism	A political ideology of extreme nationalism. The dictatorial government believes in national and/or racial superiority and in controlling citizens for social order and economic control.
Atlantic Charter (1941)	An agreement between the U.S. and Britain to fight Japan in Southeast Asia in an effort to uphold international rights and free trade against Japanese imperialism.
Nazi-Soviet non-aggression pact (1939)	The Russians made an agreement with Germany at the beginning of World War II. The Germans promised not to invade Russia. The Russians promised the Germans land to mobilize their armies. Hitler broke the pact and invaded Russia, so Russia joined the American and British alliance.
Chinese nationalists: Chiang Kai-shek and Mao Zedong	Chinese nationalists were led by Chiang Kai-shek. They wanted to modernize China with democracy and capitalism. Mao Zedong wanted China to become communist. This led to an internal civil war between Mao Zedong and Chiang Kai-shek. Eventually the communists won in 1949.
Truman Doctrine (1947)	American foreign policy to fund anti-communist groups in Greece and Turkey.
Marshall Plan (1947)	A plan to rebuild Europe after World War II. America provided financial aid to European countries to develop their industrial economies. The purpose was to increase trade in the West in order to avoid poverty and prevent the expansion of communism into Western Europe.
Berlin Airlift (1948)	Russia's Joseph Stalin cut off West Berlin from West Germany. He did this in response to America trying to unify Western Germany under one democratic government and one capitalist economic system. Truman's response was to airlift food and supplies to Western Berlin for a year until Stalin gave up.
Korean War (1950 to 1953)	North Koreans invaded South Korea in order to reunify the peninsula under communism. The Americans responded by supporting the South Koreans. General Douglas MacArthur pushed the North Koreans up to the Yalu River. Then, the Chinese got involved and pushed the Americans back to the 38th parallel.
Nikita Khrushchev (Soviet Union) (ruled 1953 to 1964)	The leader of the USSR after Joseph Stalin. He attempted to reform the Soviet Union after Stalin. He succeeded in developing Russia's cities and heavy steel industries.
Warsaw Pact (1955)	An alliance between Russia and Eastern communist countries against Western capitalist countries.
Leonid Brezhnev (Soviet Union) (ruled 1964 to 1982	The leader of the Soviet Union during the 1970s. He built up the USSR's nuclear arsenal in competition with the U.S. But then he agreed to the SALT talks with the U.S. to reduce overall nuclear arms production.
Fulgencio Batista and Fidel Castro (Cuba)	Fulgencio Batista was the military dictator of Cuba during the 1950s. He was supported by the U.S. Fidel Castro led a revolution that ousted Batista. Castro eventually turned to the USSR for political support.

POLITICAL	
Term/Concept	Brief Description
Cuba's Bay of Pigs Invasion ("Operation Mongoose")	A covert CIA operation planned under Eisenhower and then executed by John F. Kennedy. Cuban exiles would travel from Mexico to the Bay of Pigs in Cuba. The U.S. would provide military air force cover to help the Cuban exiles join with other Cubans to overthrow Castro. But Castro found out before the invasion and was waiting for the exiles at the Bay of Pigs.
Ho Chi Minh, the Viet Minh, and Dien Bien Phu (Vietnam)	Ho Chi Minh was the communist leader of the Viet Minh or liberation army in North Vietnam. It eventually surrounded the French at their fort, Dien Bien Phu, and forced the French to leave Vietnam.
Gulf of Tonkin	President Lyndon Johnson claimed that the Vietnamese had attacked two American battleships, USS C. *Turner Joy* and USS *Maddox*, in international waters. He argued that this justified Americans sending combat troops to Vietnam.
Pentagon Papers	Daniel Ellsberg released these secret documents in 1971, showing that Lyndon Johnson had lied about the scope of the Gulf of Tonkin. The two battleships were within North Vietnamese waters. One ship was attacked with little damage, and the other's radar malfunctioned due to a weather storm.
Great Leap Forward (1958 to 1962)	Mao Zedong tried to collectivize farming by putting people on common farmlands of 10,000 people. This led to a misallocation of resources and the deaths of millions of Chinese in a manmade famine.
Cultural Revolution (1966 to 1976)	Mao Zedong trained young "Red Guards" to go to local villages and put traditional Confucianists on trial for betraying the revolution. This was done to distract from his failure in the Great Leap Forward.
Mikhail Gorbachev (Soviet Union) (ruled 1985 to 1991)	The leader of Russia after 1984, Gorbachev tried to reform communism to make it more like Western socialism.
Glasnost and perestroika	Two reform movements in Russia. Glasnost was meant to provide opportunities to share new ideas. Perestroika was intended to give businesses more freedom for innovation and competition.
Tiananmen Square (1989)	Young Chinese students tried to protest and reform the Chinese communist government. They built a statue honoring the Statue of Liberty in the U.S. The Chinese troops were sent in to crush their rebellion and arrest the leaders.
Developing world vs. developed world	The developing world is largely in the Southern Hemisphere. These countries are starting to industrialize; they tend to have authoritarian governments. Developed countries are industrialized or post-industrial with service economies; they have democratic governments.
Decolonization	The process by which previous colonized countries break away from the imperial European countries.
Mohandas Gandhi (India) (1869 to 1948)	The leader of the non-violent nationalist movement in India. He advocated for using *satyagraha*, or the Hindu spiritual philosophy of using non-violence, to pressure the British to leave India. He was also known as Mahatma, meaning "great soul."
Zionism and Theodor Herzl (Israel)	Theodor Herzl was the leader of the Jewish movement for having a nation-state. The impetus was due to the anti-Semitism faced in Europe and Russia. Herzl believed that if the Jewish people had a nation-state, they would have the protection to stop future attacks on their people.
War for independence in 1948	The Jewish people declared the UN partition plan of Palestine to be valid. Six months later, Israel fought the invading armies of Egypt, Jordan, Syria, and Lebanon. Israel won the war and declared itself an independent state.

Continued

POLITICAL	
Term/Concept	**Brief Description**
Gamal Abdel Nasser and Anwar Sadat (Egypt)	Gamal Abdel Nasser led a coup against the king of Egypt, Farouk. Nasser then led a pan-Arab movement meant to gain Middle Eastern independence from European control and influence. Anwar Sadat was the leader of Egypt during the 1970s. He led the Egyptians in the Yom Kippur War in 1973. Sadat worked with the U.S. and Israel to create a peace agreement at Camp David in 1978.
Camp David Accords (1978)	The meeting between Egyptian President Anwar Sadat, Israeli Prime Minister Menachem Begin, and U.S. President Jimmy Carter. They agreed that Egypt would never again invade Israel if Israel turned over the Sinai Peninsula to Egypt.
Mohammad Reza Pahlavi and Mohammad Mossadegh (Iran)	The Pahlavi family ruled over Iran from 1945 to 1979. The Iranian people elected the socialist leader Mohammad Mossadegh to nationalize the oil companies. The CIA, fearing communist influence, overthrew Mossadegh in 1953 and installed the Pahlavi family back in power.
Ayatollah Khomeini (Iran) (ruled 1979 to 1989)	A Shiite cleric who led the Muslim part of the revolution against the Pahlavi family in the Iranian Revolution in 1979.
Kurdistan Workers' Party (PKK)	A political organization in Turkey that advocates for the right to Kurdish self-determination.
National Liberation Front (NLF)	The Vietnamese nationalist independence movement in South Vietnam. It started as a non-violent movement to oppose U.S.-backed leader Ngo Diem. The NLF eventually became a militant ally to the North Viet Minh. They were called the Viet Cong.
Kenyan African National Union (KANU)	The nationalist independence movement in Kenya led by Jomo Kenyatta.
Apartheid	A racial hierarchy set up in South Africa by the Dutch Afrikaners following World War II. The Afrikaners created a series of laws that defined black South Africans as unequal and segregated them into townships.
Nelson Mandela (ruled 1994 to 1999)	The leader of the black South African movement for equal rights and an end to apartheid. He started with a non-violent movement but then turned to violence after the Sharpeville Massacre. Mandela was put into Robben Island prison from 1964 to 1982. He was then imprisoned in South Africa at Pollsmoor and Victor Verster prisons until 1990. After his release he ran for and won the South African presidency.
African National Congress	The movement created by middle-class Africans at the beginning of the 20th century to create a way to gain independence for Africa from European imperialism.
Institutional Revolutionary Party (PRI)	The Mexican national party started after the Mexican revolution in 1929. It adopted a socialist government and nationalized the country's oil for development.
National Action Party (PAN)	A Mexican political party that emerged to compete with the PRI in the 1990s. Its leader, Vincente Fox, argued for free markets, fewer tariffs, and a privatization of the Mexican government's oil company.
Devolution	The belief that nation-states have grown too large. Since the end of the Cold War, many nationalist movements have argued for the breaking down of nation-states into more regional and local areas of governance.

RELIGIOUS	
Term/Concept	**Brief Description**
Sayyid Qutb (1906 to 1966)	An Egyptian Muslim reformer in the 1950s who argued for a more "pure" Islam based on theocracy. His ideas became the basis of the Muslim Brotherhood, Al-Qaeda, and ISIS.
Egyptian Brotherhood	An Islamic group that started in Egypt as a way to unite Arabs around a "pure" Islamic theocracy. They hoped to move Muslims away from modern secular culture toward a more literal following of the Quran.
Osama bin Laden (1957 to 2011)	A Saudi Arabian Muslim who helped to create and lead the international terrorist group Al-Qaeda, which believes in creating an Islamic caliphate.
Al-Qaeda	A terrorist group made up of Islamic extremists whose objective is to overthrow non-Islamic regimes from North Africa to Southeast Asia.

IDEOLOGICAL	
Term/Concept	**Brief Description**
Imperialism	The control of other countries, especially in the Southern Hemisphere, for the purpose of extracting resources for mass production.
Social Darwinism	A belief based on the theory of natural evolution. Herbert Spencer argued that groups of people inherit genetic traits that make them superior or inferior to other groups.
Terrorism	The use of violence by religious and secular groups against non-military citizens in order to achieve a political goal. The 21st-century examples have been the Muslim groups Al-Qaeda, ISIS, Hamas, and Hezbollah. In the past, the Irish independent movement (Irish Republican Army, or IRA) also used this means against the British for independence.

TECHNOLOGICAL	
Term/Concept	**Brief Description**
Thomas Edison (1847 to 1931)	An American inventor who created the lightbulb. This resulted in more illumination, allowing for factory work to be increased in time and efficiency.
Alexander Graham Bell (1847 to 1922)	An American inventor who created the telephone in 1876, opening up possibilities for more efficient and quicker communication over distances.
Alexander Fleming (1881 to 1955)	An American scientist who discovered penicillin. This form of medicine helped to fight bacterial diseases. It also meant the switch from the fluids theory to the germ theory in medicine.
The Wright brothers	Two American inventors who developed airplane travel in 1903.
Mechanized weaponry	Weapons that were created and mass-produced through the Industrial Revolution. The most deadly were the automatic guns, especially the Maxim gun.
Maxim gun	An automatic gun that could fire multiple rounds without any interruption. This weapon was used in trench warfare in World War I.
Poison gas	Weapon used in World War I by the Germans and French. The most common was mustard gas. This type of chemical warfare was deadly due to its impact on the human biological system.
U-boats	The Germans created this form of naval warfare. It was a submerged ship that could be used to sneak up on battleships and ram them, causing them to sink.

Continued

TECHNOLOGICAL	
Term/Concept	**Brief Description**
Airplanes	During World War I, all countries used this new form of transportation to drop dynamite on the opposing army's trenches.
Tanks	A new technology created by the World War I powers to break the trenches. Tanks were seen as movable fortresses that could cross the field with soldiers on the inside.
Iceboxes	Refrigerated boxes that could be used to keep produce fresh and avoid spoilage.
Atomic bombs: Manhattan Project	A project to break atoms apart in order to create a massive explosive impact including radiation.
Arms race	The development of nuclear bombs by the U.S. and USSR during the Cold War. Both sides would race each other to develop weapons for greater global influence.

ECONOMIC	
Term/Concept	**Brief Description**
Charles Dawes' Plan (1923)	Charles Dawes was a banker after World War I. He developed a plan to lend money to the European allies to develop European industry and consumer markets.
Installment plans	Consumers would buy goods by paying incrementally each month. They would take out a loan from a bank or business and then pay back that loan with interest over time.
Buying on the margin	Investors would borrow part of the price on a stock and pay for a small part directly. Typically, it was a 90% loan and a 10% payment.
Gold standard	Currencies were backed by a hard metal, gold. The purpose was to maintain a balance of trade among countries.
Globalization	A process of connecting global economic and political trade based on lowering tariffs to increase the flow of goods, information, and resources.
Bretton Woods Conference (1944)	A meeting in Bretton Woods, New Hampshire, to establish a global economic system that would be managed by the World Bank, International Monetary Fund, and the American dollar.
International Monetary Fund (IMF)	A global economic institution that sets up rules for free trade and global loans for development.
World Bank	An international economic system that provides loans to developing countries to industrialize in order to increase global trade.
Comparative advantage vs. dependency theory	**Comparative advantage** is an economic theory stating that countries should develop what they do well and trade with the developed world. **Dependency theory** argues that developing countries become dependent on the developed world due to transnational companies exploiting cheap labor in the developing world.
General Agreement on Tariffs and Trade (GATT)	An agreement in 1947 to lower tariffs in order to increase international trade.
European Union (EU)	A common market created in Europe among countries to lower tariffs and create efficient trade between the countries.
Suez Canal	The Suez Canal was a manmade canal between the Mediterranean Sea and the Red Sea through the Isthmus of Suez. The canal was constructed in Egypt by the French. It was seized by the British. In 1957, Gamal Abdel Nasser nationalized the canal for Egypt.

ECONOMIC	
Term/Concept	Brief Description
World Trade Organization (WTO)	An organization created in 1995 among countries to create an international court to assess countries' lowering of tariff rates.
Absolute poverty vs. relative poverty	**Absolute poverty** is the measurement of the poor by the actual minimum amount of money that a person has. **Relative poverty** is the measurement of a person's income in relation to another individual or group.
PEMEX	The Mexican oil company owned by the government. The Mexican government nationalized the oil and tries to use the oil for national development.
OPEC	A group of Arab countries including Venezuela that tried to use oil production to influence global politics. In the 1970s, OPEC reduced oil production to raise gas prices and force political influence on the U.S. and Europe.
NAFTA (North American Free Trade Agreement) and CAFTA (Central American Free Trade Agreement)	Free trade agreements for the Western Hemisphere. **NAFTA** is an agreement between the U.S., Mexico, and Canada to lower tariff rates to increase trade (1994). **CAFTA** is an expansion of this agreement between the U.S. and Central America.

Chapter Review

The changes in the 20th century led to a scientifically and technologically advanced modern world. The design of new machines and technologies helped to mass-produce luxury goods and services, but advancements also altered the environment. Inventor Thomas Edison created the lightbulb, allowing factories, homes, and cities to operate on a power grid much longer into the night. Alexander Graham Bell created the telephone, allowing for quicker and more widespread communication. Alexander Fleming discovered the antibiotic penicillin, leading to a cure for multiple types of diseases. All of these outstanding advancements gave people an expectation that the future was bright, but this would come to an end in 1914. Dormant political and social underlying energies were present around the world, but no one could have anticipated that the developed nations were on the brink of total war.

This chapter covers key events that led to 20th-century world wars, the division and decolonization of territories, the role of fluctuating world economies, and the interconnections of globalization.

World War I (1914 to 1918)

An extreme form of nationalism was emerging in France, Russia, and especially Germany that led to World War I (known as the Great War). When the war erupted in 1914, most of the people in Europe were predicting that new technologies would help to quickly resolve the conflicts. Young men went to war believing that they would return home as heroes for their respective nations. Instead, soldiers soon realized that the war was violent, inhumane, and demoralizing. Europeans' high regard for technological accomplishments was shattered by the same mechanized technology that was supposed to advance humankind.

> ## Heads Up: What You Need to Know
>
> On the WHAP exam, it's important to know the four main causes of World War I. The acronym MAIN will help you remember the causes.
>
> **M**echanized weaponry
>
> **A**lliances: Triple Entente and Triple Alliance
>
> **I**mperialistic control for territories
>
> **N**ationalism of extreme nature

Okay, now let's discuss the four main causes of World War I.

Key Facts about the Causes of World War I

Mechanized weaponry. Many nations were prepared for war with mechanized weaponry and Germany had the most powerful military in the world, which threatened nations like Britain. The invention of mechanized weaponry made the old form of warfare obsolete. In the past, sides would charge against each other in the open battlefield using foot soldiers and cavalry. Now, automatic guns like the Maxim gun led to the massacre of soldiers. For example, the total casualties from just the Battle at the Somme in France was 1 million people in 1916. Another reason for these mass casualties was a new form of warfare called **trench warfare,** in which battle was executed at close range to hold defense lines. The two sides had set up 300 miles of trenches in the northern part of France. The strategy was to hold the battle line and wear out the other side until it was possible to overtake the enemy. Unfortunately, the actual effect was a stalemating of both sides with massive casualties—a constant war of attrition for both sides.

Technology proved to be a deadly instrument for prolonging warfare and committing massive casualties. Other weapons that mechanized warfare and made it far more dangerous included:

- **Poison gas:** France and Germany experimented with using chlorine, phosgene, and mustard gas killing massive numbers of soldiers. These gases would literally liquefy a person's lungs over several days.
- **U-boats:** Germany developed primitive submarines that could travel close to the surface of the water. Germans used these submarines to ram British ships that were being used to carry war supplies to France.
- **Airplanes:** Powered aircraft invented by the Wright brothers changed the role of aircraft and military warfare. Prior to World War I, airplanes were used for sport. At the 1899 Hague Peace Conference, it was decided that dropping explosives from the air was prohibited. Airplanes could only be used for reconnaissance. Military strategists soon realized that air strikes would influence the outcome of the war. During World War I, pilots flew over trenches and dropped dynamite on the opponent's side in order to break up trench warfare. The air strikes were massively destructive.
- **Tanks:** Both sides of the conflict developed military tanks to carry soldiers across the middle of the land between trenches. However, the tanks turned into death traps because they were fabricated with thin metal. Tanks moved too slowly to flee from the line of fire. When tanks were fired upon, the metal was too thin to protect the soldiers inside. The bullets passed through the tank's thin exterior and ricocheted, killing the people inside.

Alliances. The Great War started one month after Austro-Hungarian Archduke Ferdinand's assassination. The European nations had created alliances (secret pacts) in order to avoid war in the imperialized areas of the world. The idea was that no countries would attack another one if they were allied with partners ready to commit to war. Secret pacts and double-dealing among nations created an atmosphere of distrust. World War I had two major alliances. The **Triple Entente** included Russia, France, and Serbia. The **Triple Alliance** included the great powers of Germany, Hungary, and Italy. Once Archduke Ferdinand was assassinated, the alliance system was triggered and country after country started to declare war on one another.

Imperialism. Another reason for this sense of nationalism had to do with the previous century of imperialism. In 1914, Europe was a world power and many nations sought to control the remaining free territories of the world for increasing raw materials and gaining economic power. The fight for increased power led to colonial rivalries. With rival colonies in Africa, Asia, and the Middle East, European powers approached the brink of war several times. Rivalry was especially contentious between Britain and Germany in Africa and between France and Germany in Morocco.

Nationalism. Nationalism is the love for one's nation based on common interests and identity. The idea of nationalism grew out of enlightened thinking during the French Revolution of 1789 when people aspired to unite their nation and reject monarchical authority. Extreme nationalism gained momentum at the beginning of the 19th century when France's army, led by Napoleon Bonaparte, invaded many nation-states across Europe. The people of these defeated nations felt demoralized and humiliated by Napoleon's annihilation, especially the Germans and Italians. Napoleon's conquests inadvertently fueled the fire for an extreme nationalistic attitude that carried over to World War I. By 1914 the essence of nationalism became radicalized with extreme views of "us versus them."

A philosophy called **social Darwinism** also contributed to extreme nationalism. Social Darwinism argued that certain groups of human beings were superior to others. Based on this theory, the superior groups' biological traits made them intellectually, culturally, and artistically superior. Some Europeans believed that their discoveries during the Enlightenment, the Scientific Revolution, and industrialization were proof that they were biologically superior, and they believed that God had given them an obligation to civilize and control the parts of the world that today we call the developing world (Africa, Latin America, India, and Southeast Asia).

TEST TIP: Many AP students make a big mistake on the WHAP exam by misunderstanding the cause of World War I. Students point to the assassination of Archduke Ferdinand of Hungary on June 28, 1914, as the cause of the war. Ferdinand's assassination provoked the war between Austria-Hungary and Serbia, but it was not the main cause of the war. World War I started one month after this tragedy on July 28, 1914, and Germany declared war on Russia on August 1, 1914.

The underlying main cause of the war was the formation of an alliance system that obligated certain nations to defend other allied nations.

Key Facts about the End of World War I

The United States declared war on Germany. Eventually, the United States joined the war on April 6, 1917. Germany's military built a fleet of technologically advanced navy ships and continued to sink British unarmed luxury liners using their U-boat technology. One was a civilian ship called the ***Lusitania*** en route from New York to England. The ship was torpedoed by the Germans on May 7, 1915, and more than 1,100 passengers and crew members died, including 120 U.S. citizens. Although this provoked the United States, it did not join the war until two years later when it was threatened by Germany's proposal to Mexico. The British intercepted the **Zimmermann Telegram,** correspondence from Germany to the German ambassador to Mexico. Germany wanted to stop the United States from entering the war, and promised Mexico that it would return its lands in the southwest of the United States if Mexico joined the war with the Germans and the Triple Alliance. This led to the United States, under President Woodrow Wilson, declaring war on Germany. The entrance of fresh U.S. troops turned the war around and Germany surrendered in 1918.

The lost generation. The young men and women who had experienced World War I were extremely disillusioned in the old truths they had been taught to believe. Based on ruthless experiences, most people began to feel the opposite sentiment of the hope that they began with at the start of the war. This generation of men and women who came of age during the war became known as the *lost generation.* About 10 million soldiers had been killed and another 21 million soldiers had been injured. In addition, about 6 million to 13 million civilians had been killed; this included the **Armenian genocide** (1915–1917) of over 1.5 million Armenians who were slaughtered by Young Turks soldiers. The promise of advanced technology had turned into a nightmare of mass slaughter with new weaponry.

> TEST TIP: In the aftermath of World War I, post-war sentiments about a lost generation and the madness of war were mounting. American writer, Ernest Hemingway, famously wrote *The Sun Also Rises,* and German writer, Erich Maria Remarque, wrote *All Quiet on the Western Front.* On the WHAP exam, use these outside source examples in your free-response essays to illustrate the post-war worldview of the brutality of war.

The Fourteen Points. There was, however, some hope that the war would bring a new consciousness about the need for global peace. U.S. President Woodrow Wilson led the Allies at a Paris peace conference in the hope of creating a global peace settlement. Wilson proposed **Fourteen Points** that outlined principles for world peace, including:

1. Free and open trade.
2. National self-determination for people.
3. Public treaties to slow down the production of weaponry.
4. An end to secret alliances.
5. A new global institution to secure peace—the League of Nations.

Wilson could not enforce all of the points, especially since he did not really believe in *self-determination* (the right for a nation to determine its own government) for people in Africa and Asia. The British and French just saw the end of the war as a means to take German colonial possessions. Although Wilson's progressive ideas in the Fourteen Points failed, its framework was used to negotiate the Treaty of Versailles.

TEST TIP: The League of Nations (1920–1946) is an important international organization to remember on the WHAP exam as you provide examples in free-response questions about 20th-century wars. The League was created after World War I with the purpose of preventing aggression that might cause another great war. For the WHAP exam, it's important to know that the League failed to ratify the Treaty of Versailles, and Germany and Russia were not allowed to join at the time. In the 1930s, the League failed to prevent another world war. After World War II, the League of Nations was replaced by the United Nations in 1946.

The Treaty of Versailles (1919). Germany and Austria-Hungary were not invited to take part in the peace conference. The main nations that attended the peace process were France, Britain, Italy, and the United States. The Treaty of Versailles was established to restore the European balance of power and promote peace, but the British and French wanted to punish Germany. Germany was forced to give up colonial territories to Britain and France. Another punishment that Germany had to accept was to pay for all of the damages of World War I. Most importantly, Germany was forced to accept complete responsibility for starting the war in **Article 231.** These terms humiliated and angered Germans for many years. When the United States decided not to support the League of Nations, the other two members of the Big Three (David Lloyd George from Britain and Georges Clemenceau from France) decided to simply strengthen their colonial possessions around the world.

Heads Up: What You Need to Know

The consequences of World War I changed the political, social, and economic course of world history. Some of the important long-term consequences that you should be familiar with for the WHAP exam include:

- Millions of lives were lost due to the advancements in weaponry, and people became cynical about the future of the world. Young people who survived the war became known as the "lost generation."
- The Russian Communist Party was formed under Joseph Stalin (see the next section).
- Germany's fury mounted about its punishment and being excluded in the peace process during the Treaty of Versailles. These resentments laid the groundwork for World War II.
- The balance of power shifted, the population declined, the economy collapsed, new nations formed, and territories were remapped.

The Russian Revolutions and the Rise of Communism

During World War I, one of the best examples of the disillusionment of human progress came with the Russian revolutions.

Workers and farmers (who were mostly peasants) grew disillusioned with the Romanov monarchy because they were losing the war and people were starving at home. Russian soldiers were killed in massive numbers, and soldiers began to desert the front lines. In February 1917, before the end of World War I, a civilian revolution broke out to overthrow the monarchy in order to get out of the war. The revolutionaries quickly established a provisional government that included socialists, liberals, and conservatives. Their hope was to establish a socialist government that would help Russian farmers end serfdom and create equality. The provisional government became increasingly unstable.

The Rise of Communism

Russian revolutions came to an end and Vladimir Lenin began a communist rule in Russia.

Vladimir Lenin (Russia's Leader 1917–1924)

The German government had its own strategy on how to undermine Russia. The Germans took the radical **Vladimir Lenin,** who had been exiled by the provisional government, and put him on a locked train back to Russia. Lenin went into the countryside and rallied the farmers to his Marxist cause of a new radical communist government. Lenin led the **Bolshevik Revolution** (also known as the October Revolution), which overthrew the provisional government. Lenin's movement was called the **Bolshevik Party.** The Bolshevik Party believed that an *intelligentsia* (well-educated group of communist leaders) could lead peasant farmers into a utopian revolution. Lenin became known as the founder of communism. This Russian civil war pitted the *Whites* (monarchists and anti-Bolsheviks) against the *Reds* (Bolsheviks and their allies). It lasted for 2 years and had casualties on both sides.

The new government under Lenin promised a utopia of social and economic equality, and many people outside of Russia hoped that this new form of government would be the culmination of all of human beings' hopes and visions for a perfect society—communism.

Leon Trotsky (Collectivization) vs. Nikolai Bukharin (Cooperatives)

Before Lenin died in 1924, he had hoped that a new charismatic leader could replace him and carry out Russia's progression to a communist utopia. However, after Lenin's death there was a struggle for power between **Leon Trotsky** and **Nikolai Bukharin.**

Trotsky had different beliefs on how to achieve utopia. In an effort to industrialize the Soviet Union, Trotsky believed that the Russian society should consolidate its farming, called **collectivization** (*kolkhozy* in Russian). To overcome the food shortage and strengthen the nation's economic power, peasant households were forced to combine farms, land, and labor into a collective agricultural enterprise. That meant that Russian farmers would farm together on land that was publicly owned, and their productivity would be taxed. The taxes would be used to invest in rapid industrialization. Collectivization was intended to destroy the wealthy peasant class (***bourgeois***). By 1927, there were 14,000 collective farms in the Soviet Union.

Trotsky's opposition was Nikolai Bukharin. Bukharin believed in **cooperatives.** Cooperatives resulted in the same outcome as collectivization, but it was far slower. In cooperatives, the idea was to allow farmers to keep their private property and tax them at lower rates. The eventual goal was the same—industrialization.

Neither Trotsky nor Bukharin would ever take control of the Soviet Union. Someone else would, someone who held a government position and rose to power to outmaneuver his rivals—Joseph Stalin.

Did you know? The Russian *kolkhozy* and Israeli *kibbutzim* may appear similar because they are both collective farms, but they are radically different due to their nations' different political ideologies. The Soviet Union is a communist society; therefore, Russia's kolkhozy is <u>forced</u> collectivization. On the other hand, Israel is a democratic socialist society; therefore, Israel's kibbutzim is <u>voluntary</u> collectivization.

Joseph Stalin (1929–1953)

Joseph Stalin changed the Soviet Union from a peasant society into a world superpower, but in the process he caused the worst manmade famine in world history due to his forced industrialization program. Stalin had no original ideas; he was a rigid bureaucrat who wanted power. He claimed to support Bukharin and had Trotsky exiled. Stalin then took credit for the idea of collectivization claiming that it was his idea, not Trotsky's. Stalin placed Bukharin and his supporters on trial for betraying the revolution. Stalin either killed or imprisoned all of his political opponents.

By 1928, Stalin was in control of Russia. Stalin implemented the collectivization policies, and the removal of private property led to a backlash by farmers in the Ukraine. Stalin had his secret police take the farmers' production and then he blockaded the roads. All of this was done in winter when new crops could not be grown, so millions of farmers starved to death—20 million to 40 million people died of starvation.

The Post-War Era

During the early 1920s, European countries honored the Treaty of Versailles for 5 years and hoped to preserve peace to avoid a recourse of war. To achieve peace, it was important to decrease the tensions in the Middle East and to reintegrate Germany into Europe as a peaceful partner. But by the end of the 1920s, strong divisions had begun to emerge and nations were eager to attain self-government.

Key Facts about the Post-War Era

The Dawes Plan. After World War I, the United States' economic boom spread to the global market and boosted European businesses. The United States and European powers agreed to enact the Dawes Plan in 1923 to give loans to European countries for war reparations. Germany and other countries would receive loans to infuse their economies, develop industries, and repay the British and French for war loans. This benefitted European nations by boosting their economies, but it also helped the United States' economy since global consumers could buy more goods and services in trade.

The Mandate System divided the Middle East. The Ottoman Empire had sided with the Germans during World War I, and when the Germans lost the war, the Ottoman Empire finally collapsed. The British and the French divided up the Middle East and created the nations that we see today under what was called the **Mandate System.** The British acquired Jordan, Iraq, and Iran, and the French acquired Syria and Lebanon.

The biggest problem was the conflict between the people living in the Palestinian region and the incoming Jewish migration. The British promised the Jewish population a homeland under the **Balfour Declaration** (a letter written by British Foreign Secretary Arthur James Balfour in 1917 expressing support for a Jewish homeland in Palestine), but previously in late 1915 they also promised the Arabs that they would protect their interests. At the time, Palestinians comprised 90 percent of the population, and by 1920 Palestinians began to revolt. In the end, the British appeared to be dividing the populations in order to gain access to oil, and this led to increased tensions in the Middle East.

Weaponry treaty violations. After World War I, nations agreed to the terms of the Treaty of Versailles to reduce armed forces to low levels. Britain, France, and the United States did lower their production of weaponry, but Germany and Japan violated the agreement and increased the productivity of their weaponry and battleships. This action would eventually make their imperial navies equal to the powers of Britain, France, and the United States, and prepared Germany and Japan for a new war.

Invasion treaty violations. The weak League of Nations was not ready to stop the rise of new imperial powers. Japan would invade China in the 1930s, Germany would invade Eastern Europe in the 1930s, and Ethiopia would invade Northern Africa in the mid-1930s. By the late 1930s, a new Italian-German axis formed an alliance system that was ready for a new global conflict.

In the late 1920s, a series of events turned fortunes into the worst global economic decline of the 1900s—the Great Depression.

The Great Depression (1929–1939)

The Great Depression of 1929 caused millions of people to lose their savings overnight. People panicked, made poor judgments, and felt resentful.

Key Facts about the Causes of the Great Depression

Overspending. After World War I, the global economy seemed to be on a strong upswing. The United States began an economic boom with an increase in the production of goods. New domestic technologies such as the icebox, telephone, and radio were manufactured quickly and modestly. In addition, more and more people moved from **urbanization** to **suburbanization** (the movement of people into suburban homes), and the working-class and middle-class populations were overspending to purchase luxury items.

Consumer debt. The economy was based on an unstable economic foundation of consumer overspending. With rapid advancements in technology, most companies were now using machines instead of human labor to lower their labor costs. People were working less and didn't have the money to spend, yet they kept buying. How did people buy goods with no money? A new method of financing was available—credit. Consumers continued buying and investing using **credit installment plans** (early forms of credit cards) to pay for products.

Lack of demand for goods. The competition among manufacturers increased, but it caused an oversupply of goods—the supply of goods exceeded the demand. This caused a collapse in prices and forced many manufacturers out of business, especially in agriculture. As factories closed, unemployment spiked.

Increased interest rates. The final straw appeared in the international economic system. The international economic system was based on the **gold standard.** The gold standard meant that every nation's currency was backed up by gold reserves. The United States had emerged from World War I with the strongest economy in the world so it was able to store up more gold. However, by the end of the 1920s, the other nations' economies had recovered from war reparations. The U.S. **Federal Reserve** feared that investors from other countries would buy up gold and take it back to their nations, so the Federal Reserve raised interest rates. Other nations were forced to take their currencies off of the gold standard, and interest rates dramatically increased. The increased interest rates caused two massive shocks to the stock market in 1928 and 1929.

Stock market crash (1929). Investors used a system called **buying on the margin.** Investors would pay a small percentage for a loan while borrowing the rest. This was used to invest in the stock market and created a sizeable surge in stock prices. This unrealistic economic surge created a stock market *bubble,* and because the bubble was based on unrealistic stock values, the stock market eventually collapsed. When the bubble burst, investors experienced extreme losses and people frantically tried to pull their investments out of the stock market.

The stock market crash alone did not cause the Great Depression. Over the next couple years, the incredible amount of consumer debt and bank failures led to economic crisis. When the stock market failed, people could not pay off their loans, purchases, and credit installments. Home values depreciated and people lost their possessions, even their homes. People tried to take their savings out of their bank accounts, but banks collapsed because government regulations at the time did not insure the money in bank accounts. The banks did not have enough money for millions of people and people did not have enough money to pay off their debts.

The Great Depression led to a major impact on global ideologies and governments that would change everything in the post-war era.

The Road to World War II

Many students mistakenly believe that World War I and World War II were essentially the same. This is understandable given that both were global wars and both used extremely destructive advanced weaponry, but the effects of the two wars were very different. The effects of World War II shaped the rest of the 20th century—and possibly even some of the conflicts that we are witnessing in the 21st century.

The Rise of Fascism

During World War I, totalitarianism existed in the world, but two other ideologies arose as potential solutions to the Great Depression and World War I: the ideologies of **communism** and **fascism.** Communism was rejected by most nations because it was seen as an atheistic philosophy that contrasted with most people's traditional beliefs, but some countries chose to follow fascism even though it was based on the ideology of racial superiority. The rise of fascism was a step toward World War II.

Did you know? Fascism is usually associated with the horrible moral and human tragedy of genocide, especially of the Jewish population (see p. 220). Did you know that fascism had both positive and negative social attributes? Students often make the mistake of not learning the pros and cons of fascism ideology. It is important to understand why people would choose to accept such an intolerant belief system.

Critical Thinking Question: Why was fascism so popular during the 1930s?

People were inspired because fascism had a positive social appeal for the following reasons:

- The government leader was initially well-liked because he emphasized nationalism, unity, and the love for one's country.
- The government created jobs by expanding the military, creating a constant demand for more industrial production.
- The government prevented civil disobedience by strictly enforcing laws.
- The government contracted private businesses to create military goods, which helped bring about economic growth, employment, and eventual foreign expansion.
- The government helped businesses by preventing labor unions and workers from demanding higher wages.
- The government emphasized traditional conservative values, including male dominance and racial dominance.

World War II began in 1939, and by 1940 German fascism controlled most of Europe due to Germany's occupation in most of continental Europe. One possible reason for the appeal of German fascism was its ability to develop a growing economy. While the democratic United States economically suffered a 25% unemployment rate, fascist Germany only had a 2% unemployment rate. By 1940, only Britain remained outside of German control. In Europe, Britain stood alone in its democratic ideology .

Heads Up: What You Need to Know

A frequent question on the WHAP exam asks you to compare and contrast political ideologies. Political ideologies are important because these beliefs divided the nations of the world. Refer to the "Political Ideologies" chart below to understand the similarities and differences among fascism, communism, and totalitarianism. The information in the chart will help you provide specific evidence and examples to support your written free-response.

Political Ideologies				
Ideology	Brief Description with Examples	Form of Government	Positive Social Appeal	Negative Social Results
Communism	A social-economic system of government of a classless society. Examples: Russia (1917), China (1921), Cuba (1965), North Korea (1948), and Vietnam (1976).	A one-party state, with the state controlling all aspects of life. Communism eliminates social classes, capitalism, unequal wealth, and all forms of religion. For example, the USSR (today known as the Russian Federation) was a communist nation where all major decisions were made by the one-party state.	Communism was intended to be a form of modern-scientific socialism—a system of a perfect sharing community. It is based on social reform and economic equality. Communism especially appealed to the working classes and those in poverty who did not own land. Communism was founded by the work of Karl Marx and Friedrich Engels in *The Communist Manifesto*. The original purpose of communism was based on Marx's assertion that many problems of a society were largely due to the unequal wealth and social classes.	Communists called to overthrow all other forms of governments. Communism found individualism destructive because people might pursue individual wealth through capitalism. Communists had extreme governmental control. Although communism was based on social equality, it is not based on political equality. All decisions are made by a one-party state, and this party owns everything in the nation as a "custodian of the nation."

Ideology	Brief Description with Examples	Form of Government	Positive Social Appeal	Negative Social Results
Fascism	A radical form of extreme nationalism that believes in national or racial supremacy to all other nationalities. Examples: Italy and Germany (1919–1945).	A radical form of dictatorship whereby the head of state has the "absolute government authority" over the nation. Fascist governments believe they are superior over other nations. People are not allowed to disagree with their government. Fascism is a subcategory of totalitarianism. All fascist states are totalitarian.	Fascism promoted nationalism at a time when people sought to believe in unity and a sense of belonging. People were happy because the increased military created jobs and economic growth. Fascism appealed to the wealthy, who were threatened by losing their wealth to a more democratic political system. People initially felt safer with a military government to keep law and order. The dictators are often charismatic, project confidence, and are admired by the people. People often look for a hero to save their nation.	Fascism was extremely militaristic and was built on controlling people with fear. Fascists did not believe in individualism because it might promote democracy and individual liberty and rights. Fascism advocates political, economic, and social control over all aspects of the nation. Fascists believe they are superior over other races or ethnicities. Fascists do not accept democracy and do not tolerate opposition. Fascists are anti-democratic and anti-communistic.
Totalitarianism	A system of government that requires complete submission to the ruling monarchy or state. Examples: the Soviet Union led by Stalin (1925–1953) and China led by Mao (1966–1976).	A single-party government that has complete civil and political control over the people's rights. In totalitarianism, one political party dominates and exercises complete authority over its citizens (and their activities). Totalitarianism is similar to fascism, but not all totalitarian states are fascist.	The conformity of people prevented chaos, violence, and crime. The goal is to create a perfect society.	It is a centralized dictatorship that requires absolute obedience. The state controls all social aspects of its citizens, including private attitudes, values, and beliefs. Believed in the "axe rule" (anyone who disagreed with the leader was killed). Did not tolerate opposition and adopted aggressive foreign policies. Totalitarians are anti-democratic.

World War II Axis Power Leaders

Italy (Mussolini)

The people of Italy were unhappy with their unfair treatment during the Treaty of Versailles. **Benito Mussolini** organized the fascist party **Black Shirts** and rallied for Italians' nationalist sentiments by putting the economy on a course of restoration. He used violence and intimidation to seize power in Italy in 1923. By 1926, Italy had the first political fascist party. Mussolini made dramatic changes in the constitution and strengthened the Italian military to ensure his authoritative power over Italy.

Germany (Hitler)

After the Great Depression, **Adolf Hitler**'s Nazi Party became much more popular and took over the government through democratic elections in 1932 and 1933. By 1933, Germany was ruled by Hitler and the **Third Reich** (Nazi Party). Hitler began to modernize the German economy, build a powerful military, create a racial hierarchy persecuting Slavs, Africans, Gypsies, and Jews, target his political opponents, and target the mentally and physically disabled who were viewed as financial burdens on the state's economy.

Did you know? In 1926, Hitler wrote an autobiographical book entitled *Mein Kampf* ("my struggle"), which detailed his political ideology of fascism and social Darwinism. This book became the Nazi bible during World War II and detailed Hitler's anger about Germany's treatment in the Treaty of Versailles. Remember that after World War I, the Treaty of Versailles (1) forced Germany to accept blame for starting the war, (2) forced Germany to pay for war reparations, (3) seized German territories, and (4) forced Germany to demilitarize. Most Germans welcomed Hitler's nationalistic views from *Mein Kampf* because they were unhappy about the treaty.

Soviet Union (Stalin)

As discussed in a previous section, Joseph Stalin changed the Soviet Union from a peasant society into a world superpower under a communist rule. Communism promised equality, cooperation, and political freedom, but instead Stalin created a **totalitarian** government, a new political class of communist leaders, and a terror-based state system. Citizens were too terrified to oppose the regime because Stalin targeted political dissidents. Stalin was a dictator of the Union of Soviet Socialist Republics (USSR) from 1929 to 1953. Estimates are that 40 million to 60 million people were killed under Russian communism under Stalin's orders.

Japan (Hirohito)

In Southeast Asia, an ideological movement similar to fascism arose in Japan—imperialism. Japan had been industrializing and expanding since 1853 and the rise of the Meiji Restoration. However, during the 1930s under the leadership of **Emperor Hirohito,** Japan brought a new form of Japanese imperialism into power. The Great Depression led to a lack of European and Western consumer demand for Japanese luxury goods. This caused a massive crash of the Japanese economy, and a new conservative group of militaristic leaders arose who promised centralized leadership to the people of Japan.

Japanese imperialism, called *Imperial Way Faction,* was different from European imperialism. European imperialism was founded on exploration and colonization, whereas the new imperialistic Japan was fueled by social Darwinism and beliefs of racial superiority. Similar to fascists, imperialists believed in racial superiority and extreme nationalism. Japan's ruthless invasion of Northern China is an example of its destruction. In Nanjing, Japanese soldiers raped women and killed over 300,000 disarmed civilians in this city (now known as the **Nanjing Massacre,** which still causes political arguments today). Japan wanted to create the Southeast Asian Co-Prosperity Zone and claimed this was an attempt to remove European imperialists, secure Western respect, and bring civilization to other nations. However, it was really a way to replace European imperialists with Japanese imperialists.

Heads Up: What You Need to Know

On the WHAP exam, it is important to identify the main causes and events that led up to World War II.

- **The Great Depression.** The global economy had suffered, and this created unstable governments.
- **Japan's expansion.** The increased growth of Japan was not supported by its natural resources or land. Japan sought out imperialistic expansion by invading China and Manchuria; then in 1937, Japan formed an alliance with Germany.
- **The rise of fascism.** The strengthening of new nationalistic thinking throughout European nations, especially Germany and Italy, changed the political ideological climate of Europe.
- **Appeasement.** By 1933, Hitler and the Nazi Party started to build military strength in Germany, but European leaders failed to enforce the Treaty of Versailles. Nations like Britain and France hoped to keep peace at any cost in order to prevent war. Germany invaded the Rhineland in 1935 to take back its territory lost during World War I, but still the European leaders said nothing.
- **Munich Conference.** Hitler demanded that Czechoslovakia surrender Sudetenland (a region that was taken away from Germany in World War I), but Czechoslovakia refused. In 1939, Hitler met with European leaders at the Munich Conference. He promised the leaders that he only wanted to reunify the western side of Czechoslovakia, Sudetenland. British Prime Minister Neville Chamberlain believed that this small appeasement would satisfy Hitler. In order to avoid war, Hitler was given Sudetenland if he would agree to stop expanding and invading other nations. Instead, Hitler invaded Czechoslovakian territories and then turned his sights north to take over Poland.

World War II (1939 to 1948)

The fascist forces were extremely successful at the beginning of the global conflict in 1939. This was partly due to Germany's military mobilization and the lack of a response from Europe and the United States to the growing threats in Europe. On the WHAP exam, you may be asked to identify some of the developments that began World War II.

Key Developments at the Start of World War II

Anschluss (1938). Hitler demanded that Austria join the Third Reich to strengthen Germany, called the Austrian *Anschluss* (annexation of Austria).

Nazi-Soviet non-aggression pact (1939). Hitler formed an alliance with the Soviets and agreed that he would not invade the Soviet Union. Stalin feared that the capitalistic nations would team up against the Soviet

Union, and he made a pact with Hitler. In this pact, the two nations agreed to divide conquered Eastern European nations, and not to attack each other.

Germany invades Poland (1939). Hitler was unstoppable and did not keep his promise from the Munich Conference. Tension between Germany and Poland had been increasing since World War I. In September 1939, Poland was under attack by German troops. After the invasion, the Third Reich executed over 60,000 Polish officers and activists. All diplomacy had failed. Britain and France were forced to declare war on Germany. This ushered in World War II.

Germany invades France (1940). Following the victories in Czechoslovakia and Poland, Hitler's tank divisions carried out a *blitzkrieg* (lightning war) to quickly crush France's army. Hitler's forces established an occupation in most of France with a small French fascist party, the **Vichy Regime,** which controlled central France. Hitler had successfully taken over all of Western Europe by 1939 except for Britain.

The Holocaust. Germany's persecution of the Jews had begun before the war, but during the war Hitler's anti-Semitic Nazi Party destroyed Jewish synagogues, businesses, and homes. Hitler's belief in fascism convinced many German citizens that Jews were an inferior race. Hitler's terrifying Nazi destruction and propaganda did not stop on the battlefields. As Germany fought against its enemies, Hitler and his regime enacted the **Final Solution** to the "Jewish problem," attempting the genocide of the Jews of Europe. Hitler set up death camps across Nazi-occupied Europe that engineered the death of more than 6 million Jews, along with other undesirables such as homosexuals, Gypsies, the disabled, Slavs, and others.

TEST TIP: It is important to remember the key players of World War II.

- The Allied Powers (called the *Allies*). The big three Allies included Great Britain, the United States, and the Soviet Union (joined in 1941 after Germany's betrayal). Other nations included Belgium, the Netherlands, Denmark, Norway, Greece, Yugoslavia, Poland, nationalist China, Canada, Australia, New Zealand, and France (until 1940).

- The Axis Powers: Germany, Italy (joined 1940 until 1943), Japan, Hungary, Bulgaria, Finland, and Romania.

Key Facts about the Events of World War II

The United States and Great Britain's Lend-Lease Act (March 1941). The European and North American alliance began to take shape after these fascist successes in Poland and France. The United States had become isolationist in the 1930s; however, President Franklin Roosevelt knew that the United States would eventually become involved in the fight against fascism. Roosevelt established policies that situated the United States on the edge of involvement. In March, Roosevelt began the **Lend-Lease** program, in which the United States would lease military arms, ammunitions, and naval destroyers to Britain in exchange for 99-year leases to eight British military bases in the Western Hemisphere. The lease program became known as "an arsenal of democracy." Secret U.S. and British talks started about the U.S. engaging in the war.

The United States joins the war (August 1941). The United States collaborated with Britain in the **Atlantic Charter,** an agreement that established a post-war commitment to human rights, post-war mutual disarmament, free trade, and no territorial gains without the consent of the nations concerned. Most importantly, Roosevelt and British Prime Minister Winston Churchill became both political and personal friends. By 1941, the United States was on the verge of involvement in World War II, but the Japanese attack on December 7, 1941, at Pearl Harbor, Hawaii, provided the justification that Roosevelt needed to finally become involved in World War II.

Germany invades the Soviet Union (June 1941). Remember that Hitler and Stalin made a non-aggression pact in 1939. The treaty included a promise that Germany would not invade Russia if the Soviet Union remained neutral, but Hitler broke his promise and invaded the Soviet Union. Hitler decided to invade the Soviet Union in *Operation Barbarossa*. The massive invasion was designed to quickly conquer the communist state and take advantage of its resources to support Germany's war efforts. However, Hitler's plan was dismantled because Hitler severely underestimated the logistics of battling in the Soviet Union terrain and severely cold weather conditions.

Northern African campaign (1940–1943). Military strategies by the Allies were primarily conceived by the United States and Britain. The Allies decided to use a Northern Africa strategy in 1943 to eliminate Hitler's tank divisions. This was a turning point in the war. The goal was to remove Italy from the war and isolate Germany. The United States would invade Europe from the Western Front, and the Soviets (who had become part of the Allied powers) would invade on the Eastern Front. Initially, however, the Northern African campaign sparked Stalin's paranoia. Stalin wrongly believed that the Allies were attempting to get rid of both fascism and communism by prioritizing a Southern European invasion before relieving Russia of the German invaders. The Allied push from the west and east forced more than 250,000 Italian and German soldiers to surrender.

The Asian-Pacific war front. A second strategy in World War II involved the Pacific theater and the Japanese expansion. The Japanese had used an incident near a railroad in Mukden to justify an invasion of China. The attack on the Japanese railway was done by either Chinese dissidents or Japanese acting as Chinese. Either way, it was a way for Japan to justify its real desire to invade Manchuria for strategic reasons and to search for oil resources. Japan then brutally took over Chinese northern cities. This led to a Chinese alliance between the **Chinese nationalists** under **Chiang Kai-shek** and the communists under **Mao Zedong.** This alliance was too weak to stop the Japanese. Eventually the Japanese expanded deep into China. The United States and Britain responded with the Atlantic Charter and froze oil sales to Japan. This led to failed negotiations between the United States and Japan. Japan then planned for and completed a successful attack on the U.S. battleship fleet at Pearl Harbor. Japan then went further and invaded the United States territory of the Philippines. In response, U.S. General Douglas MacArthur and Admiral Chester Nimitz developed **island hopping,** a military strategy to invade small islands and secure military bases. Their strategy was to use the American navy to take out the small satellite islands supporting Japanese expansion. When this was finished, the United States would directly attack the Japanese island nation.

So, did these strategies succeed? The short answer is yes, but these war strategies were extremely difficult to implement.

The invasion of Normandy (June 1944). The Northern Africa strategy was a success. Italy proved to be very weak and easy to remove from the war. However, the eventual invasion from the west through the beaches of Normandy, France, in 1944 was extremely difficult and almost failed when Britain and the U.S. conducted the largest seaborne invasion, called "D-Day." Hitler's forces had entrenched themselves in concrete bunkers on the ocean's coast. Even after a massive artillery bombardment from battleships, the Allied forces faced the cliffs at Normandy. Still, the invasion succeeded, and the United States drove through France into Germany, defeating the German armies on May 8, 1945.

The United States bombs Japan (August 1945). The war continued to drag on for months with Japan. The United States defeated Japan, but at an extreme cost. The United States removed one island after the next in the Pacific. Finally, the contest came down to Okinawa and Iwo Jima. At Iwo Jima, the Japanese lost 20,000 men and the Americans lost 6,000 men. At Okinawa, the Japanese lost 110,000 men and the Americans lost over 82,000 men.

However, what was more important was the revelation of what the Japanese were willing to do in order to win. The Japanese culture was based on the Bushido code, which gave all loyalty to the emperor. This meant that the Japanese military was willing to fight until the death to honor the will of the Japanese leadership, which they considered to be godlike. There would be no end to the war unless the emperor announced an official decree. And this brings up the historical debate about the United States' use of an **atomic bomb** on Japan.

To end the war, the United States dropped a bomb on the city of Hiroshima, Japan, on August 6, 1945, killing more than 100,000 people. This was the first time in history that an atomic bomb was used in warfare, so most people subjectively debate about the United States dropping two atomic bombs on Japan (a second bomb was dropped on August 9, 1945, on Nagasaki, killing an estimated 40,000 people). Some argue that it was wrong to drop the bombs because they killed so many people. Others say that the atomic bombs were necessary to end the war.

HISTORIOGRAPHY. *Both arguments about the United States dropping atomic bombs on Japan have a point, but let's look at this issue from a historian's point of view. The chart below illustrates the two historical sides of those in support and those in opposition of the atomic bombings on Japan.*

SUPPORT "Truman Was Right"	OPPOSE "Atomic Diplomacy"
This group of historians argues that Truman was forced to drop the atomic bombs on Japan due to the Japanese Bushido culture. Historians argue that the Japanese civilian population would not concede, regardless of their annihilation by the United States military. The Japanese military would not surrender until the emperor declared a surrender. The problem was that the advisors for the emperor still thought they could win the war. Therefore, the atomic bombs served as a tactic to shock the Japanese leadership into a surrender. What if we had not done this? Well, the result may have been a land invasion of Japan that would have led to about 1 million deaths of American soldiers and probably far more Japanese civilian and military casualties.	This group of historians argues that the Japanese military was defeated by 1945, although they agree that the emperor had to issue a surrender before soldiers would concede. Historians from this school of thought assert that the emperor wanted to surrender. The problem was that the Americans would only accept an unconditional surrender in which the emperor would have to completely remove himself from office. This move would undermine the Japanese culture and the respect for their emperor. The emperor's advisors were split. Three generals believed the war could be won, and three generals wanted to surrender. According to this school of thought, Japan could have offered a conditional surrender to allow the emperor to remain in a symbolic position of power, but this negotiation would have undermined the first group of generals who claimed that they could win the war. However, this wasn't the underlying issue; the problem was that the U.S. was motivated to use the atomic bombs to scare the Russians from invading Southeast Asia.

The End of World War II

The war came to a close in 1945 when the Axis powers were defeated. After the war, Allied leaders met to discuss the post-war settlement. The Big Three of the Grand Alliance—Franklin Delano Roosevelt (U.S.), Winston Churchill (Britain), and Joseph Stalin (Soviet Union) wanted to weaken Germany, but not to allow a resurgent Germany to rise up to cause a World War III. Nazi leaders were taken to court and tried as war criminals. German resources were to be used to repair damages inflicted on other nations. At the **Yalta Conference,** the Big Three agreed to split up Europe between Soviet spheres of influence and British spheres of influence.

The Yalta Conference set the stage for the dividing up of Europe and Germany. This opens up the next big conflict of the 20th century—the Cold War. Before we cover the Cold War, let's discuss some of the global changes that took place after World War II.

Post–World War II

The Establishment of Global Organizations

Many nations, such as Germany and France, were completely destabilized after World War II. The end of war led to a global reorganization that was significantly different from the end of World War I. The leaders of the United States, Britain, and France decided that the cause of World War II was "economic," not the problem of military production after World War I. These world leaders came together to form international institutions to regulate the global economy, especially in the developing world. Three major institutions were established after World War II: the **United Nations,** the **International Monetary Fund,** and the **World Bank.**

The United Nations (UN). The United Nations was formed in 1945 to replace the failed League of Nations. The UN was established as an organization that promoted international diplomacy. It included a large global parliament called the General Assembly. After the war, the power of the UN was held by a Security Council, a group of four principal nations: the United States, the Soviet Union, China, and Great Britain. The goal of the Security Council was to mediate and make military decisions when necessary to keep the peace around the world. To avoid conflicts, each nation was allowed to cast one vote during the decision-making process. The UN also had the ability to help refugees, settle global disputes through an International Court of Justice, and provide healthcare benefits for people in numerous countries. During the Cold War, however, the conflict between the United States and the Soviet Union often paralyzed the Security Council.

International Monetary Fund and the World Bank. Although the UN was important for peacekeeping, the real power was set at the **Bretton Woods Conference** in New Hampshire. This is where the International Monetary Fund (IMF) and the World Bank were established to unite countries economically. The UN believed that if countries shared a common economic interest, they would be less likely to engage in war. The goal of the IMF was to lay down the ground rules for economic aid to countries, but countries had to comply with the rules (fight inflation, industrialize to build their economies, and lower tariffs). If the countries could accomplish this, they were able to receive financial aid for development from the World Bank. This economic influence led to the power of the Northern European and American countries over the developing world. During the Cold War, this economic influence was used as a strategy in negotiating with the Soviet Union. The idea was to advance countries into a global market of trade.

The Cold War (1945 to 1955)

The Cold War was between the two world superpowers—the United States and the Soviet Union—and their major differences in ideologies and economics. The United States' democratic views opposed Russia's communist views. In the Cold War, tensions mounted with the unprecedented prospect of a nuclear war between these two superpowers.

Key Facts about the Cold War

The Soviet Union sought territorial expansion to spread communism. The Cold War was somewhat of a misunderstanding. While there is no question that the leader of the Soviet Union, Joseph Stalin, was a murderous leader, even to his own people, the fear among Western leaders was that Stalin wanted to invade

Western Europe for territorial expansion and communist influence. However, Stalin lacked the military manpower to engage in another war. Stalin was mistrustful and wanted to protect his mother Russian country from attacks so he strategically placed soldiers at Russia's borders to prevent Russia from a possible invasion.

The United States sought to "contain" communism. In response to Stalin's actions, the United States president, Harry Truman, adopted the strategy of **containment** (the idea that communism could not be allowed to spread). The idea was developed by George Kennan who had lived in Russia during the 1930s and 1940s. Kennan argued in his "long telegram" to Truman that Stalin was not looking to take over the world like Hitler, but he was dangerous because he wanted to spread communism in strategic areas to protect Russian nationalism. Kennan suggested that the United States surround Russia with military bases in Western Europe. Kennan argued that the United States should use propaganda, secret services, and the military to remove the threat of potential Soviet Union communist allies in the developing world.

Heads Up: What You Need to Know

The key events about the Cold War to remember for the WHAP exam are as follows: the Truman Doctrine, the Marshall Plan, the Berlin Blockade and the Airlift Crisis, the Warsaw Pact, the Iron Curtain, and China's fall to communism.

The Truman Doctrine (1947). The Truman Doctrine was a United States plan that called for Congress to fund anti-communist groups in Turkey and Greece. The fear at the time was that Stalin was secretly coordinating with communist groups in Southern Europe. In fact, Stalin was not secretly communicating with other nations, but this perception led to an American desire to keep communism in Eastern Europe by providing political, military, and economic support to democratic nations in Southern Europe.

The Marshall Plan (1947). The United States offered financial assistance to Western Europe to assist in rebuilding the infrastructure and stimulating European economies from the devastation of World War II. The Soviet Union was also offered this assistance, but Stalin rejected the help because the offer came with conditions that required capitalist trade. The main strategy of the Marshall Plan was to develop a marketplace for industry and global trade. One of the goals of the United States was to prevent what happened at the Treaty of Versailles after World War I. If European nations were stable, then they might be less likely to turn to fascism and communism.

The Berlin Blockade and the Airlift Crisis (1948). After World War II, Stalin's military and secret police enforced communist rule throughout the Soviet Union and expanded communism in some countries like Germany. After Germany's defeat, Germany was divided into four Allied-occupation zones. Eastern Germany went to the Soviet Union, while Western Germany went to the United States, Great Britain, and France, with Berlin as the capital city. The city of Berlin was also split into sectors: East Berlin (occupied by the Soviet Union) and West Berlin (occupied by the United States, Great Britain, and France).

The United States reunited Western Germany in order to have a single economic market and government, but Stalin saw this as a precursor to an American democratic invasion in Eastern Germany; he saw the United States as enemies rather than allies. Therefore, Stalin then set up a blockade to cut off West Berlin from Western Germany. All water, food, and railroads were blocked. America responded by airlifting food and supplies into West Berlin for a year. The principal allies of the U.S. (Britain, Canada, and Australia) used airplanes to deliver food and supplies to the people of West Berlin. Stalin had no more leverage, and near the end of 1949 he had to give in, having gained nothing but turning Germans against Soviet rule.

The Warsaw Pact (1955). After a year, Stalin stopped the blockade and the United States led the effort to form **NATO (North Atlantic Treaty Organization).** This was a group of Northern European and American countries that promised to respond to any Soviet aggression into Western Europe. The Soviet Union responded with the **Warsaw Pact** (formally known as the Treaty of Friendship, Cooperation, and Mutual Assistance). The Warsaw Pact was an Eastern European military defense pact between communist nations to defend against the threat of Western democratic invasions. The Soviet Union was the leader. It unified the Soviet Union with many other Eastern European nations: Poland, East Germany, Czechoslovakia, Hungary, Romania, Albania, and Bulgaria. In the 1990s, the Warsaw Pact officially disbanded after several countries had withdrawn from all military interventions.

> **TEST TIP:** On the WHAP exam, using organizations like NATO as an example in your DBQ response can help show historical connections over time. Although NATO was organized in 1949, it continues today as an intergovernmental military and political organization to safeguard and resolve international conflicts. NATO was originally organized by the United States and other democratic nations as a response to communist threats. Today, the United States contributes to three-fourths of NATO's budget.

The Iron Curtain (1945–1991). The Berlin Blockade destroyed the Soviet Union's reputation throughout Europe. As tensions grew among nations, Stalin's suspicions grew about Western incursion. Europe was divided nearly in two by what was symbolically called the **Iron Curtain.** Winston Churchill described the Iron Curtain as a metaphorical boundary that symbolically divided Europe into two competing ideologies: Western democracy and Eastern Soviet Union totalitarian communism. The Iron Curtain was heavily guarded with armed military and looked like a tall border wall. The most famous portion of the Iron Curtain was the **Berlin Wall.**

China falls to communism (1949). The *Communist Party of China* (later called the *People's Republic of China*) was established in 1949 to unite the poor and destroy the wealthy. Mao Zedong was the leader of the communist revolution that forced the collapse of China's nationalist government. The Soviets tested their first successful nuclear bomb in 1949, and North Korea invaded South Korea in 1949. This led to the United States coalition of the United Nations landing in South Korea to push the North Koreans back past the 38th parallel. By the early 1950s, the Americans and Western Europeans believed that Joseph Stalin and his ally Mao Zedong were "setting up a set of dominos." This metaphor suggested that communists wanted to overtake one country at a time, like falling dominos, so that each neighboring country would fall to communist ideology.

Heads Up: What You Need to Know

In the aftermath of World War II, the United States and the Soviet Union superpowers continued to compete for allies in the developing world—democracy versus communism. On the WHAP exam, you should be aware that many of the underlying political, social, and economic world conflicts from the 1950s through the 1990s were prompted by democratic or communistic ideological beliefs. The United States and its Western allies feared that communism would take over the world in the *domino theory* (if one country fell to communism, others would fall like dominos). China fell to communism in 1949, and as you will see in the next section, several other countries fell to communist rule. Today, only five countries remain communist states: China, North Korea, Cuba, Laos, and Vietnam.

The 1950s and 1960s

The Soviet Union: Khrushchev (1953 to 1964)

In 1953, Joseph Stalin died. A new Soviet leader, **Nikita Khrushchev,** came to power and seemed to signal a massive change in Soviet policy. Khrushchev called for the reformation of communist Russia and addressed the Soviet parliament, the *Duma,* to condemn Stalin for murdering millions of Russians and damaging the efforts of the communist revolution. Khrushchev called for improving the strained international tensions so that the communist government could work on domestic reforms and a collectivization system.

Communist Uprisings in Eastern Europe (1956)

Khrushchev's transparency for communist reformations had negative consequences in Eastern Europe. Soviet satellites in Eastern Europe heard Khrushchev's speech to the Russian parliament, the *Duma,* and were threatened by his words of improving global relations. In 1956, Poland's leader of the Communist Party, **Wladyslaw Gomulka,** ended forced collectivization. In the same year, Hungarian leader **Imre Nagy** announced Hungary's withdrawal from the communist Warsaw Pact, and revolutions broke out in Hungary. In 1968, **Alexander Dubcek,** the Czechoslovakian communist leader, responded to his citizens' demands and withdrew from the Warsaw Pact. Faced with uprisings throughout Eastern Europe, Khrushchev sent Soviet military tank divisions to invade Hungary and force the country back into the Warsaw Pact. The Soviet Union crushed each of the major political independence movements, and Hungary's leader, Nagy, was captured and executed.

The Soviet Union: Brezhnev (1964–1982)

In 1968, a new Soviet leader, **Leonid Brezhnev,** brought stability to Russia, and when anti-communist protests emerged in Czechoslovakia to take over the government, Brezhnev sent a Soviet army to crush the Prague revolution (known as the **Prague Spring**) and restore the Communist Party. Brezhnev established the **Brezhnev Doctrine** to secure the Warsaw Pact by using military force to intervene if a country tried to leave the Soviet-led alliance.

Throughout the 1950s, the **arms race** between the United States and the Soviet Union was heated. As discussed in the Cold War section, while the two countries had limited their nuclear arms to atomic fission in the 1940s, a new type of bomb was invented, a *fusion bomb*. These hydrogen bombs were far more destructive than previous bombs. Both countries eventually developed a more efficient means of delivering these weapons, and both created *transcontinental ballistic missiles* to carry nuclear payloads to the enemy. By the end of the decade, both countries had the ability to destroy the entire world seven times each.

Then, two events came close to creating a complete unraveling of any hope for peace and improved tensions: Operation Mongoose and the Cuban Missile Crisis.

Did you know? Long-range ballistic missiles are now known as *intercontinental ballistic missiles,* or ICBMs. Modern ICBMs have nuclear and chemical/biological weapons delivery capabilities. Today, several countries have ICBM capabilities—the U.S., Russia, Britain, France, China, India, Pakistan, Israel, and North Korea. The communist nation of North Korea continues to test-launch ICBMs and threaten the world with nuclear warfare.

Cuba: Batista (1933–1944 and 1951–1959) and Fidel Castro (1959–2008)

In the late 1950s, the Cuban government was led by the military dictatorship of **Fulgencio Batista.** Batista made a fortune for himself, but he created massive poverty in Cuba so multiple revolutionary groups were looking for a change in government. Batista is known as the Cuban president who was overthrown by **Fidel Castro.** In 1959, Castro overthrew Batista when he orchestrated a revolutionary movement with guerrilla warfare.

Bay of Pigs Invasion: A U.S. plan to overthrow Castro (1961). Castro became the new dictator of Cuba. When Castro first took command, Cubans welcomed the change of regimes because Castro improved education and healthcare. But Castro soon began to brutally persecute and imprison anyone who opposed his regime. This caused thousands of Cubans to flee Cuba. As a new leader, Castro turned to the Soviet Union for military and economic support for domestic policies. The Soviet Union inspired Castro to form the *Communist Party of Cuba* (formerly the Integrated Revolutionary Organization) and Castro reduced American economic influences in Cuba. This led to a strained relationship between the United States and Cuba. Remember, Cuba's island is only about 100 miles from the United States, and even though Batista was a repressive dictator, he was against communism and was considered an ally to the United States.

The United States president, Dwight D. Eisenhower, coordinated a plan with the CIA to secretly overthrow the Castro regime. The covert operation was called *Operation Mongoose*. The plan included an invasion at the Bay of Pigs in Cuba, but then Eisenhower's term came to an end. Eisenhower handed off the plan to his successor, John F. Kennedy, but Castro found out about the plan and thwarted the attack.

Cuban Missile Crisis (October 1962): In response to the attempted Bay of Pigs invasion, the Soviet leader Khrushchev and Castro placed nuclear ballistic missiles in Cuba to stop any future United States attacks. Kennedy saw this as a threat to the balance of power in the Western Hemisphere. Kennedy used a naval blockade of Cuba to force the Soviet Union to stop supplying nuclear arms and to remove the ballistic missiles on the Cuban island. The plan almost came to a nuclear war strike between the two superpowers of the United States and the Soviet Union, but behind closed doors, diplomacy led to an agreement that the United States would never again invade Cuba if the Soviet Union removed all nuclear ballistic missiles.

Korean War (1950–1953)

Korea was liberated from Japan in 1945 just after World War II. The country was divided into southern (occupied by the United States) and northern (occupied by the Soviet Union) territories because of their differing political ideologies. North Korea (*Democratic People's Republic of Korea*) was communist, and South Korea (*Republic of Korea*) was democratic. When the communist North Korea invaded democratic South Korea in 1950 in an effort to impose communism, this started the first military conflict of the Cold War. The Korean War pitted the United States against the Soviet Union. The United Nations stepped in and the United States used its policy of containment to block communism from taking over South Korea. The United States aided South Korea, and China aided North Korea. More than 2.5 million people were killed during the Korean War.

China (1949–1976)

In the 1950s and 1960s, China continued to dissolve into a failed state. **Mao Zedong** wanted to use the country's traditional farmers to develop a communist state. Zedong created a policy called the **Great Leap Forward** (1958–1960). The intention was to have massive collectivized farms of 10,000 farmers. He believed that the farmers could produce enough farm goods for the country as well as for international trade. Instead, the policy led to a massive misallocation of resources and depression for the farmers. The result was a manmade famine that killed about 40 million people.

Typically, when an authoritarian leader fails to this degree, he is removed and killed by his political opponents. However, Mao developed a way to protect himself. Mao claimed that traditional Confucianists undermined the communist program; he set up armies of young Chinese students who overran local villages and prosecuted people. This period, called the **Cultural Revolution,** was as an attempt to move the Chinese from Confucianism to communism. In reality, it was a political strategy for Mao to get rid of his political opponents. Mao survived this period and remained in power until his death in 1976.

Vietnam: Ho Chi Minh (1945–1969)

France occupied Vietnam in the late 1800s and was briefly replaced by Japan during World War II. In the 1950s, the French returned. The communist leader, **Ho Chi Minh,** led the **Viet-Minh** in North Vietnam (called the Democratic Republic of Vietnam) against the French using guerrilla warfare. Ho is most known for the longest and most costly battles against French colonization. This meant that his soldiers, who lacked modern weaponry, would hide out in the Vietnam forests and engage in sudden attacks on the French army to steal their weapons. Eventually the Vietnamese soldiers surrounded the French at their northern fort, **Dien Bien Phu.**

Vietnam Conflict (1959–1975)

At the center of the conflict was North Vietnam's aspirations to unify the entire nation of Vietnam under one communist regime that was modeled after the Soviet Union or China. The French agreed to leave Vietnam and allowed the Vietnamese to reunite the country through a national election, but the United States feared that Vietnam would fall to communism. Even though the French decided to withdraw, the United States under the Kennedy administration established an ally in South Vietnam. The United States decided to support the South Vietnamese regime, led by Ngo Diem, who was corrupt and not well liked by the Vietnamese. In one instance, Diem tried to close down Buddhist temples, which led to massive protests, including one monk setting himself on fire.

A big change in Vietnam resulted when Lyndon Johnson became the president of the United States. In 1964, Johnson claimed that the North Vietnamese had attacked two United States battleships at the **Gulf of Tonkin.** Johnson asked Congress for an escalation of combat troops; after this declaration, the number of American troops in Vietnam rose to 500,000 soldiers. From 1965 to 1969, Johnson's goal was not to go to war with North Vietnam, but to prevent communism. Johnson sent American troops to bolster South Vietnam's military defenses against North Vietnam (called the *Viet Cong*). The United States found itself in an unprecedented dilemma between the North and South Vietnamese. In addition, American troops were militarily limited because, just like the French, the U.S. could not conduct a serious ground assault in a jungle war against the Viet Cong. In small jungle villages, U.S. soldiers found it nearly impossible to determine who the enemy was. In the meantime, the Soviet Union and China supplied the North Vietnamese with ammunition, supplies, and political advice. The casualties were growing.

Over the next several years, American foreign policy was unable to bring the war to a successful end, and American leaders feared Chinese involvement. The United States limited attacks to an air offensive called **Operation Rolling Thunder.** This strategy was extremely destructive, and more bombs were dropped on North Vietnam than during World War II. But the Viet Cong continued to fight.

In the United States, several revelations late in the war caused a "credibility gap" with the American government. A release of the **Pentagon Papers** showed that Lyndon Johnson had not been honest about the attacks at the Gulf of Tonkin. The first attack caused no damage and was largely inconsequential.

The second attack was actually a radar that malfunctioned during a weather storm. The news also revealed that one of the American platoons had massacred Vietnamese civilians (women, children, and the elderly) at My Lai, and the military had covered it up. Although the United States government had assured its citizens that the North Vietnamese were weakened, in 1968 the Ho Chi Minh forces led massive surprise invasions in South Vietnam, called the **Tet Offensive.** The war became increasingly unpopular in the United States, and many Americans protested to exit the Vietnam War. By 1973, the United States withdrew from Vietnam, and Vietnam shortly thereafter fell to communist control.

By the end of the Vietnam War, the Americans lost 60,000 soldiers, more than all of the previous American wars combined. About 2 million North and South Vietnamese lost their lives. Southeast Asia was destabilized and communism spread into neighboring Laos and Cambodia. War hawks (people who favor going to war) claimed that their fears of the domino theory were true. Later, China and Vietnam engaged in war over boundary differences.

The 1970s, 1980s, and 1990s

Key Facts about Developing World Events in the 1970s, 1980s, and 1990s

The Soviets invade Afghanistan. During the 1970s, the United States and the Soviet Union tried to lower tensions by following a policy called **Détente.** This policy attempted to open up trading relationships between the United States and the Soviet Union, but at the end of the 1970s, the Soviet Union invaded Afghanistan. Afghanistan is close to the oil-rich countries of Iraq and Iran, as well as the Persian Gulf. American leaders feared that this was a sign of a new Soviet aggressive stance in the Middle East.

Anti-communist groups in Latin America. In the 1980s, U.S. President Ronald Reagan came into office promising to use a more aggressive stance against the Soviet Union. Reagan funded anti-communist groups in Latin America and led a war against the small Latin American island nation of Grenada. Reagan claimed that the Soviet Union was building an airstrip on the island of Grenada so it could move into the Western Hemisphere.

Changes in Soviet leadership. Throughout this period, changes were occurring within the Soviet Union. In the early 1980s, the Soviet leaders were replaced due to the deaths of previous presidents. The Communist Party was now dominated by older people who had become isolated from the younger Russian generation's modern ideas. **Mikhail Gorbachev,** the new Russian president, introduced a series of reforms to transform Russian communism into a new and more modern society. He realized that he had inherited many problems in the Soviet Union. Gorbachev used *perestroika* (increased awareness of the economy) to provide some economic freedoms for new businesses. He also introduced *glasnost* (transparency and openness to the public) to open up more freedom of thought, but much of this new freedom only brought greater demands from the Russian people for even more freedom from the communist government.

The Warsaw Pact dissolved. Eastern European communist governments began to break away from the old Soviet Warsaw Pact. The most symbolic was when Eastern Germany broke away, and Germans destroyed the Berlin Wall in 1989. Following this, Lithuania, Georgia, Romania, and Czechoslovakia abandoned the Warsaw Pact.

The end of Soviet communism. By 1991, the Russian government was facing an internal crisis and the communist leaders put Gorbachev under house arrest. Russians no longer agreed with their communist leaders, so there was a peaceful protest outside of the Kremlin that led to a combined union of the military and the populace. In one weekend, the communist regime of the Soviet Union came to an end.

China and communism. At the same time, China was facing its own challenge. In 1981, the new leader of China, **Deng Xiaoping,** had developed a new idea for reform. Xiaoping ended the failed policies of collectivization and allowed peasants to lease their own land and sell crops to the international market for some profit. The leader also retained the power of the Communist Party and justified all of this through references to traditional Confucianism. His economic policies began to show promise as the country moved into an industrial revolution.

However, many young Chinese students wanted greater social and political freedoms. The students looked to Western Socialist Europe for economic trends, and they looked to the United States for social and political freedoms. Chinese students began to demonstrate their protest against communism at **Tiananmen Square** in 1989. Unlike Russia, however, they did not get the support of the military. Instead, the student leaders were arrested, and their movement was ended by the Chinese military.

China has maintained its communist ideological politics while providing for more competitive markets. China has remained a global competitor with the United States. Today, the Chinese are trying to create leadership in Southeast Asia and Eastern Africa.

The end of the Cold War. The end of the Cold War arrived in 1991. Everyone in the world was surprised by how quickly the conflict came to its conclusion. The surprise was best exemplified by CIA officials saying that they found out that the war had ended by turning on the television and seeing the announcement on the television news station CNN.

Decolonization

One of the most important outcomes of World War II and the Cold War were the independent movements of nations from the developing world toward decolonization. World War II brought an end to fascism, and it also challenged the ideology of social Darwinism or racial purity. The United States and some European nations could not both fight Hitler's racial ideology and justify the "White Man's Burden" of civilizing the countries in Africa, Asia, and Latin America.

HISTORIOGRAPHY. *Historians refer to "The White Man's Burden" (1899), a poem by Rudyard Kipling. Kipling was referencing the imperialist motives of the "evolved" United States and its colonization of the Philippine Islands. Kipling was a friend of President Roosevelt and believed that the United States was called to humanitarian action in underdeveloped territories. The "white empire" of the United States should take up the moral responsibility to advance industrialization in colonized civilizations.*

> TEST TIP: What may be difficult for you to remember on the WHAP exam is that there were many different movements that led to decolonization and the independence of nations from the developing world. The number of self-ruling countries grew from 90 to 170 by the year 2000.

Let's take a look at the most important countries and regions (and their leaderships) during the 20th century.

India

India became independent in 1947. India represents the leadership of the movement because it was one of the first successful countries to break away from imperialist rule without the use of violence. The Indian independence movement spanned 190 years (1757 to 1947). You might remember from the previous chapter that India formed the **Indian National Congress (INC)** political party in 1895. It was divided between those who wanted immediate independence and those who wanted to take a more gradual approach toward independence. In 1920, this divide started to break away with the rise of the charismatic and non-violent leader **Mohandas Gandhi.** Gandhi preached the idea of *satyagraha* (the "third path" approach) that rejected both violence and passive non-action. Gandhi argued that Indian Hindus should embrace the positive aspects of British culture while rejecting its occupation. He reached out to all of the diverse groups in India to form a coalition that would oppose British occupation using non-violent strategies.

Gandhi's non-violent movements attracted international attention when the British attacked demonstrators in the courtyard of Amritsar in 1919, called the **Amritsar Massacre.** The British brigadier-general's troops killed almost 400 non-violent protestors when the British wanted to ban demonstrations and meetings. When the world heard about this massacre, there was public pressure put on the British to give the Indians their independence. Gandhi then formed a Non-Cooperation Movement from 1920 to 1922. People were urged to boycott British courts and schools and refuse British government employment. The end of the British rule in India was in 1947, but India was partitioned into subdivisions.

Developments in India

Since gaining its independence in 1947, India has faced several significant social, religious, and economic difficulties:

- The religious division between the Hindus and the Muslims. For example, Mohandas Gandhi was assassinated in 1948 by a fellow Hindu who was upset that Gandhi was willing to embrace Muslims.
- The continued fight over the boundaries in Northern India.
- Both India and Pakistan have nuclear weapons.
- The question of economic identity. Gandhi wanted to retain India's traditional agricultural economy, but the successor to the leadership after Gandhi's death, **Jawaharlal Nehru,** wanted India to industrialize and join the international trade market.

This has led to a continued question about how to move the growing rural population in India into central industrialized cities. Due to extreme poverty, India has lost many of its middle-class professions when many people immigrated to Britain and the United States. Today, India is one of the top competitive economic nations in the world, so many of India's problems may soon be resolved through economic trade.

Pakistan

Up until 1947, Pakistan was a territory of the British Indian Empire. Following World War II, the British agreed to give India its independence, but internal divisions arose over ethnic and religious differences. **Muhammad Ali Jinnah,** an Indian Muslim, organized fellow Muslims against what he perceived to be the Hindu majority. He called for a separate Muslim homeland, which eventually evolved into a British partition of Northern India into the Hindu-dominated boundaries of Northern India and the Muslim country of Pakistan. The work of various movements led to the **Indian Independence Act of 1947,** which called for a separate Muslim state of Pakistan.

Pakistan itself would eventually fall into a civil war in 1971 between the West Pakistanis, who spoke Urdu, and the East Pakistanis, who spoke Bengali. This led to two divisions in Pakistan: Pakistan (West Pakistan) and Bangladesh (East Pakistan). To make the issue more complicated, there is Kashmir (an area just south of Pakistan), a Muslim population that was governed by Hindu leaders. This created the context for an ongoing boundary war between Pakistan and India ever since 1948.

Israel and Palestine

One of the most contentious fights between two different independence movements has been between **Jewish Israelis** and **Muslim Palestinians** after the collapse of the Ottoman Empire.

Key Facts about the Conflict Between Israel and Palestine

Divided land. After World War I, the Europeans created the mandate system that divided the land into areas:

> British control: Iraq, Iran, Jordan, and Palestine
>
> French control: Syria and Lebanon

The British began to make competing promises to the Arabs and the Jewish immigrants. First the British promised the Jews that they would eventually create a homeland in the Balfour Declaration. Then they promised the Arabs that they would maintain Arab sovereignty. These competing promises created the two opposing groups, both without clear leadership.

Zionist movement. The Jewish immigrants from Europe had long wanted a homeland since they had been removed by the Romans in the Jewish Diaspora in the 1st century. Jews faced anti-Semitism in Europe for many centuries. By the late 1800s, there was a religious and political movement, **Zionism** (a movement for the establishment, development, and protection of a Jewish nation), that argued that Jews would only find protection once they created a homeland with a recognized government and military. **Theodor Herzl** was the leader of the Zionist movement and pointed to two examples to demonstrate his argument.

The first example occurred after the Franco-Prussian War. After the French lost the war to the Germans, they claimed that someone in the military had handed over secrets to the Germans. French **General Alfred Dreyfus** was tried and sentenced to life imprisonment on Devil's Island. Eventually, Dreyfus was cleared of any wrongdoing when it was discovered that the espionage was coming from another source, but it took over a decade of evidence to demonstrate his innocence. It was clear the resistance to Dreyfus' innocence was coming from prejudices directed at his Jewish identity.

The second example was from Russia. A Russian tzar had faced multiple failures at the beginning of the 20th century, so his generals forged a group of papers, called the **Protocols of the Elders of Zion.** These papers claimed that Jewish rabbis met to plot how to take over the world. These papers were used by anti-Semites, including fascists, to create fears and attacks against Jews.

Israel became an official country in 1948. The most important event to change the direction of the Zionist movement was the Jewish Holocaust of World War II. The attack on the Jewish population by Germany's fascist Nazi Party appeared to validate Jewish fears of never being accepted. After World War II, Zionist leaders pushed for a final resolution to the partition of Palestine at the United Nations. Eventually, the Zionist leaders accepted a UN plan to separate Palestine into Western and Eastern partitions. In 1948, the Jewish Zionists claimed the Western half of Palestine as the new nation of Israel.

Israeli and Arab wars. In response, the Arab countries united to attack Israel on three different occasions. The first was directly after the **War for Independence** in 1948. The second was the **Six-Day War** in 1967, and the third was the **Yom Kippur War** in 1973. In each case, Israel won the wars and acquired more land.

> TEST TIP: For the WHAP exam, the most important of the three wars was the Six-Day War, when the Israelis responded to Jordanian attack by taking over territory in the West Bank. This area became the place where we see continued tensions today between the Israeli occupation and the Palestinians.

The leader of the movement against the Israelis was the nation of Egypt. In 1952, **Gamal Abdel Nasser** led a coup against the Egyptian king. He promised to unite all Arabs in a **pan-Arab movement.** Nasser appeared to be successful when he was able to nationalize the **Suez Canal** and stop Britain from taking it back. One of his goals was to eventually remove the nation of Israel and return the land to the Palestinians. However, during the Six-Day War, his armies were soundly defeated by the Israelis, who also gained territory in the **Gaza Strip** just north of Egypt. The people of Egypt lost faith in Nasser and he was replaced by **Anwar Sadat.** Sadat also tried to invade Israel during its high holy day of Yom Kippur, but he too lost the battle against the Israelis. Even though Sadat lost the battle, he had shown some signs of success early in the war, so the Egyptians believed he might eventually fulfill Nasser's promises.

Peace negotiations between Egypt and Israel. Sadat decided to go in another direction to improve the tensions between the Arabs and Israel. Sadat met with U.S. President Jimmy Carter and the Israeli Prime Minister **Menachem Begin** at the **Camp David Accords.** At the end of the meeting, these nations concluded that Egypt would no longer invade Israel if Israel returned the land taken from Egypt during the Yom Kippur War. To most of the Western world, this appeared to be a major breakthrough in Middle Eastern tensions. However, for a newly rising radical Islamic movement, this was a betrayal, and in 1981, Sadat was assassinated by members of the **Egyptian Brotherhood.**

The rise of radical Islamists. Sadat's assassination revealed a very different movement that had been brewing in the Middle East since the 1950s. A radical Islamist movement had been growing under the influence of the writings of **Sayyid Qutb.** Qutb argued that the attacks on Israel failed due to the secularization of Arab nations. His writings eventually influenced terrorist groups, including the Egyptian Brotherhood and **Osama bin Laden's Al-Qaeda**. What really made Al-Qaeda stand out was its emphasis on creating an international terrorist organization, and bin Laden's goal went even further than hatred for Israel. Bin Laden wanted to create a new Muslim *caliphate* (Islamic government ruled by a person who is the successor of the prophet Muhammad). Today's conflict with ISIS is a continuation of this new religious *zealotry* (fanatical religious and political devotion).

Iran

Iran (known as Persia before 1935) had a relationship with Britain since the 13th century. Iran was one of the countries created during the mandate system following World War I. In 1921, **Reza Kahn** seized power and declared himself the leader of Iran. During World War II, he considered joining with Hitler's axis powers, and this led to a British seizure of Iran.

Key Facts about Iran

The British-owned oil industry in Iran. Britain placed Reza Kahn's grandson, **Mohammad Reza Pahlavi,** in control of the government. Britain then used this connection to place a British-owned oil industry in Iran. During the 1950s, the Iranian population complained that the British oil industry was shipping both oil and Iranian wealth out of the country, so the Iranians elected socialist **Mohammed Mossadegh** into power. Mossadegh and the Iranian parliament voted to take over the oil industry. This created fear in the United States that Iran was intending to join the Soviet Union during the Cold War. This move could mean a serious shift in the power over oil in the region. The CIA created a program that eventually led to the secret removal of Mossadegh; he was replaced by Mohammad Reza.

Iranian reforms. Reza led Iran during the 1960s and 1970s and instituted several reforms to modernize Iran. For example, women gained the right to vote, a welfare system was created, and the religious Mullahs were separated from governmental power. The separation of religion from the state led to anger among the traditional Muslims. In addition, Reza's use of the *SAVAK* (secret police) increased Iranian anger toward him since the SAVAK was used to round up Reza's opposition and torture them in prison.

Khomeini overthrows Reza. By 1979, tensions in Iran led to a revolution against Reza. The revolution was initially led by a coalition of liberals, communists, socialists, and Muslims. Then the Shiite cleric **Ayatollah Ruhollah Khomeini** took over the movement and imprisoned or killed all of the non-Muslim Iranian leaders. Iran became a religious *theocracy* (a system whereby religious priests rule the government in the name of God). Khomeini pursued an aggressive foreign policy to expand Shiite influence in the Sunni-dominated region.

Modern-day Iran. Iran has recently gone through tremendous domestic changes. The growing youth of Iran have shown signs of positive views toward the Western world.

There appeared to be an opportunity for political change in 2009 during the **Iranian Green Revolutionary Movement** (green is the symbol of unity and hope) against the Islamic clerics. Resistance protesters demanded the removal of President Mahmoud Ahmadinejad after he was elected with over 60% of the votes. Protesters of the movement claimed that the results were fixed by government officials because the outcome was announced so quickly. Thousands of protestors demonstrated, but Iran's Ayatollah blamed the United States for interfering in Iran's politics. It took 9 months to stop the protestors, but in the end the revolution failed. Over 10,000 people were arrested. Clerics increased their hard-line response to the revolution and started to pursue a nuclear program, which they claimed was started to expand Iran's energy sources.

In 2016, Iran's nuclear program nearly led to a war between Iran and Israel over the fear of an Iran nuclear arms program. The United States Obama administration worked with Iran to stop the program, but Iran continues to be very aggressive in its attempt to expand Shiite influence in the region.

Turkey

Turkey emerged as a nation-state at the end of the Ottoman Empire. The leader, **Atatürk,** hoped to forge a closer alliance with Western Europe after World War II and also wanted to modernize the country by creating a greater secularization of the state from Muslim clerical control. Turkey was successful in joining NATO in 1955 and the European Union in 1989.

Key Facts about Turkey

Turkey continues to face a number of critical concerns for its future.

- Turkey did not accept responsibility for the perpetration of genocide against the Armenians during World War I. This issue continues to keep the West from welcoming Turkey to a favored nation status for trade.

- Turkey continues to battle with the Kurdish population in the South. The Kurds want to break away from Turkey and form their own nation, and have created a political party called **Kurdistan Workers' Party (PKK).** The PKK have fought an armed struggle against the Turkish government that has led both the Turkish and United States governments to declare the PKK a terrorist organization. However, with the recent terrorist threats, the United States needs both the support of air bases in Turkey and the Kurdish land to fight against ISIS.

- Turkey has had a constant internal fight regarding the influence of Islam over the government. In 1997 and 2007, the military intervened in order to stop Islamic influence on the government. During the summer of 2016, there was an unsuccessful military coup to remove the president, **Recep Tayyip Erdogan;** it was feared he was allowing too much Islamic influence in the government.

Today, Turkey faces two major issues. One major issue is whether or not it can keep a mutually beneficial relationship with the United States and Western Europe. A similar and interrelated issue is whether or not the Turkish government can maintain its secular governmental status.

African Region

The process of decolonization was complicated in the African region since this was the central place for European efforts to organize its control during the Age of Imperialism. Let's take a look at several different countries independently, and then let's see if there are any common patterns or any differences.

Ghana

Ghana is located in Western Africa. It is one of the leading countries of Africa because of its natural resources: gold, timber, diamonds, and cocoa. The **Gold Coast** combined with British Togoland in 1957 to create independent Ghana. The Gold Coast is the name for this part of Africa because the gold trade with Europe made it possible to develop Ghana in the 17th century.

Ghana gained independence from Britain in 1957, but like many new countries, it faced many challenges. The first president of Ghana was **Kwame Nkrumah,** a charismatic leader who called for a **Pan-African union.** Nkrumah hoped that Africa could eventually form a federal system similar to that of the United States and pursued public works programs for Ghana. However, Nkrumah was eventually criticized for corruption and the rising public debt. In 1963, Nkrumah declared dictatorial powers, and 3 years later, the military overthrew him. After Nkrumah's rule, Ghana was governed by military dictators. After 25 years, Ghana returned to a democratic rule in 1992.

Algeria

Algeria is located in Northern Africa. It was originally under the control of the Ottoman Empire, but in the 19th century, France invaded and seized Algeria (1830 to 1962). In 1954, the Algerians fought France for independence, but it wasn't until 1962 that Algeria gained independence from France. A small group of French settlers called for French military resistance and the **National Liberation Front (FLN)** fought to force France out of Algeria. In France, the French Communist Party called for French President **Charles de Gaulle** to give the Algerians their independence. De Gaulle eventually bypassed the French legislature and went straight to the people through referendum to vote for Algerian independence.

Algeria became a one-party state led by the FLN. This eventually inspired a radical Islamist movement against the Algerian government in 1991. The Islamic Salvation Front won an election but was prevented from holding office. The new president, placed in power in 1999, tried to include some moderates from the Islamic community. However, violence continues between the different groups.

Kenya

Kenya is located in Eastern Africa. It is located on the coastline by the Indian Ocean, making it very important strategically and historically for trade. Kenya is one of the most rapidly increasing populations in the world. In the late-19th century, Kenya was under the control of the British government as part of the East Africa Protectorate. Then in 1952, the **Mau Mau rebellion,** under British colonial rule, started a movement that used guerilla warfare to attack British settlements. This rebellion stirred terror throughout the Kenyan population. The British abandoned Kenya in 1963, leading to the election of **Jomo Kenyatta.**

A significant East Asian population had migrated to Kenya to work on its **Mombasa-Kisumu Railway** in the late 1800s. After the project was completed, they settled on unoccupied lands. Throughout the 1960s, there were tensions between different tribal groups: **Kikuyu, Luhya,** and **Luo.**

In 1982, Kenya was officially a one-party dictatorship led by the **Kenyan African National Union (KANU).** The Kenyan government began to "Africanize" the Kenyan labor markets. Asians were required to obtain a work permit, and employers were not allowed to hire Asians unless there were no qualified Kenyans for the job. This forced many Asians to relocate to Britain. After Kenyatta's death, the next leader, **Daniel Moi,** was president for over 24 years. Moi's government was criticized for its debt and corruption. Today, Kenya is considered one of the top human rights violators in the world, and there is a coalition government that is attempting to reform the problems of the mid-20th century. Even the International Monetary Fund (IMF) has threatened to remove loans if the country does not reform.

Angola

Angola is located in Southern Africa. In 1482, Angola was colonized by the Portuguese, whose primary interest soon turned to slave trading. Many historians agree that Angola was probably the largest source of slave trading in the world in the 15th century. By the end of the 19th century, slave labor had morphed into a forced labor system, which continued until it was outlawed in 1961. In 1975, Angola gained its independence. Different tribes began to fight one another and were supported by the different superpowers of the Cold War. These included the Mbundu tribe backed by the Soviet Union and Cuba, the Bakongo tribe backed by the United States, and the Ovimbundu tribe backed by South Africa. These external influences provoked a civil war that lasted for 27 years until 2002. The war devastated the country and displaced about 4 million people. Today, Angola's economy is slowly improving, but the country is faced with rebuilding its infrastructure and disarming the thousands of existing landmines left from the war.

Nigeria

Nigeria is located in Western Africa. It gained its independence from Britain in 1960. Although there are about 200 ethnic groups in Nigeria, after Nigeria gained its freedom from Britain, Nigeria was torn between the **Igbo tribe** (a westernized Christian group) and the **Hausa-Fulani tribe** (an Islamic group). These two groups fought a civil war for a decade over possible secession of the Igbo tribe. Military coups were common in Nigeria, and the Igbos were defeated. Military generals took over the country until 1990, when the country elected a civilian government. In 1999, a new constitution was formed and democracy was regained.

The leaders of Nigeria tried to create a federation of 36 different states, and they allowed for a dual legal system that would incorporate both secular and Islamic Sharia legal codes. The constitution has also tried to encourage intermarriage between ethnic groups.

South Africa

In 1652, South Africa was colonized by the Dutch. The Dutch believed that God had led them to the new Jerusalem. However, they had tensions with the local **Zulu tribes** until the Dutch found gold mines. This discovery led to the **Boer Wars** (*Boer* means Dutch settlers) between the British, Dutch, and Zulus over the territory. At the conclusion of the wars, the British allowed Dutch settlers to govern the local African population if the British gained control over the gold mines.

The Dutch control evolved into an all-white government **apartheid system** (racial "separateness") established after 1948. The apartheid system was established through laws that required black South Africans (the majority of the population) to carry identity papers, live in separate homelands, and remain segregated from the white **Afrikaner** population. These laws remained in effect for almost 50 years. In response, the **African National Congress** was formed. One of its key leaders was **Nelson Mandela,** who favored Gandhi's non-violent approach to end apartheid. However, on March 21, 1960, after the South African police killed hundreds of protestors at the **Sharpeville Massacre,** Mandela chose to revolt with violence. This led to his arrest and imprisonment on Robben Island for 27 years.

Heads Up: What You Need to Know

Nelson Mandela is a key figure in world history and his story is among the most remarkable in world history. Mandela dedicated his life to fight for equality and helped to bring an end to apartheid in South Africa. He was imprisoned from 1963 to 1990 (27 years) as a consequence for his protests against a white-controlled government, but he was released from prison and quickly became an international figure for anti-apartheid. In 1993, Mandela (and F. W. de Klerk) were jointly awarded a Nobel Peace Prize for their efforts to peacefully end apartheid. In 1994, Mandela became South Africa's first black president.

By the 1980s, international pressure had mounted against the South African apartheid system. Western students, rock stars, and businesses divested their financial investments in the South African economy. The new president, F. W. de Klerk, decided to negotiate with Nelson Mandela for an integrated South Africa. De Klerk knew he needed to work with Mandela to create a reconciliation with South African rebel forces if peace were to be created. In 1991, he freed Mandela from prison.

Mandela called for a peaceful transition to an integrated state. In 1994, he ran for and won the office of the presidency, and he then pursued a "rainbow coalition" of blacks and whites in reforming the government.

Latin America

The turmoil and instability from the period of imperialism and colonialism were obstacles to Latin America's development. However, there have also been great hopes for the economic improvement in many of the Latin American countries.

Key Facts about Latin America

Latin American dictatorships. Many Latin American countries have had problems of single-party dictatorships. After Mexico's rebellion in 1917, the **Institutional Revolutionary Party (PRI)** became a single-party leader until the 1990s. There was brief competition from the **National Action Party (PAN)** that led to the election of Mexico's President **Vincente Fox** in 2000. However, the PRI returned to power in 2006. In Venezuela, **Hugo Chavez** came to power from 1999 to 2013 and created the United Socialist Party. Chavez promised land reforms and an empowerment of small farmers. Instead, he ended up creating a dictatorship.

Latin American economies. Many Latin American countries have chosen the economic program of state-run economies or industries. Cuba became a communist dictatorship in the 1960s. When the Soviet Union collapsed in 1991, the Cuban economy was left without its greatest benefactor. However, Cuba gained a brief period of support from Venezuela. Venezuela created a state-run oil industry and largest oil export in the Western Hemisphere with the hope of using its revenues to empower small farmers. Oil revenues accounted for 95 percent of Venezuela's revenue, but when oil prices dropped by 50 percent in 2015, this led to a devastating collapse of the Venezuelan economy. Since the Venezuelan economy collapsed, Cuba was once again in a state of crisis. Mexico created **PEMEX** in 1938, a state-run oil company.

Latin American free trade agreements. The Latin American region has become a part of free trade agreements. Mexico joined with the United States and Canada in 1994 in the **North American Free Trade Agreement (NAFTA).** The Bush administration expanded the U.S. regional free trade agreements in the 2000s with a **Central American Free Trade Agreement (CAFTA).** Recent debates in the United States have been about the issues of free trade, economic growth, and transnational companies seeking out areas of cheap labor.

Latin American drug cartels. Another downside to the increased activity between North America and Latin America has been the rise in drug cartels, especially in Mexico and Central America. Large drug cartels have been active in kidnappings, massacres, and the takeover of local governmental systems.

Globalization

Globalization has been a positive step for individuals and countries, but it has also had some significant disadvantages that have required responses from local political and social leaders. But what is globalization?

Many students think that globalization is international trade, but this is an incorrect and limited view of globalization. Trade has existed since the first day humans migrated out of Africa. Globalization is really about the process of connecting economic and political developments throughout the world. Globalization eliminates boundaries to trade, cultural exchange, and information. This can be accomplished by nation-states lowering tariff taxes in order to spread trade, technology, labor, and information across international boundaries. The assumption behind globalization is that when boundaries are removed, a mutual exchange across boundary lines is promoted.

Critical Thinking Question: How did globalization happen and what are its effects?

International economic institutions formed. Globalization really began at the end of World War II. The victorious leaders of the Allied forces argued that World War II was caused by an economic collapse that inspired radical leaders and regimes. In 1947, these leaders met at the *Bretton Woods Conference* to create two international institutions to stabilize the global economy: the **International Monetary Fund** (IMF) and the **World Bank**. As discussed on p. 223, the IMF set the rules for countries to develop their economies by changing from an agrarian society to an industrialized society. If countries followed these rules, they could receive financial loans from the World Bank.

Treaties formed. After these important institutions were formed, the next step in globalization was the formation of major treaties among countries to lower tariff rates. *Tariffs* are taxes on the imported goods or products that arrive in a country. Most countries implement tariffs to protect their industries from foreign competition.

Heads Up: What You Need to Know

On the WHAP exam, globalization may be one of the most significant developments of Period Six. Here are some reasons why:

- Globalization ties together all of the major events during this period, including World War II, the Cold War, and decolonization.
- Globalization has dramatically changed the face of almost every nation in the world, including governments, culture, technology, and economic relationships.
- Globalization was created by international agreements to lower tariffs including: GATT, EU, NAFTA, CAFTA, and WTO.
- Many current global controversies are tied into the framework of globalization. There is increasing divide between wealthy developed nations and poorer developing nations.
- New technologies that led to globalization include fossil fuel energies, digital technologies, satellites, and fiber-optic cables.

Theories about the Effectiveness of Globalization

There are two theories about whether or not these types of policies are effective: comparative advantage theory and dependency theory.

Comparative Advantage Theory

The economic theory of **comparative advantage** is the ability of a country to produce and sell goods and services for trade at a lower price than a competing country. Therefore, the country would have an advantage over its competitors. Economists argue that comparative advantage is good for international trade because a country can focus on what it is best at for production and services. For many countries in the developing part of the world, this means a very limited group of raw resources, agricultural goods, or technology. For example, the United States buys services in India's call centers because it is cheaper; both countries benefit. Comparative advantage allows the developing country to focus on its productivity and encourage foreign investment. Eventually, the developing country will use that new investment to broaden its economic options. According to this economic theory, international competition raises the living standards of everyone through economic growth over time.

Dependency Theory

A second theory argues that the logic of comparative advantage makes sense but masks the reality of global trade and inequality. According to the **dependency theory,** the countries in the developing world are competing against each other and the countries of the developed world are competing against each other. Why is this a bad thing? The resources of the poor underdeveloped countries flow to the wealthy developed countries. The developing world lowers costs for foreign businesses, lowers taxes, implements business regulations, and does not allow labor unions. This encourages wealthy transnational corporations (TNCs) to come to the developing world countries to establish factories in the poor underdeveloped countries. These factories create three disadvantages. First, the companies hire workers at very low wages. Second, these companies do not pay taxes, so the governments do not get money for development. Third, the companies send their profits back to the base of their corporation in the wealthy developed country. According to the dependency theory, international trade creates growing inequalities among nation-states around the world.

Treaties and Agreements

The leaders of globalization tend to abide by the comparative advantage theory, promoting lower tariffs in order to increase trade, industrialization, and the transmission of information from one nation to the next. There have been a number of significant treaties or agreements related to lower tariffs. Here are the big ones to remember for the WHAP exam:

Global Economic Treaties, Agreements, and Organizations	
GATT (General Agreement on Tariffs and Trade)	The GATT was an agreement among countries to lower their tariffs in order to promote international trade following World War II.
EU (European Union)	Western Europe started to form a coalition of countries that would lower their tariff rates and follow common business rules in order to create regional trade in Europe.
WTO (World Trade Organization)	This legal organization was formed in the 1990s. It is an international court where countries can sue one another if they don't abide by the international rules on tariffs and trade.
NAFTA (North American Free Trade Agreement)	In response to the EU, the United States created a regional bloc of countries including itself, Mexico, and Canada. These countries agreed to lower tariffs and allow for easier business movement among the countries.
OPEC (Organization of Petroleum Exporting Countries)	In an effort to coordinate and unify the oil industry, OPEC was established in 1960. OPEC negotiates with oil-rich countries (mostly in the Middle East, like Saudi Arabia) to regulate oil prices, production, and exportation. Before 1960, the oil industry was controlled by large companies that were able to charge high prices and export to anyone who paid these prices. Oil-rich countries became wealthy, but poor countries experienced oil shortages as a result.

Critical Thinking Question: Do trade agreements really work?

Well, it depends on what you are looking at for the assessment.

Absolute poverty. On the one hand, globalization has led to some amazing positive social and economic developments. For example, absolute poverty has decreased over the last 40 years. Absolute poverty is the measurement of how much money you actually have. It is a measurement of the growth (or decline) of income in your pocketbook. Across the world, since globalization started, absolute poverty has decreased dramatically. Why has this happened? Most likely because so many economically disadvantaged people have moved from farmlands into industrial cities, where they have opportunities to increase their income over time.

Relative poverty. On the other hand, globalization has also led to a growth in relative poverty. Relative poverty is based on a person's economic status compared to other members of society. People are considered relatively poor if they fall below the prevailing standard of living based on where they live in the world and their income. The gap between what people need to live on in the developed world versus the developing world has been widening over the last 30 years. Some argue that this does not matter because as long as economies are growing; who really cares if people are making different amounts of money as long as people have enough to support their physical needs. Another possibility to consider, though, is that even if people are no longer living in extreme poverty, they may not have sufficient income to consume enough goods, both for their own countries and the global economy.

Key Facts about the Challenges of Globalization

Nation-state devolution. We have been living in nation-states for a relatively short period of time—nation-states became the primary way of organizing societies and people only about 200 years ago. The problem is that we have attempted to force people of many different cultures, religions, and languages under one government, one set of laws, and one nationality. This does not always sit well with cultural minorities who aspire to self-govern and form their own identity. A movement similar to the separatist movement started in the 1980s and lasted until the early 2000s called the devolution movement. It was a movement to return power to individual states. **Devolution** is when a central government gives power and property to local groups, thus breaking down nation-states into more regional and local areas of governance.

In the 1990s, Yugoslavia divided into Serbia, Bosnia, and Croatia. In Spain, the Basque minority has been fighting against the Spanish government. In Russia, the Southern ethnic group of Chechens fought for their independence from the Russian Confederation. In Iran, Iraq, and Turkey, the Kurdish minority is fighting to break away and form its own nation of Kurdistan. In each of these cases, small minority groups wanted to claim their own cultural self-determination separate from their originating nation-state.

Genocide. As countries have attempted to develop a sense of national identity, they have often turned against racial and ethnic minorities who are different. During the 1950s, in Rwanda, Belgian colonists had categorized a group of Africans as **Tutsis** who controlled the state. The Belgians believed the Tutsis looked like them and this led to a conflict with the African majority, **Hutus.** Rwanda gained its independence in 1962, but animosities remained over the conflict between these two groups. In 1994, the Hutus shot down their own president's airplane and laid blame on the Tutsis; they then started a brutal battle of genocide and began to hunt down and kill the Tutsi minority population.

In 2003, Darfur in Sudan was divided into two groups: Arab Muslims in the North and non-Arab Christians in the South. The non-Arab group took up arms against the Muslim government, so the Arab Muslim government allowed for a Muslim militia called the **Janjaweed** to attack the non-Arabs in the South. This led to the displacement of 1 million people and the slaying of over 200,000 people.

Terrorism. Closely aligned to the separatist movement is the political action of terrorism. Global terrorism has a distinct definition: It is the politically motivated and intentional violence perpetrated on innocent people in order to destabilize governments. Modern-day terrorism has increased in frequency and has had a global reach. Terrorism has existed for centuries, but modern global terrorism is very different. Coming from a **Wahhabis** religious sect of Islam, global terrorism has been carried out in the name of religion. Radicalized Islamic leaders believe they can create a pure Islam that will bring back the days of the *caliphates* (government controlled by a Muslim leader). According to radicalized terrorists, their acts of violence will be forgiven by God. Their goal is to create this pure Islamic governance from Northern Africa to Indonesia. Modern-day terrorists have arisen during the period of globalization as an attack on the Western boundaries that were established by the Europeans after World War I.

Global warming. One of the biggest challenges to globalization has been the concern over the heating up of the earth. The scientific theories of global warming posit the negative side effect of using CO_2 gases for industrialization. The theory is that CO_2 is released into the atmosphere and traps heat in the environment.

This heat then has positive feedback. Positive feedback is defined as a system that loops around to cause something similar to happen. For example, the positive feedback of increased heat causes the melting of the glaciers. This then leads to excess water in the oceans, and the oceans heat up, expanding the water molecules. Then the hot air evaporates the water, leading to more water molecules in the air. This traps more heat. The eventual result is rising sea levels, displacement of coastal populations, and a growing global average of heat. Critics of global warming have either called for alternative energies (nuclear, wind, solar, or thermal) or more radical solutions such as stopping industrialization.

Heads Up: What You Need to Know

Below is a summary of the common themes and issues for Period Six:

- Political ideologies, such as extreme nationalism and fascism, led to a tumultuous era of extremes in the 20th century.
- The world economic decline in the 1900s caused unstable governments that led to World War II. As a result, world financial organizations were established: the United Nations, the International Monetary Fund, and the World Bank.
- The "total wars" of World War I and World War II were the most brutal in world history due to new tactics and advanced technologies.
- The United States dropped the first atomic bombs on Japan in an effort to end World War II.
- The United States and its Western allies feared that communism would take over the world in the *domino theory*. This nearly caused World War III during the Cold War between the United States and Russia.
- Developing world nations led revolutionary movements to decolonize.
- Globalization, terrorism, and global warming have changed the face of almost every nation in the world.

Chapter Review Practice Questions

The practice questions show the types of questions that may appear on the exam. On the actual exam, the questions are grouped into sets. Each set contains one source-based prompt and two to five questions.

Multiple-Choice Questions

Questions 1–3 refer to the following passage.

> Independence for the Gold Coast was my aim. It was a colony and I have always regarded colonialism as the policy by which a foreign power binds territories to herself by political ties, with the primary object of promoting her own economic advantages . . .
>
> Thus we have witnessed the greatest awakening ever seen on this earth of suppressed and exploited peoples against the powers that have kept them in subjection. This, without a doubt, is the most significant happening of the twentieth century.
>
> —Source: Kwame Nkrumah, excerpt from "Ghana: The Autobiography of Kwame Nkrumah," 1965. Statement about the fight for Ghana's independence.

1. Which of the following best explains the context of Nkrumah's statement above?

   A. The leader was expressing support for the capitalist powers in their fight against the Eastern communist bloc.
   B. The passage references the alliance between the Western powers against fascism during World War II.
   C. This statement was issued to challenge Woodrow Wilson to uphold his belief in self-determination.
   D. The leader was referencing the decolonization process that occurred after World War II.

2. Which of the following best expresses the reason Ghana's leader was successful in attaining his goals?

   A. Leaders in the developing world were able to create successful movements to unite whole regions.
   B. The developing world sided with either the communist or capitalist bloc during the Cold War.
   C. New technological innovations emerged from the developing world during globalization.
   D. The defeat of Adolf Hitler in World War II created a questioning of the moral legitimacy of social Darwinism and racial hierarchies.

3. Which of the following provides the best argument to dispute Nkrumah's passage?

   A. Nelson Mandela led a non-violent resistance movement against the Afrikaners' apartheid system in South Africa.
   B. Most African countries were led by military dictators after the decolonization movement ended.
   C. African countries became a part of the non-aligned movement, siding with the U.S. or Russia based on national self-interest.
   D. International pressure for decolonization increased when military force was used at the Amritsar and Sharpeville massacres.

Questions 4–6 refer to the following passage.

The inspirers of the "Cold War" began to establish military blocs—the North Atlantic bloc, SEATO, and the Baghdad pact. [They claim] they have united for defense against the "communist threat." But this is sheer hypocrisy!

We know from history that when planning a re-division of the world, the imperialist powers have always lined up military blocs. Today the "anti-communism" slogan is being used as a smoke screen to cover up the claims of one power for world domination.

The United States wants, by means of blocs and pacts, to secure a dominant position in the capitalist world. The inspirers of the "position of strength" policy assert that it makes another way impossible because it ensures a "balance of power" in the world. [They] offer the arms race as their main recipe for the preservation of peace!

It is perfectly obvious that when nations compete to increase their military might, the danger of war becomes greater, not lesser. Capitalism will find its grave in another world war, should it unleash it.

—Source: Excerpt from a speech by Soviet Premier Nikita Khrushchev
in 1956 in which he explains his point of view on U.S. actions.

4. Which of the following best summarizes what Khrushchev is responding to in his speech?

   A. The U.S. leading a United Nations coalition into Korea during the Korean crisis
   B. The use of atomic bombs by the United States to end World War II with Japan
   C. The U.S. airlift of materials into Western Berlin during the Berlin Blockade
   D. The U.S. formation of NATO as a defensive alliance against possible USSR expansion into Western Europe

5. Which of the following best illustrates the "re-division of the world" that Khrushchev references in the <u>second paragraph</u> of his speech?

    A. The developed world and the developing world were divided by the need for industrial development.

    B. The United States aided Europe through the Marshall Plan after World War II to redevelop following post-war damage.

    C. The USSR and the U.S. formed a bipolar East-West world following World War II.

    D. Following World War II, the old imperialist powers let go of the developing world colonies for self-determination.

6. Which of the following best describes the context of the conflict that is described in Khrushchev's speech?

    A. The U.S. and USSR fought each other indirectly through proxy powers in the developing world.

    B. European powers created alliances as a form of deterrence to stop future wars.

    C. The allies came together to form an international institution for diplomacy to stop future global wars.

    D. Regional national and non-state powers fought each other over boundaries and national identity.

Document-Based Question

1 question

60 minutes

Reading Time: 15 minutes (brainstorm your thoughts and organize your response)

Writing Time: 45 minutes

Directions: The document-based question is based on the seven accompanying documents. The documents are for instructional purposes only. Some of the documents have been edited for the purpose of this practice exercise. Write your response on lined paper and include the following:

- **Thesis.** Present a thesis that supports a historically defensible claim, establishes a line of reasoning, and responds to all parts of the question. The thesis must consist of one or more sentences located in one place—either the introduction or the conclusion.

- **Contextualization.** Situate the argument by explaining the broader historical events, developments, or processes that occurred before, during, or after the time frame of the question.

- **Evidence from the documents.** Use the content of at least three to six of the documents to develop and support a cohesive argument that responds to the question.

- **Evidence beyond the documents.** Support or qualify your argument by explaining at least one additional piece of specific historical evidence not found in the documents. (Note: The example must be different from the evidence used to earn the point for contextualization.)

- **Analysis.** Use at least three documents that are relevant to the question to explain the documents' point of view, purpose, historical situation, and/or audience.

- **Historical reasoning.** Use historical reasoning to show relationships among the documents, the topic question, and the thesis argument. Use evidence to corroborate, qualify, or modify the argument.

Based on the documents that follow, answer the question below.

Question 1: Compare and contrast the reactions to the decolonization process after World War II.

Document 1

Source: The United Nations, "Declaration on the Granting of Independence to Colonial Countries and Peoples," 1960.

Mindful of the determination proclaimed by the peoples of the world in the Charter of the United Nations to reaffirm faith in fundamental human rights, in the dignity and worth of the human person, . . . Solemnly proclaims the necessity of bringing to a speedy and unconditional end colonialism in all its forms. To this end Declares that:

1. The subjection of peoples to alien subjugation, domination and exploitation . . . is contrary to the Charter of the United Nations and is an impediment to the promotion of world peace and co-operation.

2. All peoples have the right to self-determination; by virtue of that right they freely determine their political status and freely pursue their economic, social and cultural development.

Document 2

Source: Excerpt from "Charter of the Organization of African Unity," May, 25, 1963.

We, the Heads of African States and Governments assembled in the City of Addis Ababa, Ethiopia,

Convinced that it is the inalienable right of all people to control their own destiny,

Conscious of the fact that freedom, equality, justice and dignity are essential objectives for the achievement of the legitimate aspirations of the African peoples,

Conscious of our responsibility to harness the natural and human resources of our continent for the total advancement of our peoples in all spheres of human endeavour,

Inspired by a common determination to promote understanding among our peoples and cooperation among our states in response to the aspirations of our peoples for brother-hood and solidarity, in a larger unity transcending ethnic and national differences,

Convinced that, in order to translate this determination into a dynamic force in the cause of human progress, conditions for peace and security must be established and maintained,

Determined to safeguard and consolidate the hard-won independence as well as the sovereignty and territorial integrity of our states, and to fight against neo-colonialism in all its forms,

Dedicated to the general progress of Africa,

Persuaded that the Charter of the United Nations and the Universal Declaration of Human Rights, to the Principles of which we reaffirm our adherence, provide a solid foundation for peaceful and positive cooperation among States,

---

Desirous that all African States should henceforth unite so that the welfare and well-being of their peoples can be assured,

Resolved to reinforce the links between our states by establishing and strengthening common institutions,

Have agreed to the present Charter.

Document 3

Source: Patrice Lumumba, "The Truth about a Monstrous Crime of the Colonialists." Speech at the Ceremony of the Proclamation of the Congo's Independence, June 30, 1960.

. . . Although this independence of the Congo is being proclaimed today by agreement with Belgium, an amicable country, with which we are on equal terms, no Congolese will ever forget that independence was won in struggle, a persevering and inspired struggle carried on from day to day. . . . We are deeply proud of our struggle, because it was just and noble and indispensable in putting an end to the humiliating bondage forced upon us. . . . We have experienced forced labor in exchange for pay that did not allow us to satisfy our hunger, to clothe ourselves, to have decent lodgings or to bring up our children as dearly loved ones. Morning, noon and night we were subjected to jeers, insults and blows because we were "Negroes." . . . We have not forgotten that the law was never the same for the white and the black, that it was lenient to the ones, and cruel and inhuman to the others. . . . We have not forgotten that in the cities the mansions were for the whites and the tumbledown huts for the blacks. . . . All that, my brothers, brought us untold suffering. But . . . we tell you that henceforth all that is finished with. The Republic of the Congo has been proclaimed and our beloved country's future is now in the hands of its own people.

Document 4

Source: Excerpt from The Governments of the Arab League, "The War of Independence: Arab League declaration on the invasion of Palestine," May 15, 1948. Written one day after Israel gained independence and Arab forces were advancing into Palestine to establish law and order.

1. Palestine was part of the former Ottoman Empire subject to its law and represented in its parliament. The overwhelming majority of the population of Palestine were Arabs. There was in it a small minority of Jews that enjoyed the same rights and bore the same responsibilities as the [other] inhabitants, and did not suffer any ill-treatment on account of its religious beliefs. The holy places were inviolable and the freedom of access to them was guaranteed.

2. The Arabs have always asked for their freedom and independence. On the outbreak of the First World War, and when the Allies declared that they were fighting for the liberation of peoples, the Arabs joined them and fought on their side with a view to realising their national aspirations and obtaining their independence. England pledged herself to recognise the independence of the Arab countries in Asia, including Palestine. The Arabs played a remarkable part in the achievement of final victory and the Allies have admitted this.

Document 5

> **Source: David Ben-Gurion, Israeli Minister of Foreign Affairs, broadcast to the nation after the Arab invasion, May 15, 1948.**
>
> . . .
>
> Finally, we must prepare to receive our brethren from the far-flung corners of the Diaspora; from the camps of Cyprus, Germany, and Austria, as well as from all the other lands where the message of liberation has arrived. We will receive them with open arms and help them to strike roots here in the soil of the Homeland. The State of Israel calls on everyone to faithfully fulfil his duties in defence, construction, and immigrant absorption. Only in this way can we prove ourselves worthy of the hour.

Document 6

> **Source: Shah of Iran, Mohammad Reza Pahlavi, 1973. Under Pahlavi's reign, Iran was modernized, women were granted voting rights, and literacy became a priority.**
>
>

Document 7

> **Source: Mustafa Kemal Atatürk, "Atatürk Speeches and Statements," 1923. Speech to reform and industrialize the Republic of Turkey.**
>
> The reason for the lack of success of our society lies in the indifference towards our women. Man comes into the world to live as long as his destiny allows him. To live is to act so if an organ of a society acts while the other lies idle, then it means that society is paralyzed. A society must accept all the conditions and necessities on which its success in life depends. So, if science and technology are necessary for our society, our men and women must equally master them. As you know, division of labor is necessary in social life as it is in all the other fields. In general division of labor, women should not only carry out their duties, but they should also take part in efforts for the prosperity and welfare of the society.
>
> The most important duty of women is motherhood. If we remember that a child's first school is his mother's bosom, we can understand the utmost importance of this duty better. Our nation has decided to be a powerful one. One of the ways to ensure a powerful nation is to make sure our women are competent in every aspect. For that, our women will acquire scientific and technical information, and complete every phase of education that men complete. Thus women and men will walk side by side in social life helping and protecting each other.

Answers and Explanations

Multiple-Choice Questions

1. **D.** Kwame Nkrumah was the leader of the independence movement for the African country of Ghana. He was speaking of the desire for national independence following World War II.

2. **D.** Kwame Nkrumah was referencing the developing world's desire for freedom. This was supported by the developed world because Adolf Hitler, who promoted racial theories of superiority, had just been defeated. The prevailing U.S. and European policies could no longer support social Darwinism beliefs.

3. **B.** One of the many difficulties following decolonization was the rise of corrupt leaders and military dictatorships. This tended to undermine the movements for national liberation since the real goal was development for the people of the developing world.

4. **D.** The U.S. formed NATO in 1949 in order to protect from communist invasions of Western Europe. This was done in reaction to the cutting off of West Berlin to West Germany. Communist Russia saw this as a potential move for future invasions of the USSR, so it formed the Warsaw Pact as its own defensive group against the Western powers.

5. **C.** After World War II, the world was divided into two global powers, the U.S. and the USSR. This was known as a bipolar world, with the two superpowers creating their own alliances. Winston Churchill would label this as the Iron Curtain in Western and Eastern Europe.

6. **B.** European powers, the U.S., and the Soviet Union created NATO (North Atlantic Treaty Organization), SEATO (Southeast Asian Treaty Organization), and the Warsaw Pact, respectively, as regional alliances to deter the other superpower from attacking.

Document-Based Question

DBQ Scoring Guide

To achieve the maximum score of 7, your response must address the scoring criteria components in the table below.

Scoring Criteria for a Good Essay	
Question 1: Compare and contrast the reactions to the decolonization process after World War II.	
Scoring Criteria	**Examples**
A. THESIS/CLAIM	
(1 point) Presents a historically defensible thesis that establishes a line of reasoning. (Note: The thesis must make a claim that responds to **all** parts of the question and must **not** just restate the question. The thesis must consist of **at least** one sentence, either in the introduction or the conclusion.)	A good response to this question will have a central thesis that historically shows comparisons and contrasts about decolonization in the developing world. Remember that the essay thesis must address BOTH comparison and contrast to receive full credit. The sample essay provides a coherent thesis that is supported throughout the essay with a logical line of reasoning of both comparing and contrasting the similarities and differences among different nations. The main argument presents supporting evidence about the ideology of self-determination that played a significant role in the movement toward independence from imperial domination.
B. CONTEXTUALIZATION	
(1 point) Explains the broader historical context of events, developments, or processes that occurred before, during, or after the time frame of the question. (Note: Must be more than a phrase or reference.)	A good response should include the historical context of broader developments relevant to decolonization and independence movements. This sample essay starts by setting the context as post–World War II and places the essay in the context of the reaction to Hitler's failed racist ideology. The essay also discusses how the decolonized countries were attempting to remain neutral in the Cold War in order to gain benefits for their people.
C. EVIDENCE	
Evidence from the Documents **(2 points)** Uses at least **six** documents to support the argument in response to the prompt. OR **(1 point)** Uses the content of at least **three** documents to address the topic prompt. (Note: Examples must describe, rather than simply quote, the content of the documents.)	To earn the highest possible points, the sample response addresses all seven of the documents and relates the documents back to the thesis. Documents 1, 2, 3, and 5 reference the reactions of nations that applaud their newly formed inalienable rights to self-govern. Document 4 shows how Arab leaders feared imperialism, and Document 7 addresses the internal struggles within a nation based on religious beliefs.

Continued

Scoring Criteria	Examples
C. EVIDENCE	
Evidence Beyond the Documents **(1 point)** Uses at least one additional piece of specific historical evidence beyond those found in the documents relevant to `the argument. (Note: Evidence must be different from the evidence used in contextualization.)	Each paragraph provides outside details to show the inspiration for the documents. The essay begins by explaining how the Berlin Conference set up imperialism. The Arab-Israeli conflict is explained with the Balfour Declaration. The internal fight over modernization is explained with examples of the Wahhabi movement. The essay goes on to compare the external-internal issues to those of the Enlightenment and the Haitian Revolution. The author shows how the French Revolution also stated the grand proposal of universal rights. However, these came into conflict with their colonial holding in Haiti. Also, the last paragraph makes a comparison between the internal conflicts in Haiti among different classes to those in the decolonized countries.
D. ANALYSIS AND REASONING	
(1 point) Uses at least three documents to explain how each document's point of view, purpose, historical situation, and/or audience is relevant to the argument. (Note: References must explain how or why, rather than simply identifying.)	The essay uses a variety of analyses to explain the primary point of view or purpose of several documents. For example, Documents 1 and 2 show statements of independence. Document 4 was written by members of the Arab League to secure Arab unity. Document 7 was a speech by the president founder of the Republic of Turkey who wanted to implement Western reforms to industrialize Turkey based on European models. Each of these documents provides a point of view based on attribution and purpose.
(1 point) Uses historical reasoning and development that focuses on the question while using evidence to corroborate, qualify, or modify the argument. (Examples: Explain what is similar and different; explain the cause and effect; explain multiple causes; explain connections within and across periods of time; corroborate multiple perspectives across themes; or consider alternative views.	The essay addresses both reasoning skills, comparison and contrast, and provides complex explanations that both corroborate and modify the argument. The sample response essay has a comparison based on the common acceptance in the UN Charter for universal self-determination. The contrast is on whether the reaction was against European imperialism or due to internal fights over traditional and modern ways forward. In addition, the second paragraph qualifies the argument by providing a dissenting view from some historians—that is, the objective in decolonizing was to regain natural resources.

DBQ Sample Response

After World War II, there was a worldview shift in thinking about imperialism and colonization. The superpowers of Europe and the United States had defeated Hitler and his ideological views about social Darwinism, racial hierarchies, and world dominance. As recognized by the United Nations (Document 1), it was time for the world to refocus imperialistic objectives and begin the process of decolonization. At the same time, leaders in the developing world called out for decolonization and self-determination. Colonies no longer wanted to be exploited for natural and labor resources. Colonial leaders sought to gain cultural, political, and economic independence from imperialistic powers (Documents 2, 3, 4, and 5). These leaders began to form movements that would pressure for independence. And, in the midst of the Cold War, they claimed a non-aligned movement with either the capitalist or communist powers. The comparison of their reaction is an embrace of the universal statements for local self-determination of cultures and nations. However, while some nations fought against the legacy of imperialism, others had to deal with internal divisions based on religious beliefs and drives for modernity (Document 7).

Some historians will argue that decolonization occurred only because of the desire for regaining the resources taken from the developing countries by European powers. However, the leaders of the developing world based their movements for national freedom on the UN charter following World War II. In Document 1, the purpose of the universal call for national freedom was to counter the social Darwinist philosophy that led to Hitler's rise and the global conflict that the Allies had just won.

Developing countries looked to the UN charter and claimed a common belief in the equality of all people, including their protection of rights. Document 2 expressed the point of view of the African leaders who wanted to form their own independence in both culture and resources. In the late 1800s, the Europeans had carved up Africa in the Berlin Conference. But new leaders like Jomo Kenyatta and Kwame Nkrumah maintained that Africans had a right to develop their own national governments and take control of their natural resources for local development. Document 3 was written from the perspective of the newly elected socialist leader in the Congo, Patrice Lumumba, who wanted to strengthen the local African populace against the racist ideologies of the Belgian colonizers. Lumumba made this argument in order to end both the European colonization of the Congo and the Belgian extracting of Congo's diamonds. In all of these cases, the African leaders pointed to the UN charter to justify the universal demand for freedom and national self-determination.

There was often a difference within the historical context of decolonized countries over who would be considered to be a legitimate part of the new nation-state. Document 4 comes from the point of view of the Arab leaders, who feared both European imperialism and the new fight with Eastern European Zionism. The Arab leaders claimed that the fall of the Ottoman Empire had allowed for Europeans to exploit the differences in the region. This was a reference to the European mandate system. The British had carved up the lands that were formerly under the Ottoman Empire. Then, the British promised the Jewish people a new nation-state under the Balfour Declaration while promising the Arabs access to Mediterranean trade. This was done to pit the groups against each other for the British advantage of getting oil. In Document 5, Ben-Gurion would disagree with the Arab claim because he saw the Jewish people themselves as victims of anti-Semitism in various areas of the world. His document has the purpose of inviting Jewish people to escape the global diaspora and persecution by coming to the newly created Jewish nation of Israel. This led to a difference between the Arab and Jewish people over who should legitimately hold land in the Middle East.

Another difference that occurred within the historical context of decolonized countries was between the traditional and modernist groups that wanted to define the future of self-determination. Document 6 is a picture of Shah Pahlavi in Iran. This picture shows the authority of the Pahlavi family in the 1960s. Pahlavi tried to create a more modern Iran based on Western ideals of women's education, technological creation, and new markets. Similarly, Document 7 came from the perspective of a secular modernizer in Turkey. Atatürk argued that the Muslim nation would only advance forward if women's traditional roles as mothers were updated to include modern education in technology and science. Within Islamic nations, this has been fiercely contested by the rise of more traditional purist movements. The Wahhabi movement in Saudi Arabia has argued for a literal interpretation of the Quran. This has led to radical religious groups that want the Muslim world to adopt a more theocratic, not Western, approach to decolonization.

The majority of the developing world nations had a common desire to gain self-determination and independence. However, some developing countries faced greater obstacles from the legacy of European imperialism while others needed to address internal religious and ethnic divisions.

Chapter 11

Full-Length Practice Exam

This chapter contains a full-length practice exam that will give you valuable insight into the types of questions that may appear on the WHAP exam. As you take this practice exam, try to simulate testing conditions and time limits for each of the following sections:

Section	Questions	Time
Section I: Part A—Multiple-Choice Questions	55 questions	55 minutes
Section I: Part B—Short-Answer Questions	3 questions	40 minutes
Section II: Part A—Document-Based Question	1 question	60 minutes
Section II: Part B—Long-Essay Question	1 question	40 minutes

Answer Sheet for Multiple-Choice Questions

1 Ⓐ Ⓑ Ⓒ Ⓓ
2 Ⓐ Ⓑ Ⓒ Ⓓ
3 Ⓐ Ⓑ Ⓒ Ⓓ
4 Ⓐ Ⓑ Ⓒ Ⓓ
5 Ⓐ Ⓑ Ⓒ Ⓓ

6 Ⓐ Ⓑ Ⓒ Ⓓ
7 Ⓐ Ⓑ Ⓒ Ⓓ
8 Ⓐ Ⓑ Ⓒ Ⓓ
9 Ⓐ Ⓑ Ⓒ Ⓓ
10 Ⓐ Ⓑ Ⓒ Ⓓ

11 Ⓐ Ⓑ Ⓒ Ⓓ
12 Ⓐ Ⓑ Ⓒ Ⓓ
13 Ⓐ Ⓑ Ⓒ Ⓓ
14 Ⓐ Ⓑ Ⓒ Ⓓ
15 Ⓐ Ⓑ Ⓒ Ⓓ

16 Ⓐ Ⓑ Ⓒ Ⓓ
17 Ⓐ Ⓑ Ⓒ Ⓓ
18 Ⓐ Ⓑ Ⓒ Ⓓ
19 Ⓐ Ⓑ Ⓒ Ⓓ
20 Ⓐ Ⓑ Ⓒ Ⓓ

21 Ⓐ Ⓑ Ⓒ Ⓓ
22 Ⓐ Ⓑ Ⓒ Ⓓ
23 Ⓐ Ⓑ Ⓒ Ⓓ
24 Ⓐ Ⓑ Ⓒ Ⓓ
25 Ⓐ Ⓑ Ⓒ Ⓓ

26 Ⓐ Ⓑ Ⓒ Ⓓ
27 Ⓐ Ⓑ Ⓒ Ⓓ
28 Ⓐ Ⓑ Ⓒ Ⓓ
29 Ⓐ Ⓑ Ⓒ Ⓓ
30 Ⓐ Ⓑ Ⓒ Ⓓ

31 Ⓐ Ⓑ Ⓒ Ⓓ
32 Ⓐ Ⓑ Ⓒ Ⓓ
33 Ⓐ Ⓑ Ⓒ Ⓓ
34 Ⓐ Ⓑ Ⓒ Ⓓ
35 Ⓐ Ⓑ Ⓒ Ⓓ

36 Ⓐ Ⓑ Ⓒ Ⓓ
37 Ⓐ Ⓑ Ⓒ Ⓓ
38 Ⓐ Ⓑ Ⓒ Ⓓ
39 Ⓐ Ⓑ Ⓒ Ⓓ
40 Ⓐ Ⓑ Ⓒ Ⓓ

41 Ⓐ Ⓑ Ⓒ Ⓓ
42 Ⓐ Ⓑ Ⓒ Ⓓ
43 Ⓐ Ⓑ Ⓒ Ⓓ
44 Ⓐ Ⓑ Ⓒ Ⓓ
45 Ⓐ Ⓑ Ⓒ Ⓓ

46 Ⓐ Ⓑ Ⓒ Ⓓ
47 Ⓐ Ⓑ Ⓒ Ⓓ
48 Ⓐ Ⓑ Ⓒ Ⓓ
49 Ⓐ Ⓑ Ⓒ Ⓓ
50 Ⓐ Ⓑ Ⓒ Ⓓ

51 Ⓐ Ⓑ Ⓒ Ⓓ
52 Ⓐ Ⓑ Ⓒ Ⓓ
53 Ⓐ Ⓑ Ⓒ Ⓓ
54 Ⓐ Ⓑ Ⓒ Ⓓ
55 Ⓐ Ⓑ Ⓒ Ⓓ

Section I

Part A—Multiple-Choice Questions

Multiple-choice questions are grouped into sets. Each set contains one source-based prompt (document or image) and two to five questions.

55 questions

55 minutes

Questions 1–3 refer to the following passage.

> If a patrician has knocked out the tooth of a man that is his equal, his tooth shall be knocked out.
> If he has knocked out the tooth of a plebeian, he shall pay one-third of a mina of silver.
> If a man's wife be surprised with another man, both shall be tied and thrown into the water, but the husband may pardon his wife and the king his slaves.
> If a man wishes to separate from his wife who has borne him children, then he shall give that wife her dowry, and the right to use the field, garden, and property so she can rear her children.

> —Source: Adapted from the *Code of Hammurabi,* 1754 B.C.E.

1. Based on the passage and your knowledge of world history, the *Code of Hammurabi* was written in response to which of the following changes in early Mesopotamian societies?

   A. This was a law code that was written to regulate trade between nations.
   B. This was part of a religious text that was justifying clerical authority.
   C. This passage represents an agreement between the monarch and his nobility over the sharing of power.
   D. This was a law code that set out rules and punishments for a land-based empire in Mesopotamia.

2. Which of the following best exemplifies the social relationships of the Babylonian society?

   A. The passage is a justification for landowners' power in society.
   B. The passage is a reflection on the nature of slavery for the purpose of labor.
   C. The passage justifies different social classes and gender hierarchies through legal punishments.
   D. The author of the passage was attempting to organize and define kinship relationships.

3. Which of the following conclusions can be drawn from the passage?

   A. The author of the passage was a monarch attempting to provide legal definition to social classes.
   B. The passage was written to solve treaty negotiations between countries.
   C. The passage was intended to provide a legal understanding of the state of slavery in society.
   D. The purpose of the passage was to explain society's religious beliefs.

Questions 4–6 refer to the following two passages.

Passage 1

The Master said, "Govern the people by regulations, keep order among them by chastisements, and they will flee from you, and lose all self-respect. Govern them by moral forces, keep order among them by ritual and they will keep their self-respect and come to you of their own accord."

—Source: Excerpt from "The Analects of Confucius," 5 B.C.E.

Passage 2

The sage in governing the people considers the springs of their action, never tolerates their wicked desires, but seeks only for the people's benefit. Therefore, the penalty he inflicts is not due to any hatred for the people but to his motive of loving the people. If penalty triumphs, the people are quiet; if reward overflows, culprits appear. Therefore the triumph of penalty is the beginning of order; the overflow of reward, the origin of chaos.

—Source: Han Feizi, Chinese Legalist Scholar, 3 B.C.E.

4. In reference to societal governance, how do the author's views in <u>Passage 1</u> contrast with the author's views in <u>Passage 2</u>?

   A. Passage 1 calls for a strict regulation of human behavior in order to curb self-interest.
   B. Passage 1 calls for the use of social kinship bonds for community over strict authoritarian rules.
   C. Passage 1 argues for a centralization of authority in order to form social stability.
   D. Passage 1 argues that the government needs to create standardized rules to regulate the economy.

5. Taken together, the context of the two passages addresses which of the following historical issues?

   A. Centuries of warfare between noble classes who were fighting over political control of China
   B. A resolution to a religious conflict in which reformers were challenging traditional clerical control
   C. The rise of a new middle class that challenged the owners of business in the society
   D. The fear in China of outside Northern invaders bringing in a different culture

6. Taken together, the two passages represent what major conflict within society from c. 5 B.C.E. to 3 B.C.E.?

   A. The attempt to devise rules for social obligations between the peasant and ruling classes of China.
   B. The fight between clerical leaders and religious reformers
   C. The competing use of either science or faith to resolve questions in the society
   D. The difference over centralizing power or using kinship relationships for governance

Questions 7–9 refer to the following passage.

"Daughter, show us the secret cave where the spirits are hidden," said the father, "and teach us the magic words you have learned from the old woman. We shall take the spirits to another place, and we shall have the power."

And so it was. The father took the totems from that place and hid them in another cave. He became the *kirman,* the song leader, and he taught the people the sacred dances and ceremonies. To him they brought their problems and he judged between them when they quarreled. And, to this day, the men have kept the power.

—Source: "The Man-Eater: The Mutjinga Myth," Anonymous, c. 1000 B.C.E.

7. Based on your knowledge of world history, the passage reflects what type of recorded history during the period of human beginnings?

    A. Written records used for telling history and recording official documents
    B. Oral history and the mythical "origin stories"
    C. Legal documents and codified statements of societal order
    D. Priestly recordings of religious holy books

8. Which of the following can be reasonably concluded about the social relationships that the author is describing in this myth?

    A. The author is justifying those who hold land and the rental system to peasants.
    B. The author of the passage provides a rationale for expansion into local empires.
    C. The author's point of the story is to explain the gender hierarchy.
    D. The author's story provides an understanding of why the culture needs to remain isolated and pure.

9. Based on your knowledge of world history and the passage, which of the following is the basis of political authority in early communities?

    A. A political leader gains power through military conquests.
    B. A leader must gain the trust of the people through a democratic vote.
    C. The leader is given power through a holy book sanctioned by a deity.
    D. The leader gains power by a sacred adventure that demonstrates his wisdom and abilities.

Questions 10–12 refer to the following passage.

Darius came forward, and spoke as follows:

Take these three forms of government: democracy, oligarchy, and monarchy; and let them each be at their best. I maintain that monarchy far surpasses the other two. What government can possibly be better than that of the very best man in the whole state? The counsels of such a man are like himself, and so he governs the mass of the people to their heart's content; while at the same time his measures against evil-doers are kept more secret than in other states. Contrariwise, in oligarchies, where men vie with each other in the service of the commonwealth, fierce strife is apt to arise between man and man, each wishing to be leader, and to carry his own measures; whence violent quarrels come.

—Source: Herodotus, "The Persians Reject Democracy," 5 B.C.E.

10. The developments described in Herodotus' passage about Athenian democracy show that he is considering which of the following?

   A. The question of how to keep cultural purity in a world of international trade
   B. The different military strategies needed to defend the city-states against a foreign empire
   C. Different types of governance and their ability to manage struggles for power
   D. Questions about social stability and how to maintain strong kinship relations

11. Based on your knowledge of world history, Herodotus' argument was written as a response to which of the following?

   A. The invasion of steppe people from the Northern regions into the Southern countries
   B. A fight between city-states and large land-based empires over resources
   C. The rise of peasant rebellions against large landowners
   D. A fight between the emperor and the noble landowners over the high cost of taxes

12. Which of the following provides the best support for Darius' argument in the text recorded by Herodotus?

   A. The city-states only allowed for the wealthy landowners to participate in civic affairs.
   B. Democracy allowed for a widespread engagement with government.
   C. Democracy encouraged the development of civic virtue.
   D. Merchants had the greatest influence over government due to their productivity.

Questions 13–15 refer to the following image.

Source: Pre-pottery Neolithic granary. Jordan Valley (near the Dead Sea), 11,500 to 10,550 B.C.E.

13. Which of the following best describes the type of society that would have used the type of storehouse for grain depicted in the image?

    A.   A hunter-gatherer society that moved according to the seasons

    B.   A large land-based empire in the Middle East

    C.   The steppe communities that moved out of Central Asia into India and Northern Africa

    D.   A sedentary society that created a surplus of grains

14. Which of the following best explains why this ancient civilization developed such a storage facility?

    A.   The fear of empires that would conquer the society

    B.   The need to store the scarce amount of grains that were produced

    C.   The need to save the surplus of food for periods of shortage due to the flooding of local rivers

    D.   The lack of food due to the desert climate

15. Based on your knowledge of ancient civilizations, what significant political development emerged as a result of building grain storage facilities?

    A.   The development of religious symbols and rituals related to food

    B.   The creation of political offices and bureaucracies to manage water and food sources

    C.   The expansion of militaries to conquer other civilizations and their food resources

    D.   The creation of a naval fleet to protect trade on the Dead Sea

Questions 16–18 refer to the following image.

Source: Early Egyptian civilization, c. 2000 B.C.E.

16. The activity depicted in the image above best represents what significant change in early human civilizations?

    A.   The move of people from urban to suburban cities
    B.   The development of centers for mass production of textile goods
    C.   The interaction of large empires in trade over the Silk Roads
    D.   The development of surpluses of food through new uses of natural resources

17. Which of the following best reflects the political developments that may have resulted due to the actions depicted in the image?

    A.   The creation of bureaucracies to manage storage, records, and land use
    B.   New forms of citizen engagement with government in local city-states
    C.   The rise of centralized monarchs who used their power to expand the kingdom
    D.   Social movements that would demand a more equitable sharing of resources

18. Based on your knowledge of world history, what significant social change may have occurred in this civilization as gleaned from the activity in this image?

    A.   Women were given a more equitable position in society due to their help with hunting and gathering.
    B.   Social classes arose centered around land ownership.
    C.   A new middle class arose due to the increased economic opportunities and competition.
    D.   Merchants climbed up in social status due to their economic contributions to society.

Questions 19–21 refer to the following passage.

His father said to him: "Svetaketu, as you are so conceited, considering yourself so well-read, and so stern, my dear, have you ever asked for that instruction by which we hear what cannot be heard, by which we perceive what cannot be perceived, by which we know what cannot be known?"

"What is that instruction, Sir?" he asked. …
"Fetch me … a fruit of the Nyagrodha tree."
"Here is one, Sir."
"Break it."
"It is broken, Sir."
"What do you see there?"
"These seeds, almost infinitesimal."
"Break one of them."
"It is broken, Sir."
"What do you see there?"
"Not anything, Sir."

The father said: "My son, that subtle essence which you do not perceive there, of that very essence this great Nyagrodha tree exists."

—Source: Upanishads, 800 B.C.E.

19. The Nyagrodha tree mentioned in the <u>third paragraph</u> of the passage is associated with which of the following major axial belief systems in world history?

    A. Confucianism
    B. Daoism
    C. Buddhism
    D. Hinduism

20. Based on your knowledge of world history, the context of the author's short story may be a direct result of which of the following events?

    A. The invasion of Northern steppe people from Mongolia into the kingdom
    B. The constant changes brought from trade and migrations of people from Central Asia
    C. The collapse of the Roman Empire and the fragmentation of kingdoms
    D. Internal wars over land between the emperor and the nobles

21. Which of the following best supports how the people who practice this belief system might react to world trade (Silk Roads trade or Indian Ocean trade)?

    A. The leaders would call for isolation and cultural purity.
    B. The military would call for an expansion of the empire to access new resources.
    C. The priests would call for a religious proselytizing of people who hold different beliefs.
    D. The author would call for a tolerance and acceptance of change as a part of the natural flow of life.

Questions 22–24 refer to the following passage.

The manners of the tradesmen are inferior to those of rulers, and far removed from manliness and uprightness. We have already stated the traders must buy and sell and seek profits. This necessitates flattery, and evasiveness, litigation and disputation, all of which are characteristics of this profession. And, these qualities lead to a decrease and weakening in virtue. As for trade, although it be a natural means of livelihood, yet most of the methods it employs are tricks aimed at making a profit by securing the difference between the buying and selling prices, and by appropriating the surplus.

—Source: Ibn Khaldun, Muslim scholar, 14th century C.E.

22. Khaldun's quotation can best be understood as a reaction to which of the following geographic areas?

   A.   China and the steppe region
   B.   Indian Ocean trade route
   C.   Trans-Saharan and Northern Africa trade routes
   D.   Andean Mountains trade route

23. Which of the following best explains Khaldun's attitude about trade described in the passage?

   A.   He was impressed by the technological innovations that resulted from trade.
   B.   He was fearful of the negative impacts on women from European explorers.
   C.   He promoted the sharing of religious beliefs across trade routes.
   D.   He feared how trade and the profit motive would weaken traditional Islamic beliefs.

24. Which of the following supports Islam's religious point of view about trade during the 1300s?

   A.   The Prophet Muhammad was a merchant himself and advocated for fair and just trade.
   B.   Muhammad argued that all trade was selfish and immoral according to Quranic teachings.
   C.   Muhammad called for unlimited trade for the development of progress.
   D.   Muhammad advocated for the sharing of religious and cultural beliefs through international trade.

Questions 25–27 refer to the following passage.

Their trappings and arms are all made of iron. They dress in iron and wear iron casques* on their heads. Their swords are iron; their bows are iron; their shields are iron; their spears are iron. Their deer carry them on their backs wherever they wish to go. These deer, our lord, are as tall as the roof of a house.

The strangers' bodies are completely covered, so that only their faces can be seen. Their skin is white, as if it were made of lime. They have yellow hair, though some of them have black. Their beards are long and yellow, and their moustaches are also yellow. Their hair is curly, with very fine strands.

* *helmets*

—Source: Excerpt from "The Broken Spears: The Aztec Account of the Conquest of Mexico," 16th century C.E.

25. Which of the following offers the best interpretation of the passage above?

   A. It provides an example of cultural diffusion through religious missionaries along trade routes.
   B. It demonstrates how new uses of metallurgy led to changes in farming and military techniques.
   C. It depicts cultural conflicts due to the different religious and cultural perspectives of civilizations engaging in exploration.
   D. It depicts the changing gender roles in societies.

26. Based on your knowledge of world history, which of the following best expresses the result of the interactions between the Aztecs and Spaniards?

   A. Both societies opened up trade and an exchange of cultural ideas.
   B. Spain was able to conquer the Aztecs and then create *encomiendas* with native Aztec labor.
   C. China sent out its explorer Zheng He to discover trade routes and land in Africa and India.
   D. Europeans created a Trans-Atlantic slave trade in order to develop their exploitation of the sugarcane market in the Caribbean.

27. Based on your knowledge of world history, which of the following reasons best explains why the Aztecs were conquered by the Spaniards?

   A. The Spaniards possessed a large invading population.
   B. The Spaniards had superior technology that overwhelmed the Aztecs.
   C. The Aztecs lacked a significant and well-organized army.
   D. The Spaniards' diseases decimated the Aztecs, which allowed them and local native tribes to conquer the Aztec Empire.

Questions 28–30 refer to the following passage.

Also, discussion has occurred here concerning the best arrangements that could be made for the Crown to receive revenue from the said country with less vexation to its natives, and in particular whether those [Indian pueblos] which do not have the capacity to pay the tributes and taxes they owe Us in gold should be required to provide people to work in the gold or silver mines that are assigned to the Crown, supporting them there at their cost to mine the metal for Us. This would be if they have the capacity for it; and if they do not, they could provide only the people to work in the mines or only the supplies, so they would not be so overburdened. Also [it has been discussed] whether other pueblos should support a number of slaves in the mines. You should discuss [all] this with our judges, officials, and other reasonable people who have knowledge of the country; and you should arrange things with all the care and moderation that is necessary in this case, doing what is most acceptable to the Indians and most profitable for Our treasury, and you should advise Me, what you agree on and what you do.

—Source: Spain's royal instructions for Viceroy Mendoza, 1535.

28. The instructions given from the king of Spain to the viceroy of New Spain demonstrate which of the following types of governance over the colonies in the 16th century?

    A. The king had a direct rule and management over New Spain.
    B. The colonists in New Spain established family settlements for long-term development.
    C. The landowners established local rule through assemblies.
    D. The king issued orders to a representative, who then managed the local population.

29. Which of the following best explains the economic organization of the king of Spain's mandate for the local native population?

    A. The local natives were allowed to run their own markets through competition.
    B. The colonists would find raw resources to send back to Spain for mass production of finished products.
    C. The local population was placed on farms and worked in silver mines to extract raw resources for the imperial power.
    D. The middle class of the country was given incentives to join in international trade.

30. Based on your knowledge of world history and the passage, what was the difference between Mexico's native population labor and the Atlantic slave trade labor?

    A. The labor in Mexico was based on the extraction of resources, while the Atlantic slave trade was based on a racial objectification of human labor.
    B. While the native labor in Mexico could be used across family generations, African slavery could not.
    C. Native labor tended to last longer due to the lack of disease transfer.
    D. African labor was not as reliable because Africans had been transported so far from their home territory.

Questions 31–33 refer to the following passage.

Natives and newcomers interacted in unexpected ways, creating biological bedlam. When Spanish colonists imported African plantains [a tropical plant that resembles a banana] in 1516, the Harvard entomologist Edward O. Wilson has proposed, they also imported scale insects, small creatures with tough, waxy coats that suck the juices from plant roots and stems. About a dozen banana-infesting scale insects are known in Africa. In Hispaniola, Wilson argued, these insects had no natural enemies.

In consequence, their numbers must have exploded—a phenomenon known to science as "ecological release." This spread of scale insects would have dismayed the island's European banana farmers but delighted one of its native species: the tropical fire ant *Solenopsis geminata*. *S. geminata* is fond of dining on scale insects' sugary excrement; to ensure the flow, the ants will attack anything that disturbs them. A big increase in scale insects would have led to a big increase in fire ants.

Source: Charles Mann, *1491: New Revelations of the Americas before Columbus,* 2012.

31. Mann's environmental study is a response to which of the following unintended results of European exploration in the Western Hemisphere during the 15th century?

   A. Europeans introduced new crops to the environment that modified nutrition.
   B. Europeans changed the trade and environmental patterns from crops to precious metals.
   C. Europeans introduced new species of wildlife that changed the ecological relationships in Mesoamerica.
   D. Europeans interacted with native populations that changed social relationships.

32. Which of the following European imports had the largest negative impact on the Mesoamerican communities in the 1600s?

   A. Spanish horses were used by natives during battles between tribal groups and the kingdoms.
   B. Spanish porcelain changed the types of trade between tribal groups and the kingdoms.
   C. Spanish ideas led to the rejection of all traditional native Aztec beliefs.
   D. Spanish diseases led to a widespread dying off of the native Aztecs.

33. Based on your knowledge of world history, which of the following consequences is similar to the unintended outcome of "biological bedlam" described in the first sentence?

   A. The introduction of the potato from Mesoamerica to Europe led to a massive growth in population in Ireland.
   B. The introduction of the flea through the Mongol expansion in Central Asia led to the spreading of the Black Death.
   C. Zheng He's travels from China to Eastern Africa led to an expansion of the Indian Ocean trade route.
   D. Ibn Battuta's travels throughout the Muslim world led to a greater understanding of the different Islamic cultural communities.

Questions 34–36 refer to the following map.

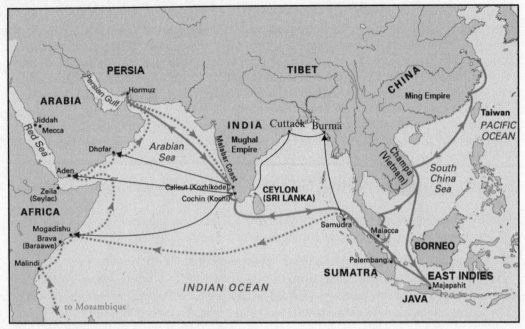

Source: China's Expeditions of Zheng He (1405–1422).

34. Based on the map and your knowledge of world history, what major change developed in global economic relationships during the 1600s?

    A.   The Portuguese began to dominate in the colonization of the Eastern Hemisphere.

    B.   The Ming Dynasty expanded China's influence to Eastern Africa.

    C.   The Mongols reopened the Silk Roads trade routes through military conquest of Central Asia.

    D.   Major port cities in the Eastern Hemisphere began to trade for the first time in global history.

35. Which of the following offers the best explanation why Chinese exploration declined after the 1600s?

    A.   The Chinese lacked the internal investment to continue to fund such voyages.

    B.   The Europeans were easily able to conquer the Eastern Asian empires.

    C.   Chinese ships started wars with other empires, leading to a drain on imperial resources.

    D.   China's leaders stopped voyages to focus on the threat of Northern invaders.

36. Which of the following was one of the most significant impacts of the trade depicted in the map?

    A.   Disease traveled from region to region, causing massive population decreases.

    B.   A diffusion of culture occurred between port cities in India, China, and Eastern Africa.

    C.   Imperial wars increased in the fight over territory and resources.

    D.   The religion of Islam became the predominant belief system in the region.

Questions 37–40 refer to the following image.

Source: British Industrialization Factory, 1790.

37. The image above is best understood as an example of which of the following large-scale demographic changes in Europe during the 1700s?

    A.   People were producing a surplus of agricultural goods due to a new concept, the rotation of fields.

    B.   People were moving from rural areas into cities.

    C.   Immigrants were moving from the developing to the developed world for job opportunities.

    D.   People were moving from urban centers into suburban neighborhoods.

38. Which of the following is the most reasonable explanation for the developments depicted in the image?

    A.   The use of new energies like coal allowed for the mass production of goods.

    B.   The creation of new metals like bronze and iron allowed for new agricultural techniques.

    C.   The use of new ship navigational techniques allowed for the extraction of raw resources from colonies.

    D.   The use of new digital technologies allowed for the rapid transmission of information across borders and boundaries.

39. Which of the following best describes one disadvantage of the actions depicted in the image?

    A.   An increase in absolute living standards for people moving from farming to urban centers

    B.   Opportunities for women to enter into the workforce

    C.   A rapid use of energy that led to a depletion of resources

    D.   Unsafe working conditions, especially for children in mines and factories

40. Based on the image and your knowledge of world history, which of the following best characterizes the changes in the family structure during the 1700s?

   A. Women remained in the household due to traditional values.
   B. Children went to school to gain a technical education for the future.
   C. Families grew less religious due to the economic pressures of making money.
   D. Families decreased in size due to the increase in the cost of living.

Questions 41–43 refer to the following passage.

   The fourth and latest wave of globalization began with the demise of the Soviet Union in 1991, and has proceeded since then largely under U.S. auspices.

   With the Soviet Union and European socialism gone and China abandoning the socialist model, the goals pursued by the United States—global free trade, privatization of state-owned enterprises (e.g., land and factories) in all states, and more open ("transparent") political systems—have more closely integrated the former socialist world and the third world into the rhythms and needs of the global capitalist world.

   In this latest round, globalization means the expansion—led by the United States—of capitalism into every nook and cranny of the world.

   —Source: Robert Marks, "Origins of the Modern World: A Global and Ecological Narrative from the Fifteenth to the Twenty-first Century," 2007.

41. Marks' quotation is best understood in the context of which of the following?

   A. European desires to colonize areas in Africa and India for natural resources
   B. The opening of global markets for trade by lowering tariff restrictions
   C. The use of coal for the creation of mass manufacturing in urban areas
   D. The competition of the United States and Soviet superpowers over areas in the developing world

42. Which of the following global innovations best supports the context of Marks' comments?

   A. The discovery of coal in England for steam-powered engines
   B. The use of new metals like iron and bronze for agricultural innovations
   C. The use of electricity for powering up urban centers
   D. The new forms of digital information through the Internet

43. The global expansion led by the United States that Marks mentions in the third paragraph helped to initiate which of the following global institutions?

   A. The League of Nations and its collective security principle
   B. The United Nations Security Council and its desire to create international peace
   C. The IMF and its rules for developing countries to receive loans for development
   D. NATO and its mission of deterrence from communist invasion into Northern Europe

Questions 44–46 refer to the following chart.

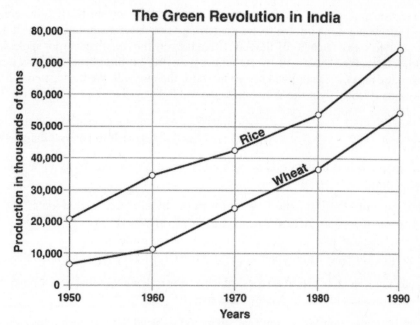

The Green Revolution in India

Source: Library of Congress, Federal Research Division (adapted).

44. Which of the following best describes the changes illustrated during the period of 1950 to 1990?

   A.   India experienced a massive migration of Muslims to the North after its independence from Britain.
   B.   India faced the obstacle of British tariffs on cotton during the British colonization of India.
   C.   New techniques in mass production of farming goods led to an increase in basic food resources in India.
   D.   The population in India grew rapidly following its increase in industrialization.

45. Which of the following best explains the direct causes for increased rice and wheat production depicted in the chart?

   A.   The rapid movement of farmers into urban centers
   B.   The use of coal for increased transportation
   C.   The use of imported trade goods from the West into India
   D.   New modifications to agricultural goods

46. Based on the chart and your knowledge of world history, which of the following historical events was similar to the changes depicted in the chart?

   A.   The increase in food surplus during the sedentary societies due to new irrigation and fertilization practices
   B.   The use of mass-produced industrial goods to build a middle class
   C.   The demand of tributary taxes from tribes to the central empire
   D.   The use of African slave labor for the production of sugarcane in the Caribbean

Questions 47–49 refer to the following passage.

Now I have seen that some of you fear to go forward and fight for our King. If it were in the brave days of the old, chiefs would not sit down to see their King taken away without firing a shot. No White man could have dared to speak to chiefs of the Ashanti in the way the British governor spoke to your chiefs this morning. It is true that the bravery of the Ashanti is no more? I cannot believe it. Yea, it cannot be! I must say this; if you the men of Ashanti will not go forward, then we will. We the women will. I shall call upon my fellow women. We will fight the White men. We will fight until the last of us falls on the battlefield.

—Source: Yaa Asantewaa, Queen Mother of the Ashanti Tribe,
speech to chiefs, Ghana, West Africa, 1900

47. Asantewaa's speech is best understood in the context of the Ashanti tribe as a reaction to which of the following developments?

    A.   The influence of Hinduism and Islam through the Indian Ocean trade route
    B.   The invasion of Eastern Africa by Italy during World War II
    C.   The enslavement of Africans along the Trans-Saharan trade route
    D.   The European attempt to conquer areas of Africa during the Age of Imperialism

48. Based on your knowledge of world history, which of the following global developments is most similar to the circumstances referenced in Asantewaa's speech?

    A.   The Self-Strengthening Movement that attempted to blend Western technology with Eastern ideas
    B.   Traditional leaders' resistance to Western individualism and democracy in Southeast Asia in the late 1800s
    C.   The imposing of tributary relationships by the Aztecs on local tribes in Mesoamerica
    D.   The Meiji Restoration's attempt to bring Western technology to Japan for the development of the military

49. Which of the following international agreements led to the problems that Africa's Ashanti Queen Mother is referencing?

    A.   The Treaty of Paris ending the Seven Years' War
    B.   The Declaration of the Rights of Man at the beginning of the French Revolution
    C.   The creation of the League of Nations to establish national sovereignty
    D.   The Berlin Conference establishing the European rules for carving up Africa

Questions 50–52 refer to the following table.

Year	Hand-Spun Yarn (millions of pounds)	Machine-Spun Yarn (millions of pounds)	Handwoven Cloth (millions of yards)	Machine-Made Cloth (millions of yards)
Production of Cotton Yarn and Cloth in India, 1884–1914
1884	150	151	1,000	238
1894	130	381	1,200	429
1904	110	532	1,286	545
1914	90	652	1,405	1,140

—Source: Data gathered by British colonial authorities.

50. Based on the data presented in the table, which of the following interpretations can be concluded about the production of cloth in India in the late 1800s?

   A. Indian mass production of cloth declined throughout the period.
   B. Indian urbanization declined, with fewer new machines or factories.
   C. Indian mass production of cloth decreased due to the traditional farming resistance to new machines.
   D. Indian industrialization allowed for the introduction of the country into the international trading marketplace.

51. Which of the following is a true statement based on the data in the table?

   A. Most Indians still remained in the rural farmlands even though there was an increase in the rate of urbanization.
   B. Indians lacked any machinery for mass production.
   C. Indian culture was resistant to the new technologies for increasing cloth production.
   D. Mass production of new cloth overtook rural production of cloth.

52. Based on your knowledge of world history and the data presented in the table, which of the following best explains the changes in Indian gender roles in the late 1800s?

   A. Women moved from urban areas into rural areas at a higher rate.
   B. Women did not have as many opportunities in the cities due to traditional values.
   C. Women were gaining new opportunities to move into the urban factories at a higher rate.
   D. Women gained new opportunities for higher education in India during the early 1800s.

Questions 53–55 refer to the following passage.

> The cricket field has many lessons to teach in other walks of life. The brotherly feeling that prevailed throughout the play was remarkable and I hope that our Hindu brethren as sportsmen would be no less pleased but also rejoice at the Muslims winning the championship.

> —Source: Muhammad Ali Jinnah, leader of the All-India Muslim League and later first leader of Pakistan, commenting on the Quadrangular Tournament, a cricket competition in which sides representing Europeans, Hindus, Muslims, and Parsis competed against each other, 1924.

53. According to Jinnah, the primary 20th-century conflict in India is reflected in which of the following?

    A. The Indian criticism of British tariffs that were restricting local textile production
    B. The internal religious-ethnic conflict between Muslims and Hindus following Indian independence in 1948
    C. The fight between Mohandas Gandhi and Jawaharlal Nehru over the future economic path for India
    D. The question over partition between Pakistan and Bangladesh

54. Based on your knowledge of world history, which of the following represents the outcome of the conflict depicted in the passage above?

    A. India was partitioned into a Northern Muslim Pakistan and Southern Hindu India.
    B. India became a multi-ethnic state that had a sharing of power between all the major ethnic groups.
    C. Britain established a military rule over the local population with indirect rule through middle-class Hindus and Muslims.
    D. Britain remained in control due to the potential conflict between Hindus and Muslims.

55. Which of the following historical developments is most similar to the ideas expressed in this passage?

    A. The development of countries in the Southern Hemisphere using loans from the World Bank to industrialize
    B. The non-aligned countries that would side with neither the U.S. nor the USSR during the Cold War
    C. The ethnic-religious conflict between Muslims and Jewish people in Palestine over their holy lands
    D. The fights over citizenship as migrants moved from the Southern Hemisphere to the developed world looking for work

IF YOU FINISH BEFORE TIME IS CALLED, CHECK YOUR WORK ON THIS SECTION ONLY. DO NOT WORK ON ANY OTHER SECTION IN THE TEST.

Part B—Short-Answer Questions

3 questions

40 minutes

Reading Time: 10 minutes (brainstorm your thoughts and organize your responses)

Writing Time: 30 minutes

Directions: Write your responses on lined paper. The short-answer questions will *not* require that you develop and support a thesis statement. Some short-answer questions include texts, images, graphs, or maps. Use complete sentences—bullet points or an outline are unacceptable. Write answers for the first and second questions and then answer EITHER the third or fourth question (not both). Answer **all** parts of the questions to receive full credit.

Question 1. Use the passage below to answer all parts of the question that follows.

> From 1792 onward laws were passed all around the Caribbean and in North America restricting immigration from strife-torn Saint Domingue. Even when the likelihood of direct interference was not considered strong. Slave owners feared the revolution's inflammatory example. Within a month of the August 1791 revolt, slaves in Jamaica were singing songs about the uprising, and before long whites in the West Indies and North America were complaining uneasily of a new "insolence" on the part of their slaves. Several plots and insurrections were partly inspired by events in Saint Domingue and the Emancipation Decree of 1794. Most notable of these were the conspiracies organized by free colored in Bahia (1798), Havana (1812) and Charleston (1822). However, many factors were at work in the slave rebellions of the period, and to suppose that mere inspiration from abroad was critical in provoking resistance would be to underestimate the difficulties confronting dissidents in this age of strong colonial garrisons.
>
> —Source: David Patrick Geggus, historian, "The Haitian Revolution: A Documentary History," 2008.

1. **(a)** Identify ONE piece of historical evidence regarding the Haitian Revolution (not specifically mentioned in the passage) that shows the significance of its global effect on forced labor in the 1700s.

   (b) Provide ONE piece of historical evidence (not specifically mentioned in the passage) that compares the Haitian Revolution to a similar revolutionary movement of the time period.

   (c) Provide ONE piece of historical evidence that would undermine the author's point.

Question 2. Use the maps below to answer all parts of the question that follows.

Map A: Population Density, England, 1801.   Map B: Population Density, England, 1851.

2. **(a)** Briefly identify and explain ONE <u>change</u> that took place in England from 1750 to 1900 that is illustrated in the maps above.

   (b) Briefly identify and explain ONE specific reason for the <u>change</u> illustrated in the maps above.

   (c) Briefly identify and explain ONE social <u>continuity</u> in England that persisted into the 20th century based on the information provided in Map B.

Question 3 OR Question 4

Directions: Choose EITHER Question 3 or Question 4 and answer all parts of the question.

Question 3

3. **(a)** Identify ONE significant <u>difference</u> in the social structure between nomadic hunter-gatherers and sedentary societies.

   (b) Explain ONE <u>similarity</u> in the political management system between nomadic hunter-gatherers and sedentary societies.

   (c) Describe ONE way in which early human civilizations changed as a result of their surrounding natural environment.

Question 4

4. **(a)** Provide ONE <u>similar</u> reason that developing countries demanded independence after World War II.

   (b) Compare similar motives of two specific countries that demanded independence after World War II.

   (c) Contrast the motives of two specific countries that demanded independence after World War II.

IF YOU FINISH BEFORE TIME IS CALLED, CHECK YOUR WORK ON THIS SECTION ONLY. DO NOT WORK ON ANY OTHER SECTION IN THE TEST.

Section II

Part A—Document-Based Question (DBQ)

1 question
60 minutes

Reading Time: 15 minutes (brainstorm your thoughts and organize your response)
Writing Time: 45 minutes

Directions: The document-based question is based on the seven accompanying documents. The documents are for instructional purposes only. Some of the documents have been edited for the purpose of this practice exercise. Write your response on lined paper and include the following:

- **Thesis.** Present a thesis that supports a historically defensible claim, establishes a line of reasoning, and responds to all parts of the question. The thesis must consist of one or more sentences located in one place—either the introduction or the conclusion.
- **Contextualization.** Situate the argument by explaining the broader historical events, developments, or processes that occurred before, during, or after the time frame of the question.
- **Evidence from the documents.** Use the content of at least three to six of the documents to develop and support a cohesive argument that responds to the question.
- **Evidence beyond the documents.** Support or qualify your argument by explaining at least one additional piece of specific historical evidence not found in the documents. (Note: The example must be different from the evidence used to earn the point for contextualization.)
- **Analysis.** Use at least three documents that are relevant to the question to explain the documents' point of view, purpose, historical situation, and/or audience.
- **Historical reasoning.** Use historical reasoning to show relationships among the documents, the topic question, and the thesis argument. Use evidence to corroborate, qualify, or modify the argument.

Based on the documents that follow, answer the question below.

Question 1: Compare and contrast how land-based empires managed different ethnic and cultural minorities and explain the extent to which incorporating different minorities into the political systems was effective.

Document 1

> **Source: Han Yu, leading Confucian scholar and official at the Tang imperial court, "Memorial on Buddhism," 819 C.E.**
>
> Now the Buddha was a man of the barbarians who did not speak Chinese and who wore clothes of a different fashion. The Buddha's sayings contain nothing about our ancient kings and the Buddha's manner of dress did not conform to our laws; he understood neither the duties that bind sovereign and subject, nor the affections of father and son. If the Buddha were still alive today and came to our court, Your Majesty might condescend to receive him, but he would then be escorted to the borders of the nation, dismissed, and not allowed to delude the masses. How then, when he has long been dead, could the Buddha's rotten bones, the foul and unlucky remains of his body, be rightly admitted to the palace? Confucius said: "Respect ghosts and spirits, but keep them at a distance!"

Document 2

> **Source: Edict on the Collection of Swords; Laws Governing Military Households; Closed Country Edict, Tokugawa Hideyoshi Regime, Japan, 1615 C.E. The Edict on Swords has come to be known as the "sword hunt," that prohibited farmers from carrying arms. This decree guaranteed that the samurai elite would have a monopoly on armament.**
>
> 1. Great lords, daimyo, the lesser lords, and officials should immediately expel from their domains any among their retainers or henchmen who have been charged with treason or murder. Wild and wicked men may become weapons for overturning the state and destroying the people. How can they be allowed to go free?
>
> 2. Henceforth no outsider, none but the inhabitants of a particular domain, shall be permitted to reside in that domain. …
>
> 3. Whenever it is intended to make repairs on a castle of one of the feudal domains, the shogunate should be notified.

Document 3

Source: The Travels of Mansa Musa, Sultan of the Mali Empire, c. 1300 C.E.

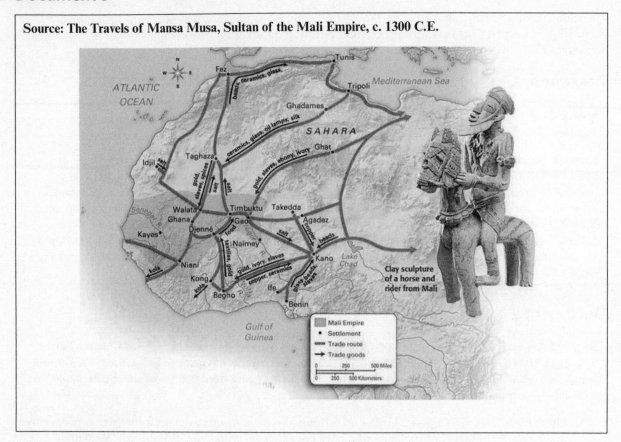

Clay sculpture of a horse and rider from Mali

Document 4

Source: Ogier Ghiselin de Busbecq, Hapsburg Ambassador to Suleiman the Magnificent, Constantinople, from letters sent to the Austrian Emperor, 1554 to 1562.

The sultan's hall was crowded with people, ... but there was not in all that great assembly a single man who owed his position to anything save valor and merit. No distinction is attached to birth among the Turks. ... In making his appointments, the Sultan pays no regard to any pretensions on the score of wealth or rank, nor does he take into consideration recommendations or popularity. He considers each case on its own merits, and examines carefully into the character, ability, and disposition of the man whose promotion is in question. ... Those who receive the highest offices from the Sultan ... do not believe that high qualities are either natural or hereditary, nor do they think that they can be handed down from father to son, but that they are partly the gift of God, and partly the result of good training [in state schools], great industry, and unwearied zeal. ... Among the Turks, therefore, honors, high posts, and judgeships are the rewards of great ability and good service. If a man be dishonest, or lazy, or careless, he remains at the bottom of the ladder. This is the reason that they are successful in their undertakings ... and are daily extending the bounds of their empire.

Document 5

> **Source: Tang Tiazong, second emperor of the Tang Dynasty, c. 600 C.E.**
>
> As for Sui Wen-ti [founder of the Sui Dynasty], I would say that he was politically inquisitive, but mentally closed. Being closed-minded, he could not see truth even if it were spotlighted for him; being over inquisitive, he was suspicious even when there was no valid reason for his suspicion … I want all of you to know that I am different. The empire is large and its population enormous. There are thousands of matters to be taken care of, each of which has to be closely coordinated with the others in order to bring about maximum benefit. Each matter must be thoroughly investigated and thought out before a recommendation is submitted to the prime minister, who, having consulted all the men knowledgeable in this matter, will then present the commendation, modified if necessary, to the emperor for approval and implementation.

Document 6

Source: Map of the Ottoman Empire, 1350–1683.

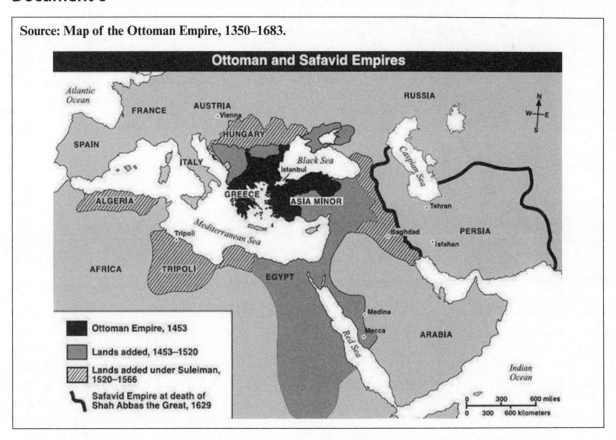

Document 7

Source: Justinian Law Code, 535 C.E. A collection of laws developed by the Byzantine Eastern Roman emperor, Justian I.

Justice and Law.

JUSTICE is the constant and perpetual wish to render every one his due.

1. Jurisprudence is the knowledge of things divine and human; the science of the just and the unjust.

2. Having explained these general terms, we think we shall commence our exposition of the law of the Roman people most advantageously, if we pursue at first a plain and easy path, and then proceed to explain particular details with the utmost care and exactness. For, if at the outset we overload the mind of the student, while yet new to the subject and unable to bear much, with a multitude and variety of topics, one of two things will happen—we shall either cause him wholly to abandon his studies, or, after great toil, and often after great distrust to himself (the most frequent stumbling block in the way of youth), we shall at last conduct him to the point, to which, if he had been led by an easier road, he might, without great labor, and without any distrust of his own powers, have been sooner conducted.

3. The maxims of law are these: to live honestly, to hurt no one, to give every one his due.

IF YOU FINISH BEFORE TIME IS CALLED, CHECK YOUR WORK ON THIS SECTION ONLY. DO NOT WORK ON ANY OTHER SECTION IN THE TEST.

Part B—Long-Essay Question

1 question

40 minutes

Directions: Write your response on lined paper. You must demonstrate your ability to use specific historical evidence and write an effective essay to support your argument. Your essay is considered a first draft and may contain some grammatical errors that will not be counted against you. However, to receive full credit, your essay must demonstrate historically defensible content knowledge and the following:

- **Thesis.** Provides a thesis that is a historically defensible claim, establishes a line of reasoning, and responds to all parts of the question—rather than merely restating or rephrasing the question. The thesis must consist of one or more sentences and must be located in one place—in the introduction or the conclusion.

- **Contextualization.** Describes how the historical context is relevant to the question. Relates the topic to broader historical events, developments, or processes that occurred before, during, or after the time frame. (Note: Must include more than a phrase or reference.)

- **Evidence.** Supports and develops the argument by identifying specific and relevant historical examples of evidence related to the topic of the question.

- **Historical reasoning.** Uses historical reasoning (comparison, causation, or continuity/change over time) to structure the argument that addresses the question.

- **Analysis.** Demonstrates a complex understanding of the historical development that focuses on the question to corroborate, qualify, or modify the argument. (For example, analyze multiple variables, explain similarities/differences, explain cause/effect, explain multiple causes, explain both continuity and change, explain connections across periods of time, corroborate multiple perspectives across themes, or consider alternative views.)

Choose ONE of the three long-essay questions below. The three questions apply to different time periods. Write ONE essay on the topic of EITHER Question 2, Question 3, or Question 4 that follows.

Question 2: Evaluate the causes and consequences of the diffusion and merging of ideologies and the extent to which ideologies changed political hierarchies over time during 600 B.C.E. to 600 C.E.

Question 3: Evaluate the causes and consequences of the transmission of disease and the extent to which disease changed the social and economic systems during the period of 1300 to 1700.

Question 4: Evaluate the key changes in labor systems and the extent to which these changes led to social changes over time from 1750 to 1900.

IF YOU FINISH BEFORE TIME IS CALLED, CHECK YOUR WORK ON THIS SECTION ONLY. DO NOT WORK ON ANY OTHER SECTION IN THE TEST.

Answer Key for Multiple-Choice Questions

1. D	12. C	23. D	34. B	45. D
2. C	13. D	24. A	35. D	46. A
3. A	14. C	25. C	36. B	47. D
4. B	15. B	26. B	37. B	48. B
5. A	16. D	27. D	38. A	49. D
6. D	17. A	28. D	39. D	50. D
7. B	18. B	29. C	40. D	51. A
8. C	19. D	30. A	41. B	52. C
9. D	20. B	31. C	42. D	53. B
10. C	21. D	32. D	43. C	54. A
11. B	22. C	33. B	44. C	55. C

Answer Explanations

Section I

Part A—Multiple-Choice Questions

1. **D.** Choice D is correct because it refers to the notion of retribution in the law code, and it is directly referencing Hammurabi's empire of Babylonia. Choice A is about a law code, but it is incorrect because Hammurabi's law codes were about internal, domestic relationships, not international laws. The passage was written by a secular king, and has no reference to religious authorities (choice B). Choice C is incorrect because the passage does not say anything about sharing power; this answer choice would be more relevant to the Magna Carta in England during the Post-Classical Era.

2. **C.** The passage references the context of different class and gender relationships, choice C. Hammurabi provided for various incentives based on social hierarchy. Choice A is close to being correct, but the passage is not strictly about landowners. There is nothing in the passage that reflects on slavery or its regulations (choice B), and there is nothing in the passage about familial relationships (choice D).

3. **A.** The passage is about the social hierarchy and what justifications were given for the position of different social and gender groups, choice A. Choices B and C are incorrect because there is nothing in the passage about international relationships or slavery. Choice D is incorrect because there is no reference to religion or spiritual issues.

4. **B.** Passage 1 references social and familial piety, which is about Confucianism and its family bonds. Passage 2 references Chinese Legalism. Choice B is the only choice that refers to this contrast. Choices A and C refer to Chinese Legalism, and choice D refers to moral persuasion and social bonds, not government laws.

5. **A.** The two passages reference Chinese Confucianism and Chinese Legalism. These two philosophies were a part of the Hundred Schools of Philosophy meant to solve the problem of the Era of Warring

States in China, choice A. Choice B is incorrect because both Chinese Confucianism and Chinese Legalism tried to avoid religious and clerical issues. Neither of the passages discusses the importance of the middle class; therefore, choice C is incorrect. Although there was a fear of the steppe people from the Northern areas, choice D is incorrect because these passages are not about stopping foreign invasions; they are about internal governance.

6. **D.** Choice D references the clear difference between Chinese Legalism and Chinese Confucianism. Choice A is incorrect because the two passages are not about a class conflict in society. There is nothing referenced on religion since the issue in China was not about religious leaders (choice B). Science versus faith (choice C) was more of an issue for the European Enlightenment during the 1600s.

7. **B.** This type of mythical story was told through oral traditions, choice B. Choice A is incorrect because the passage is a myth told by hunter-gatherer societies that did not rely on written records. Choices C and D are incorrect because this myth was told by hunter-gatherer groups and they would not have written records or possess holy books.

8. **C.** The passage is about mythical explanations for reasons that males held power in societies, choice C. The mythological story comes from the beginning of human civilization, so choices A, B, and D are incorrect, as they all refer to developments that occurred after this time period. Property issues arose when people settled into sedentary societies (choice A). Land empires arose when people settled into cities and villages (choice B), and societies in Southeast Asia and the Middle East feared losing culture due to international trade (choice D).

9. **D.** Leaders during the hunter-gatherer periods would gain authority through experience, charisma, and signs of courage, choice D. Hunter-gatherer societies had not developed professional armies that conquered lands (choice A). Democracy (choice B) did not exist until the Greek city-states, and there were no holy books (choice C) to demonstrate beliefs during the hunter-gatherer early civilization period.

10. **C.** The passage is about a contrast of the types of governance between Persia and Greece, and demonstrates the point of view of superiority of Greece during the Persian invasion, choice C. The author is not thinking about issues of international trade or the diffusion of culture (choice A). There is nothing in the passage about military strategies (choice B). Choice D is incorrect because there is nothing in the passage about social familial relationships.

11. **B.** Choice B is correct because Darius' argument is referring to the fight between the Greek city-states and the land-based empire of Persia. The fight described in the passage is not about China or the problems of the steppe people invading Central Asia (choice A), and the fight is not about the internal conflict between landowners and peasants (choice C). Choice D is incorrect because the fight is more about the conflict in China between the emperor and the nobles over land and power, not taxes.

12. **C.** The major Greek thinkers argued that democracy created better citizens since people were engaged with governance, choice C. Choice A is incorrect because the point of the passage is that the majority of people engage with the government. Choice B is incorrect because democracy was limited to about one-third of the people who were citizens: males and landholders. Choice D is incorrect because merchants were suspect due to their self-interests in trade.

13. **D.** Sedentary communities created storage facilities for food surpluses, choice D. Choice A is incorrect because hunter-gatherers moved with seasonal changes and would not have developed a storage facility. Large land-based empires would not have created small-scale granaries (choice B). Steppe communities (choice C) were nomadic and did not have storage facilities.

14. **C.** The unpredictable nature of rivers, such as the areas near the Tigris/Euphrates, led to flooding and the destruction of crops, choice C. Sedentary societies did face some warfare, but the warfare was limited since empires had not yet been established (choice A). Choice B is incorrect, as societies did produce surpluses of grain. The desert climate (choice D) was a problem, but sedentary societies created surpluses through irrigation systems and new iron/bronze tools.

15. **B.** Political offices and management systems were created to record the production and distribution of food, choice B. Sedentary societies did create monuments and symbols for religious faith (choice A), but these were not connected directly to storage facilities. Expansive militaries (choice C) did not arise until the creation of empires, along with bases for taxation. Navies (choice D) did not develop until empires developed, and the empires needed to be adjacent to coastal regions.

16. **D.** The image depicts an irrigation system that was needed for the growing of more food or food surpluses, choice D. It does not represent the demographic movement of people into suburban areas (choice A), nor does it show the interaction of different empires in trade (choice C). Choice B is referring to the changes in the Industrial Revolution of the 1700s.

17. **A.** The rise of new irrigation systems required recording and management systems, choice A. Choice B is referring to democratic systems that would not arise until centuries later with the Greek city-states. Centralized monarchs (choice C) arrived after this time when sedentary societies combined into empires. Social movements demanding equality (choice D) did not arise until after the Industrial Revolution in the 1800s.

18. **B.** New irrigation practices led to land ownership and social classes of landowners and renters, choice B. Women were placed into a more inequitable condition, as they were expected to raise children for farm work, making choice A incorrect. A middle class did not arise until the Industrial Revolution in the 1800s (choice C). Merchants did not climb in social status (choice D), as they were suspect for what was seen as their self-serving business practices until the Age of Exploration in the 1600s.

19. **D.** The Upanishads are the holy texts of the Hindu faith, which is the only religion among the answer choices with direct references to the Nyagrodha tree, choice D. Confucianism (choice A) was a political philosophy in China. Daoism (choice B) was a spiritual belief in China. Buddhism (choice C) was a belief system in India; it did surface later as a reform of Hinduism.

20. **B.** India is located in the middle of the Central Asian Silk Roads and Indian Ocean trade area. As a result, its spiritual beliefs expressed the extreme changes brought from trade and migration, choice B. The Upanishads were written in Classical India; the invasion of the Northern steppe people (choice A) came from the Chinese or Eastern Asian region. The Upanishads are from Central Asia, not Western Europe (choice C). The fights between the emperor and the nobles (choice D) are more relevant to China.

21. **D.** The author's argument is based on the Hindu belief in multiple paths to understanding the brahma or universal truth, choice D. Choice A refers to later movements in countries like China to close off exploration and return to traditional cultural purity. The passage does not refer to the need for control through the military (choice B). Religious proselytizing or trying to persuade people to join the faith (choice C) is more common in monotheistic faiths like Christianity and Islam.

22. **C.** Islamic influence was most heavily felt and monolithic in the Northern African and the Trans-Saharan region, choice C. The author is Islamic and not coming from the Chinese region (choice A). Islam was influential in the region of the Indian Ocean (choice B), but the area had such a mixture of religions that it made it difficult to find a call for religious purity. Islam was not found in the Andean Mountain range (choice D).

23. **D.** Ibn Khaldun's tone is negative toward the loss of religious virtue due to the profit motive, choice D. Ibn Khaldun was expressing a fear of cultural syncretism and loss of purity, not admiration for technology (choice A). Ibn Khaldun was discussing a more negative tone of trade's effects on culture; however, this passage was written long before European exploration (choice B). Ibn Khaldun's tone is critical of the loss of faith and not open to sharing of ideas (choice C).

24. **A.** Muhammad was a part of the trading Quryash tribe in the Saudi Arabian desert. He did criticize the leaders of trade for being unfair in their trading practices, but he himself was a merchant and viewed trade as necessary and good if it followed the rules of the Quran, choice A. Muhammad argued that certain practices that exploited people were unjust, not trade itself (choice B). Muhammad did preach for the just treatment of the poor, but he was not open to unlimited trade (choice C). Mohammed believed in the central truth of a monotheistic faith, so he never advocated sharing beliefs (choice D).

25. **C.** The passage shows the different cultural perceptions of the two groups and implies how these perceptions affected their encounter, choice C. The initial encounter between the Aztecs and Europeans was between natives and explorers, not missionaries (choice A). The passage is about perceptions of the cultural differences, not technological differences (choice B). The passage is about the encounter between natives and explorers, not between genders (choice D).

26. **B.** Spain was able to conquer the Aztecs and then use Aztec labor for farming and silver mining, choice B. The encounter between the Aztecs and Hernan Cortes was one of the eventual conquering of the Aztecs, not an opening of cultural diffusion (choice A). Choice C is not relevant to the Spanish exploration and encounter with the Aztecs. The Trans-Atlantic slave route (choice D) occurred much later and was centered more in Caribbean islands and Brazil for sugar production.

27. **D.** The Aztecs were weakened by Spanish diseases, and the Spanish were supported by local native tribes who were averse to Aztec domination, choice D. The Spanish only had about 300 military personnel, while the Aztecs had thousands of warriors, making choice A incorrect. The Spanish did have rifles and cannons, but the technology was not developed well enough to defeat the Aztecs (choice B). The Aztecs were the dominant empire in the Mesoamerican region, with a well-established and centralized army, making choice C incorrect.

28. **D.** The governance system was to establish a local viceroy who would manage local affairs but have allegiance to the king, choice D. Choice A is incorrect because the Spanish management of Mesoamerica was not direct. Choice B is incorrect because family settlements were true for English settlements, but not for the Spanish or French settlements. Although landowners would establish a nationalist revolt for local power (choice C), this did not occur until the 1800s.

29. **C.** The economic organization of the local population consisted of farming and silver mining, choice C. The other choices are incorrect. The Spanish established a colonial relationship that was based on the exploitation of labor and local natural resources; local natives were not allowed to run their own markets (choice A). The production of raw resources for manufactured goods (choice B) was more of a later economic system in the 1700s under mercantilism. The development of the middle class (choice D) did not take place until the Industrial Revolution in the 1700s.

30. **A.** Choice A accurately describes labor in Mexico versus the Atlantic slave trade. Choice B is incorrect: Atlantic slave trade was based on the belief that African slaves and their children were property; natives and other slaves were not changed culturally into property. Choice C is incorrect because natives tended to die due to their lack of immunities to European diseases; Africans were able to survive European diseases due to the centuries of contact through the Mediterranean and the Indian Ocean trade. Choice D is incorrect because African labor was exploited to farm sugar, cotton, and tobacco and was used for centuries.

31. **C.** Europeans brought cattle, pigs, and horses, which led to major changes in ecological relationships, choice C. Choices A and B are incorrect because Europeans did not bring many crops (choice A), and they did not change the trading in North America to precious metals (choice B). Although it is true that Europeans changed the type of social relationships (choice D), this is not the main point of Mann's argument.

32. **D.** Spanish diseases had the greatest impact on the native population, causing deaths from smallpox and influenza, choice D. Although the Spanish did bring horses (choice A), the native Aztecs did not use horses for battle in the 1600s. (Note: Natives in the Midwest section of North America used horses for hunting, but not in Mesoamerica.) The natives used ceramic pottery, but they did not use or trade porcelain (choice B). Although Spanish Catholicism impacted natives' beliefs, the natives did not reject their traditions; most natives found a way to blend the ideas of traditional Aztec faith with Catholicism (choice C).

33. **B.** The unintended transmission of the flea that carried the Black Death is similar to Mann's overall argument about the "biological bedlam" in Europe of the transmission of small insects and disease, choice B. Although it is true that the potato had a huge impact on nutrition and livelihoods (choice A), Mann's argument is more about the small, unintended effects of the transmission of insects and bacteria. Zheng He's travels (choice C) are not relevant to Mann's main argument. Ibn Battuta had an impact on the diffusion of culture and religious faith, not the transmission of disease or small insects (choice D).

34. **B.** Fifty years before Portugal's Vasco da Gama sailed up the east coast of Africa, the powerful Ming Dynasty sent out Zheng He's fleet in the 1400s. He's expeditions opened major trade routes into eastern Africa, choice B. These expeditions were unmatched in world history, with some of the largest wooden ships ever built. Choice A is incorrect because the dates for the spread of the trade routes do not correspond to the expansion of the Portuguese into the Eastern Hemisphere that occurred in the 1500s. Choice C is incorrect because the Mongols opened up the Silk Roads several centuries prior, and the Silk Roads were on the land, not the sea. Choice D is incorrect because major port cities had been open for centuries earlier in Africa and along the Indian Ocean trade route.

35. **D.** Chinese leaders stopped Zheng He from further exploration for fear of losing cultural purity and the need to stop the advance of the steppe people, choice D. Choice A is incorrect because China was very wealthy during this time period, and its wealth would continue as the silver market inflated its economy. Choice B is incorrect because Europeans had great difficulty conquering Southeast Asia due to the strong organization of governments in that region. Choice C is incorrect because the navy was not involved in the conquering of countries; this took place with armies in areas like the Korean peninsula and Vietnam.

36. **B.** Most historians agree that the powerful Ming Dynasty's emperor sent out naval expeditions to boost China's wealth and power, but one of the significant impacts was trade and the expansion of port cities in India and Eastern Africa, which allowed for a diffusion of culture, choice B. Choice A is incorrect because disease was significant in the 14th century during the Black Death, but it was not an issue in the 15th and 16th centuries. Choice C is incorrect because trade in the Indian Ocean did not include imperial wars until the exploration of the Portuguese. Choice D is incorrect because Islam spread in Northern Africa and the Middle East, not along the Chinese treasure routes.

37. **B.** The Industrial Era saw a massive migration of people from the rural farmlands into cities, providing a large supply of labor and allowing for factory mass production, choice B. Choice A refers to the three-field system of the Post-Classical Era that led to greater production of crops; this is not relevant to the Industrial Era. Choice C refers to the migration of people during the period of globalization in the 20th and 21st centuries. Choice D is incorrect because during industrialization, people migrated from rural to industrial areas.

38. **A.** Coal was used to fuel mass production in the cities by increasing use of new transportations and factory work, choice A. Choice B refers to metals that were discoveries during early human civilizations. Choice C refers to ship navigation technologies that were more relevant to the European Exploration period when the Polo family brought back these new technologies from the Yuan Dynasty. Choice D refers to digital technologies that are relevant to 21st-century globalization.

39. **D.** The main disadvantage was poor working conditions for women and children such as in the mines, choice D. Choices A and B were advantages. People experienced an overall increase in living standards by moving from rural to industrial areas (choice A). Women did enter into the workforce (choice B), which opened more opportunities, especially education for women. Energy was used more rapidly with coal and steam (choice C), but this did not noticeably deplete resources in this time period.

40. **D.** Families decreased in size due to the reduced need for farmhands and the higher cost of living, choice D. Choice A is incorrect because women entered the workforce more, not less, to increase household family income. Choice B is incorrect because children worked in factories and did not attend school. Choice C is incorrect because families remained religious despite poor living conditions.

41. **B.** Marks addresses the post–Cold War world when the United States became the unipolar power that managed a new globalized economy of lowered tariffs and increased trade, choice B. Choice A is incorrect because European powers had largely given up their colonies by this time period. Choice C is not relevant to the period that Marks is describing, as the use of coal was largely a product of the change toward the Industrial Revolution of the 1700s. Choice D refers to the Cold War, not the post–Cold War.

42. **D.** The use of digital technologies is the unique hallmark of the globalized economy that Marks is describing, choice D. The other choices describe events that are outside of the globalization period. Discovery of coal (choice A) is relevant to the Industrial Revolution. The use of new metals for domestication of animals and farming (choice B) is relevant when people settled into sedentary societies. The use of electricity (choice C) became important during the Second Industrial Revolution of the late 1800s and early 1900s.

43. **C.** The IMF sets the rules for the World Bank that lends money to developing countries. This was a part of the Bretton Woods' conference agreement to develop the global economy, choice C. The League of Nations (choice A) was an institution created after WWI to stop future global conflicts. The United Nations Security Council (choice B) was created after WWII to stop global conflicts, not economic issues. NATO (choice D) was created in the late 1940s to stop future Soviet aggression into Europe. NATO was not about economics; it was about possible military conflict during the Cold War.

44. **C.** The Green Revolution is credited with new farming techniques and genetic modification that led to increased wheat and rice output, choice C. The graph is about the increase or output of agricultural goods, not human migration (choice A). India did not face the problem of British tariffs (choice B); this was prior to its independence in 1948. The graph is not about population increase (choice D); populations decreased when industrialization was introduced to the region.

45. **D.** The Green Revolution is the main cause of increased wheat and rice in India and Mexico due to new farming techniques and genetic modification of foods, choice D. Choice A is incorrect because it is more of an effect than a cause; while there has been a large movement of farmers into urban centers, most people in India are still in the rural areas. Choice B is incorrect because coal was the cause of industrialization in the late 1700s during the Industrial Revolution. Choice C is incorrect because the developing world has used a policy of import substitution from the developed world; this was not the cause of increased grain production in India.

46. **A.** This type of question asks you to synthesize information over time. Choice A is most similar since it refers to an agricultural revolution based on new technologies. The human beginnings used new irrigation techniques and new metals for farming like iron and bronze. Although choice B is similar, it refers to the development of class-based systems; the graph is about an increase in crop production. Choices C and D are not relevant.

47. **D.** The correct answer is specific to the European efforts to imperialize Africa and the responses of native groups, choice D. Asantewaa's speech is about the influence of European nations on Africa during the Age of Imperialism. This would not involve India or Hinduism (choice A). The invasion of Ethiopia by Italy did not occur until World War II under Mussolini (choice B). The speech addresses the Age of Imperialism, which was about 100 years after Atlantic slavery and several centuries after the Trans-Saharan slave trade (choice C).

48. **B.** Traditional leaders often resisted the ideas of the West by proposing their traditional beliefs in wisdom, communalism, and strong centralized leaders. This is most like the queen's desire for total resistance to Europeans, choice B. Choice A is a good guess since the Self-Strengthening Movement was a native attempt to deal with imperialism, but the movement was about blending technologies from the West with Eastern ideas, not total resistance. Choice C is more from the perspective of the conquering group, in this case, the Aztecs creating a subordinating tax on local tribes. Meiji attempted to blend Western ideas in technology with Eastern ideas (choice D), which is not relevant to total resistance associated with the queen's comments.

49. **D.** The Berlin Conference was specifically about dividing Africa for European imperial possessions, choice D. The treaty ended the Seven Years' War in Europe (choice A) and the French-Indian War in Northern America, but the context was more about the eventual wartime debt that led to the American, French, and Haitian revolutions. The Declaration of the Rights of Man (choice B) referred to the French Revolution and the problem of fights between farmers and urban dwellers in France before the French Revolution. The League of Nations (choice C) was founded after WWI to stop future global conflicts.

50. **D.** India's continued participation in the Industrial Revolution led to its increased role in both cotton production and textile production for the global economy, choice D. The chart demonstrates a continued growth of mass-produced cloth in India during the Industrial Revolution, not a decrease (choice A). An increase in mass-produced cloth would suggest an increase, not a decline, in farmers moving into urban areas and working in Indian factories (choice B). The chart shows that machine-made cloth increased throughout the period. This would mean that Indians were not resisting new technologies (choice C).

51. **A.** Most Indians remained in the rural areas even though there was an increasing rate of migration to the cities, which could explain the continued production of cloth by hand, as machines were not available in rural areas, choice A. The table indicates that Indians did have some sort of machine for mass production and this was a product of the Industrial Revolution, making choice B incorrect. According to the table, the Indian culture incorporated new technologies for the mass production of cloth and yarn (choice C), and machine-spun yarn overtook hand-spun yarn. However, handwoven cloth continued to be of higher quality than machine-woven cloth, making choice D incorrect.

52. **C.** Choice C is the correct description of the increased opportunities for women as they moved into urban areas. Women moved from rural to urban areas, not the other way around, eliminating choice A. Women gained more opportunities in the cities because they had to work to support their families, making choice B incorrect. While women did gain new opportunities in the factories, higher education would take place in the 20th century, not the 1800s (choice D).

53. **B.** Choice B provides the correct description of the religious and nationalist fears of the Muslim minority before the independence of India. Muhammad Ali Jinnah criticized the Hindu majority, who he believed would dominate over the Muslim minority. The issue was about religion and culture, not tariffs (choice A). This passage is not about the fight between the Hindu leadership and the question of India's future economic relationships (choice C). Jinnah was the leader of the Pakistani partition; however, this happened later, after independence in 1948. Bangladesh and Pakistan partitioned even later due to an internal Muslim fight, making choice D incorrect.

54. **A.** Eventually, the independence movement created a civil war between Hindus and Muslims that led to a partition of Pakistan (the Muslim state) and India (the Hindu state), choice A. Gandhi wanted a multi-ethnic state (choice B), but the civil war that erupted between Muslims and Hindus prevented this from happening. Britain did establish a middle-class leadership (choice C), but this was during the Raj; the question is about the outcome after the independence movement. Britain left India in 1948, and the effect afterward was a civil war between Hindus and Muslims, eliminating choice D.

55. **C.** The internal fight over holy lands due to different ethnic and religious identities is the most similar to the ideas Jinnah expresses in this passage, choice C. Choices A, B, and D are incorrect because they are not about the religious-ethnic conflict, but rather economic development during globalization (choice A), how nations sided with other nations during the Cold War (choice B), and immigration over global regions (choice D).

Part B—Short-Answer Questions

Question 1

This question is asking you to read a secondary source from a historian who is interpreting the Haitian Revolution. Then you have to analyze what this interpretation tells you about the revolution. After that, you have to compare this revolution to others of its time period. Finally, you have to show that you can argue with or dispute the author's particular interpretation of the revolution.

To receive full credit, you must address all three parts. The sample responses for parts (a), (b), and (c) in the table below are for instructional purposes only. On the actual exam, you must write ONE complete short-answer essay.

Part	Task	Explanation	Sample Response
(a)	Identify ONE piece of historical evidence regarding the Haitian Revolution (not specifically mentioned in the passage) that shows the significance of its global effect on forced labor in the 1700s.	Part (a) asks you to historically show the global importance of the Haitian Revolution.	The Haitian Revolution was the first successful "black" slave rebellion against the plantation owners who owned African people for labor. The leader of the Haitian Revolution, Toussaint L'Ouverture, had the ability to create a "black"-led republic and global uprising. The revolution inspired slaves in America and Mesoamerica and ended European occupation of Haiti.
(b)	Provide ONE piece of historical evidence (not specifically mentioned in the passage) that compares the Haitian Revolution to a similar revolutionary movement of the time period.	Part (b) can be answered by comparing the Haitian Revolution to slave rebellions in North America, the Mestizo rebellion in Mexico, or the peasant rebellion in France.	The effects of the Haitian Revolution were similar to the revolutionary movement of Father Miguel Hidalgo's "Cry of Dolores" in Mexico. Hidalgo led thousands of Mexican peasants, Indians, and farmers against both Spain and the _Criollo_ (Creole) elite class. Hidalgo argued for independence, local representation, and freedom from the Creoles, who owned most of the land and had the most power in Mexico.
(c)	Provide ONE piece of historical evidence that would undermine the author's point.	Part (c) can be answered by choosing a specific example from the time period that would argue with or dispute the author's interpretation.	Geggus argues that the rebellions took place due to local cultures of resistance. However, the slaves were inspired by the French Enlightenment ideals and the supposed hypocrisy of the French not living up to their own universal rights in the Declaration of the Rights of Man.

Question 2

Reasoning skill: *Continuity and change over time.*

This question asks you to interpret two maps and explain the demographic, technological, and social changes in England, in the span of 50 years from 1801 to 1851.

To receive full credit, you must address all three parts. The sample responses for parts (a), (b), and (c) in the table below are for instructional purposes only. On the actual exam, you must write ONE complete short-answer essay.

Part	Task	Explanation	Sample Response
(a)	Briefly identify and explain ONE change that took place in England from 1750 to 1900 that is illustrated in the maps above.	Part (a) can be answered by considering the significant impact of the Industrial Revolution and by explaining how industrialization created economic productivity.	The two maps show the changing demographic pattern that took place during the early and middle parts of the Industrial Revolution. The map of 1801 shows how most people worked on farms and lived in rural areas of England. But because of industrialization, by 1850 millions of people were forced to move into the new city centers, as the map for 1851 indicates. The population of most major cities doubled from 1800 to 1850.
(b)	Briefly identify and explain ONE specific reason for the change illustrated in the maps above.	Part (b) can be answered by focusing on the specific cause for the change; for example, the discovery of new energies or the use of new technologies for mass production.	One possible reason for the dramatic change in England's demographics was the discovery and use of coal that led to the use of steam-powered engines. This created the ability to mass-produce materials in factories in urban centers. This in turn attracted more labor into the cities.
(c)	Briefly identify and explain ONE social continuity in England that persisted into the 20th century based on the information provided in Map B.	Part (c) can be answered by choosing a specific example from the social changes that continued due to the new forms of labor, demographics, social class roles, women's roles, or migration.	One social outcome of industrialization that persisted into the 20th century was the problem of relative economic inequalities in the cities. Poor farmers who migrated to the cities worked long hours for little pay due to the principle of laissez-faire government, or a government that was minimally involved in the economy. Factory workers included women and children, and they worked in ghastly conditions with no government protection.

Question 3

Reasoning skill: *Comparison*.

This question asks you to analyze the differences in early human social relationships in the context of a particular time period. You are being asked to compare and contrast the changes of hunter-gatherers to the period right after it with the sedentary societies. And, you are being asked to discuss the significant effects of these changes.

To receive full credit, you must address all three parts. The sample responses for parts (a), (b), and (c) in the table below are for instructional purposes only. On the actual exam, you must write ONE complete short-answer essay.

Part	Task	Explanation	Sample Response
(a)	Identify and explain ONE significant difference in the social structure between nomadic hunter-gatherers and sedentary societies.	Part (a) can be answered by analyzing one specific part of the social organization of early human societies in the hunter-gatherer era.	The nomadic hunter-gatherers of pre-history would likely have been organized around a kinship system of about 20 to 30 people from the mother's side of the family (matrilineal). These groups tended to have more equitable relationships due to their interdependence in finding scarce food resources. The roles of men and women were equal in hunter-gatherer societies compared to sedentary societies. Sedentary societies formed societies around "clans" or family obligations and began to set up social hierarchies, whereby men became the leaders of the clan. Sedentary societies formed the first patriarchy class system around fathers and prominent male figures.
(b)	Explain ONE similarity in the political management system between nomadic hunter-gatherers and sedentary societies.	Part (b) can be answered by providing one specific comparison about the political similarities between hunter-gatherer societies and sedentary societies.	The hunter-gatherer societies were similar to the sedentary societies in the populations' need for basic resources like food and water. Hunter-gatherers were politically equal, but when sedentary societies developed early forms of agriculture in order to help produce a surplus of food for a growing population, this led to the first political system of government. Early forms of farming in the sedentary agricultural revolution led to governing classes among the male-dominated society.
(c)	Describe ONE way in which early human civilizations changed as a result of their surrounding natural environment.	Part (c) can be answered by providing reasons that the immediate environment caused early human civilizations to move and adapt for survival.	Early civilizations tended to move with the seasonal changes in their area in order to find local food, animal resources, and good climate. As a result of their environment (climate and land), early humans moved into Eurasia in the Fertile Crescent where the soil was rich and water was abundant. Humans migrated to seek out safe areas to protect their populations and grow food to survive. Humans adapted to their environment to be able to survive by planting, plowing, and irrigating land.

Question 4

Reasoning skill: *Comparison.*

This question asks you to compare and contrast the motives for decolonization following World War II.

To receive full credit, you must address all three parts. The sample responses for parts (a), (b), and (c) in the table below are for instructional purposes only. On the actual exam, you must write ONE complete short-answer essay.

Part	Task	Explanation	Sample Response
(a)	Provide ONE similar reason that developing countries demanded independence after World War II.	Part (a) can be answered by an overall comparison of the developing countries' economic, social, or political motives for independence.	In the years following World War II, the movement toward decolonization increased, and by the turn of the century, the number of developing nations that gained independence from their imperialistic powers almost doubled. One of the main motives why many developing countries demanded independence from their overseas powers was to escape economic dependence and oppression from European imperialism. For example, after the British colonized in India, India lost its middle-class. Today, India has one of the largest economies in the world, but its diverse population still faces extreme poverty.
(b)	Compare similar motives of two specific countries that demanded independence after World War II.	Part (b) can be answered by providing a specific example from the time period that compares the motives of two countries seeking independence.	The British had a firm control over both Ghana and India, but after being motivated by nationalism inspired by other countries during World War II, both India and Ghana fought for independence from British occupation. Both nations were motivated by national sovereignty because they wanted to be able to rule over their own governments, rather than following laws from the British crown.
(c)	Contrast the motives of two specific countries that demanded independence after World War II.	Part (c) can be answered by providing examples from **two** countries that had different motives for decolonization and independence.	Each developing nation had different motivations and reasons for wanting to gain independence and separate from their imperial country. The people of some nations were culturally and religiously motivated, while others were politically and economically motivated. South Africans wanted independence to end cultural and racial inequalities, but Iranians wanted to become independent to set up a religious, political theocracy based upon Shia Islam.

Section II

Part A—Document-Based Question

DBQ Scoring Guide

To achieve the maximum score of 7, your response must address the scoring criteria components in the table that follows.

Scoring Criteria for a Good Essay	
Question 1: Compare and contrast how land-based empires managed different ethnic and cultural minorities and explain how empires were effective in unifying different minorities into the political systems.	
Scoring Criteria	**Examples**
A. THESIS/CLAIM	
(1 point) Presents a historically defensible thesis that establishes a line of reasoning. (Note: The thesis must make a claim that responds to *all* parts of the question and must *not* just restate the question. The thesis must consist of *at least* one sentence, either in the introduction or the conclusion.)	The thesis must answer all parts of the question while following a line of reasoning. The essay begins with a strong thesis argument about the importance of unification for peace and stability among the empire. The essay has coherent arguments in each body paragraph and makes logical connections to the topic of managing various groups of minorities and focuses on historical evidence to show the effective and peaceful methods for integrating minorities in government political systems.
B. CONTEXTUALIZATION	
(1 point) Explains the broader historical context of events, developments, or processes that occurred before, during, or after the time frame of the question. (Note: Must be more than a phrase or reference.)	A good response provides historical context to give the reader an overview of the topic. The essay begins by providing the time frame relevant to this topic: after 600 C.E. The essay also discusses the context for China's development of ideas after the Era of Warring States, the development of ideologies like Neo-Confucianism, the Ottoman Empire's use of the Wazir and Janissary Corps, and the Byzantine Empire's place in the Middle East.
C. EVIDENCE	
Evidence from the Documents **(2 points)** Uses at least *six* documents to support the argument in response to the prompt. OR **(1 point)** Uses the content of at least *three* documents to address the topic prompt. (Note: Examples must describe, rather than simply quote, the content of the documents.)	A DBQ response needs to address at least six of the documents to receive the highest possible points for this component. This essay uses all of the documents and shows elements from the historical context of the empires of the Post-Classical Era with the first empires in China, Japan, and the Middle East and the Roman Empire.

Scoring Criteria	Examples
C. EVIDENCE	
Evidence Beyond the Documents **(1 point)** Uses at least one additional piece of specific historical evidence beyond those found in the documents relevant to the argument. (Note: Evidence must be different from the evidence used in contextualization.)	This essay includes several pieces of outside evidence to explain the different ways that the Ottomans incorporated minorities as advisors to the sultan. For example, to help the Christians and Jewish communities feel included, they were allowed to serve in major positions in the Ottoman military, the Janissary Corps, and the empire's advisory group, the Wazir.
D. ANALYSIS AND REASONING	
(1 point) Uses at least *three* documents to explain how each document's point of view, purpose, historical situation, and/or audience is relevant to the argument. (Note: References must explain how or why, rather than simply identifying.)	The documents are analyzed for their purpose, historical situation, and the author's point of view. For example, Documents 1, 2, 4 and 7.
(1 point) Uses historical reasoning and development that focuses on the question while using evidence to corroborate, qualify, or modify the argument. (Examples: Explain what is similar and different; explain the cause and effect; explain multiple causes; explain connections within and across periods of time; corroborate multiple perspectives across themes; or consider alternative views.)	The sample essay argues that rulers used a variety of techniques to create national unification and identity using common ideologies, including different groups into political offices, and providing legal codes to assimilate groups into the empire. The essay qualifies the argument to address that while some historians would point to economic causes for unification, cultural and political tools for unification were far more effective. The essay also compares and contrasts different ways in which land-based empires managed minority groups.

DBQ Sample Response

Empires were formed during the Classical Era when rulers combined people together into larger political systems. Rulers used legal codes, religion, and local political elites to centralize power and unify empires. Based on the foundations of a centralized authority, after 600 C.E. these land-based empires expanded through military conquest and trade and their larger government political systems joined with several regions. This resulted in new challenges. After expanding their territories, empires in China, the Middle East, and Africa had many people from different ethnic, language, cultural, and religious groups. This meant that the rulers might encounter instability or even rebellion among the people due to the mixing of diverse groups. Leaders in these empires used a variety of techniques to promote peace and stability. Some leaders tried to unite the people of the empire by creating a common national identity, while others used political rewards and incentives to create loyalty to the empire. The primary goal was to create a national unification that would obligate all of the various groups of people to feel an alliance to a centralized leadership. Since these empires continued to exist for centuries, assimilating different ethnic and religious groups in the political system proved to be a stabilizing force.

As illustrated in the maps of Documents 3 and 6 depicting empire expansion and trade, some historians might argue that the emperors' primary approach to create unity was through economic trade so that people might be contented with economic gains and new types of luxury goods. However, trade was only one way that rulers created approval among the people in their empires. Rulers also gave minorities political positions, justified their rule through religious beliefs, and created a common sense of identity for all people that helped to obligate people to the ruler. For example, in Document 4 the Sultan's ambassador provides evidence in a letter to the Austrian Emperor illustrating that people were not compensated for inherited traits, rather people in the empire were rewarded for their "great ability and good service."

Many leaders used civil and religious beliefs to justify a national identity. For example, one of the key problems in China was uniting people around a common understanding. This was due to the 100 schools of philosophy that had spread out during the Era of Warring States. Further, China had been open to the trade of goods and ideas from India. Buddhism had been culturally diffused into China for centuries. In Document 1, a leading Confucian scholar faces the possibility of Buddhism undermining the practical obligations of the national belief system. The purpose of Han Yu's statement was to characterize Buddhism as a foreign ideology that did not fit with the Chinese Confucian identity. Eventually, Confucian scholars would mix some of the Buddhist supernatural beliefs of Confucianism, but this neo-Confucianism was created to serve the purpose of integrating numerous groups of people from the present day Manchuria, Tibet, Afghanistan, Vietnam, and Korea. Document 3 shows a similar type of ideological centralization except in Western Africa. Mansa Musa had used the Islamic belief system to centralize rule over Mali as well as the trade routes that he created across Northern African and the Middle East. This was especially important since Africa had been home to numerous polytheistic faiths. Mansa Musa's adoption of Islam allowed him to create a central hub for his empire that would be stable but also attract trade from the polytheistic "stateless" societies in Central Africa.

Other rulers used national political positions to centralize the different populations of people but under one nationality. The best example of this was the Ottoman Empire which spread out over the Middle East and Northern Africa (Document 6). The empire included numerous ethnic groups and Christians and Jewish communities. The map in Document 6 shows the difficulty that the Sultan had to keep such a large area under central control. The Sultan accomplished this by allowing Jewish and Christian individuals to serve in major positions in the Ottoman military, the Janissary Corps, and the empire's advisory group, the Wazir. The purpose of doing so was to incorporate the individuals from different groups into one national identity of political and social obligation. A similar type of political centralization is seen in Document 4 through the point of view of a visiting European dignitary. This individual expressed a tone of admiration for the Sultan of the Ottoman Empire due to his ability to use the advice from various different groups in his courtroom. This is especially significant given that the European leader was praising a foreign adversary. The author's tone suggests that the use of different offices for these individuals helped to create national consolidation. Similarly, in China, the civil service exam was given in order to recruit and promote talented bureaucrats and leaders from the noble class. Document 5 demonstrates how the Chinese emperor used the system of political offices to create loyalty to him from amongst the powerful.

Another technique of early land-based emperors was to create a sense of political authority that could be respected by all members of the society. For example, Japan always faced the problem of being a decentralized island. Most of the islands were ruled, not directly by an emperor, but by local governors or daimyos. In Document 2, a legal code was created with the purpose of removing the power of local leaders. The document calls for the local leaders to give their allegiance to the national shogunate or military authority. Similarly, in Document 7, Justinian used a legal code to establish his religious and secular authority over the Byzantine Empire. Byzantium was a trade city located in the central crossroads of the Turkish peninsula. It constantly faced the threat of invasion by a variety of different peoples. The use of Justinian's Law Code helped to create an orderly society that could be protected while engaging in trade.

The expansion of land-based empires brought the challenge of assimilating diverse groups of minorities into societies who had diverse ethnic, cultural, and religious backgrounds. Leaders handled this integration by creating a national identity of a common ideology, promoting people into government political positions, and creating respectable national offices of authority.

Part B—Long-Essay Question

Long-Essay Scoring Guide

Each point is earned independently (for example, you can earn a point for developing your argument and earn a point for providing evidence). To achieve the maximum score of 6, your response to ONE topic should use the scoring criteria that follow as a checklist to make sure you have included all of these elements in your essay.

> **Note: The directions asked you to choose ONE of the three LEQ topic options. The sample essay below is written for LEQ Question 4, but you can use some of the suggested ideas presented in the table that follows, "Scoring Criteria for a Good Essay," to formulate your written responses for Question 2 or Question 3.**

Scoring Criteria for a Good Essay

Question 1: Evaluate the key changes in labor systems and the extent to which these changes led to social changes over time from 1750 to 1900. (*Reasoning skill: Continuity and change.*)

Scoring Criteria	Examples
A. THESIS/CLAIM	
(1 point) Presents a historically defensible thesis that establishes a line of reasoning. (Note: The thesis must make a claim that responds to *all* parts of the question and must *not* just restate the question. The thesis must consist of *at least* one sentence, either in the introduction or the conclusion.)	A good response to this question has a central thesis that must provide at least two changes for labor systems. It must also show at least two effects that are specific to social changes. This thesis addresses the changes due to the use of new coal-burning energy—the leading technology inspired by the Industrial Revolution. The essay focuses on the changes in the first generation of labor systems established in Britain's factories during industrialization, but expands the argument to include key changes of labor systems over time throughout the world.
B. CONTEXTUALIZATION	
(1 point) Describes the broader historical context of events, developments, or processes that occurred before, during, or after the time frame of the question. (Note: Must be more than a phrase or reference.)	A good essay looks at the context of the big picture. This essay provides a context about the specific change from feudalism to the Industrial Revolution. The essay provides a specific description of feudalism as centered in land ownership. This allows the writer to lead into the changes brought on by coal and industrialization to the social relationships of landowners and peasants to factory owners and workers.
C. EVIDENCE	
(2 points) Supports the argument in response to the prompt using specific and relevant examples of evidence. OR **(1 point)** Provides specific examples of evidence relevant to the topic of the question. (Note: To earn 2 points, the evidence must *support* your argument.)	The essay must provide multiple examples that will support the argument. This essay discusses the examples of new energy sources like coal and steam that led to new technologies of mass production and new labor systems. The writer also provides examples of changes to labor migration from farms to urban centers and other countries and points to traditional social values, child labor laws, and reform movements. In addition, the author provides examples of changes for young women immigrating into urban centers in India, Japan, and Southeast Asia.

Scoring Criteria	Examples
D. ANALYSIS AND REASONING	
(2 points) Demonstrates a complex understanding of historical development that addresses the question and uses evidence to corroborate, qualify, or modify the argument.	This essay demonstrates a complex understanding of the topic. It qualifies the changes in the Industrial Revolution to those happening in globalization and connects the argument to the broader historical context of social developments during pre-industrialization (agrarian society) and developments that followed industrialization (new labor laws, middle class, and government reforms).
(Examples: Explain what is similar and different; explain the cause and effect; explain multiple causes; explain connections within and across periods of time; corroborate multiple perspectives across themes; and consider alternative views.) OR **(1 point)** Uses historical reasoning (comparison, causation, or continuity/change over time) to frame and develop the argument while focusing on the question. (Note: Must be more than a phrase or reference.)	The essay also addresses the historical reasoning of changes and continuities. The essay addresses the changes of labor systems related to energy and technology during the Industrial Revolution, and it evaluates the continuity and changes regarding the effects of traditional labor systems, class structures, gender structures, and family structures.

Long-Essay Sample Response for Question 4

During the 1600s, most societies were structured around social hierarchical relationships known as feudalism. In this social and labor system, people agreed to work, rent, and farm centralized land from noble landowners. In this agrarian system, landowners held land in exchange for labor and service. This was justified through the ideological beliefs of social obligations. In addition, people worked mostly out of their homes, using basic hand tools to manufacture and produce goods like clothing. In the 1700s, the labor system changed. The European production of coal, led by the British, fueled a new Industrial Revolution that fundamentally changed the social and labor systems worldwide. Industrialization played a large role in the massive change in manufacturing. New forms of machinery made possible through new forms of energy increased the volume and variety of manufactured goods. This led to the migration of farmers into urban centers, where these new populations became employed as factory workers in a new labor city. Throughout this time period, factory workers faced challenges from social and economic inequalities.

Britain was the first to industrialize. The British discovered large deposits of coal in the north and used coal to operate its steam-run manufacturing machines. The discovery of coal rapidly transformed societies from rural farming communities to cities. New methods of using fuel-burning coal became increasingly important as a source of power for factory machines, steam engines, and furnaces. The new technologies were faster and more efficient. Affordable coal-fueled machines were able to quickly produce power that led to the mass production and transportation of goods for export, like textiles.

As the new forms of energy production and technology spread out across the world, business owners sought out cheap, unskilled labor in the cities. The business owners soon realized that there was a need for more people to work in the factories to maintain and run the machines. At the same time, the mass production of crops changed the agricultural labor systems due to technological innovations of landowners (crop rotation). Smaller farmers lost their lands and many farm workers were displaced. Urban businessmen attracted displaced farm laborers from rural areas to urban centers by promising work and higher wages. Young farming men and women migrated into cities and found new types of unskilled labor in the factories. Women and children began working for the first time. The dramatic shift from agrarian-based societies to industry-based societies caused the populations of cities to grow at a fast pace. The industrialized coal-powered factories ushered in technological innovations, but these innovations were frequently at a cost to the social and economic impact of the first generation of workers. City housing conditions became unsanitary and unsafe, and diseases and illnesses quickly spread. Women, children, and young men began working in industrial centers for minimum compensation, working long hours in hazardous conditions. The demands of human labor being used in coal-fueled factories gradually changed over time, and traditional social hierarchies, family roles, gender roles, and labor laws also changed. For example, in 1847 a law was passed to limit the number of hours that children could work. Although child labor is permitted in some parts of the world in the 21st century, all developed countries have prohibited the use of child labor.

The innovations of the Industrial Revolution had far-reaching effects in other parts of world. As industrialization spread to the other regions of the world, it changed traditional organizations of land ownership and class systems. A rising middle-class began to emerge throughout Europe, and other regions of the world also began experimenting with new machinery, which impacted the social, cultural, technological, and economic way of life. Those regions of the world who chose not to implement industrial innovations suffered socially, economically, and politically. For example, Russia chose not to modernize. Even though they had enormous potential, Russia fell behind politically and economically because it couldn't compete technologically and militarily compared to other European powers of the 20th century. In addition, large landholders in Southeast Asia and India consolidated land and used new machinery to mass-produce farm goods for sale on the international market. This led to small landholders losing their land to economic competition. Those farmers then migrated throughout the world to places like the Americas, South Africa, India, and Southeast Asia to seek jobs on large plantations. The widespread impact of industrialization led to both a centralization of land ownership and reform movements from people seeking different forms of labor systems.

Innovations in the labor systems during the Industrial Revolution also opened new opportunities for women due to the need for their work in cities. Families in places like India, Japan, and China needed to supplement their farming incomes and would send their young daughters into the major cities to work in factories. This led to both a change and continuity in gender relationships. Daughters brought back their wages from factory work to their traditional farming families. This maintained the patriarchal relationships in the Indian Caste system, the Chinese Confucian system, and the Japanese Shinto system. However, while working in the cities, these same women experienced an appreciation for independence from traditional family roles. This eventually led to their camaraderie with other young women and shifts in social ideologies.

The broad social impact of industrial competition in the global economy, which started as a capitalistic mission to benefit wealthy businessmen, helped to maintain some traditional social values, but it also changed labor systems and opened the doors for people in cities across the world. Labor reform movements started and created the foundation for social movements like the suffragettes, women who demanded voting rights. In addition, labor and social reform movements created greater educational opportunities for young women. Changes in social labor systems also led to changes in labor laws, changes in family roles, opportunities for women to climb the social and employment ladders, the rise of a middle class, and new government reform policies throughout the world.